ATTACK ON PEARL HARBOR

ATTACK ON PEARL HARBOR

STRATEGY, COMBAT, MYTHS, DECEPTIONS

ALAN D. ZIMM

Graphics by
MATT BAUGHMAN

CASEMATE

Philadelphia & Newbury

Published in the United States of America and Great Britain in 2011 by
CASEMATE PUBLISHERS
908 Darby Road, Havertown, PA 19083
and
17 Cheap Street, Newbury RG14 5DD

ISBN 978-1-61200-010-7
Digital Edition: ISBN 978-1-61200-021-3

Cataloging-in-publication data is available from the Library of Congress
and the British Library.

10 9 8 7 6 5 4 3 2 1

Printed and bound in the United States of America.

For a complete list of Casemate titles please contact:

CASEMATE PUBLISHERS (US)
Telephone (610) 853-9131, Fax (610) 853-9146
E-mail: casemate@casematepublishing.com

CASEMATE PUBLISHERS (UK)
Telephone (01635) 231091, Fax (01635) 41619
E-mail: casemate-uk@casematepublishing.co.uk

CONTENTS

CHARTS AND DIAGRAMS

FOLKLORE, VIEWED WITH A CRITICAL EYE . . .

An Attack "brilliantly conceived and meticulously planned"
As a shock wave of catastrophe surged from Pearl Harbor's burning waters to engulf a stunned US nation, judgments were made about what had befallen America's Fleet. A young naval aviator recorded his impressions just hours after the attack:

> What a day—the incredulousness of it all still gives each new announcement of the Pearl Harbor attack the unreality of a fairy tale. How could they have been so mad? . . . If the reports I've heard today are true, the Japanese have performed the impossible, have carried out one of the most daring and successful raids in all history. . . . The whole thing was brilliant.[1]

So it seemed, the whole thing was brilliant.

The Pearl Harbor attack is depicted as the culminating act of a suspenseful, character-driven drama, a Greek tragedy of heroic champions and maladroit bunglers maneuvering the future of navies, nations, and empires, men making monumental decisions emanating from their strengths, their weaknesses, and their foibles. On the Japanese side there are the hesitant, traditionalist "battleship admirals," whose reluctance to acknowledge the emerging dominance of the aircraft carrier is overcome by Admiral Yamamoto the daring gambler, supported by Commander Genda the brilliant planner and Commander Fuchida the intrepid warrior. On the American side are Admiral Kimmel and Lieutenant General Short, depicted as blundering, or making questionable decisions, or as men failed by their subordinates, or derelict in their duty, or ill-treated by bad luck, or the hapless victims of a conspiracy of scheming British and Washington-insiders to bring America into the war.[2]

According to a consulting historian to the US Navy, "the attack was almost textbook perfect." Others judged that it was "brilliantly conceived and meticulously planned," the plan was "bold and original." A television commentator informed his audience that "The Japanese aerial attack was an unqualified success," and that "The attack plan was brilliant."[3]

Across a wide range of histories, publications, and films the "brilliant" label is accepted as an incontrovertible fact. The recorded narration on a tour boat plying Pearl Harbor assured visitors that the attack was "brilliantly conceived and executed." A historian judged that the execution of the attack "had been almost perfect; like a flashing samurai sword . . ." Another asserted that "Pearl Harbor had been reduced to a pile of smoking rubble and sunken ships," while others joined in concluding, "In the Japanese attack on Pearl Harbor in 1941, the US Navy battle line was destroyed."[4]

Mostly derided as an example of battleship-centric conservatism is the fact that naval professionals on the Japanese Navy General Staff believed the operation to be reckless.[5] Fearful of the outcome, the chiefs of staff of the First and Eleventh Air Fleets recommended, in writing, that the raid be abandoned. One of those protesting was Rear Admiral Onishi Takijiro, who near the end of the war formed the first Special Attack (Kamikaze) Squadrons—in other words, the objections came not just from "conservative battleship admirals," but from men willing to take risks and endorse unorthodox actions. Onishi, knowing that Japan could only win through a negotiated peace, told Yamamoto that Japan should "avoid anything like the Hawaii operation that would put America's back up too badly."[6]

After a round of wargames, the flag officer assigned to execute the attack and most of the Naval General Staff wanted nothing to do with it. When the decision was made irrevocable, officers on the Naval General Staff feared disaster; they enjoined Admiral Nagumo, the commander of Japan's carrier-centered Mobile Force *(Kido Butai)*, to "exert every effort to save the force if events turned against him."

Similarly dismissed with a nod to Japanese fatalism are the assessments of many of the Japanese aviators: "Most of the flying officers thought they would never come back alive." The Japanese strike commander estimated that his men had a 50-50 chance of surviving.[7] The aviators' apprehension echoes over the years in veterans' accounts: "Goodbye, *Kaga,*" one recalled whispering as he departed his carrier on the morning of the attack, "return to Japan safely. We will probably never land on you again."[8]

Previous accounts have concentrated on personalities and the human drama of the battle. Given the presumption of brilliance, the planning and execution of the Pearl Harbor attack has never been subjected to anything like an impartial critical analysis. Can a plan be judged "brilliant" without passing a detailed examination and critique? How can an operation be lauded as "textbook perfect" without understanding what was in the textbook, and what would constitute perfection?

Instead, applying backwards logic, the drama of sunken, shattered ships has directed the superficially obvious answer: brilliant results come from brilliant planning, training, and execution. Three respected historians applied this reverse reasoning when they wrote, "in the final analysis one point has to be made. The fact that in the end everything—everything, that is, except for the American carriers—came together in the attack of Sunday 7 December 1941 provides justification of the system: the system worked."[9]

Did it really?

Common Knowledge, Presumptions, and Modern Analytic Approaches

For modern-day naval officers, the end of a combat operation or training exercise initiates a follow-on process of evaluation and criticism. In the United States Navy part of the process is called a "Hot Wash-Up." All major participants gather together to scrutinize events and decisions, detect errors, analyze flaws, note deficiencies, and record what has been learned. Questions are probing, criticisms are unsuppressed. The data is often turned over to professional Operations Research (OR) analysts for further study.

If a Hot Wash-Up had been held immediately after the Pearl Harbor attack, the assessments of Short, Kimmel, Yamamoto, Nagumo, Genda, Fuchida, the Japanese plan, the execution of the plan, the risks and the anticipated results might well be significantly different.[10]

Was the operation executed properly? Were there flaws in the planning or execution or battle damage assessment? Might these flaws portend things to come? Was anything forgotten or neglected in the planning? Was the plan state-of-the-art, or were existing useful attack techniques ignored? Why not? What was the balance between risk and reward? Were Japanese expectations reasonable, or the products of overoptimism, or even self-delusion? Did the attack meet expectations? Meet its potential? What could have happened if the Japanese attack had not benefited from the fortuitous American blunders? What could have been the effect on the course and outcome of the war if different results had been realized?

Many untested presumptions have become established as unchallenged truth. Myths have arisen and bounced about in print, on the Internet, and television. "A volume of folklore has developed around the Pearl Harbor attack as stories and 'facts' are passed from source to source with little critical examination."[11]

For example, it has been taken as a certainty that the Japanese blundered when they did not send a third-wave attack against the Pearl Harbor's repair facilities and oil storage tanks. The failure of the Japanese to launch such an attack has been described as the Americans' "only bright spot in the whole debacle."[12] One author boldly states that if the oil storage tanks had been destroyed "the US Navy would almost certainly have abandoned Pearl Harbor, and withdrawn to California,"[13] a judgment repeated in a television program.[14]

Other myths abound. Among them: the Japanese aviators, known in their homeland as the *waga arawashi,* "our angry eagles,"[15] were all elite pilots hardened by China War experience; it was a blessing that the Pacific Fleet was in port rather than at sea, where all the battleships would have been sunk in deep water;[16] sinking a warship in the channel would have blocked Pearl Harbor and made it useless; Japanese midget submarines torpedoed two battleships;[17] an incompetent typist delayed the Japanese declaration of war until after the commencement of hostilities, making Pearl Harbor a "sneak attack" which triggered implacable American public anger against Japan.

Rather perversely, both the Americans and the Japanese had reason to overestimate the number of hits. The Japanese aviators all wanted credit for individual success, and their commanders wanted to sing the praises of carrier air power in their competition with more conventional surface gunnery ships. On the American side, more hits would suggest that their ships were tough and well designed.

Scope and Limitations

This study is not an exercise in revisionist history—it is not intended to be a history at all, but rather an analysis of selected aspects of the attack. No attempt is made to recount all the events of that day.

The primary objective is to examine the Japanese planning, execution, and post-battle analysis of the attack, in the context of their overall strategy.

The naval engineering involved in getting *Kido Butai* within range of Hawaii is an impressive tale, but one that is outside the scope of this work, as are the many stories of individual bravery on both sides. There is no discussion of the various "conspiracy theories" regarding code breaking, pre-battle warning or "who knew what and when."

What is intended is a professionally oriented, fact-grounded, post-event review of the kind conducted many times by the author while on active duty in the Navy and afterwards as an Operations Research analyst. The methodologies used can reveal unsuspected strengths and weaknesses of forces, expose institutional problems, and provide clues as to the reasons underlying later events. Facts and calculations are central. It is not opinions in conflict with other opinions, as is the case in most revisionist disputes; rather, it is analysis and calculation designed to validate or discredit ungrounded opinions.

Context

In employing this process problems have been found with the Japanese planning and execution of the Pearl Harbor strike. The problems had a variety of sources: from the mindset of the planners, from doctrinal deficiencies, and from erroneous assumptions, things that were simply not known at the time and would be revealed only in the course of subsequent battles. They also came from inadequate training, a failure to anticipate, and from lapses in discipline.

In early 1941 the effectiveness of air power at sea was unpredictable and inconsistent; air power itself was greatly in flux. New aircraft types were the cutting edge of aviation, only to be considered obsolete death-traps two or three years later. Tactics were under constant revision as the capabilities of the aircraft and weapons changed. Doctrine publications lagged the state of the art significantly. The progress each year was immense.

Between the World Wars there were no truly representative combat trials between ships and aircraft. The problem was the human element. It was simply not known how the conditions of combat would influence human performance, as the experiences of the First World War were eclipsed by stronger and faster aircraft, bomb sites, and heavier and more accurate defenses. It just was not known, for example, how anti-aircraft (AA) fire would affect a bombardier's accuracy, or how closely a pursuit pilot would press his attack in the face of a bomber's defensive machine guns. The limited experiments and training that were conducted—like making bombing runs against target ships that were not shooting back, or firing AA at unmanned radio-controlled aircraft or towed sleeves or balloons—gave results that were misleading, or unrepresentative of combat, or eclipsed by the rapid rate of change of the underlying technologies.

In addition, there were, and remain to this day, distortions by aviation- and battleship-oriented ideologues promoting their spin on events. Aviation propagandists, especially in the army-oriented air forces and the emerging "strategic" bombing forces, took it as a matter of faith that bombers would always get through, bombing would always be accurate, and bomb damage would be devastating.[18] Carrier enthusiasts claim aviation was "unfairly" held back by ultra-conservative members of the battleship "Gun Club."[19] These worldviews are lenses through which the events leading up to 7 December 1941 are distorted.

The Japanese collected some air war experience against China and in their "incidents" with the Soviets, but it was an odd sort of experience, against foes with very irregular quality of personnel and equipment, under circumstances not likely to be reproduced in a naval war against the United States. They found these lessons easier to discard than accept, and mostly their airmen reverted to the old ways and did not adapt.

Westerners, with only isolated, laudatory exceptions, largely ignored what was going on in the Far East.

After the war began in 1939 there were hints of air power's potential. The British air raid on Taranto that sank three Italian battleships provided a significant nudge in the ribs, but there were also many cases where ships survived air attacks unscathed. The battleship could not be ruled as obsolete after two German battlecruisers gunned down a British aircraft carrier, taking no damage themselves. By late 1941 there was still much to be discovered, much still in flux, no conclusion yet possible regarding the relative effectiveness of aircraft v. ships.

Regarding the Pearl Harbor attack, care must be taken when pointing out what might be seen as errors or omissions on the part of the Japanese planners or participants. These warriors were breaking new ground without the benefit of the knowledge available now, or the perspective of experience from the many air battles of WW II. The state of the art at that flash of time must be kept in focus. This is difficult. Because of the rapid rate of change, the front-line operational tactics, techniques, and procedures outstripped written doctrine. Doctrine might not even exist on paper, with the current "best practices" only in the minds of the aviators. This study includes some detective work, along with an inevitable element of informed speculation.

One cannot but retain great respect for those challenged to plan and execute the attack, with no precedent to guide them and many technical and tactical problems to overcome. Such respect, however, should not deter a full critical analysis, pointing out where they succeeded and where they failed. This contributes to a better understanding of the combatants, making the War in the Pacific more comprehensible. Analysis can also help reveal the thought processes and mindset the Japanese brought into the battle, and what they took out of the experience.

Mental Models, Cultural Factors and Processes

One of the most important things a commander must be able to do is have an idea of the range of probable results when given combinations of forces engage. He must do this to decide if an engagement is worthwhile, if a given force can defeat the enemy.

This mental process is accomplished by an (often subconscious) application of the commander's mental models of engagements, models that are developed during his training and over his experience in the service, or perhaps from his perception of his luck, destiny, and place in the pantheon. In addition to being predictive, these mental models act as filters to the data presented to the commander. Things that agree with the preconceptions the commander carries into battle will be seen and registered and considered; those that do not agree can be rejected as invalid and not cognitively processed, can be ignored, or can be rapidly passed over as unimportant in the press of events, in what is known as confirmation bias. The preconceptions a commander carries can also alter his mental condition. Data received that does not agree with the preconceived mental model can cause mental discomfort, agitation, distress, confusion, and a reduced capability to make good decisions, a condition known as cognitive dissonance.

These mental models can be seen as valuable tools to predict the future, or as miserable baggage getting in the way of an accurate assessment of reality. It is important to understand the mental models that a commander has stocked in his mind going into combat. The effects and consequences of some of these pre-conceived mental models can be observed in the course of the Japanese raid on Pearl Harbor. A detailed analysis provides clues regarding the respective commanders' mindsets, attitudes, and expectations that would influence future decisions.

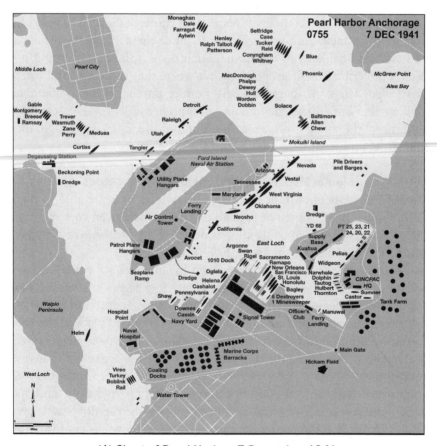

(1) Chart of Pearl Harbor, 7 December 1941

CHAPTER ONE

STRATEGIC AND OPERATIONAL SETTING

Early Rumblings

An attack on Pearl Harbor as an opening move in a war between Japan and the United States was not a new or unusual concept in Japanese military circles.

The Japanese Navy had a tradition of opening wars with surprise attacks without a formal declaration of war. This was exemplified by their attack on the Russian fleet at Port Arthur, delivered two days after breaking off relations with Russia and two days before their formal declaration of war in the Russo-Japanese War.[1]

In 1927 *Kaigun Daigakko*, Japan's naval staff college, wargamed an attack on Pearl Harbor by two carriers, one of which was lost. That same year, Lieutenant Commander Kusaka Ryunosuke, later as a Rear Admiral to serve as the Chief of Staff of the Pearl Harbor attack force, presented lectures on an aerial attack on Pearl Harbor.[2] The following year, Yamamoto Isoroku, a captain who was to rise to command the Combined Fleet, in a lecture at the Navy Torpedo School, said "In operations against America, we must take positive actions such as an invasion of Hawaii,"[3] and discussed striking Pearl Harbor. The subject was examined anew in "A Study of Strategy and Tactics in Operations against the United States," a 1936 Naval Staff College analysis which suggested that Japan should open the war with a surprise attack on Pearl Harbor.[4]

On the civilian side, between 1910 and 1922, books about imaginary wars were in vogue. After a lull in the late 1920's, there was an unprecedented outpouring of these books after the London Naval Conference and the Manchurian Incident of 1931, when Japan replaced Russia as the dominant power in South Manchuria. In 1934 alone at least 18 such books were promoted in magazines and newspapers, describing a future war with Russia, the United States, or both.[5] Japanese authors such as Hirata Shinsakyu used a pre-emptive attack against Pearl Harbor to begin fictional depictions of war between Japan and the United States.[6]

Similar attacks were postulated by American and British authors as early as 1909.[7] Novelists Ernest Fitzpatrick in *The Conflict of Nations* and Homer Lea in *The Valor of Ignorance* depicted Imperial Army soldiers arriving in the Hawaiian Islands as immigrant workers, wiping out the American garrison in a surprise attack, and proceeding to invade the American mainland.[8] Bywater's *The Great Pacific War*, written in 1925, had the US Asiatic Fleet hit by a surprise attack at Pearl Harbor to open the war.[9]

One curious aspect was that in many of the Japanese novels the Japanese were defeated, while many American novels had the Americans ignominiously booted out of the Pacific. "Rouse the populace by describing the horrors of defeat" was the message of this genre, predicting disaster if actions were not taken to forestall the threat.

The critical nature of Hawaii was well understood. Pearl Harbor was America's central position in the Pacific, situated 2,074 nautical miles (nm) from San Francisco, 2,200nm from San Diego, 5,000nm to the Philippines and 3,350nm from Tokyo. First established as a U.S. naval base in 1908, it had been the headquarters of the Pacific Fleet since 1940, a crucial repair and logistics facility, and a vital link in the sea and air lines of communication between the United States and the Philippines. It was the ideal springboard for an American counterattack against Japan and the last line of defense before America's mainland. Hawaii was considered by the Japanese as part of their Greater East Asia Co-Prosperity Sphere, and portrayed as a legitimate object of Japanese expansion—160,000 of its 400,000 population were *doho*, or ethnic Japanese, presumed to be yearning for reunification with their Japanese roots.[10]

Pearl Harbor and Oahu were developed as major bases, with the US Navy taking advantage of Hawaii's good weather for training. The

Pacific Fleet used raids on Pearl Harbor as a component of several Fleet Exercises from 1928 on.[11]

Japanese Naval Strategy in the 1920s and 1930s

Under the terms of the Washington Naval Treaty, Japan's fleet of battleships was limited to 60% of the tonnage allocated to America and Great Britain. A disparity of forces was something the Japanese had overcome before. At the beginning of Japan's war with China in 1894, the Japanese had fewer and smaller ships, on aggregate less than two-thirds of the Chinese tonnage, but they prevailed on the strengths of better gunnery and better tactics. In the Russo-Japanese War the Japanese again began as the weaker side, with half the number of capital ships and one-third the tonnage, and again they emerged victorious.[12]

With this heritage the Japanese were confident they could develop a strategy to defeat the United States. Two assumptions were central in their strategic planning. First, they believed that an attacking fleet required twice the combat capability of the defending fleet in order to prevail. This was to them confirmed by the travails of the Russian Baltic Fleet, which traveled halfway around the world only to be destroyed in the famous battle of Tsushima, the first defeat of a major Western naval force by an Asian navy.

Second, they believed that combat power was the square of the size of the force. This concept was similar to Frederick Lanchester's modeling of air-to-air battles from the First World War, although the Japanese likely paid more attention to the writings of Rear Admiral Bradley Fiske, who worked out similar mathematical relationships. Fiske also advocated wargaming as a means of working out tactical and strategic problems in advance, a practice the Japanese embraced with enthusiasm. Thus, by squaring the proportions of force, the 10:6 ratio required by the terms of the treaties became 100:36 in terms of combat power, almost 3 to 1, which the Japanese viewed as sufficient for an attacking force to defeat them.[13]

To win, the Japanese had to change these odds. These assumptions would come into play later in their justification for the Pearl Harbor attack.

The Japanese strategy called for luring the American Pacific Fleet from San Diego out to the Western Pacific, where it would be defeated in a decisive battle. According to Agawa:

. . . the orthodox plan of operations called for the navy to throw its strength first into an attack on the Philippines. Then, when the US fleet came to the rescue and launched the inevitable counterattack, the Marshalls, Marianas, Carolines, Palaus, and other Japanese mandates in the South Pacific would be used as bases for whittling down the strength of the attacking American forces with submarines and aircraft so that finally, when they had been reduced to parity with the Japanese forces or even less, they could be engaged in a decisive battle in the seas near Japan and destroyed. This was much the same concept as underlay the Battle of the Japan Sea in which, in 1905, Japan had taken on and annihilated the Russian Baltic Fleet off Tsushima.[14]

The Japanese would invade the Philippines to secure their sea line of communications to the southern resource areas, and as a means to lure out the American fleet into an immediate movement to relieve the islands.[15] The Americans would concentrate their warships to protect the large numbers of oilers, supply ships and auxiliaries needed to support the move. As this huge fleet steamed west a battle would develop, in several phases over perhaps several weeks.

In the first phase Japanese submarines, some uniquely equipped with search planes, would locate and track the American Fleet. The submarines, faster on the surface than the American battleline, would converge and deliver repeated attacks. Japanese long-range medium bombers based out of the Mandates would further bleed the American fleet. This was called "The Strategy of Interceptive Operations."[16]

Contact between the surface ships of the two fleets would initiate the second phase. Japanese cruisers and destroyers would launch a series of night attacks, firing massive volleys of 120 or more long-range torpedoes, 25% of which were expected to hit. The Americans were expected to suffer heavy losses that would shatter their morale.

In the final phase, the Japanese battleline, now equal or superior in strength to the Americans, would complete the destruction in a long-range gun battle, using their superior speed to isolate portions of the American fleet. The Japanese expected this final battle to be decisive, leading to a negotiated peace. The Americans would be forced to acknowledge Japan's dominant position in the western Pacific and Asia. This was *Zengen Sakusen*, or "The Great All-Out Battle Strategy."[17]

This basic strategy became fixed in the minds of the Japanese Navy General Staff, changing little between 1925 and 1941. In 1936 Great Britain was added as an enemy. However, up through 1940, while American territories in the western Pacific were to be invaded and taken, and in spite of the popular exhortations of the novelists, the Naval General Staff's Concept of Operations never considered Hawaii as a target.[18]

The Japanese expected to win through better tactics, better weapons, and higher-quality ships and personnel. Their training was intensive and realistic, often eschewing safety precautions: for example, destroyers practiced torpedo attacks at night and in poor weather at high speed, and had some dreadful collisions. During 1938 to 1940 training was particularly intensive, "as though a major war were in progress." The stakes were high. For example, a new exercise was introduced where the fleet would enter harbor at night without illuminating the ships' running lights, a risky undertaking. Should an error cause damage to one of the ships it was possible that the officer in charge would be "obliged to commit ritual suicide."[19] Night bombing attacks were practiced with an emphasis on realism. Searchlights from air defense sites would dazzle the pilots, which caused mid-air collisions and the loss of aircraft and lives. After several such incidents the program was questioned, but ultimately training continued as before. The losses were accepted.

Japanese ships were customized for the specific conditions and location of the expected encounter. The final decisive battle was to occur near home waters, so Japanese ships characteristically had only moderate endurance and low habitability and were expected to be able to operate largely out of their home ports. Hull strength, damage control fittings, stability, and other attributes were sacrificed to attain very high top speeds and very heavy armament. Ships were loaded with weapons far out of proportion to the ship's displacement.

Sometimes the designs pushed armament loads too much. In 1934 the torpedo boat *Tomozuru* capsized in heavy seas. The design had to be revised, and the stability margins in other classes re-examined. Many ships were required to take aboard hundreds of tons of ballast to lower their center of gravity.

An attack on Pearl Harbor was not included in *Zengen Sakusen*. Japanese ships generally did not have the fuel to sail from Japan to Pearl Harbor and back. Since the decisive battle was to be fought near Japanese home bases, there was no imperative to develop underway replenishment methods or to build the specialized auxiliaries needed for remote operations.

The advent of the Southern Operation—the plan to capture the petroleum and resource producing regions of Malaya, Borneo and Java—delivered a shock to the Japanese Navy. Now the fleet was expected to take the offensive thousands of miles away from Japanese home waters, capture enemy territory, and hold it. Outlying areas that were expected to be lost in the course of the Interceptive Operations now were to be held.

The Naval General Staff adapted. The Decisive Battle was moved thousands of miles from Japan, before the Southern Resource Areas could be recaptured. *Zengen Sakusen*, the darling of the Naval General Staff, still applied.

However, with a change in command of the Japanese Combined Fleet came a change in the Fleet's concept of how to open the war. The new commander was Admiral Yamamoto—the same Yamamoto Isoruko who had lectured on attacking Pearl Harbor in 1928. His thoughts returned to Pearl Harbor, considering the idea of a pre-emptive attack against the American Pacific Fleet employing *Kido Butai*, the concentrated carrier striking force. "It took someone in the Japanese naval high command of his position, stature, and heretical outlook to make the argument at the highest levels, and then push it through to activation."[20]

To Attack Pearl Harbor: Yamamoto's Objectives

Yamamoto believed that Japan should "fiercely attack and destroy the US main fleet at the outset of the war, so that the morale of the U. S. Navy and her people" would "sink to the extent that it could not be recovered." He went on to say, "We should do our very best at the outset of the war with the United States . . . to decide the fate of the war on the very first day." More ominously, he predicted that "If we fail, we'd better give up the war."[21]

With the spectacular success of the Pearl Harbor attack, such fatalism has been discounted. Yet, Yamamoto himself—"short, plump, superstitious, a womanizer and a passionate gambler"—expressed that "half calculation, half luck" played a major role in his decision making.[22]

What were these calculations? How much luck did the ardent poker player need? What did Yamamoto expect to achieve, and at what cost?

Addressing these and similar questions will help reveal whether the attack was a deservedly successful, finely calculated operation, or a spin of the wheel.

Objective #1: Sink a Battleship

The first objective was, simply, to sink a battleship.

Yamamoto, lauded as the "Father of Japanese Naval Aviation," believed that battleships were "white elephants." He opposed the construction of the superbattleship *Yamato*, echoing his aviators that "the three great follies of the world were the Great Wall of China, the Pyramids, and the battleship *Yamato*."[23]

However, he also believed that the battleship was fixed in the minds of the American public as the *sine qua non* of sea power, and that the battleship had "intangible political effects internationally as a symbol of naval power."[24] Should the Japanese succeed in sinking one of these behemoths, Yamamoto expected the Americans to be so shocked and demoralized that their will to continue the war would submerge with the shattered battlewagon. This, Yamamoto believed, would lead to the same ending as that achieved by Togo after the Battle of Tsushima: a peace conference leading to a negotiated end to the war.

Yamamoto concentrated on sinking battleships; carriers were not part of his picture. His utterances about sinking carriers were largely an afterthought.

At one time in the planning process, Yamamoto remarked, "Since we cannot use a torpedo attack because of the shallowness of the water, we cannot expect to obtain the results we desire. Therefore, we probably have no choice but to give up the air attack operation."[25] The shallowness of the water would not have prevented dive bomber attacks against carriers, which the Japanese believed could be destroyed by four 250-kg GP bomb hits, but torpedoes were required against battleships. He would cancel the attack if he could not torpedo battleships, even if there were carriers that could be sunk by dive bombers. Yamamoto's objective was the battleships, not the carriers.

There were other clues later in the war that seemed to indicate that Yamamoto was not such an all-out carrier proponent. "For all his lip service to the principle of the offensive and to naval air power, he still, perhaps subconsciously, visualized the battleship as the queen of the fleet."[26]

Yamamoto recognized that there were risks involved in attacking Pearl Harbor. In particular, there was a significant chance that American land-based bombers would strike *Kido Butai*, possibly before the raid could be launched. Yamamoto in particular and the Imperial Navy in general believed in the lethality of land-based bombers against warships. Part of their Strategy of Interceptive Operations was predicated on the presumed capabilities of island-based medium bombers.

Yamamoto did not see how the Japanese carriers could deliver strikes during the Interceptive Operations without themselves being attacked by the American carriers. Because of the fragility of aircraft carriers, this would only result in the carriers' mutual destruction with no subsequent advantage to Japan. What was needed was a way to strike the Americans outside the range of the American carrier-based aircraft.

Beginning in December of 1935 Yamamoto was assigned as the Chief of the Aeronautics Department of the Navy Ministry. He initiated the development of what was to become the G3M1 Type 96 Nell Attack Bomber.[27] This was a breakthrough aircraft—a high performance twin-engine land-based monoplane that could carry a torpedo on exceptionally long-range missions. In its combat debut on 14 August 1937, a strike into China, the G3M1 Nell flew a round trip of 1,200 miles, an extraordinary achievement for the period.

With this range capability, airfields on the Mandates could be used as "unsinkable aircraft carriers." In theory, aircraft could be transferred rapidly between airfields and concentrated ahead of the advancing US fleet. Massed medium bombers would strike well outside the enemy's capability to retaliate.[28] If the G3M1 Nell could eliminate the enemy carriers, then Japan's carriers would have the freedom to strike the American fleet with impunity.

Yamamoto had considerable faith in the capabilities of this aircraft. A practical example was his reaction to the news that the British battleship *Prince of Wales* and battlecruiser *Repulse* had arrived at Singapore on 2 December 1941. These ships were a direct threat to several huge Japanese convoys about to depart for the invasion of Malaya. The stakes were high. His countermove was to deploy squadrons of G3M1 Nell medium bombers from the Empire to Indochina. Yamamoto did not redeploy any of his surface combatants or his reserve of battleships. He thought the medium bombers would be enough.[29]

The Japanese projected the effectiveness of their medium bombers onto the American aircraft, a tendency called mirror-imaging. Assuming the American bombers would have similar effectiveness as their own, they expected to lose at least one and likely more of their fleet carriers in any attack on Pearl Harbor. The risk to *Kido Butai* was accentuated by the distance to the nearest Japanese base. Towing a crippled carrier home would be out of the question—distance, winter weather, and a shortage of fuel, much less continuing American attacks, would scuttle any attempt. Any Japanese carrier sustaining significant engineering or floatation damage would have to be scuttled. With Japanese intelligence reporting 550 aircraft on Oahu,[30] the Japanese carrier force could not be expected to escape unscathed.

The rather startling implication is that Yamamoto, portrayed as one of the most air minded of all the Japanese commanders, the "Father of Japanese Naval Air Power," once the commanding officer of the fleet carrier *Akagi*, was willing to trade one, or half, or possibly all of his fleet carriers for a small proportion of the enemy's battleship force. His operational orders to attack even if the carriers were detected 24 hours before the raid underline this willingness. In the actual event, when Japanese intelligence agents reported that all the American carriers had departed Pearl Harbor before the attack, Yamamoto was disappointed, but did not recall the attack. Sinking American aircraft carriers was a good thing in his mind, but not the overriding consideration. Yamamoto wanted a battleship, and was willing to pay in carriers.[31]

Even more startling was the fact that Yamamoto's planners at one time seriously contemplated a one-way mission. Since all of Japan's carriers did not have the unrefueled range to sail from Japan to Pearl Harbor and back, the planners considered sending in the carriers, launching the strike, recovering the aircraft, transferring the crews to other ships, and then scuttling those carriers without sufficient fuel for the return trip. One A6M Zero pilot related that "Genda-san told me that he was actually thinking that we would have to do a one-way attack in the beginning."[32] This option was dropped when means were found to provide the carriers sufficient fuel for a round trip, by overloading them with fuel at the outset and providing underway refueling.

Objective #2: Immobilize the Pacific Fleet

A second objective was to immobilize the US Pacific Fleet for at least six months. This was to prevent flank attacks interfering with the Japanese advance into the resource-rich areas in the far south. Was there actually a realistic threat to the Southern Advance by the US Pacific Fleet? If so, what would immobilize them?

Available Japanese Resources for the Southern Advance

The Japanese fleet was fully employed at the outset of the war. On 8 December 1941, the day of the attack west of the International Date Line, 93% of the Japanese large surface combatants and carriers were underway—ten of ten battleships,[33] nine of ten carriers, eighteen of eighteen heavy cruisers, and eighteen of twenty light cruisers. There were no operational ships left in Empire ports other than one escort carrier loading aircraft to ferry forward, and a few small patrol ships.

The fleet's reserve was the battle force, six battleships, two light carriers, two light cruisers, and ten destroyers, cruising south of Japan near the Bonin Islands. This force would remain in Empire waters until June of 1942.

The mobile striking force was a concentration of power: six fleet carriers, two fast battleships, two heavy cruisers, one light cruiser and nine destroyers. The Naval General Staff originally planned to have these carriers neutralize American air units in the Philippines, the most powerful enemy concentration of air power in the theater. Operating off the coast of Luzon, the carriers were to strike Clark Field and the surrounding complex of airfields, and afterwards provide direct support to the main invasion force at Lingayen Bay.

The Japanese would need all of their warships to successfully face the main American fleet, but much of their fleet would be committed as far away as the South China Sea supporting Army operations. It would take weeks for the Japanese Navy to concentrate enough force to oppose a move against the Marshall or Caroline islands, even if they cut free from their obligations to support the Army.

The Japanese advance south was a mountain torrent crashing into a desert plain. The surface forces of the US Asiatic Fleet consisted of only one heavy and two light cruisers with fourteen destroyers, while other Allied forces in the immediate invasion areas had only one battleship, one battlecruiser, one heavy cruiser, eight light cruisers (mostly obsolescent WWI types under 5,000 tons, suited only to protect convoys from auxiliary merchant raiders), with 13 destroyers.

There were other Allied forces scattered about—another two heavy cruisers and four light cruisers in outlying areas such as Sydney, Auckland, and South Africa. There were also a few cruisers and destroyers under repair or being refitted at Singapore, Sydney, and other locations. Some would be ignominiously towed to India to escape the Japanese advance.

	BB & BC	CA	CL	DD
Japanese invasion and cover forces	2	16	15	71
Allied Pacific Forces near invasion areas	2	2	10	27

BB = battleships; BC = battlecruisers; CA = heavy cruisers;
CL = light cruisers; DD = Destroyers

Against this the Japanese invasion and covering forces (excluding the carrier striking force) totaled two fast battleships, sixteen oversized heavy cruisers, fifteen light cruisers and seventy-one destroyers. In addition, the Japanese would have a light carrier and ten seaplane tenders, along with land-based air. The Japanese could expect to have air superiority, if not air supremacy, early in the advance.

The Japanese Southern Advance appears to have a surplus of surface combatants on a comparative basis, but this was incorrect. The ships' mission was to hunt down the Allied surface ships, but they also had to protect the numerous invasion forces, each of which would need covering forces. The Allies might concentrate nearly anywhere. However, if the two Allied capital ships were eliminated, the excellent Japanese heavy cruiser fleet would dominate the theater.

In turn, the Allied opposition was weaker than the numbers suggest. Its assets were mostly aging or obsolescent ships and aircraft suffering under divided command. The different nations had different objectives and different ideas, mostly contradictory, regarding the employment of their forces.

For example, the Dutch, facing the invasion of their homes in Java, wanted to concentrate all forces and fend off the Japanese invasion fleets in a last-ditch, to-the-death defense of Java. In contrast, the British and Americans took a longer view, using their surface ships to protect their convoys from armed merchant raiders as they redeployed their ground and air forces. Their ships would be scattered between India and Australia and all points between. They sought to preserve their ships for a war that would continue long after Java fell. Ultimately, decisions on strategy and employment were made often for transitory political considerations rather than a unified strategic vision.

The ABDA (American, British, Dutch, and Australian) "Fleet" had no common doctrine, no common language, and could barely communicate with each other. Comparing the ABDA forces to a speed bump would be to exaggerate its power.

In the climactic major surface battle of the Southern Advance, the Battle of the Java Sea on 1 March 1942, only three months after the beginning of the war in the Pacific, Japanese forces were present in overwhelming strength. The Japanese had five carriers, four battleships, twelve heavy cruisers, six light cruisers, and 33 destroyers either engaged or within a day's steaming of the battle. The ABDA coalition mustered two heavy cruisers, three light cruisers and nine destroyers—60 to 14 by ship count, nearly 10 to 1 in tonnage.

After only three months of fighting, the Japanese could have moved carriers, heavy cruisers and fast battleships to oppose any flank attack without unduly risking the Southern Advance.

Comparative Force Levels and the Pearl Harbor Attack

Battleships were the primary target in the Pearl Harbor attack.

The Japanese had to predict the American reaction if a given number of battleships were lost in an attack on the Pacific Fleet. The presumption was that with their fleet intact the Americans planned to advance; with some smaller fleet, the Americans would not. There are clues to how they may have developed their thinking.

Sometime after the Washington Naval Conference, the Japanese obtained information on the American Pacific strategy, Warplan ORANGE. The 1920s versions called for a rapid advance across the Central Pacific to seize the Mandates, recapture the Philippines and build an advanced base as a prelude to a fleet engagement. That plan would be executed with the forces allowed under the Washington Treaty, a 10:6 tonnage ratio in battleships and battlecruisers. So, the Japanese knew the Americans were planning an advance under the 10:6 ratio.

At the London Conference the Japanese proposed a 10:7 ratio. The Americans vigorously opposed this, an indication that 10:7 was the point where the Americans believed they could not defeat the Japanese with any surety. Consequently, the Japanese may have believed that an

(2) World Distribution of Battleships 6 December 1941

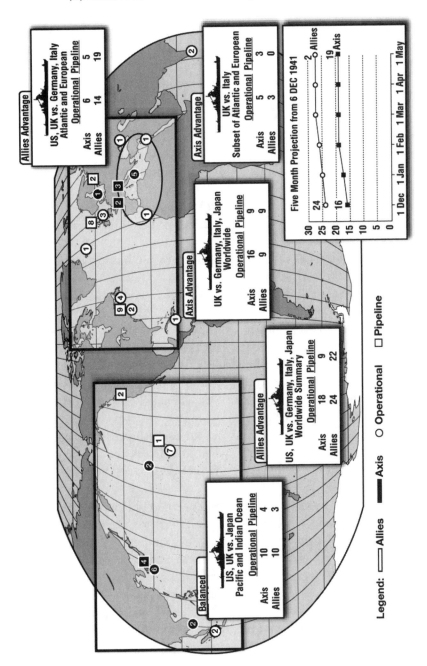

Legend: ▭ Allies   ▬ Axis   ○ Operational   □ Pipeline

Allies Advantage
US, UK, Germany, Italy
Atlantic and European
Operational Pipeline

	Operational	Pipeline
Axis	6	5
Allies	14	19

Axis Advantage
UK vs. Italy
Subset of Atlantic and European
Operational Pipeline

	Operational	Pipeline
Axis	5	3
Allies	5	0

Axis Advantage
UK vs. Germany, Italy, Japan
Worldwide
Operational Pipeline

	Operational	Pipeline
Axis	16	9
Allies	9	9

Allies Advantage
US, UK vs. Germany, Italy, Japan
Worldwide Summary
Operational Pipeline

	Operational	Pipeline
Axis	18	9
Allies	24	22

Balanced
US, UK vs. Japan
Pacific and Indian Ocean
Operational Pipeline

	Operational	Pipeline
Axis	10	4
Allies	10	3

Five Month Projection from 6 DEC 1941

Allies   Axis

1 Dec   1 Jan   1 Feb   1 Mar   1 Apr   1 May

American trans-Pacific move would be forestalled if the Americans had 14 or fewer battleships.

Yamamoto served as Japan's Chief Delegate to the preliminary talks for the Second London Naval Conference, and as a delegate to the 1934 London Naval Conference. He was intimately familiar with the arguments concerning force ratios and their implications.

On 1 December 1941 the Japanese had their capital ships deployed as shown in the chart above. The Americans had 17 battleships in commission, 14 operational, two ships in overhaul, and one in refit, of which eight (seven operational and one in refit) were at Pearl Harbor.[34] Thus, a loss of three battleships ought to draw down the American force low enough so that they would not risk a move west.

Within the six-month window for the Japanese offensive, three additional new 35,000-ton American battleships would be commissioned, of which one would complete workups and be available to participate in a Pacific offensive. An additional battleship would have to be destroyed at Pearl Harbor to compensate.

The Japanese could have used these considerations to calculate that they needed to incapacitate four battleships at Pearl Harbor.

Jumping ahead, appearance would indicate that the Japanese were correct in their estimates: after five battleships were taken out of the picture at Pearl Harbor, the Pacific Fleet did not sortie to relieve the Philippines. This has given the Japanese strategy a *post hoc ergo propter hoc* causality in the eyes of many historians. The Pacific Fleet did not move, therefore Yamamoto was right.

The Japanese set their objective at four battleships. This is confirmed from two statements. In the first, when asked why the attack on Pearl Harbor had not continued beyond the first two waves,

> Fuchida also stated that the knowledge that the attack had accounted for four battleships was also a factor since it seems the Japanese high command regarded this number as a guarantee that the Americans would not be able to contest Japanese moves throughout the western and central Pacific.[35]

In another statement, when Genda briefed the commanders of *Kido Butai* on 23 November, he explicitly stated that "the primary objective of the attack is to destroy all US carriers and at least four battleships."[36]

This substantiates the Japanese objective to destroy four battleships, a calculation that is a possible indication on how they arrived at that objective.

Note that Genda mentioned carriers before battleships. His personal objectives differed from Yamamoto's, and, as will be seen, were significant in planning the attack.

Did the losses at Pearl Harbor really immobilize the Pacific Fleet? The truth lies in more than a simple hull count.

The Americans did not see 10:7 as any kind of tipping point in the balance of power. During discussions about revising the Washington Treaty, the Japanese diplomatic code had been broken, and American negotiators knew that if they firmly opposed the new ratio the Japanese had been instructed to acquiesce. Their hard stand was not due to a particular fear of increased Japanese numbers, or a perceived threshold between the forces associated with victory or defeat.

In fact, according to US Naval War College calculations, the US battleline maintained significant superiority over the Japanese battleline even after the Pearl Harbor losses. The Japanese battleline included four lightly-armored battlecruisers that were comprehensively rebuilt in the 1930s into "fast battleships." Even with improved protection, their armor did not provide any zone of immunity against American battleship guns at less than 30,000 yards, making their gun turrets, magazines and engineering spaces vulnerable to knockout blows at the "hitting ranges" at which the battlelines would most likely fight. They were faster than the American battleline, so could choose to remain outside 30,000 yards where their deck armor was adequate, but at that range their hit rate would be miniscule and their ammunition would be expended to little effect. If they closed to hitting range they would be put out of action more quickly than any opposing American battleship.

So, American calculations showed the American battleline outclassing the Japanese battleline, even after Pearl Harbor. Warplan ORANGE could have been executed if their decision was solely based on their faith in defeating the Japanese in a battleline engagement.

Another aspect often ignored is that the Japanese were not only fighting the United States, but Great Britain as well. The chart above shows the worldwide distribution of battleships on 1 December 1941. The soon-to-be Allied nations had 24 operational battleships to oppose 16 Axis, 50 percent superiority. Five of the operational Axis battleships were

Italian ships trapped by geography, minefields, and airbases at the ends of the Mediterranean. They were technically outclassed by the British, and hampered by pusillanimous political controls, so these ships were effectively self-neutralized. Thus, the Allied advantage was greater than the numbers indicate, more like 24 to 11, or over two to one. On the other hand, four of the British battleships, the venerable "R" class, had severe operational restrictions and were the weakest of the British battleships, and certainly outclassed by the Japanese ones.

Since the destruction of *Bismarck*, the only operational Axis battleship with access to the Atlantic was *Tirpitz*. The battlecruisers *Scharnhorst* and *Gneisenau* were under repair at Brest, and so Great Britain, with nine operational battleships, looked to reinforce the Pacific. On 1 December 1941 that movement was in progress, with *Prince of Wales* and the battlecruiser *Repulse* en route to Singapore, and an "R" in the Indian Ocean.

Future trends were promising: two battleships would be coming out of refit (*King George V* and *Revenge*), two were completing workups (*Duke of York* and *Ramillies*), and one (*Warspite*) was in a US shipyard repairing battle damage and would be returning to service in February of 1942. Great Britain looked to have fourteen battleships and battlecruisers in service inside the six-month window that Yamamoto felt was needed to complete the southern operations.

If six battleships were retained in home waters to counter the Germans' three, and the situation in the Mediterranean maintained at the *status quo*, there would be five British battleships available for Far Eastern duties. Joined with the Americans' 17 it would give the Allies a total of 22. If a Pearl Harbor strike took out all eight battleships there, 14 American and British battleships would remain, right at the cusp of what the Japanese feared could defeat them. So, if the Japanese failed to achieve a "clean sweep" at Pearl Harbor, based just on superficial numbers there would be sufficient Allied battleships and battlecruisers available to form a concentration that on paper ought to be able to defeat the Japanese fleet. And, as will be seen, the Japanese could not expect to take out all the battleships in the US Pacific fleet.

There were significant impediments to concentrating the American and British battlelines. Should Singapore fall the British would not have a base from which to operate more forward than some Australian port. British battleships did not have the endurance of the kind demanded by central or south Pacific operations, and did not have the afloat logistics support—fuel and spare parts—to allow them to effectively maneuver in the vast Pacific. The Americans had plans for operations from remote anchorages, and likely could accommodate a British contingent as a substitute for damaged American ships. Fuel supply would be critical: 20 to 30 oilers would be required to support such a force, against the 11 available to support the entire Pacific Fleet. And indeed, as will be seen, it was not losses that defeated American aspirations to move west, but the steely hand of implacable logistics.

There are a number of practical things that also made such a concentration unlikely, things like a lack of a shared doctrine, incompatible command and communications, and the political willingness of the British to risk their battleships against what they saw as a secondary opponent. The chances that an effective union of the British and American fleets in the Pacific could have been realized in 1942 are miniscule.

Yamamoto treated the two fleets as independent entities. His attack on Pearl Harbor did not have the capability to draw down the total number of Allied battleships to where a combined Allied fleet could not defeat the Japanese battleline, but that was not needed. Yamamoto had the additional advantage of interior lines, should any British battleships operate out of Singapore or Java or Australia. But had the British and Americans advanced, even independently, he might have been faced with the necessity of splitting his battleship fleet. He could not be strong everywhere at once.

The next chart shows the world situation one month later, on 1 January 1942. The numbers have changed significantly. Of the eight battleships at Pearl Harbor, two were total losses and three were sunk with salvage operations likely to take six months or more. The remaining three lightly-damaged ships were sent to the West Coast for repairs and modernization. The British lost *Prince of Wales* and *Repulse* to Japanese torpedo bombers, and *Queen Elizabeth* and *Valiant* were crippled in Alexandria harbor by mines laid by Italian frogmen. In one disastrous month the Allies lost four battleships permanently with another five sidelined for long-term repairs, a loss of 38% of their operational force.

Against these losses, *King George V* and *Ramillies* completed their refits and returned to the operational forces. The Axis had the Italian *Vittorio Veneto* damaged by submarine torpedoes.

Overall, the Allied advantage evaporated. As the chart shows, Allied

(3) World Distribution of Battleships 1 January 1942

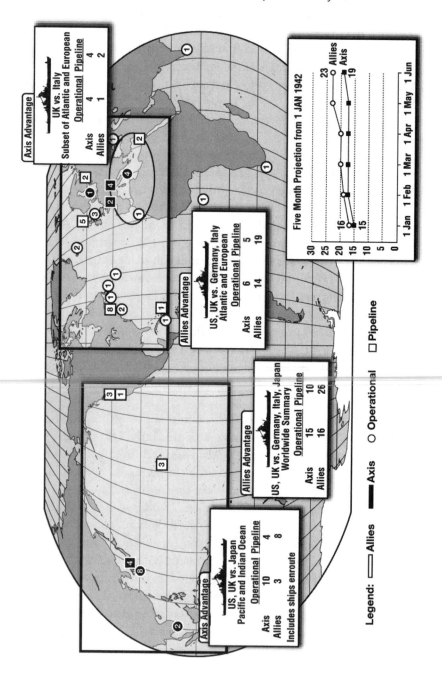

battleship strength was concentrated in the Atlantic, which will be discussed later.

Had it not been for some fortuitous, unpredictable help, Yamamoto's Combined Fleet could have been placed in a very difficult situation.

Consider the situation where the Pearl Harbor attack incapacitates four of the Pacific Fleet battleships, and the four British battleships had not been sunk at Alexandria and off Singapore. The Americans could have concentrated thirteen battleships at Pearl Harbor, while the British could have had five or more battleships in the Far East. This would have presented Yamamoto with a difficult strategic situation: split the fleet of reserve battleships, or concentrate against one and give the other enemy force freedom of action?

Had this situation developed, a likely possibility, by initiating war against both the Americans and British, the Japanese were placing their fleet in a perilous situation even with a successful Pearl Harbor strike.

The Expected Nature of the American Threat

There were four types of threats the Japanese faced from the Pacific Fleet, divided by time frame: an immediate threat (one to three months after war began), two intermediate-term threats (four to twelve months), and the longer-term threat.

Immediate Threat

Any immediate threat would come from the Pacific Fleet. Not counting ships in long-term overhaul, this would consist of three carriers, eight battleships, twelve heavy cruisers, nine light cruisers, and forty destroyers.[37] This force could mount raids on the Marshall and Caroline islands within weeks of the initiation of hostilities. It would be unlikely they could do more—they would be tethered to their base for fuel, as the demand for tankers for the European war cut the resources available to the Pacific Fleet.

However, the Japanese apparently did not consider that the Americans would be limited by such constraints, a manifestation of their famous neglectful attitude towards operational logistics. On the other hand, logistics constraints on the Pacific Fleet could be changed. If Hitler had not declared war on the United States, America might have declared war against Japan only. Many consider such an occurrence inconceivable, but it not only was conceivable, it happened—for three days, between when Congress declared war on Japan on 8 December, and Hitler declared war on the United States on 11 December. Had Hitler not twitched and allowed American rage to remain pointed to the Pacific, the "Europe First" strategy might have gone by the wayside, and the Pacific Fleet might have received a flow of resources looking more like those described in Warplan ORANGE (the original war plan for a war against Japan) rather than RAINBOW 5 (the American war plan for coalition war against the Axis).

The Japanese had received assurances from Hitler in April of 1941 that Germany would declare war on the United States, assurances repeated in November and again at the beginning of December. Hitler was anxious to bring the Japanese Navy into the war on the Axis side, while the German Navy was pressing Hitler to expand the submarine offensive beyond the restrictions imposed by American neutrality. So the Japanese could attack, secure in their assumption that the United States Navy would be engaged in a two-ocean war.[38]

Intermediate-Term Threat: The Pacific Fleet

After the war began the Americans were expected to gather auxiliaries and supply ships to allow deeper penetrations into the western Pacific. The Japanese believed they would also gather ground forces for a move directly to the Philippines. This was what the strategy of Interceptive Operations planned to defeat. The Japanese fleet could equal or exceed the Americans in battleships and battlecruisers, and outnumber them in carriers, cruisers and destroyers.

If this move occurred before units covering the Southern Advance could reinforce the battle fleet, the Japanese would only have the reserve battle force and *Kido Butai* to oppose the Pacific Fleet.

	CV & CVL	BB & BC	CA	CL	DD
US Pacific Fleet	3	8	12	9	40
Japanese Battle Fleet + *Kido Butai*	8	8	2	3	22

CV = fleet carriers; CVL = light carriers; BB = battleships; BC = battlecruisers; CA = heavy cruisers; CL = light cruisers; DD = Destroyers

In conventional terms, the Japanese would have the inferior force, being severely outnumbered in cruisers and destroyers. They would have a decided advantage in carrier decks, almost three times that of the enemy, but at this time carriers were still an unknown factor—it was not known how lethal they would prove against surface ships, and how rapidly their air groups would be depleted in combat operations. The Japanese did not have a reserve of carrier-qualified aircrew. When the carriers *Shokaku* and *Zuikaku* joined the fleet, the Japanese had to scrape the bottom of their training programs and raid schools and staffs to put together the air groups, and even then the two ships' air groups were considered to be only marginally qualified when they were dispatched on the Pearl Harbor raid.

Some theorists of the time believed that carrier air strikes at sea would suffer 50% attrition per strike. If so, the Japanese air groups would have been decimated to ineffectiveness after only two or three raids. The advantage in carrier numbers was not seen as the overwhelming force overmatch that a modern observer (knowledgeable of the subsequent carrier battles in the Pacific) would assess.

The Japanese would be badly outnumbered in cruisers, and it was from the cruisers that the Japanese pinned a good portion of their hopes toward wearing down the Pacific Fleet with massed torpedo attacks.

Overall, this was not a confrontation the Japanese preferred.

Ideally, the Japanese would want the American counteroffensive to come after the Southern Advance had concluded. This would not only free more fleet units for the encounter, but also the Japanese conquests would be "in hand" if a peace conference should begin immediately after the Japanese repulse of the Pacific Fleet. If the Pearl Harbor attack was successful in demoralizing the American public, Yamamoto believed the Americans should be brought to the negotiating table immediately after the fall of Singapore.[39]

Intermediate-Term Threat: Pacific and Atlantic Fleets Joined

A second intermediate-term possibility was that the Americans would wait to commence their movement until after the Atlantic and Pacific Fleets had joined.

Congress had refused to build up to the Washington Treaty limits, so in 1936, when the Treaty lapsed, the two navies were near to a ratio of 10:7. That would rapidly change. From the beginning of 1936 to the end of 1940 the Japanese added seven cruisers and had three battleships under construction, while the Americans added twelve cruisers and had ten battleships under construction, with many more ships planned. The Japanese fleet might be able to encounter the Americans at close to the Treaty ratio in 1941, but would see the odds tipped increasingly against them in 1942.

Long-term Threat: An Extended War of Attrition

The Americans might defer their major move west until after the fleets were reinforced by the flood of new construction due to begin arriving in late 1942. The Japanese had calculated that the Americans were building three to five tons of warships for every ton coming out of Japanese yards, and that American shipbuilding capacity would likely double during a war while the Japanese were already building at capacity. By 1944 they calculated the fleet ratio would be 10:3.[40] While awaiting force superiority, the Americans would likely restrict themselves to raids against the more remote Japanese bases, avoiding a decisive fleet encounter.

The Americans might also raid the Japanese homeland, taking the northern route via Alaska. Attacks against Japan's wood and paper cities were a frightening consideration, as was anything that directly threatened the life of the god-emperor.

Japanese Estimate of the Threat

As mentioned earlier, the Japanese had obtained information on the American Pacific strategy, but they did not have the Americans' timetable. This stimulated a hearty debate within Japanese command circles. The scenario that eventually captured the support of the Naval General Staff was one in which the loss of the Philippines would so enrage the American people that the combined Atlantic and Pacific Fleets would thrust forward without waiting for reinforcement from new construction. There was a minority view that the Americans would wait, but that view was ignored in Japanese planning.[41]

This was an American course of action that gave the Japanese a chance for victory. Japan had little chance for victory in a long war, and the Japanese knew it. They adopted a short war strategy which offered a chance to win, and built their force, trained their men and developed their tactics to support that strategy. They had no solution to the "long war" scenario—so they ignored it.

Eventually they became convinced by their own plan, and locked in by the inertia of their own bureaucracy with, as Agawa has noted, "a self-deluding formalism which assumed that the enemy would act according to predetermined conventions."[42] While confirmation bias and planning fallacy are an occupational disease of all human planners, national, historical, and military cultural factors made the problem especially prevalent among Japanese planners.

While the Japanese had the initiative in the first phase of their offensive, the Americans had control over the subsequent course of the war, and there was little the Japanese could do to influence that decision.

One look at possible Japanese thinking on the timing of the American advance can be found in the book, *The Three-Power Alliance and a United States-Japanese War*, published in Tokyo in October 1940. The author was Kinoaki Matsuo, a Japanese intelligence officer high in the Amur River Society, also called the "Black Dragon Society" after the Chinese name for the Amur River. The Society believed that the Japanese Empire should expand to the banks of the Amur. The society nurtured militaristic and aggressive aims.

Kinoaki stated that an American westward move would not happen without the joining of the Pacific and Atlantic Fleets. In his assessment, claimed to be based on information on United States naval maneuvers, it would take at least 60 days to join the two fleets, and another 60 to accumulate sufficient supplies to begin a westward offensive.

With a war beginning on 8 December, this would project the American advance to begin in early April 1942. By then, according to the Japanese warplans, both Singapore and the Philippines should have fallen, along with Java. Actual events unfolded with Singapore falling early (on 15 February), Java early (11 March), and the Philippines late (Bataan fell on 9 April). On 7 April 1942, when Kinoaki would have projected the beginning of the American thrust west, *Kido Butai* was attacking the British in the Indian Ocean, and the Japanese battle fleet was still in home waters. Kinoaki projected "a period of four months [when] the Japanese Fleet will be free to carry on its activities throughout the Pacific, and there will exist no strong opposing forces in the Pacific to interfere."[43]

American Plans

American strategy in the 1920's bounced back and forth between plans for a rapid thrust to the Philippines and for a more measured advance. The issue was resolved in December 1934, in a letter from the Chief of

Naval Operations to the Commander in Chief, US Fleet. The CNO stated that, when the warplan called for the Pacific Fleet to be "established in the Western Pacific" and "at the earliest date," these phrases should be used in conjunction with the phrase "in strength superior to that of ORANGE." The fleet would not begin a trans-Pacific movement without superiority over the Japanese, and the expectation that it would remain superior even after losses en route.

The CNO went on to drive a final stake into the heart of any plan for an immediate movement to relieve the Philippines: "In other words, after a consideration of the ratio of strength between the BLUE [US] and ORANGE [Japanese] fleets, the so called 'quick movement' for the present has been discarded."[44]

As the years progressed the schedule for a systematic advance was refined, and the schedule shortened. Fewer islands were to be assaulted and more bypassed. In plans developed before 1936, Truk was to be taken on day 75 after mobilization; later plans moved that up to day 59.

So, according to the 1930's ORANGE warplans, there was something for the Japanese to fear in American plans for an attack into the flank of their advance, even in the contingency where the quick movement to the Philippines was abandoned.

Japanese Naval Strategy to Support the Southern Advance

The Japanese strategy envisioned a decisive fleet action between battle-lines further and further away from Empire waters. In 1934 the battle was anticipated to occur near the Bonins and Marianas, 500 to 1200nm from Tokyo; in 1936, it was moved to west of the Marianas; in 1940 Yamamoto advanced the location eastward to the East Carolines and the Marshalls, 2500nm from Japan.[45]

This was a significant adjustment. Now, the Imperial Navy must capture *and hold* significant territorial conquests far from Japan. The outer defensive lines were no longer expendable, but had to become the reefs upon which the American Fleet was to be cast. The Interceptive Operations would have less depth in which to operate. The fleet would have to leave home waters and engage the Americans and British on the peripheries of their new empire.

Engaging there would be difficult, at the end of their fuel tether and with tired crews. The Japanese fleet had few salvage and repair ships to forward deploy to recover the detritus of the battle, because they were not needed under the previous concept of operations. Planning for battle further forward also meant it would happen earlier along the American's advance, leaving the Japanese less time to achieve and consolidate their gains and less time for the Interceptive Operations to work.

Why would Yamamoto agree to move the decisive battle out so far? It is likely that he acceded to the entreaties of the Naval General Staff *before* the war because he felt that such plans would be swept away as the war unfolded. Yamamoto was skeptical of the "formalistic view of tactics" that was held by the Naval General Staff. During a study meeting in 1940 he said, "Don't you think the Naval General Staff's idea of attritional operations relying fifty percent on submarines is a bit risky? I can't really believe that the idea of bringing them out to fight would work." He believed that a war centered on a "leisurely battleship sortie" just would not happen.[46]

If events did not cooperate with the Naval General Staff's scenario, Yamamoto could declare that the final decisive battle would occur in the Marshalls or Carolines or on the dark side of the moon, and it would be smoke in the wind. He could administratively announce agreement with the Naval General Staff while knowing in his heart that such announcements were irrelevant—the strategy would be, in modern US Navy parlance, OBE, "Overtaken By Events."

Meanwhile, the Naval General Staff persisted in believing they had a fair chance of success in this new, more distant Decisive Battle, while awkwardly acknowledging that there was no sure means of forcing such an encounter.[47]

Inter-service politics also intruded. The Imperial Japanese Navy's (IJN) commitment to fight the Decisive Battle far forward meant the Navy would fully support the Army's Southern Advance, and not abandon them to being bypassed and isolated while it was squatting on its conquests.

In one seminar after a joint Army-Navy wargame, an officer raised the possibility that the Americans might do something other than make a move to relieve the Philippines—for example, they might immediately launch an attack against the Japanese mainland. Surely different eventualities should also be studied? A Naval General Staff officer supervising the maneuvers replied:

> The campaign against the Philippines has already been decided on as operational policy by the imperial navy, and as such is

under study in collaboration with the army. It is highly regrettable that one should hear arguments rejecting it. We must not forget that to coordinate ideas on strategy is one of the aims of these exercises.[48]

The War in Europe's Impact on Pacific Fleet Strategy

On the American side, the ORANGE warplan was superseded by the RAINBOW series, which looked to a world war. It opens with a statement of overwhelming significance to the Pacific Fleet:

> Since Germany is the predominant member of the Axis powers, the Atlantic and European war is considered the decisive theater. The principal United States military effort will be exerted in that theater and operations of United States forces in other theaters will be conducted in such a manner as to facilitate that effort.

As a secondary effort, the Pacific Fleet was to act "offensively in the manner best calculated to weaken Japanese economic power, and to support the defense of the Malay Barrier." A "vigorous offensive," with "bold aggressive action," was desired.[49] These clarion calls were stirring in principle, but in practice would be difficult. More of the Pacific Fleet was siphoned off for Atlantic duty, scheduled arrivals of amphibious shipping and troops were delayed or redirected, merchant shipping became scarce, and the Pacific Fleet so starved for oilers that its radius of action was curtailed. With fewer ships, fewer Marines, and fewer auxiliaries, the idea of taking Truk by day 59 or day 75 or even day 180 was clearly impossible. RAINBOW forced a "long war" strategy on the Pacific Fleet.

Regardless, Admiral Kimmel, the Commander in Chief of the Pacific Fleet, planned for offensive action with carriers and battleships operating against the Marshalls, commencing only a few days after the beginning of hostilities. In addition to raiding, Kimmel had a rather fantastical plan to lure the Japanese fleet into battle by offering his aircraft carriers as bait.

Kimmel knew the Japanese would have to come to him, as he could not go to them. It would be hard for his force to work further to the west than the Mandates. The Pacific Fleet had four oilers equipped for underway replenishment of warships, but needed 25 for extended operations.[50]

With the war in Europe's insatiable appetite for shipping, and the German U-boat offensive sinking dozens of ships every month—while the American public was still addicted to its Sunday afternoon drives—shipping, particularly oilers, would be hard to snatch away.

Logistics, Forward Bases and "Unsinkable Aircraft Carriers"

If the Japanese were not totally blind to logistics, they were at least vision-impaired. They operated their forces with the barest minimum logistics support, often beginning operations with insufficient supplies to carry them through to completion. The construction of warships was always a higher priority than auxiliaries. Logistics concerns were secondary when constructing their outer lines of defense in the Pacific.

Some of the Japanese neglect stemmed from treaty restrictions. As a reward for participating in World War I, the Japanese were given the Mandate Islands in the Pacific under the League of Nations. As a price for accepting the 10:6 ratio in the Washington Naval Treaty, the Japanese insisted on a ban on fortifications in Pacific areas, denying Western powers forward support bases to operate against Japan (Article XIX). Eliminating fortifications matched both their needs and their inclinations, as it prevented a "base development race" in the Pacific that the Japanese wanted to avoid financially as well as strategically. Even after the Japanese abrogated their participation in the naval treaties and withdrew from the League of Nations, their concept of operations, where they expected to lose their outlying possessions during an attrition phase of the American advance, marked these possessions as expendable. Base development would be limited to the bare necessities to support attrition operations against the American advance.

For example, Truk, the Fourth Fleet's base from November 1939, was the strongest Japanese naval base in the Pacific. However, the Japanese "Gibraltar of the Pacific" had minimal shore repair facilities. Fuel storage was totally inadequate, eventually consisting of one 10,000-ton capacity underground tank and two above-ground 50 meter diameter by 20 meter high (250,000 bbl, 33,600 ton) steel tanks, a total storage capacity of 77,200 tons. The remains of these tanks can be seen today, though it is not known exactly when they were constructed.

To place this capacity in context, to fill one battleship would take about 5,000 tons of fuel, a heavy cruiser about 2,500 tons. If just the Japanese battleships and heavy cruisers of the Combined Fleet arrived, the fuel storage at Truk could not give them all a single ship fill. The 77,200 tons of fuel storage can be compared to the Americans' forward base in the Pacific, Pearl Harbor, with storage for 563,000 metric tons of fuel with additional capacity under construction.

During the war the IJN anchored tankers in Truk Lagoon as fuel storage "station ships." Instead of moving fuel the tankers acted as floating storage tanks, a burden on the limited Japanese tanker fleet.[51] Insufficient fuel transportation would be one of the three greatest causes of the defeat of the Japanese (the others being the inadequate wartime replacement of pilots, and the starvation of industry by the destruction of Japan's maritime transport).

The attitude of the Japanese to logistics is exemplified by an anecdote from one of their chart exercises. A unit was being advanced to contact with the enemy. To save fuel for high-speed operations in the vicinity of the opposing fleet, a slow speed of advance was initially dictated. This was criticized. The advance lacked "alacrity." Too much worry over fuel made "proper" maneuvers impossible. When forces were calculated as out of fuel, they were simply assumed to have been refueled at sea, and the swift advance continued.[52]

Logistics considerations were similarly ignored when making strategy. For example, in early January 1942 the Naval General Staff performed a study on invading, capturing, and sustaining a Japanese garrison in the Hawaiian Islands. Three million tons of cargo would be required to feed the islands' population over a year's time, and 30 ships per month to transport military equipment, a total of 60 shipments a month. A nine-knot freighter would take 36 days to make the round trip in transit time alone, not counting loading and unloading time and ship's maintenance and time spent awaiting escorts. The study concluded that Japan's overstressed merchant marine could not meet the requirement. This study did not consider that the food might not even be available from Japan, as food shortages were already a serious topic of conversation in homes throughout the Empire.[53] Obtaining food supplies directly from Indochina might double the shipping requirement.

In spite of this, members of the Japanese high command continued to advocate an invasion of Hawaii. One month after the Doolittle raid, the army joined in the decision to seize Hawaii.[54] Only the Battle of Midway put an end to their Hawaiian ambitions.

Mirror Imaging

Just as the Japanese tended to gloss over logistics concerns when making their own strategies, they tended to ignore logistics limitations confronting the enemy. The attitude of "mirror imaging" deserves mentioning. In mirror imaging, a side projects onto the enemy its own attitudes and beliefs and capabilities. In some ways this is a conservative viewpoint. Each navy tended to believe its intellectual foundation and abilities were superior to that of the enemy. If your own abilities are projected onto the enemy in a map maneuver or force calculation, and the enemy allowed to use your own concepts of operations, then you are attributing to them the "best" capabilities. If you can defeat them under those assumptions, you ought to be able to defeat them even with more assurance under actual conditions—presuming that the enemy was really inferior in that area as supposed, and they do what you expect them to do.

Both the Americans and the Japanese tended to mirror image. For example, on the American side, intelligence was rare on the performance and characteristics of Japanese warships and weapons. With no information on the performance of the Japanese 41cm (16.14-inch) guns mounted on the *Nagato* class battleships, the Americans simply assumed that it performed as well as the equivalent US 16-inch gun. When US Navy intelligence got their first sniffs of the construction of the *Yamato*-class battleships, they projected they would be quite similar to the Americans' *Iowa*-class, with 16-inch guns in triple mounts and just about the same tonnage and speed. A year after the Japanese introduced the 24-inch Type 93 "Long Lance" torpedo, Navy intelligence dismissed the idea that the Japanese could have developed an oxygen torpedo, because the Navy's Bureau of Ordinance declared such a weapon to be impossible. "Neither the British nor the Americans had yet mastered oxygen technology, so it was inconceivable that the Japanese had done so."[55]

Often this was done consciously. For example, a secret publication from 1944 dealing with the damage resistance characteristics of ships stated:

> Since practically no information is available on the defensive characteristics of Japanese ships, the best assumption that can be made at present is to assume that the Japanese ships have characteristics approximately equal to those of corresponding ships

in the U.S. Navy . . . it is believed that a large proportion of the Japanese fleet is made up of older ships with power of survival roughly equivalent to that of corresponding older ships in the U.S. Navy.[56]

In fact, this assumption was not very good. Japanese warships were optimized for speed and offensive power, and had considerably less resistance to damage and less damage control capability than comparable US Navy ships.[57] The Japanese mirror imaged when they assumed that American land-based air would be primarily directed against ships (as was the IJN's land-based air), that American submarines would be primarily used against warships in the same doctrine as Japanese submarines, and that the American move to the western Pacific would contain the same slapdash, "damn the logistics, full speed ahead!" neglect as the Japanese displayed in their own strategies.

For the Japanese, this also extended to a lack of flexibility in their assumptions, a "self-deluding formalism which assumed that the enemy would act according to predetermined conventions."[58] Anyone questioning orthodoxy was slapped down.

Development of Forward Bases and Mobile Repair Capability

Because of a lack of materials and the ships to transport them, most development of forward bases used local materials and hand labor by the garrison. The paucity of shipping meant that many islands were chronically short of food, fuel, and stores; materials for fortifying a base were sent in bulk only when a particular location was considered "next in line" for Allied attack.

Minimal also, when measured against American standards, was Japan's maritime development of Truk. Greater additional fuel storage and other facilities at Truk were certainly warranted. Some were built as the war progressed. Rather than providing piers, the fleet anchored in the lagoon. Supplies were delivered using small lighters. Having no piers or shore services—including steam, electricity, and potable water—meant the ships were constantly providing their own services, placing more wear and tear on their engineering plants, and having less availability for maintenance, less rest for the engineers, and a constant drain on the ships' fuel. Shore services could have been run on coal, which the Japanese had in abundance. Plus, coal did not require large (and vulnerable) storage tanks and pumps and piping. At Truk, the Japanese simply dumped coal in a heap near to where it was needed.

Damaged ships could get some help from a few tenders or an itinerant repair ship, but the Japanese did not have forward-deployed mobile dry docks. Ships with underwater damage had to go either to Singapore, back to the home islands, or (for some smaller ships) to captured American facilities in the Philippines. Ships damaged and not seaworthy enough to transit to one of these facilities were essentially lost for the duration—as the war progressed, scores of damaged warships and particularly merchantmen were anchored on whatever odd harbor they could reach, and there abandoned.

The Japanese inventory of forward-deployable repair ships was miniscule. *Akashi* was the only purpose-built repair ship in the fleet; she was joined by *Asahi*, converted in 1938 from a pre-dreadnought battleship, and *Yamabiko Maru*, converted from a 7,000-ton passenger steamer in 1941. Two other small ships added some repair capability. *Matsue Maru*, a 5,644-ton cargo ship, was converted into a "Specially Installed Construction Warship" in April of 1941, and *Urakami Maru*, a 4,317-ton cargo ship, was converted into a "Salvage and Repair Ship" in January of 1942.[59] These ships helped with maintenance and repair, but mostly they tried to make damaged ships sufficiently seaworthy to transit to a shoreside repair facility.

Other forward bases, the "unsinkable aircraft carriers" and "unsinkable submarine tenders," were similarly neglected prior to 1937. When given a choice between spending money on new warships or on forward bases, the Japanese placed a priority on warships. And, according to the treaties awarding control of the Mandate Islands to Japan, the islands were not to be fortified.

Even today the Japanese like to believe that the islands were unfortified. Agawa relates a story from 1937 where the American naval attaché in Tokyo sought permission to visit the Mandates but was refused, "not that [the IJN] did not want him to see installations being built in that area, but that it was afraid he might find out that there were no decent military installations at all; it wanted to leave him with the impression that some did, in fact, exist."[60]

However, this is disingenuous.

The islands in question were Class "C" Mandated Islands under the League of Nations, where the occupying nation administered the territory under its own laws, in this case as if the islands were part of Japan. They were not allowed to fortify the islands.

However, Japan withdrew from the League of Nations without returning the Mandates, and from 1937 they ignored restrictions on military development. Japan publicly insisted that it was not fortifying the islands; however, there was brisk development of ports and airfields and associated facilities for "economic development," facilities that certainly would have dual-use military applications in wartime. The exact extent of the development was difficult for outsiders to determine, since Japan discouraged travel to the islands, controlled entry rigorously, and guarded the sea approaches. Shipwrecked mariners were confined, closely guarded, and removed from the islands promptly. Westerners referred to them as "Japan's Islands of Mystery."

By June 1941, $28 million (equivalent to nearly $1 billion in 2009 dollars) had been expended throughout the Mandates, including $7 million ($250 million) on Saipan, Tinian, and Pagan in the Marianas. Facilities included airfields on Kwajalein in the Marshall Islands, Saipan in the Marianas, and Truk, along with port facilities such as piers, warehouses, and workshops. In 1939–40 seaplane tenders *Chitose*, *Kamoi*, and *Kinugasa Maru* carried construction crews and technicians to build seaplane ramps at Truk, Palau, Kwajalein, and Saipan. The tenders made several round trips to Japan to obtain additional construction supplies.

The Japanese insisted that these facilities were built for economic development. However, over the years, it was apparent that the authority controlling the location and design of coastal and island facilities shifted from civilians to the Japanese Navy. When examining the plans for such facilities as Aslito Airfield on Saipan (begun in 1934), it was found that most buildings were constructed to be bombproof and designed for easy conversion into military use, such as a facility for the assembly of aerial torpedoes. Many of these airfields, such as those on Saipan and Kwajalein, were used to launch air strikes in the opening hours of the war. The seaplane ramps facilitated operations of long-range Japanese reconnaissance flying boats such as the H8K Mavis.

While the Japanese limited development of fleet support bases, they did develop outlying islands to support offensive operations by bombers, reconnaissance planes, and submarines. In the context of the original Japanese strategy, overseas bases designed for the long-term forward sustainment and repair of the fleet would not be necessary. The war was supposed to be short, so it would be unlikely that seriously damaged warships could be repaired in time to participate in further actions. The decisive battle would be close to the Empire, so forward bases might be expected to fall to the enemy in the course of the Fabian retreat or be bypassed and isolated, so even the offensive base development was limited to the bare necessities. All that would be needed in the way of forward bases would be limited facilities to service reconnaissance seaplanes, medium bombers, and submarines. For the fleet, all that would be needed would be facilities in home waters.

This strategy was exploded when it was decided to invade and hold the forward resource areas in the Greater East Asia Co-Prosperity Sphere. Now, the Navy was being asked to take *and hold* islands thousands of miles from Japan. Under these new circumstances, the other primary reason for minimizing development of remote bases came to the fore: lack of resources, coupled with a lack of priority.

The Japanese economy was under a severe strain. They had been at war with China since 1931. Japan was smaller than the United States, in land, population, and resources. Remarkably, Japan had nearly matched US military expenditures during the interwar years with an economy no more than 15% as large. However, there was little remaining slack in the economy, and few civilian production facilities left to convert to war production. The competition for resources with the Army meant that the Navy could not have everything it needed. "The IJN was hard into the stops on the nation's total steel supply," critical for ammunition and ship production.[61]

Under those circumstances, and in accordance with their national psychology, the Japanese chose to invest in the means to attack rather than the means to defend and sustain. This makes sense on a superficial level: if the forces created to empower the attack did not succeed, any infrastructure of stores or facilities on remote bases could not reverse a setback in the Final Decisive Battle.

This logic holds only if the enemy fights the type of war that you expect, that you want him to fight. If the enemy should operate otherwise, choosing to exploit Japan's weaknesses rather than confront its strength, then the strategy is exploded, and what was a minor weakness becomes a major handicap.

The operation to invade Midway reflected Yamamoto's attempt to defeat the Americans' will to fight on his terms, with Japan on the offensive. It was to force the Americans into a decisive, morale-busting battle before the flood of new U.S. construction made the force ratios impossible. Instead, the loss of four Japanese fleet carriers made a shambles of Japanese pre-war strategies.

With the defeat at Midway the Japanese became reactionary, waiting to oppose an American fleet that they expected to concentrate into one large mass, a reversion to *Zengen Sakusen*. Instead, the war became a struggle of attrition on the fringes, a war of outposts, of cruisers and destroyers and submarines and carrier raids devoid of the massive Jutland-style fleet confrontation upon which the Japanese hopes were centered. Losses were nearly equal, losses which the Americans could replace but the Japanese could not.

Eventually, after the predicted massive American reinforcements arrived, the U.S. fleets concentrated and offered the prospect of a decisive battle, but with force ratios that the Japanese had little hope of overcoming—especially after the cruisers, destroyers, and aircraft that they had built to execute Interceptive Operations and bleed the American fleet had themselves been bled white in the war of outposts. The Marianas and Leyte became American-instigated Decisive Battles on American terms, after irreparable attrition to the Japanese forces on the periphery of the Co-Prosperity Sphere.

The lack of forward fortifications concerned the Japanese from the outset. An American move to take the Marshalls early in the war would both threaten the flank of the Japanese drive south as well as create an early breach in Japan's planned outer defensive arc. The Japanese felt that the Marshalls were not fortified sufficiently to thwart such a move. This was one of the considerations that argued for an initial strike against the American fleet at Pearl Harbor.[62]

Given the attitudes that resulted in minimalist facilities, it is not surprising that the Japanese had not considered the possibility that the destruction of port facilities or fuel transportation and storage might immobilize the American Pacific Fleet at Pearl Harbor better than a strike against fleet units. Again there was mirror-imaging in their thinking, expecting the Americans to act as they would have acted. They ignored—or were not aware of—American logistics vulnerabilities, a concern they could have discovered from open-source publications such as Thorpe's *Pure Logistics*. *Pure Logistics* featured an example problem calculating logistics requirements for a "Blue" [US] fleet of 20 dreadnoughts and 20 pre-dreadnoughts crossing a 5,000 nm ocean, with Blue having a mid-ocean base located at just about the same distance from the enemy as Hawaii.

The Japanese concentrated on destruction of the Pacific Fleet's warships, a logical approach particularly if they were aware of the CNO's dictum that a major offensive into the western Pacific would not be conducted until superior US forces were available. However, even with a successful strike at Pearl Harbor, the Japanese could not expect to reduce the American fleet (or, indeed, the Allied fleet, as they were to initiate hostilities with Great Britain and Holland as well the United States) to a combat power less than that of the Japanese fleet.

The objective of the attack was both material and psychological. The damage inflicted on the enemy was to support the territorial objectives of the war, and to inflict such losses was to establish the psychological state needed to allow the Japanese to win the ultimate victory at peace negotiations.[63]

Contradictory Strategies

Yamamoto's strategy had a significant consequence that historians have not previously recognized. The attack on Pearl Harbor by its very nature made Japan's overall concept for winning the war OBE. For *Zengen Sakusen* to succeed, the American fleet had to thrust west early in the war, before it was reinforced to overwhelming strength. And yet, the Pearl Harbor attack was to immobilize the American fleet for six months. These goals contradict.

With a six-month delay imposed upon the Americans, there was nothing to prevent them from waiting an additional six months when the arrival of newly constructed ships would give them the means to establish absolute material superiority. The Japanese concocted a narrative where an enraged American people would supposedly demand rapid revenge for the loss of the Philippines, forcing the fleet to move before it was reinforced. At the same time, the Japanese expected the Americans to be so indifferent to the Philippines that they would later barter it away during peace negotiations. From phase to phase the Japanese assumptions were inconsistent and contradictory. Assumptions changed to accommodate the goal of the moment.

This was a systemic problem within the Japanese high command. The Japanese never were good at formulating political goals and realistically determining the economic and military requirements to achieve them—witness their performance in China, Mongolia, and Korea.

The Japanese Decisive Battle strategy was questionable from the start. For example, what was to prevent the Americans from just turning around and refusing combat if they took too many losses during the Interceptive Operations? Of even greater concern, when testing their strategy in wargames, was that the Japanese found it impossible to locate the American fleet and execute their attrition attacks. In paper trials, Interceptive Operations and *Zengen Sakusen* could not be made to work. Perhaps as an expression of psychological avoidance, the basic Japanese plan was never given a trial in a full fleet exercise on the high seas.[64]

Japanese assumptions regarding the timing of the American counteroffensive consisted of unanswered questions and ill-founded premises. Why would the Americans move west after six months, with a force close to parity with the Japanese? Why would they not complete the salvage and modernization of ships damaged at Pearl Harbor and await the arrival of new construction reinforcements prior to moving west? Why would they continue an advance if heavy losses were sustained in the approach?

If Yamamoto's attack on Pearl Harbor was a success it would work against the only strategy Japan had for victory. It would be a classic case of "win the battle, lose the war"—which was exactly what happened. The choices were never so dramatically illustrated than by a photograph of the battleship *Wisconsin* tied up alongside the salvaged hulk of the *Oklahoma*. The Japanese had the dilemma of either meeting *Oklahoma* at sea early in the war, or striking Pearl Harbor and sinking a few ships like *Oklahoma*, imposing a delay on the Pacific Fleet, and so later having to face the more modern and powerful *Wisconsin* and her consorts.

Yamamoto substituted his vision of a short war coming to a negotiated end—based on the psychological shock of Pearl Harbor and the loss of the Philippines and southern resource areas—for the Naval General Staff's vision of a short war culminating in *Zengen Sakusen*. This realization gives better context to Yamamoto's statement, "If we fail [at Pearl Harbor], we'd better give up the war." He clearly had no confidence in *Zengen Sakusen*. Failure had to be defined not in terms of the results of an attack on Pearl Harbor but in terms of achieving what was needed to bring the Americans to the negotiating tables. If the attack on Pearl Harbor succeeded but did not result in negotiations, the losses caused by a successful attack would force the Americans into a long-war strategy, the very war in which Japan had no hope of victory.

It has been suggested that the strategies were actually complementary: a Pearl Harbor raid would reduce the effectiveness of the Pacific Fleet at the outset of the war, something like an early phase of Interceptive Operations, followed by the Decisive Battle that would convince the Americans that victory was not worth the necessary sacrifices. But Yamamoto did not believe that the Americans would behave in a manner to allow a Jutland-style battle at the outset, and there was no reason to believe that losses at Pearl Harbor would stir Americans into committing the fleet with inferior force ratios. Yamamoto had not thought ahead to consider a situation where the losses at Pearl Harbor did not bring the Americans to the negotiating table. The cobbled-together nature of the staff work and negotiations with the Imperial Army preceding the Midway Campaign was the result of Yamamoto's lack of foresight, as he tried to improvise his way out of the strategic situation he had imposed through the success of the Pearl Harbor attack. At least in Yamamoto's mind, there was no complementary connection between Pearl Harbor and *Zengen Sakusen.*

The psychological aspect of Yamamoto's objective (as opposed to material destruction) should not be dismissed. It played a significant role in how the Japanese would go about achieving their material objectives. In particular, the psychological aspect called for the attackers to prioritize the American battleships. Rear Admiral Onishi, Chief of Staff of the Eleventh Air Fleet, said Yamamoto believed that "Most Americans—like most Japanese—still believed battleships to be the mightiest weapons of war. The sinking of one or, better yet, a number of these giant vessels would be considered a most appalling thing, akin to a disaster of nature. Such destruction, Yamamoto reasoned, would paralyze the vaunted Yankee spirit."[65]

Yamamoto was after headlines, front page photographs of destroyed battleships. The target was the American people, a people with a prominent and vocal pacifist contingent who were placing pressure on elected representatives not to involve American troops in foreign wars. Most Americans couldn't find Luzon on a map. The Philippines were to be given their independence in five years. Why spill American blood to prevent something that was already scheduled to happen?

Yamamoto believed that if Americans could be induced to despair they would place pressure on their government to end the war, leaving Japan in possession of the southern resource areas. He asserted that "American public opinion has always been very changeable, so the only hope is to make them feel as soon as possible that it's no use tackling a swarm of lethal stingers. . . . And the one other thing we can do is to take bold risks, resigned from the start to losing up to half our own forces."[66]

Yamamoto did not understand the Roosevelt Administration. They saw things not as "the Japan problem" and "the German problem," but the problem of defeating the Axis *en toto*. There would be no contemplation of a separate peace with Japan. Pearl Harbor eliminated Japan's greatest potential negotiating tool, its offer to switch sides and join the Allies against Germany as the price of a separate peace. The Japanese assumption that a separate peace was possible was fatally flawed.

The losses at Pearl Harbor and the Philippines did not induce despair. The Americans were not interested in a negotiated, separate peace. With their pre-war assumptions exploded, Yamamoto's fallback was *Zengen Sakusen,* with a twist. He must force a final decisive battle onto the enemy by an attack on Midway, which Yamamoto thought would flush out the American battleline. Yamamoto extemporized his way into a course of action that became the greatest role reversal in history.

After six months of war he gathered together a massive fleet to steam east. He placed himself on what he had proclaimed to be that world-class "folly," the battleship *Yamato,* and led an invasion fleet against the island of Midway. He was opposed by Midway's concentrated air power and the American carriers, in what the Japanese would call an Interceptive Operation. Yamamoto took the course of action Japan had wanted the Americans to take, and the Americans' Interceptive Operations did to the Japanese what the Japanese had hoped to do to the Americans.

Even if victorious in the carrier preliminaries, Yamamoto would not have gotten his *Zengen Sakusen,* as the Americans did not commit the battleships of Joint Task Force One to defend Midway.

The Battle of Midway has to stand as the greatest irony in military history.

CHAPTER TWO

TARGETS, WEAPONS, AND WEAPON-TARGET PAIRINGS

Initial Estimates

Yamamoto initially consulted with his close friend Rear Admiral Onishi Takijiro, Chief of Staff of the Eleventh Air Fleet, asking him to begin a study of the feasibility of an attack on Pearl Harbor. They eventually discussed the concept. Yamamoto concluded from the meeting that the attack would be "so difficult and so dangerous that we must be prepared to risk complete annihilation."[1]

Onishi brought in Commander Genda Minoru, the Air Staff Officer of the First Carrier Division. Genda and Onishi were friends, and had discussed a carrier attack on Pearl Harbor several years previously. Genda was a naval aviator with a reputation for iconoclastic brilliance, but also known as "Madman Genda" at the Naval Staff College because of his radical advocacy of aircraft and his expressed belief that all battleships ought to be scrapped.[2] He was an advanced thinker regarding the employment of aircraft at sea. His theories became known in the Japanese fleet as "Gendaism."

Genda thought an attack on Pearl Harbor would be "difficult but not impossible." He worked on a draft concept of operations and preliminary assessment, which he presented to Onishi in February. He believed surprise was necessary. The main objective of the attack should be the enemy carriers, with a high priority given to land-based aircraft. The

American's main base in the Pacific was, in modern terminology, "target rich," with more worthwhile targets than could be serviced by the aircraft from Japan's four fleet carriers.[3] He recommended a balanced daylight attack employing torpedoes, bombs and fighters. There would be sufficient bombs and torpedoes only for the most important targets. Strike assets would have to be carefully allocated. Genda asserted the principle that light damage inflicted to many targets would be trivial and readily repaired, while heavy damage inflicted on key targets could be debilitating. This called for careful allocation of effort.

The key targets were generically separated into two categories: First, capital ships, the destruction of which was expected to lead to achieving the primary objectives of the attack; second, targets necessary to keep the Japanese strike aircraft and Japanese warships safe.

There was a third category, that of base infrastructure and logistics facilities. This would include things like the shipyards, drydocks, the submarine base, supply depots, administrative buildings, barracks, and fuel storage. These were not targeted. The striking aircraft simply could not carry enough bombs to do everything. The Japanese should direct their efforts against the fleet and American air power, not facilities.[4]

Onishi took Genda's draft and, after some modifications, presented to Yamamoto what we would now call a "white paper" of some ten pages. Planning began in earnest, expanding to bring in more and more subject matter experts and staff officers. Genda was eventually assigned to handle all portions of the planning relating to aviation, including studies and training.

The exact requirements of the objective are important. The American fleet was to be immobilized for six months. Heavy damage inflicted on battleships, particularly torpedo or AP bomb hits, would keep them out of the war for at least six months even if there were fully-operational repair facilities available.

One torpedo hit can put a ship out of commission for months, even if it is hit while closed up for battle. It is not just the hole in the side of the ship and the smashed equipment, but there is also wiring and insulation and pumps and motors and stuffing tubes and other sundry gear that is damaged by salt water, an insidious, corrosive liquid. Shock can damage systems far away from the torpedo hit: torpedo explosions have put gun directors high on a ship's superstructure out of commission. Pumps can be shocked out of alignment or bounced off their foundations.

A British study conducted in 1943 of torpedo hits on cruisers found that, in the 19 cases examined, the average repair time was 9.5 months.[5]

AP bombs also could immobilize a battleship for six months if they penetrated into the engineering spaces. In 1937, during damage effects experiments using the obsolete battleship *Hannover*, the Germans detonated 28cm (11-inch) and 38cm (15-inch) AP shells in her boiler and engine rooms.

The 28cm shell caused immediate debilitating damage. Burst steam piping would have forced the space to be evacuated. However, the damage was not so extensive as to preclude repair during a yard overhaul of less than six months.

The 38cm shell completely destroyed the equipment in the spaces (boilers or engines), requiring complete new installations. The repair work would have required at least six months, more if spare assemblies were not immediately available.[6]

These tests would tend to underestimate the damage effects of a shell. The shells were stationary when detonated, so that all the kinetic energy put into the shell fragments came only from the energy released by the explosive charge. The German 28cm APC shell had a bursting charge of 14.55 pounds generating about 27 megajoules, while the 38cm APC had a bursting charge of 41.4 pounds for 78 megajoules. The kinetic energy of the mass of the shell itself would depend on the residual velocity after it penetrates the armor, which would depend upon terminal velocity, armor thickness and orientation, and a host of other factors. If the shell retained 100 meters/second residual velocity (out of a striking velocity on the order of 700 meters/second), another 2 megajoules or 4.3 megajoules, respectively, or 7%, would be added to the energy total.

It is not known if the Germans passed on the results of their tests to their Japanese allies before the Pearl Harbor attack. However, the Japanese had performed similar tests against *Tosa* in June of 1924 and likely reached similar conclusions.

As will be shown in further pages, even several hundred bombs would not have placed the repair facilities out of commission. But if torpedoes and bomb hits on battleships could do the job, then striking infrastructure targets would have been unnecessary—they were irrelevant in the context of the six month objective. In fact, Japanese planners never even considered them as targets.

The first priority targets were the capital ships of the fleet, both the battleships that would provide the headlines and the aircraft carriers that could threaten the Japanese fleet with counterattack. Part of the strike would be directed against American air bases in what is known in modern terms as offensive counter-air (OCA), to keep fighters from interfering with the Japanese bombers and to prevent bombers from counterattacking.

The Japanese feared land-based air. Yamamoto originally considered a one-way attack employing only torpedo bombers. If this was not feasible, he suggested launching a full strike from 500 to 600 miles off Oahu in a one-way attack (*katamichi kogeki*). The aviators would ditch in the vicinity of Pearl Harbor and be recovered by submarines. Yamamoto estimated that when the American people saw this form of attack they would think the Japanese "such a unique and fearless race that it would be useless to fight them."

Genda rejected Yamamoto's concepts. "A one-way attack would have a bad psychological effect on the airmen if they knew their only means of survival would be the slim chance of being picked up at sea.... Ditching in enemy territory would be a needless waste of planes and highly trained airmen."[7]

With two or even four carriers, Genda's estimate was that the total aircraft available could not haul sufficient bombs and torpedoes to destroy everything. Damage estimates showed that more carriers were needed. The Japanese would have a total of six fleet carriers available in November 1941 when *Shokaku* and *Zuikaku* joined the fleet, albeit with air groups that would be "really green."[8]

However, there was competition for fleet carriers: the Operations Section of the Naval General Staff[9] felt they needed at least two fleet carriers to support the Southern Advance, especially the invasion of the Philippines, which would be opposed by a significant American air component.

Genda's conclusion was that the effort should not be made unless all available fleet carriers were thrown into the attack. The Operations Section knew that fighter support would be necessary to support the attacks on the Philippines. The conflict seemed insurmountable.

Eventually, trials with the A6M Zero naval fighter developed fuel conservation techniques that gave the fighter sufficient range to escort bombers launched from Formosa against the main Philippine military facilities at Subic, Clark Field, and Cavite. By lowering engine RPM and leaning out the fuel supply, the A6M Zero's cruising speed was reduced to 115 knots, but fuel consumption was cut from 35 gallons per hour to 17. This gave the Zero a range of as much as 1,250 nm with an endurance of 11 hours.[10] This freed the fleet carriers to strike Pearl Harbor.[11]

It was the weapon of the samurai that provided the inspiration for the attack. In the repertoire of the sword there is the "one swift stroke," *Kinshicho-Oken*, where the samurai in one motion pulls his sword from its scabbard and decapitates his opponent, then returns to his original position.[12]

Japanese Weapons, Naval Air Power, Carriers, and the China Experience

The Japanese in 1941 were leaders in carrier aviation. Their technical development was advanced relative to the other navies and seasoned by combat experience in the China War, a war which was to see the introduction of a new level of performance in naval aviation with the introduction of the monoplane, an all-metal aircraft of unprecedented performance.[13]

During the war with China, Japanese aircraft carriers ranged along the Chinese coast, launching strikes. When the war moved further inland, the air groups from *Ryujo* and *Hosho* were based inland at Kunda outside Shanghai.[14] With Japan's new high-performance fighter, the A5M Claude, and the development of a special looping turn maneuver (a displacement roll) that allowed the Claude to cut inside the turns of enemy fighters, eventually the Japanese gained control of the air.

They also gained an opportunity to test out doctrine and equipment. For example, they learned that long-range, high-altitude and high-speed medium bombers required fighter escort, and that high-altitude bombing was not always devastating, contradicting the beliefs of many Western air power theorists.

Operational experience also revealed weaknesses. Japanese aero engine technology was behind the West in making reliable high-powered engines. As a consequence, and due to a philosophy that enshrined maneuverability and eschewed "defensive" protective features such as armor plate and self-sealing fuel tanks, their aircraft were lightly built. This gave them superior maneuverability and speed and allowed them to carry heavier payloads over longer distances than other nations' aircraft with comparable engine horsepower.

However, this also made the aircraft susceptible to enemy fire. Japanese aircraft fuel tanks did not include self-sealing inner liners, making them susceptible to leaks and compression vapor explosions when hit, earning the Japanese aircraft the sobriquet of "Ronsons," the name of a popular cigarette lighter of the era. One aircraft type that was to see service at Pearl Harbor, the D3A Val dive bomber, had a fuel tank under the pilot's seat.

The Japanese viewed these as acceptable trade-offs. Their emphasis was on offensive capabilities, with defensive capabilities scorned as "not Japanese." For example, the instructions to the designers for the 12Si carrier fighter competition (that which resulted in the A6M Zero fighter), formulated after the initial Chinese combats in 1937, required no armor protection. None could be provided considering specifications that called for extreme maneuverability, speed, and rate of climb—the Japanese were just not concerned with attributes that might be considered "defensive."[15]

The Japanese tradition of personal combat, dating back to the middle ages, moved Japanese fighter pilots to chase enemy fighters and engage in dogfights, forgoing the mundane "defensive" task of escorting bombers. Bombers took severe losses in the air war as the fighters pursued personal glory.[16]

These material and doctrinal weaknesses were not considered deficiencies, but just the cost of waging war the Japanese way. Japanese society considered it a great honor to die in combat. Fallen aviators—any fallen warrior—were worshipped as deities. Death in battle was to discard what Buddhism calls the small self so as to serve the greater cause, to live in the great Imperial Virtue, resulting in a readiness for self-sacrifice that was clearly manifested in the Japanese people. Coupled with the Japanese belief that war was an act of will, and that "an iron will can accomplish anything," these concepts led almost inevitably to aircraft that emphasized offensive capabilities. Defensive characteristics were eschewed almost as if they were an insult to the aircrews' fighting spirit, *Yamato damashii*.[17]

The Imperial Army took a different direction. Early reports from the war in Europe indicated that armor protection and self-sealing fuel tanks were indispensable. Those features were included in the design of the Ki-61 Tony fighter that began production in August of 1942. It was considered a success, and over 3,000 were produced during the war.[18]

By late 1941 the Japanese had four fleet carriers available, along with one escort and two light carriers, with a total capacity of 378 operational aircraft.[19] She had five fleet carriers, two light carriers and two escort carriers either under construction or conversion, or undergoing final workups, which meant an additional capacity of 406 aircraft.[20] The light and escort carriers did not have the range to accompany an attack against Pearl Harbor.

The most modern carrier aircraft, the A6M Zero, joined the fleet in 1940. The aircraft and qualified pilots were in short supply. Aircraft were produced in a factory and towed by oxen up a winding trail through the main street of a small town to the nearest airfield. Production was slow. Some Japanese carriers would not get the A6M Zero until well into 1942.

Weapon—Target Pairings

The A6M Zero, besides being a superb dogfighter, carried a step up in armament over the previous generation of fighters. They had two 7.7mm nose-mounted machine guns, and two low-velocity 20mm cannon in the wings. The 7.7mm machine gun bullets did not have much penetrating power, nor did the 20mm, as its shell was fuzed to detonate on contact with the lightest structures. It was an effective strafing platform.

Besides the A6M Zero fighter, the Japanese carrier air wings consisted of two types of bombers. The "heavy hitter" was the B5N Kate, an aircraft with a crew of three that could be used either as a high-altitude level bomber or a torpedo bomber; payload options were one 250 kilogram (kg) high explosive general-purpose (GP) bomb and six 60kg GP bombs, or two 250kg bombs,[21] one 800kg AP bomb, or one 800kg 18-inch torpedo.

The D3A Val dive bomber was a two-seater aircraft similar in aspect to the German Ju-87 Stuka and capable of carrying a single 250kg GP bomb.

A weapons-target table is a means of summarizing which weapons are appropriate for use against each type of target. Weapons-target matching was critical in determining the roles the aircraft could fulfill. The table below summarizes the alternatives available to the Japanese planners in accordance with their doctrine. An "X" denotes an appropriate match, but should not be read to mean an optimal match—only that there was a reasonable capability with that weapon system (aircraft + ordnance) against that target. "SEAD" stands for Suppression of Enemy Air Defenses, accomplished by strafing or bombs. This is a modern term, but the tactic was available to the planners at the time.

	BB	CV	CA CL	Airfield facilities	Aircraft on ground
B5N Kate + torpedo	X	X	X		
B5N Kate + AP bomb	X				
B5N Kate + GP bombs		X	X	X	X
D3A Val + GP bomb	SEAD	X	X	X	X
A6M Zero + 20mm cannon	SEAD	SEAD	SEAD		X

Torpedoes v. Capital Ships (Battleships and Carriers)

The weapon of choice against capital ships[22] was the torpedo, and the Japanese had a good aerial torpedo in their Type 91 Mod 2 weapon.

Between 1924 and 1936 the Japanese carried out extensive experiments to determine the resistance of various underwater protection designs. Charges were placed against the hull of the incomplete battleship *Tosa* (to be sunk in compliance with provisions of the Washington Naval Treaty), and against a full-size model thought to be similar to the underwater protection scheme of the *Colorado* class battleships, as well as against many scale models. A complex formula was derived to predict the performance of underwater protection schemes against different combinations of air- and liquid-filled voids of various depths and bulkhead thicknesses.

In the tests against the *Colorado* model, a 350-pound warhead from a Type 91 Mod 1 torpedo penetrated all the torpedo defense compartments and broke through the innermost holding bulkhead.

By 1941, the Mod 2 torpedo carried a 452-pound warhead using an improved Type 97 explosive (60% TNT and 40% Hexyl). The Japanese had every expectation that their aerial torpedoes would be able to defeat the anti-torpedo protection of the American battleships.[23]

The Japanese underestimated the quality of the American anti-torpedo protection. The Type 91 Mod 2 proved to be only marginally capable against the oldest battleships, while the more advanced protection in the later Treaty battleships held. Against *Nevada* (BB-36), a hit between turrets one and two at frame 41 did not penetrate the torpedo defense system's innermost holding bulkhead, but did split seams and cause leaks. *California*'s (BB-44) holding bulkhead was deflected inward but was essentially undamaged.[24]

The Japanese believed that four or five torpedo hits would likely sink a battleship,[25] three or four a carrier.

A significant impediment to a torpedo attack was the shallow water in Pearl Harbor, 40 to 45 feet deep. Aircraft torpedoes would typically dive below 100 feet, and could go as deep as 150 to 300 feet, before rising to their intended running depth. Genda resolved to use torpedoes in the attack even before this technical problem was solved.

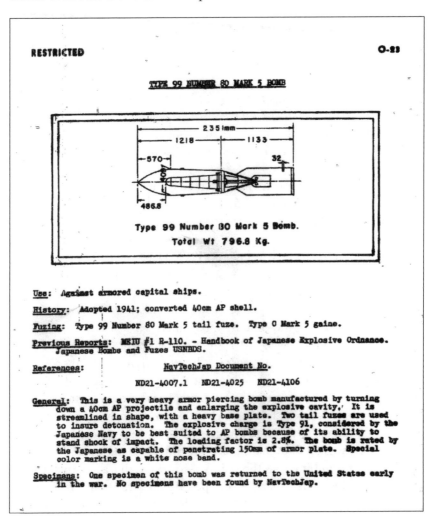

RESTRICTED   **O-23**

TYPE 99 NUMBER 80 MARK 5 BOMB

Type 99 Number 80 Mark 5 Bomb.
Total Wt 796.8 Kg.

Use: Against armored capital ships.

History: Adopted 1941; converted 40cm AP shell.

Fuzing: Type 99 Number 80 Mark 5 tail fuze. Type 0 Mark 5 gaine.

Previous Reports: MEIU #1 R-110. - Handbook of Japanese Explosive Ordnance. Japanese Bombs and Fuzes USNBDS.

References: NavTechJap Document No.

ND21-4007.1   ND21-4025   ND21-4106

General: This is a very heavy armor piercing bomb manufactured by turning down a 40cm AP projectile and enlarging the explosive cavity. It is streamlined in shape, with a heavy base plate. Two tail fuzes are used to insure detonation. The explosive charge is Type 91, considered by the Japanese Navy to be best suited to AP bombs because of its ability to stand shock of impact. The loading factor is 2.8%. The bomb is rated by the Japanese as capable of penetrating 150mm of armor plate. Special color marking is a white nose band.

Specimens: One specimen of this bomb was returned to the United States early in the war. No specimens have been found by NavTechJap.

(4) US Technical Mission to Japan Ordnance Data Page for 800-kg AP bomb[26]

AP Bombs v. Battleships

The Japanese Type 99 No. 80 Mark 5 armor-piercing bomb was converted from a 41cm (16.14-inch) gun shell, a Mark 5 or Mark 6/Type 88 APC projectile (circa 1921) used on *Nagato*-class battleships. These shells were replaced after 1931, making them available for conversion.[27]

To retain the capability to penetrate armor, most of the bomb was solid metal. The AP cap and the windscreen were removed. To reduce the weight further the body was machined down and tapered toward the base, and the thick projectile base plug was eliminated. The inside of the lower cavity was machined to accommodate a thinner base plug with two fuzes. A threaded area below the new base plug was added to attach the tail.

The old explosive was replaced by Type 91 (trinitroanisol), a more effective explosive than the older Shimose (picric acid). The explosive filler weight, 50 pounds, was less than in the original shell due to the volume of the second fuze and the room needed for connection threads for the new tail section.

This is a small explosive charge for such a heavy bomb—in contrast, the American 1,600-pound (725.7kg) AP bomb carried 240 pounds of explosive.[28] The Japanese used their Type 91 explosive due to its ability to withstand the shock of impact.[29] It was more powerful than Shimose, but less than an equivalent weight of TNT. Detonation was initiated by two independent long-delay fuzes similar to those on AP projectiles, requiring a heavy impact to set them off. If the bomb hit several thin plates before striking armor it might be slowed to the point where there was insufficient deceleration to initiate the primer.

The final assembly weighed 1,760 pounds.

US battleships carried deck armor distributed over several decks with an aggregate thickness of 5 to 6.5 inches. Testing consisted of dropping bombs against armor plate designed to replicate the protection of *West Virginia* with a combined deck thickness of 5.75 inches. In a test drop from 3,000 meters altitude, the bomb smashed through the plate.[30]

This test was an illuminating demonstration of the state of the accuracy of level bombing and the cobbled-together character of Japanese weapons testing. The Japanese dropped bomb after bomb from 3,000 meters, trying for several weeks to hit the plate without success. They were on the verge of giving up when, at the last moment, a successful hit was achieved. There is an almost comic-opera atmosphere to this incident. Other nations tested bomb penetration and fuzing by firing their bombs from a howitzer at close range, regulating the powder charge to obtain the desired impact velocity.[31]

The Japanese may not have tested fusing and detonation during these drops.

Their conclusion was that, if dropped from high enough, the 800kg bomb had the capability to penetrate into the armored citadel of a battleship. In comparison, the US 1,600 pound armor-piercing AN Mark 1 bomb was rated to penetrate 6-1/4 inches of armor when dropped from 10,000 feet (3,048 meters), with an uncertainty of plus or minus 15%.[32]

The Type 99 No. 80 Mark 5 bomb carried two base fuzes for reliability. There was a 0.2 second delay to allow the bomb to penetrate deep into the hull. The fuze was rather insensitive, requiring the bomb to hit something heavy and substantial, such as armor plate, for fuze initiation. This made the weapon unsuitable for use against carriers, cruisers, or smaller ships, where the fuze would likely not initiate. During the attack on Pearl Harbor, an 800kg AP bomb passed entirely through a ship, the *Vestal*, exploding underneath it.

According to the US Naval War College Maneuver Rules and Fire Effect Tables of the period,[33] it would take seven (using the bomb effects tables) to fourteen (using the 16-inch shell tables) penetrating hits to sink a battleship. The Japanese believed that twelve to sixteen direct hits from big guns would sink a ship in a surface battle, and that those results would likely carry over to shells converted into bombs.[34]

Later US Navy analysis determined that American AP bombs, containing three to five times the amount of explosive filler as the 800kg Type 99, had insufficient explosive power to cause extensive flooding in a battleship. AP bombs could sink a battleship only if they induced an explosion in a main or secondary magazine. Since magazine areas were 23% of a battleship's target area, six hits would give a 79% chance of sinking the ship.[35]

A challenge associated with using AP bombs is battle damage assessment (BDA). From a 10,000-foot altitude it would be difficult for bombardiers to visually follow the path of their bombs all the way to the target. Aviators would have to look for the signature of the bomb as it hit. For a miss, the signature would be an explosion on the land or in the water, visible from the aircraft unless the bomb buried itself in the ground, failed to detonate, or had a low-order explosion.

If the bomb hit and penetrated into the ship before exploding, the signature would be difficult to detect. A bomb exploding in an engineering space would mostly be marked by a cloud of white steam escaping from ventilators or open hatches, if the ship had steam up; otherwise, the smoke of the explosion might not be seen. For hits in boiler rooms, a cloud of soot and smoke forced up the ship's stacks would be the most prominent sign. Bombs could also hit the ship but not defeat the deck armor, exploding outside the citadel.

In general, prominent explosions denoted failure. Consequently, hits were estimated not by counting successes but by counting those that missed, and assuming that anything that did not miss must have exploded deep inside the target. Duds or low-order detonations would throw off the count.

It was difficult to determine if an AP bomb hit, or if a hit achieved its objective. This is a significant problem strategically. Not knowing the extent of the damage meant not knowing if the Pacific Fleet battle force was immobilized. This would influence whether Japanese forces could be dispatched south to the front lines of the advance, or had to be retained to counter possible American counterattacks from the east. If the Japanese had no assurance the Pacific Fleet was immobilized, there would have been significant impact on their operations. For example, it is unlikely that the Indian Ocean raid employing all the available carriers of *Kido Butai* would have been conducted had the Japanese thought the American fleet capable of an offensive.

GP Bombs v. Capital Ships

The Type 99 No. 25 model 1 Ordinary 250kg general purpose (GP) bomb carried by the D3A Val dive-bomber was designed to attack unarmored ships. In contrast to the 800kg AP bomb with 50 pounds of explosive, the 250kg GP bomb packed about 136 pounds of explosive, almost three times as much as the AP bomb.

The GP bomb had limited utility against battleships. According to the Japanese experts, "Nor can we expect too much from dive bombing because the [bombs] are too light to penetrate the heavy armor of a United States battleship."[36] Topside and superstructure damage was relatively easy to repair, and would not keep a battleship out of the war for the requisite six months. In the context of the Japanese objectives for the Pearl Harbor raid, GP bombs would largely be wasted against battleships.

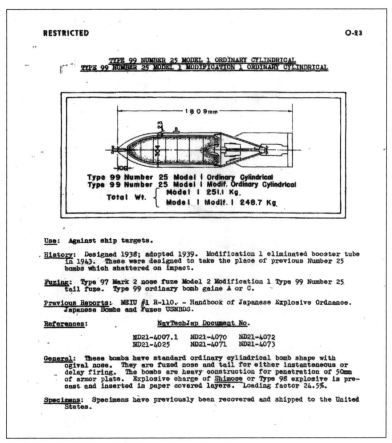

O-23

TYPE 99 NUMBER 25 MODEL 1 ORDINARY CYLINDRICAL
TYPE 99 NUMBER 25 MODEL 1 MODIFICATION 1 ORDINARY CYLINDRICAL

Type 99 Number 25 Model I Ordinary Cylindrical
Type 99 Number 25 Model I Modif. Ordinary Cylindrical
Total Wt. { Model I 251.1 Kg.
{ Model I Modif. I 248.7 Kg.

Use: Against ship targets.

History: Designed 1938; adopted 1939. Modification 1 eliminated booster tube in 1943. These were designed to take the place of previous Number 25 bombs which shattered on impact.

Fuzing: Type 97 Mark 2 nose fuze Model 2 Modification 1 Type 99 Number 25 tail fuze. Type 99 ordinary bomb gaine A or C.

Previous Reports: MEIU #1 R-110. - Handbook of Japanese Explosive Ordnance. Japanese Bombs and Fuzes USNBDS.

References: NavTechJap Document No.

ND21-4007.1   ND21-4070   ND21-4072
ND21-4025   ND21-4071   ND21-4073

General: These bombs have standard ordinary cylindrical bomb shape with ogival nose. They are fuzed nose and tail for either instantaneous or delay firing. The bombs are heavy construction for penetration of 50mm of armor plate. Explosive charge of Shimose or Type 98 explosive is pre-cast and inserted in paper covered layers. Loading factor 24.5%.

Specimens: Specimens have previously been recovered and shipped to the United States.

(5) US Technical Mission to Japan Ordnance Data Page for 250-kg GP bomb[37]

The GP bomb could be effective against aircraft carriers and cruisers. The bombs were fitted with a fuze with a 0.2 second delay, sensitive enough to initiate upon hitting the relatively thin decks of a cruiser or carrier. The bomb would penetrate 20 to 40 feet to detonate deep in the hull. In contrast, American 500- and 1,000-pound GP bombs had a 1/10th second delay, expecting 3 to 8 feet of penetration before exploding. These weapons were designed more to tear up a carrier's flight deck and shut down flight operations.

For comparison purposes, American estimates in the secret document "Striking Power of Air-borne Weapons" give an insight into the power of similar weapons. Three hits with 500-pound GP bombs had a 99%

chance of sinking a 1,630-ton destroyer, and a 70% chance of sinking a 2,100-ton destroyer. Three hits by 1,000-pound GP bombs had a 95% chance of sinking an Atlanta class light cruiser, and a 30% chance of sinking a 10,000-ton heavy cruiser. Six hits by 1,000-pound GP bombs would give an 80% chance of sinking a heavy cruiser.[38]

Why did Japan not develop an armor piercing bomb that could be employed by a dive bomber? The US Navy in 1941 had four such bombs from 1,000-pound down to 600-pound. A 1,000-pound bomb was introduced in October 1942 that could penetrate a 5-inch deck if dropped from 6,500 feet in a 300-knot 60-degree dive.[39] The exact reason is unknown, though there are some facts that may have influenced the decision (if it was contemplated at all):

1. Tests in early 1941 indicated that an 800kg bomb had to be dropped from 12,000 feet to get the penetration needed to defeat a battleship's deck armor. It may have been thought that a 250kg bomb, the design payload of the D3A Val, dropped from lower altitude in a dive, just would not be able to penetrate enough armor.
2. A shortage of special steel precluded stocking specially-made 800kg AP bombs. A steel shortage might also have deterred work on lighter AP bombs for dive bombers.

SEAD: GP Bombs and Strafing v. Air Defenses

Prior to the outbreak of the war in the Pacific, there was considerable uncertainty regarding the effectiveness of air attack against well-defended warships. Defensive fire was expected (by surface officers) to disrupt air attacks and exact horrible attrition from bombers. Some Japanese believed that the interferences from defensive fires would be so unsettling that bomber hit rates would be one-third that achieved in peacetime exercises, and losses to defensive fires would be unacceptably high.[40]

Torpedo bombers were thought to be particularly vulnerable, as they were large targets traveling slowly at low altitude and directly toward their targets, offering a greatly simplified AA fire control problem.

One solution was thought to be the employment of fighters and dive bombers to suppress AA fire. Fighters would strafe the superstructures of warships, killing or driving away AA gun crews, damaging the weapons themselves, and interrupting their ammunition supply. GP bombs exploding in a ship's upper works could be devastatingly effective against exposed gun mounts and their personnel. A 250kg bomb hit amidships on a battleship would stop most of the fire from the 5-inch and 3-inch anti-aircraft guns that were generally mounted on an open deck and unshielded. One of the highest priority modifications after the Pearl Harbor attack was to install splinter shields and gun tubs around AA guns and their crews.

Suppression of enemy air defenses (SEAD) attacks against warships were a recognized tactic during the pre-war period. The US Naval War College Maneuver Rules issued in March of 1940 included provisions for strafing to suppress warships' AA fire. An attack by 12 fighters (each with two machine guns and two 100-pound bombs) would reduce a ship's AA fire by 30% for a full day; six or more strafing aircraft would reduce the effectiveness of AA batteries by 50% against any bombing attack that immediately succeeded the strafing.[41] In June 1944 this rule was revised, reducing the required number of strafing aircraft to three, likely a reflection of the heavier .50-cal six-gun armament on modern fighters.[42]

The Japanese employed SEAD during their war against China, sending fighters against Chinese AA emplacements. This employment perhaps reflected more the lack of enemy fighters, leaving Japanese fighter pilots looking for something to do. It may not have been planned. They were not particularly effective in that role, since their training and mindset concentrated on air-to-air combat.

By 1939 the naval air forces incorporated suppression of enemy AA defenses into a system of massed aerial assault against fleet units. Fighters would strafe the ships' AA defenses, followed by level bombers, and then the near-simultaneous attack of dive bombers and torpedo bombers. The dive bombers, less vulnerable than the torpedo bombers, were assigned to both sweep away AA batteries with their 250kg bombs, and to draw AA fire away from the torpedo bombers.[43] These tactics were available to the Pearl Harbor planners.

One thing that undermined the effectiveness of the 250kg bomb in the SEAD role was its fuze setting. The 0.2 second delay meant that the bomb was supposed to penetrate well below decks before exploding, which would not be as effective in suppressing AA as the Americans' super-quick fuzing, which swept a ship's upper works with bomb fragments even if the bomb exploded in the water close aboard.

The fuze delay led some American sailors to suppose the Japanese GP bombs were delayed-action AP bombs. For example, the destroyer *Dale* was leaving the harbor during the dive-bombers' attacks on *Nevada*. Three of *Dale's* sailors recalled:

> There were bombs falling all around. And they were armor-piercing bombs, which buried themselves deep in the mud on the bottom of the channel before blowing up. The explosions sent huge fountains of water and stinking mud up higher than *Dale's* radio mast . . .
>
> The bombs that they were using were 16-inch armor-piercing battleship rounds with fins welded to them . . .
>
> One hit to starboard, and the other fell into the water right next to the boat davit where I was standing. The explosions sent up a huge fountain of stinking mud that fell all over us.[44]

The last AP bombs were dropped 45 minutes before *Dale* sortied.

Testimony of *Dale's* sailors highlights one of the problems in using eye-witness reports from veterans' memories. They can be contaminated by later reading and by their discussions amongst themselves. Sailors did not know during the attack that the Japanese were using converted battleship projectiles as AP bombs, and they certainly did not know if the fins were welded or threaded or heat-shrunk on. They remembered huge columns of mud, and they recorded they were attacked by AP bombs, since in US practice AP bombs had delayed fuzes and GP bombs did not. In this way witness reports have introduced inaccuracies into the historical record.

The Type 99 GP bomb sometimes detonated with a red cloud-like signature. Observers claimed that some appeared to be filled with flammable liquid,[45] while several officers reported them as an incendiaries.[46] *Shaw* took three hits described as "liquid-filled incendiaries weighing from 200 to 300 lbs."[47] The bomb that hit forward of the *Pennsylvania* also had noteworthy incendiary effects. However, the endorsement to *Shaw's* War Damage Report correctly concluded, "There is no positive evidence that incendiaries were used elsewhere in the attacks on ships at Pearl Harbor, and it is believed that none were dropped on *Shaw*."

A more likely answer is that the explosive pour in the bomb was done haphazardly, leaving bubbles and discontinuities, so that the explosive detonated incompletely, some burning like fireworks. Although spectacular in appearance, such displays were less lethal than if the explosive had properly detonated.

Air to Air

The A6M Zero comprised a quantum change in fighter performance. It was armed with two 7.7mm (.30-cal) machine guns firing through the propeller, and two 20mm cannon, one in each wing. The kinetic energy and explosive charge of the 20mm made it effective in the ground attack role. Ammunition was loaded with alternating armor piercing and tracer rounds, thought to be particularly effective in penetrating aircraft fuel tanks and then igniting the leaking fuel. The fuze was very sensitive, as it had to explode immediately after impact with light aircraft surfaces.

The 20mm carried only 60 rounds per gun, about 7 seconds of fire. The 7.7mm (.30-cal) guns carried 680 rounds per gun,[48] for about 40 seconds of fire. Pilots were trained to fire the 7.7mm guns first, and when on target add the 20mm for the killing stroke. In practice this could rarely be done successfully, because the initial velocities of the guns were mismatched (600 m/s 20mm rounds chasing 750 m/s 7.7mm rounds), and the velocity decay rate of the rounds were drastically different.

These defects were noted. The A6M3 Type 0 Model 32 Hamp (an updated model of the Zero) introduced an upgraded 20mm cannon with a longer barrel giving more initial velocity and better matching the 7.7mm's ballistics. The aircraft designers provided 100 rounds per gun. The A6M3 Hamp was introduced in April 1942, four months after Pearl Harbor.

The primary opposition to the A6M Zeros at Pearl Harbor was the P-40B Warhawk. The P-40B was armed with two .50-cal machine guns firing through the propeller and two .30-cal machine guns in each wing, a total of six machine guns. It was not as maneuverable as the A6M Zero, but had armor protection for the pilot, protected fuel tanks, and could take a tremendous amount of punishment. Used properly, the P-40B was an adequate-to-good fighter. If they could overwhelm or avoid the defending A6M Zeros and penetrate to the Japanese bombers, the lightly-built, vulnerable bombers would have suffered significant losses and significantly reduced weapons delivery accuracy.

A B5N Kate carrier attack bomber armed with a torpedo taking off from a carrier. This photograph has sometimes been identified as depicting one of the bombers from the Pearl Harbor attack. This is more likely a single frame from a propaganda movie about the attack. The torpedo looks an exercise round: note the prominent dent in the warhead.

Source: Naval Archives, Washington DC

CHAPTER THREE

WARGAMES

First Estimates

Early in April 1940 Yamamoto's staff officer for air discussed the attack with his opposite number on the Second Carrier Division's staff, Lieutenant Commander Suzuki Eijiro. Suzuki believed that, with surprise, the attack could succeed. However, he believed that it would cost the Japanese three of the four carriers used in the attack, perhaps all four. Suzuki calculated that if the Americans sent up 100 bombers, that *Kido Butai's* defenses could eliminate only about 40, leaving 60 to bomb the fragile carriers.[1]

Wargames

The first test of the attack's operational concept was in a series of wargames conducted in September of 1941. While other staff members in the main facility gamed the Southern Advance, 30 selected personnel— a group of the most senior commanders—withdrew to a separate room.

The specific rules used in the wargame have not surfaced, but from some of the surviving commentary it is possible to understand the basic structure the Japanese used.

First, some background. There were three styles of wargames prevalent among the navies of the period:

- Rule-based games, where all movement and combat was regulated and adjudicated strictly in accordance with specific, predetermined rules. Combat results were determined by deterministic rules, or alternately a throw of the dice or random number tables provided variability;
- Umpire-controlled games, where combat results were decided by the judgment of subject matter experts or specifically-trained officers;
- Hybrid games, a combination of rule-based and umpire-controlled games, where rule-based or randomly generated combat results can be overruled or modified by the umpire.

The leading practitioner of naval wargaming was the United States Navy. The Naval War College (NWC) held academic and analytic wargames using rules first introduced in the early 1920s and constantly updated. Wargames at the tactical and operational level constituted the majority of the time spent in instruction in the senior officer's course, lasting nine months to a year. By 1941 the rules and data filled hundreds of legal-sized pages. In contrast, the British naval wargaming rules ran to 43 pages.[2] The USN also had a simplified system used during fleet exercises.

Rules were strictly followed. An umpire had the authority to adjust results in the course of the game for those cases not handled thoroughly in the rules (which were few). When testing operational plans, the atmosphere was very interactive, with all ranks providing input and criticism. Calculations of logistic requirements were an integral part of the games.

At the NWC, strategic map wargames and tactical wargames were used for training, to test out and explore options in war planning, and to compare the capabilities of potential ship designs, test out tactics, and formulate fighting doctrine. Operationally, commanders used games to test plans for weaknesses, practice responses to enemy countermoves, and explore logistics concerns. For American naval officers, the games were intense—in the schoolhouse, reputations were made and broken; underway, admirals who blundered in fleet exercises were known to be passed over for promotion or gracefully retired from active service.

The Japanese ran hybrid games, primarily to test operational plans to see how they stood up to enemy countermoves.

The Japanese wargames could also be an intensely political process.

In the case of the games testing the Pearl Harbor plans, Yamamoto used gaming as an opportunity to socialize the plan with his senior commanders and the Naval General Staff. The game introduced the plan's concept, showed its potential, and corrected conceptual and operational errors. It allowed Yamamoto to muster his supporters and, more significantly, to flush out the opposition, drawing them into making their positions public. This prevented situations where officers could work against the plan behind the scenes—the game forced them to make their positions open and public, so Yamamoto could identify them and deal with their objections.

The plan could be changed on the spot to address some officers' issues. In other cases, with the opposition identified, Yamamoto could employ his considerable charm, and appeal to them directly for their support. Several key opponents identified during the games were convinced to withdraw their opposition.

This socialization process was of considerable significance, considering the sometimes volatile nature of Japanese decision making. For example,

> When Rear Admiral Yamaguchi Tamon, the commander of the Second Carrier Division [*Hiryu* and *Soryu*], became aware that planners were considering not including his command in the strike force bound for Pearl Harbor, he became highly intoxicated and physically seized Nagumo and, watched by a collection of officers who made no attempt to intervene, beat his commander until the latter agreed that Yamaguchi's formation would be included in the task force. In another confrontation, Yamaguchi threatened to kill Nagumo.[3]

Surprisingly (by Western standards) Yamaguchi retained his command. His desires were accommodated, not as a result of his conduct but because his conduct aligned with Yamamoto's desires. His behavior could be interpreted as the kind of "fighting spirit" the Japanese valued.

The wargaming environment also conferred a certain amount of control to the host, in this case, Yamamoto. A few words with the umpires might influence results to favor those options Yamamoto desired, and show undesired options in a bad light. With control of the assumptions and combat results, a good umpire could govern the outcome, both of the game and of the political process.

Japanese wargames tended to push logistic matters to the background. Logisticians could attend and observe the games to see what support would be required of them, but clearly they were subordinate to the combat commanders. Logistics did not drive the scenarios, as in the NWC games. The Japanese Pearl Harbor games did not totally neglect logistics, but did assume that the logistics problems would be overcome.

The Japanese staff system valued accord and promoted unanimity. Agreement with the group was a guiding principle. Dissenters had strong social and professional pressures to concur with the group. As a result, after agreement it was very difficult to later challenge assumptions or judgments. Anyone attempting such impudence would at best firmly be put in his place, at worst publicly reprimanded. Commanders might be required to execute a plan that they felt was seriously flawed.

Prange's Misinterpretation

Japanese wargaming during World War II has been given a bad reputation by Prange, who criticized the wargames that preceded Pearl Harbor and especially those held before the Battle of Midway.

In the workup to the Midway operation, Prange highlighted a game where the Japanese force was attacked and two carriers were lost. Rear Admiral Ugaki Matome, the Chief of Staff of the Combined Fleet, intervened and restored the two carriers.[4] In Prange's words, "With a sunny lack of realism . . . He did not scruple to override unfavorable rulings of other umpires."[5] Prange contends such actions were the result of overconfidence and a refusal to credit the Americans with a reasonable level of combat effectiveness. Concentrating on personalities rather than process, Prange characterizes the wargame as a contest of one-upmanship. He scolds what he sees as "war games rigged to make the enemy look incompetent, just as in the planning for Pearl Harbor."[6]

Prange did not understand operational wargaming. His interpretation is seriously flawed.

One purpose of an operational wargame is to understand what could possibly go wrong and to gather insights on how a plan might progress in the face of enemy countermeasures. Umpires' decisions are revised to take into account modifications of the plan, lessons learned, to prevent the game from departing too far from what is considered the most probable course of events, or to allow different elements of the plan to be exercised.

"Game" is an unfortunate label, as it connotes an activity with winners and losers. "Chart exercise" is a better title, with less baggage.

Consider a chart exercise where a carrier force is approaching an island for a surprise attack. During the approach the Carrier Force Commander believes he has not been spotted, so, after his strike is launched he retains his CAP (combat air patrol) fighters on deck. Unbeknownst to him, an enemy submarine spotted his force and the enemy launched their own air strike. With no fighter protection aloft, nine hits sink two of the carriers. The lesson is, "Keep CAP aloft at all times." Notes are made to change the operational order to that effect, and the results recalculated assuming the fighters were properly on station. The exercise proceeds.

Compare this with Prange's description of the wargame held prior to the Battle of Midway:

> . . . during the table maneuvers, the theoretical American forces broke through and bombed Nagumo's carriers while their aircraft were away from their mother ships attacking Midway—the very situation which had concerned Ugaki. Lieutenant Commander Masatake Okumiya, the umpire, ruled that the enemy had scored nine hits, sinking both *Akagi* and *Kaga*. But Ugaki would not suffer such *lese majeste*, and immediately overruled Okumiya, allowing only three hits, with *Kaga* sunk and *Akagi* slightly damaged. And later, when conducting the second phase practice, he blandly resurrected *Kaga* from her watery grave to participate in the New Caledonia and Fiji invasions.[7]

A wargame has many potential paths. Many could result in cancelled operations or major readjustments to a plan, since "no plan survives contact with the enemy." To prevent wasting time exploring possible (but improbable) rabbit-trails, combat results often have to be readjusted to allow the entire plan to be exercised. What Prange interprets as hubris, as "*lese majeste*," and depicts as an inability to stare unpleasant reality in the face, is actually a common and necessary practice in operational planning wargames. With two carriers sunk, the operation would likely be broken off, so continuing down that path would not have been fruitful. The objective of the wargame is not for one side or the other to "win," but rather to see how to best execute the operation and to ferret out unanticipated factors.

Prange failed to mention that the nine hits were generated by a *die roll*, not by a pre-calculated deterministic ruling.[8] The die roll may have given an extremely improbable result, a statistical outlier, a result entirely appropriate for Ugaki to overrule. On the other hand, Okumiya is said to have been surprised by the move, indicating either that it was unusual to intervene in this manner, or that the change was questionable. Japanese wargaming was hostage to the judgment of flag officers.

Consider another gaming situation. A force takes a route through shallow water and runs into a minefield. Two carriers are lost. There is an alternate route available in waters that cannot be mined. The two carriers are restored to the game, and a note made to change the operational plan to avoid the shallow water. This is not *lese majeste,* simply the accepted practice of adjusting the course of the action to account for lessons learned.

Prange accepted uncritically comments made by Fuchida that, "If any notable difficulties arose, Ugaki arbitrarily juggled them in favor of the Japanese team."[9] Without a clear understanding of operational wargaming, he did not know to ask questions that might have resulted in a more balanced assessment and a better understanding of what might require Ugaki to make adjustments to the game's combat results.

Much of this testimony comes from Fuchida. Here, as in many other places, he relates the story in a manner that places others in a bad light and intimates that Fuchida knew better all along. Fuchida was not the impartial witness needed to pass judgments on Ugaki's decisions.

As the exercise proceeded, Ugaki and his staff should have been noting lessons from the individual encounters and tabulating them to discuss after the game. Japanese culture and manners limited on-the-spot criticism. The results were likely adjusted so the exercise could continue to test the plan. Prange stated that "cheating occurred during the war games for Pearl Harbor,"[10] as if it was a schoolyard game with winners and losers. He was oblivious to Ugaki's responsibility to monitor the proceedings, and, while ensuring they did not stray far from the objective, that of exercising the entire plan.

Similarly, Ugaki "resurrected" *Kaga* to allow the officers in command of the New Caledonia and Fiji operations to undergo the crucible of simulated battle with carrier support included in their plan. In the real world, *Kaga* was lost and the New Caledonia and Fiji operations were cancelled. There was nothing to be gained in the wargame by "practicing" cancelling the operation. To exercise its part of the operation *Kaga* was needed, so *Kaga* was "resurrected."

Certainly the games can be criticized. The process of converting game lessons to planning changes appears to be less effective than it ought to have been—it may not have been formalized at all. The usual American practice was to include note-takers capturing all such issues in preparation for discussions afterward; we do not know if the Japanese had a similar formal practice. Their practice was likely more informal, with individual officers installing changes to their parts of the operational order based on their personal observations and discussions with their counterparts.

A trap of wargaming is the assumption of godlike powers by umpires and admirals. Games proceed under conditions that they deem realistic, even if they are based on judgments that others might question. In the Japanese games there were disagreements over some decisions, but the purpose of a chart exercise is to bring such disagreements out into the open for consideration.

The game's Japanese critics should not be ignored. There were flaws in the game and gaming process, and judgment calls by the umpires and admirals that were questionable. However, the Japanese wargaming effort was more robust, less arbitrary, and more productive than Prange's interpretation would suggest. Certainly it was not perfect; in the Midway game there were elements of the "Victory Disease" that infiltrated Japanese attitudes and thinking, along with a sense they would win regardless of what the Americans threw in their path.

Victory Disease had yet to taint the environment when Yamamoto held the first of several wargames to examine the Pearl Harbor attack—more the opposite, as most Japanese naval officers were in awe of the magnitude of what they were about to attempt. These wargames seemed genuine, with perhaps some staging by Yamamoto to help socialize acceptance of his plan with other senior officers. They were games to explore operational alternatives, and not merely to put an existing plan to the test. As such there appears to be fewer interventions by senior officers, although there were some rather improbable judgments that, as will be seen, reflected the role the gods were assigned to play.

The First Games

The first of the wargames were played on 16–17 September 1941. The

Japanese allocated all four of their active fleet carriers to the striking force. The carriers were spotted before they launched their attack, alerting Pearl Harbor's defenses. The Japanese strike met heavy resistance from interceptors and AA. Half the strike aircraft were shot down,[11] losses on the order of 106 to 127 aircraft (depending on the composition of the strike). Only "minor" damage was inflicted. Counterattacks by US aircraft sank two carriers and damaged the other two. The attack was a disaster.

The next day the game was re-run with some modifications. The plan was modified so that the carriers made a high-speed overnight approach to arrive at the launch point before the American scouts were in the air for their morning search. Surprise was achieved. The strike was judged to have sunk four battleships and severely damage one, sunk two carriers and severely damaged one, and sunk three cruisers, with three cruisers heavily damaged. One hundred and thirty US aircraft were destroyed,[12] 50 in the air and 80 on the ground. US counterattacks sank one carrier and severely damaged another. While withdrawing, a fortuitous (probably umpire-generated) rain squall screened the Japanese fleet from further damage.[13]

The attack was deemed feasible, but heavy Japanese losses were expected.[14]

Details of the game rules and damage assessment formulae, along with details of the composition of the strike, are not known, along with details such as how many B5N Kate bombers carried torpedoes, and what proportion of the D3A Val dive bombers were allocated to hit ships and what proportion were allocated to airfield targets. The D3A Val dive bomber had at this time demonstrated (in training) a 50 to 60 percent hit rate, but B5N Kate torpedo bombers had yet to solve the shallow water problem. Rigorous training in April of 1941 had increased the B5N Kate level bombing hit rate from 10% to 33%.[15] But, with the uncertainties in how the Japanese composed their strikes, there is insufficient information to reproduce the calculations for each weapon, and how the stated result was achieved.

The wargame serves as a benchmark to what the Japanese believed an attack with four carriers might accomplish. If the enemy was alerted and had their air defenses ready, the Japanese felt that there would only be "minor" damage inflicted. If surprise was attained, the damage inflicted by the four carriers would be enough to immobilize the main body of the US Pacific Fleet for the needed six months. But only 130 of the es-timated 550 American aircraft on the island would be destroyed, leaving sufficient air power for strong counterattacks. Consequently, the risk was deemed high. "At the September war games, even with the umpires bend-ing over backwards in favor of the home team, all had agreed that they must anticipate the sinking of several carriers."[16]

Part of the "bending over backwards" perhaps involved the antici-pated hit percentages against the fleet. In this wargame, four Japanese carriers accomplished more damage against warships than was accom-plished in the actual attack with six carriers.

It may have been that the Japanese saw that the level of effort used in this wargame achieved sufficient damage against the fleet targets, but there were shortfalls in the damage inflicted on American air power. So, when *Shokaku* and *Zuikaku* became available, they were pulled into the attack plan, and the bulk of their aircraft was directed to the offensive counter-air (OCA) role.

Another alternate possibility is that the aircraft in the actual strike did not achieve the hit rates and fire distribution expected of them, so the six carriers, in reality, caused less damage then was predicted for the four carriers in the wargame.

Another optimistic assumption was that one A6M Zero was the equivalent of three enemy fighters—when one officer tried to challenge "such stupidity" he received a "sharp admonition."[17]

Another Round of Games

Beginning 13 October 1941 another wargame was held on the flagship *Nagato*, with Yamamoto as host. This time the striking force had only three fleet carriers—*Akagi* was pulled out at the insistence of the Naval General Staff to support the attack on the Philippines.[18]

In this game surprise was achieved, but only "moderate damage" was inflicted. How the damage was assessed is again unknown, as is the thres-hold between "major," "moderate," and "minor" damage. The Japanese warships took no damage, but the operation was seen as "less than sat-isfactory."[19]

One might suspect that Yamamoto welcomed the verdict of "mod-erate damage" inflicted by the three carriers—that is, if he hadn't set up that outcome—since that usefully established the need for more carriers in the minds of the attending Naval General Staff officers. In addition, the Japanese force escaped without damage, another result that Yamamoto would welcome in his campaign to obtain approval for the attack.[20]

A few weeks later Yamamoto asked for and got all six fleet carriers.

Not all the discussion was on the expected offensive results of the operation. Many of the planners emphasized bringing the precariously vulnerable carriers back to home waters quickly and safely. The need for repeated attacks against Pearl Harbor did not come up during the wargames, although two of Yamamoto's planners—Genda and Commander Sasaki Akira, Yamamoto's Air Staff Officer—talked about the possibilities before and after the exercises. Nevertheless, in front of the flag officers the exercise concentrated on what could be accomplished against the American fleet units in a single strike of two waves, and the costs in terms of aircraft and carriers damaged and sunk.[21]

Summary

The wargame results established mental models of expected outcomes (cause and effect) in the minds of the attending officers. These models can be summarized as follows:

# of IJN CV	Surprise?	Unit Type	US Losses Sunk	Damaged	IJN Losses Sunk	Damaged
4	No	BB: CV: CA/CL: Aircraft:	"Minor"		2 ~127 (50%)	2
4	Yes	BB: CV: CA/CL: Aircraft:	4 2 3 130	4 1 3	1	1
3	Yes	BB: CV: CA/CL: Aircraft:	"Moderate"		No Damage	

The possible Japanese losses were daunting—they were losses on a strategic level, losses that could influence the course and outcome of the war as a whole. And yes, there were opportunities for the umpires to inject bias—Admiral Kusaka thought "the results depended too much on the various personalities of the umpires."[22]

The Japanese were never ones to allow calculations of material forces (or a roll of the dice) to take precedence over their deeply held belief in the primacy of fighting spirit and the unquantifiable superiority of Japanese crews and equipment. These games were "mere mathematical exercises." They ignored the factors of luck and divine guidance, factors that the proponents were sure favored the Japanese.[23]

In spite of the gods' expected bias, the word that filtered down to the aviators was that they faced a fifty-fifty chance of dying for their Emperor.[24]

To Yamamoto, whatever the circumstances, whatever the potential for losses, the effort had to be made. He was adamant. The issue went beyond logical argumentation. In an exchange with one of his most intransigent opponents, Yamamoto "put a hand on Kusaka's shoulder and said with an air of utter sincerity, 'Kusaka—I understand just how you feel, but the Pearl Harbor raid has become an article of faith for me. How about cutting down in the vocal opposition and trying to help me put that article of faith into practice?' "[25]

Western readers, grounded in theories of total war based on calculations of material superiority and firepower, might dismiss this approach as something akin to superstition, an outmoded, backward belief system. If so, they have eluded understanding.

In war, there are only three ways to win: by annihilating the enemy, totally incapacitating him, or by eliminating the enemy's will to fight. The first two are more in line with Western theories of war, but occur in a tiny number of cases historically. Few wars or battles have been won by annihilation or total incapacitation of the enemy. The overwhelming majority conclude when one side decides to quit.

The Western way of war strives for annihilation but accepts the enemy's surrender well before annihilation. Changing the enemy's will to fight is a by-product of material losses. Instead, the Japanese recognized the primacy of the will to fight from the outset, striving for means to convince the enemy to quit without requiring overwhelming incapacitating losses to settle the issue. If this could be accomplished, as in the Russo-Japanese War or the Sino-Japanese War, their relatively small country could successfully win against opponents many times their size. Just because their approach did not work in World War II does not invalidate it—it simply demonstrates that the course to winning a war based on the psychological defeat of the enemy must be carefully charted.

Yamamoto sought to induce despair in the volatile American voting public by destroying an inviolate symbol of naval supremacy, the battleship. He was convinced he had taken the measure of a population that was vocally pacifistic. He did not understand that the loudest voices in the American polity may not be the most representative.

Several times after the wargames he reasserted his determination to make the attack, in one instance announcing, "As Commander-in-Chief I have resolved to carry out the Pearl Harbor attack no matter what the cost."[26]

CHAPTER FOUR

PLANNING THE ATTACK

Limitations and Constraints

The attack plan was limited by material, force level, and doctrinal constraints.

Carrier Capacity

Eventually, at Yamamoto's insistence, all six of Japan's fleet carriers were assigned to the operation. Added to the four large carriers employed in the wargames were the new carriers *Shokaku* and *Zuikaku*, to be completed only weeks before the departure date, barely sufficient time to work up their flight deck crews. These air groups would be "as green as spring grass." But these aircraft could carry the volume of bombs needed against targets that did not demand high skill levels.

All six fleet carriers provided the planners with 417 aircraft. Spare aircraft were on each carrier, but they were disassembled and crated and would take a day or more to assemble.

As seen in the chart that follows, the numbers of each type of aircraft are nearly balanced, and reflected the normal complement of the carriers.

Carriers	Carrier Attack	Dive Bombers	Fighters
Akagi	27	18	27
Kaga	27	27	27
Soryu	18	18	27
Hiryu	18	18	27
Shokaku	27	27	15
Zuikaku	27	27	15
Total	144	135	138

Tailoring the Air Groups for the Attack

Only three of the Japanese carriers had sufficient range to make the transit from Japan to Hawaii and back without refueling.[1] Genda had considered breaking up the normal carrier air groups to preferentially load one type of bomber on those carriers designated for the attack. At one time he considered sending two or three carriers loaded with only fighters and B5N Kates with torpedoes. When the problems with launching torpedoes in shallow water appeared insurmountable, he considered leaving home all the B5N Kates and loading up a few carriers with just D3A Val dive bombers.

Both concepts would require shuffling aircraft and aircrew between carriers, a violation of normal Japanese practice. Aircraft and aircrew were considered a part of the carriers' complement under the command of the ship's commanding officer, and not an independent command as in the American practice. This was a decided handicap. Later in the war, in cases where Japanese air groups were decimated, as happened to *Zuikaku* and *Shokaku* at the Battle of the Coral Sea, the entire carrier had to be withdrawn from operations until a new air group could be assembled and trained. The American practice of independent air groups that could be assigned to any carrier was much more flexible and effective. For example, *Saratoga's* air group was shifted to *Yorktown* in the days just before the Battle of Midway, and it was operationally effective in a matter of days.[2]

There were transfers from the light carrier air groups to fill out the fleet carrier complements, particularly to obtain sufficient A6M Zero pilots, but a wholesale transfer of B5N Kate or D3A Val complements from one carrier to another had never been previously done, and would likely have generated an instinctive rejection from most senior aviators.

If the B5N Kate aircrews were all concentrated on a few carriers for the attack and then lost at Pearl Harbor, all the surviving carriers would have to carry on the war with an unbalanced air complement. Without B5N Kates, the remaining carriers would not have a killing capability against battleships.

An attack on Pearl Harbor with just the D3A Vals would have lacked killing power against battleships, but could have destroyed carriers and cruisers. This was acceptable to Genda, who considered the carriers the main objective, but would not satisfy Yamamoto.

It is not surprising that both concepts were rejected.

Deck Capacity

With 30 knots of wind across the deck, about 250 feet of deck run was required to launch a fighter, more for the heavily-laden bombers. With carrier flight decks 750 to 850 feet long, 500 to 600 feet were available to stage the aircraft to be launched in one "go."[3]

The first deckload of aircraft would launch and immediately form up and depart to the target. The aircraft remaining in the hangars would be lifted to the flight deck and positioned aft, and then have their engines started for warm-up, a process lengthy enough to eliminate thoughts of having the first group loiter awaiting the second launch so the attack could proceed in a single wave.[4] Spotting the deck took approximately 40 minutes, limited by the cycle times of the elevators, with *Kaga*'s the slowest. Engine warm-up took 20 minutes. With these restrictions, the second wave was expected to launch about one hour after the first.[5]

Doctrine

In 1941 Japanese doctrine had carriers operating in two-ship divisions. Search missions and local patrols would be carried out by battleship and cruiser float planes as much as possible, augmented by carrier aircraft when necessary, reserving the carrier aircraft for offensive missions. The practice was to spot on deck some fighters for CAP and strike escort duties, along with the entire ship's complement of one type of bomber. One carrier would launch its entire complement of D3A Vals and the other its complement of B5N Kates, whereupon they would join into a single combined-arms strike. This allowed unit integrity, with each bomber type under its own commander from its own ship operating with the men they knew and with whom they had trained. Their attacks would have a greater cohesion than if each carrier launched mixed groups of bombers.

This was good doctrine. Throughout the war the Japanese were able to launch and form up strikes in a minimum of time, something with which the Americans had problems until later in the war.[6] But it did constrain the Japanese from deploying their aircraft largely on a unit basis. In contrast, the American practice was more "mix and match," launching deckloads of mixed bomber types and mixed squadrons to meet the requirements of the specific mission and immediate availability of aircraft.

Vulnerable Torpedo Bombers

The torpedo bombers had to lead the attack. These aircraft were restricted to an unusually "low and slow" attack profile to accommodate the narrow launch envelope required by the modified shallow-water torpedoes, making them easy targets for AA gunners. The torpedo bombers had to slip in their attack before the AA gunners were awake, oriented, armed, and firing.

Aircrew Training and Experience

The air groups on *Zuikaku* and *Shokaku* were only recently formed and many of the aircrews were young and inexpert. In the words of one Japanese pilot, they were "really green" with "very little flight experience."[7] It would be most reasonable to assign them the easier and less critical missions requiring less skill and precision—which meant OCA, airfields and aircraft.

Fighter Employment

The Japanese fighters were considered offensive weapons, not defensive, in the sense that they were expected to range out and attack the enemy, not sit back in a defensive role as escorts or CAP. Their thinking was that "offense was the best defense" when it came to ensuring that their bombers made it through.

As previously mentioned, SEAD against ground targets was a neglected capability and not really in their repertoire or their mindset in

1941. However, the fleet practiced SEAD in attacking warships at sea. An "out of the box" thinker might see the need to apply this cooperation in the Pearl Harbor attack.

Genda, the lead planner, was a fighter pilot. For all his reputed brilliance, his thinking was firmly within the usual Japanese fighter pilot paradigm, locked in the box.

"Stovepipe Thinking"

Japanese doctrine characteristically lacked a combined arms approach, a deficiency called (in modern terminology) stovepipe thinking. There was little inclination to solve problems in a mutually cooperative manner. Dive bombers, torpedo bombers, and fighters all had their separate missions. The concept of having one type assist another type perform a mission was not in their worldview. They certainly considered the best order for the aircraft types to deliver their attacks, but this was to facilitate the individual attacks and reduce mutual interference, more than out of any motives of cooperation or mutual support.

The Japanese would recognize the need to break out of their stovepipe thinking later in the war, but would never really succeed.

Air-to-Air Communications

Important planning considerations rested on the ability of aircraft to communicate. Inter-aircraft communication capabilities define how much control a commander has over his forces aloft, his ability to adjust to circumstances, the flexibility to take advantage of unforeseen errors by the enemy, or even just to allow switching from one plan to another. Good communications allow better coordination of forces and dissemination of sighting reports and on-scene intelligence. Most significantly to the Pearl Harbor attack force, it would allow control of the force by a commander with better overall situation awareness, in particular, the ability to control fighters and the ability to control the distribution of the bombers to gain the best effect from each bomb and torpedo.

This is a significant capability. The attack would be the first combat action for nearly all the Japanese aviators, as most of the aviators on the newly commissioned carriers were young, mostly under 20, and would need supervision by more experienced hands, but also because the second wave would need information on the damage caused by the first wave to optimize their targeting.

It wasn't until 1940 that the Japanese Navy first established its own capability to produce and install radio sets for aircraft, and 1941 when plans were established to retrofit radio sets into existing aircraft on a large scale. Even then, their production goals were woeful—for 1942 they planned to produce four types of long-range aircraft HF radios for a total of 1,000 sets per month, and only 100 short-range aircraft radiotelephones per month, at a newly established plant at the Numazu Ordnance Depot.

The standard was to have each multi-seat carrier aircraft carry an HF set and a radiotelephone, and each fighter carry a radiotelephone, by December 1941. All the aircraft of the *Kido Butai* may not yet have been fitted in time for the attack.[8]

The standard of installation was poor. The radios were practically unusable. The bulky sets were jammed into aircraft not designed to accommodate them, and little consideration was given to ensure the sets could be worked. Controls often could not be manipulated to exact settings. The sets did not fare well in a high-vibration environment that varied from steamy hot to sub-zero. Controls might be awkward to reach and dial scales out of sight. Vibration caused knobs to drift off their settings. Operating the sets at high altitude was nearly impossible. The aviators complained that some installers were more interested in getting credit for the installation than in leaving a working radio. Testing was perfunctory and haphazard. Careless supervision and poor installation resulted in wiring problems and electrical grounds. The discharges of engine spark plugs would interfere with reception.

Lieutenant Commander Arima Keiichi, a dive bomber observer assisting the research department in 1944 to develop communications equipment, testified:

> I feel strongly that Japan was inferior to the United States regarding wireless communication. During the war Japan mainly used Morse code, but American aviators were able to use voice modulation gear. We were not able to use voice modulation gear well, but regarding Morse code we were superior.[9]

The air crews, particularly fighter pilots, became indifferent to the use of their radiotelephones.[10] Radios interfered with fighter pilots' concept of themselves as independent samurai warriors. Lieutenant (junior grade) Harada Kaname, a *Soryu* A6M Zero pilot, related that at the time of Pearl Harbor:

> We had a radio communication system, but it was primitive, so we didn't use it much. Japan had limited technology, and we were told to use the Morse signal. If the enemy came the signal was like to-to-to, but this signaling was difficult to do sometimes, so we often used hand or facial signals. You could do these types of signals within a small group, but if we tried to communicate with another small group it was very difficult. Hence, each small group made decisions with the guidance of their leader, in accordance with the situation.[11]

Radio communications problems were not unique to the Japanese Navy. CDR Scott Smith, speaking of the first six months of the war, attested that "radio communications in those days was just short of miserable."[12] In particular, intermittent communications between the escort fighters and the bombers at the Battle of Midway was a contributing factor in the horrendous losses suffered by the torpedo bombers.

These problems continued and were evident particularly at the Eastern Solomons and Santa Cruz battles. American aircraft radios tended to drift off the precise frequency required by the sensitive voice transmitter. After the Battle of Santa Cruz, one angry flight commander who had lost communications with two-thirds of his aircraft, wrote:

> The present radio equipment cannot be set exactly on frequency in war waters, and unless it is, all future attacks will be doomed to similar failure. The set is too complicated for aircraft operation. The rear-seat gunner has plenty on his hands without fiddling with all of the radio dials in flight . . . If radio equipment is so complicated that it cannot be operated by personnel in flight, it should be thrown out and changed immediately.[13]

American radios were superior to Japanese equipment. Judging from the Americans' problems, one can imagine the challenges Japanese aviators faced.

The Japanese mostly ignored their nearly inoperable voice radio equipment. Anecdotally, it appears that little (if any) use of the radiotelephone was included in Japanese plans for Pearl Harbor, or used in practice. Communications appeared restricted to limited HF continuous wave radio, Morse signals, and visual signals. The famous attack order, *Tora Tora Tora*, was sent over keyed HF. Flares were used to communicate "surprise" or "no surprise." When the flares were misinterpreted, veterans did not mention any attempts via radiotelephone to correct the error and bring the formations back under control.[14]

A poignant incident during the attack shows the norm for Japanese aerial communications. A fighter was leaking fuel and the pilot knew he had no chance to return to his carrier. To his wingman, he pointed to his mouth (the sign for fuel), gestured that his fuel was low, smiled, waved, and rolled his plane into a final suicide dive. There was no attempt to use the radiotelephone, even for last words.

Certainly radiotelephones were in ill repute among Japanese naval aviators at least through 1943, and it is unlikely that they would rely on the equipment for anything tactically critical. There are stories during the Solomons campaign of Japanese fighter pilots personally tearing out their radio equipment in order to lighten their aircraft and gain a bit more speed and maneuverability.[15]

Radiotelephone limitations restricted Japanese planning. Communications deficiencies restricted how ship-killing ordnance could be coordinated. In particular, it forced more responsibility on the leaders of *shotai* and *chutai* in selecting targets and directing the attack. There simply were no reliable communications with higher leaders.

Target Selection and Weapons Delivery

With limited inter-aircraft communications, much responsibility was placed on the shoulders of the aircraft commanders when it came to target selection. The Japanese bombers operated in *shotai* of three aircraft. The *shotai* leader—or, in larger attacks, the *chutai* leader of three *shotai*—would select the target, and the other aircraft would simply follow. However, individual aircraft commanders had the authority to select a different target.

For the D3A Vals, the *shotai* was an important unit, as their dive-bombing technique had the following aircraft adjusting their aim point based on the fall of the leader's bomb. If the *shotai* became separated, significantly reduced dive-bombing accuracy could be expected.

Limitations and Constraints—Summary

The planners had significant constraints, some imposed by their equipments, some from their doctrine, and some from the limitations of their own thinking. Recognizing self-limitations was not an area in which the Japanese excelled—a culture where errors could result in suicide tended to limit thinking outside of societal norms.

This analysis will proceed to compare the Japanese planning and attack against what was theoretically possible, while noting the source of the shortfall, whether from doctrinal constraints, mental errors, or errors in execution. An alternative approach, determining a perfect attack within the constraints of Japanese doctrine and thinking, would be very problematic, since characteristically there might be many reasons behind a shortfall, and it might be impossible to determine them all. As will be seen, most of the Japanese shortfalls had solutions that could have been achieved within the technology of the period, if only the problem had been recognized and some thought given to its solution. In most cases the planners were restricted in their ideas of what was possible, and accepted their limitations as a matter of course.

Within the above constraints, the planners had the flexibility to determine the aircraft types to employ in each wave, what targets to hit and in what order, what weapons to use on each aircraft type against each class of target, and how fighters were to be allocated and employed. These issues were significant challenges alone.

Planning for Pre-strike Reconnaissance

The Japanese plan included submarine and aerial reconnaissance immediately prior to the attack.

A submarine would scout the Lahaina Roads anchorage off Maui a day prior to the attack and transmit a report. This would be a fairly low-risk mission, and the information would be critical. If the fleet was located off Maui at anchor, the attack would have to be redirected and the armament mix changed. The level bombers would not be needed, and those fifty aircraft re-armed with the more lethal torpedoes. If only part of the fleet was out, the attack would have to be split and armed accordingly.

Two cruiser float planes would be launched in the pre-dawn hours before the attack. One was to scout Lahaina Roads again, presumably to check if the fleet had departed the anchorage since the submarine's report, while the other went to Pearl Harbor for reconnaissance and to transmit a weather report.

Shortly after 0600, with hardly any light to mark a horizon for the pilots, the carriers were to launch the first wave of the attack. At 0630 the battleships and heavy cruisers would launch 16 float planes to scout to the east, south, and west. Japanese reconnaissance doctrine differed from that of the Americans, in that float planes were more used for long-range reconnaissance, while the Americans used carrier aircraft. The Japanese doctrine was good, in that it preserved the carriers' aircraft for offensive operations, maintained unit integrity, and kept carrier decks from being tied up to recover the reconnaissance aircraft. Its weakness was that the float planes from the battleships and heavy cruisers were stored exposed to the weather, and were not as reliable. In addition, the float plane aviators got fewer hours and were not the same quality as carrier aviators.

Later, at Midway, the American system showed its warts when the three American carriers could not put together a coordinated strike, as one carrier had to delay her launch while recovering reconnaissance aircraft. But the Japanese system made the critical error. A reconnaissance float plane was delayed in launching, making it fatally late in discovering the American carriers.

The second wave would be launched at approximately 0730, one hour after the departure of the first wave.

Fuchida's Claim Regarding Level Bombers

Fuchida was first introduced to the Pearl Harbor attack plan in a meeting with Genda in late September 1941, immediately after Fuchida was transferred to serve as the strike leader aboard *Akagi*.

According to Fuchida, the plan Genda showed him did not include level bombers with AP bombs. "The Japanese Navy had a terrible record of hits using this technique,"[16] scoring less than 10% hits in exercises the previous June. In addition, AP bombs had a tiny charge of explosives compared to torpedoes. Aviators in the IJN had argued for some time that level bombing was an inefficient use of resources and would not score enough hits to justify its use. At one point the First Carrier Division recommended that horizontal bombing should be abolished.[17]

Fuchida, a level bombing specialist, claimed he pressed Genda to add level bombers. AP bombs, Fuchida asserted, would be needed against ships inaccessible to torpedoes. He pointed out to Genda two things: torpedo nets could protect all the ships from torpedoes, while double-berthing ships side-by-side would shield the inner battleships.[18] Fuchida claimed his arguments convinced Genda, and as a result level bombers were included in the attack plan.

This conversation likely did not occur.

First, Fuchida spoke as if Genda was not aware of the implications of double-berthing battleships or of torpedo nets. Considering Genda's reputation for brilliance, such gaps in his knowledge are highly unlikely.

Second, the Japanese were working on an armor-piercing bomb for the Pearl Harbor attack well before Fuchida's meeting with Genda in late September 1941. Early in 1941, a 20-meter-square armor plate was set up to test a bomb made from a converted 40cm battleship shell. Tests refined the modifications to improve its penetration capability. At that time it was thought that a release altitude of 12,000 feet was required to get the desired penetration. Production of the bomb was started, and by mid-September 150 had been produced.

Genda had indeed almost given up on horizontal bombing in March of 1941 due to the low hit percentage, which was under 10%. Considering that 12 to 16 hits were considered necessary to sink a battleship, at that rate all the carrier attack planes from all six carriers would be required to sink one battleship. This was unacceptable.

In April, Lieutenant Furukawa Izumi arrived aboard *Akagi* after passing through the bombing course at Yokosuka. In addition, a special team consisting of Chief Petty Officers Watanabe Akira and Aso Yanosuke was formed to work the problem. These men improved the coordination between the pilot and the bombardier. Bombing accuracy improved dramatically, rising in trials to as high as 33% hits. In early June, Genda recommended that the level bombing leaders go to Kagoshima Naval Airfield to train on the techniques developed by Watanabe and Aso. In other words, in June of 1941 Genda put the wheels in motion to include level bombing in the Pearl Harbor attack.[19]

Another set of tests were in process at the time that Fuchida reported for duty at his new post.

The Navy held experiments beginning around the end of September to test a special missile converted from 16-inch shells. . . .

These tests had been going on for about ten days, with no hits achieved, when [Rear Admiral] Ueno [Keizo] requested Nagumo to send some of his best pilots with their own aircraft to Kashima to see if they could brighten the picture.[20]

Why was another set of tests being run in September when the earlier tests already approved the bomb for production? Evidently, the planners wanted the level bombers to attack from 3,000 meters instead of 4,000 meters to improve their accuracy, but it was not known if the bomb could penetrate enough armor at that altitude.

Fuchida makes the tests a thing of high drama, starring Fuchida. He claimed that Nagumo sent for him immediately after he was informed of Ueno's problem, saying that the experiment was vital, and "upon it depends the success or failure of the Pearl Harbor attack." Fuchida and five others hastened to Kashima, and on the third day, from 3,000 meters, scored a direct hit which smashed through an armored plate replicating the *West Virginia's* deck protection.

The September testing was to determine the altitude from which the level bombers would attack, not whether or not they would be included in the attack. Fuchida did not change Genda's mind about including level bombers in the attack. The decision had already been made, the bombs already manufactured. When Fuchida arrived on the scene it was just a question of refining the details.

Third, by late September the plan had to have progressed well beyond the point where the Japanese considered that the numbers of torpedo planes and level bombers could be juggled. The B5N Kate carrier attack bombers could fulfill four roles: employing torpedoes against capital ships, AP bombs against capital ships, 250kg GP bombs against cruisers or carriers, or 250kg and 60kg land attack bombs against ground targets. There was undoubtedly considerable calculation regarding the allocations, since they constituted the killing power against battleships or the majority of bombs against ground targets. The idea that Genda accepted a new idea to employ B5N Kates with AP bombs at this late date is not credible. It would have required a complete revision of the strike plan, which had to be near its final form.

The training program began just after Fuchida's arrival. Training as intensive as the Japanese air groups conducted was not something that just happened, but had to be planned. Airfields had to be prepared, aircraft stationed and prepped, fuel and maintenance and weapons staged, maintenance personnel assigned, housed and fed, and other considerations. The outline of the training plan—locations, aircraft allocations, fuel and maintenance and the like—was likely promulgated well before Fuchida's arrival. The allocations of B5N Kate bombers between torpedo and AP bombs and OCA had to have been made earlier for the training plan to be ready in late September.

Fuchida's claim that he was responsible for including level bombers with AP bombs in the strike plan cannot be correct.

Aircraft Allocations

The aircrews were allocated their roles probably early in September. Genda allocated the numbers assigned to each task and each target area.[21] He also had the authority to draw additional aviators into the planning process, so he called in a number of experts to help formulate the tactical orders. In addition, he could bring in select *Hikotaicho*—translated literally as "air unit commanding officer," a position similar to the CAG (Commander Air Group) on US carriers. Although normally there would be only one *Hikotaicho* assigned to a carrier, Genda changed this to as many as three per carrier or as few as none, depending on the plan's needs.

The B5N Kate units were divided between torpedo bombers and level bombers, two very different skill sets. The late-September start allowed six weeks to resolve problems and train the aircrews for their tasks.

A Two-Wave Attack

Carrier Striking Force Operations Order No. 3 specified 351 aircraft to be launched in two waves.[22] One hundred and sixty-two were to be directed at fleet units (battleships, carriers, and cruisers), and 189 against aircraft and airfields.

If four carriers launched 90 carrier attack planes armed against battleships, the other two carriers could contribute 54 more B5N Kates, or alternately 45 to 54 D3A Val dive-bombers to the first wave. The Vals were chosen, and sent against airfields to shut them down and prevent fighters from getting into the air, and to disrupt any counterattack preparations.

1st Wave:

The first wave was to consist of 189 aircraft.

90 aircraft would go against the Pacific Fleet:

- 40 B5N Kates carrying 40 torpedoes, 24 primarily targeted against the battleships and 16 against carriers;
- 50 B5N Kates carrying 50 800kg AP Bombs, targeted against inboard battleships; 99 would be directed at enemy airfields or to attack enemy fighters in the air:
- 54 D3A Vals carrying 54 250kg GP bombs directed at airfields;
- 45 A6M Zero fighters.

2nd Wave:
The second wave was to consist of 171 aircraft:
- 81 D3A Vals carrying 81 250kg GP bombs were to go to Pearl Harbor and attack warships. They were primarily after carriers. Alternate targets were cruisers and battleships;
- 54 B5N Kates, carrying either one 250kg GP and six 60kg GP bombs or two 250kg bombs each, targeted against airfield hangars and facilities;
- 36 A6M Zeros.[23]

Allocations

The following table shows aircraft allocation across the missions.

	Fleet—Torpedoes	Fleet—Bombs	OCA
B5N Kate	40	50	54
D3A Va		81	54
A6M Zero			81

The torpedo bombers constituted only 28% of the available B5N Kate carrier attack bombers. Thirty-five percent would carry AP bombs, and the remaining 38% would attack airfields.

Of the 280 bombers, 171 (61%) were sent against fleet targets.

The aircraft assigned to offensive counter-air were allocated as follows:

- 54 first wave D3A Val dive-bombers, against the Ford Island and Wheeler airfields;
- 54 second wave B5N Kate carrier attack planes against the airfields at Kaneohe, Ford Island, Barber's Point, and Hickam.

The next table shows how the ordnance was directed.

	Torpedoes	AP Bombs	250kg GP Bombs	60kg GP Bombs
Fleet targets	40	50	81	
OCA targets			126	108

The bombers were carrying a total of 315 bombs. By number, 74% of the bombs were assigned to OCA. By payload, 92,250kg (71%) of the ordnance (bombs and torpedoes) was directed against the fleet and 37,900kg (29%) for OCA. The B5N Kates carried 65% of the total bomb payload of the attack.

The OCA effort was augmented by 81 A6M Zero fighters. Including fighters, 66% of the aircraft were assigned to OCA.

Offensive Counter Air v. Fighter Cover

Strategically, destruction of aircraft in this early part of the war was of some value to the Japanese because of the overall shortage of Allied aircraft. The Americans were attempting to rebuild their military while simultaneously supplying arms to Britain and Russia in the war against Hitler. There were many demands on an aircraft industry that was still gearing up for full production. New aircraft were doled out among claimants in penny lots. No demands were fully satisfied, a situation that would remain critical for at least a year.

Aircraft destroyed at Pearl Harbor were aircraft that could not be shifted to the Philippines or Java to oppose Japan's offensive. However, this did not justify attacking Pearl Harbor just to destroy aircraft. The value of destroyed aircraft was transitory. Aircraft could be replaced quickly with the proper prioritization of industrial output—America would produce over 12,000 aircraft in 1941, five times that of Japan. The Japanese could hope to destroy at Oahu only a few hundred at best, six day's production. Many of the aircraft on Oahu were older, obsolescent types of limited military worth.

Japan could not afford a battle of attrition with the United States; destroying aircraft alone was not worth the risk of a trans-oceanic attack. Every bomb targeted against aircraft or airfield facilities was one less weapon directed against the destruction of the Pacific Fleet battleships. Battleships took years to replace. Hangars could be rebuilt in weeks, aircraft in days.

Trained aviators took longest to produce and were the most limiting factor. Destroying an aircraft on the ground did not mean that the aircrew was lost, so squadrons could be quickly rebuilt with new (and more modern) aircraft.

Perversely, a Japanese success against the American aircraft on Oahu would serve as a powerful stimulus to allocate more production to the Pacific. The Pacific would get more modern aircraft as replacements diverted from aircraft intended for Europe, so the intermediate term benefits would be seen more by the Germans than the Japanese.

The Japanese had reason to limit the number of munitions expended against aircraft. An (overly simplistic) calculation can illustrate the point. Consider the choice of having a D3A Val dive-bomber attack either an eight-ton medium bomber or a 10,000-ton cruiser. It might take two Vals to destroy the bomber, for a return of four tons of industrial production per bomb. Against the stationary cruiser, four hits might be needed requiring eight dive-bombers, for a return of 1,250 tons of industrial production per bomb. That is over a 300-times better return for attacking the cruiser. And, while the Americans had thousands of aircraft, the Pacific Fleet had only 21 cruisers, and were much harder to replace.

This simplistic comparison does not take into account a host of factors, including relative availability of the different construction materials, cost per ton, production rates, complexity of construction, replacement production rates, labor requirements, and the different capabilities of requirements for the different platforms. But it does illustrate how a planner considers allocations on the basis of "return per weapon expended." Given eight D3A Vals to allocate, the potential return was either four enemy bombers or one cruiser.

Most naval officers of the period—even aviators—would have agreed that every one of the Japanese weapons could have been profitably employed against fleet targets. But strategic, operational, and tactical needs can conflict. All the weapons could not be concentrated against the fleet because there were other needs to consider. The aim of the OCA effort was short-term, tactical, and transitory: to suppress the American aircraft long enough to allow the Japanese to deliver their attack, recover their aircraft, and move beyond retaliation range. Their wargames had illuminated the potential damage that could be inflicted by an aerial counterattack. Losing two or three carriers at the outset of the war could have significant ramifications.

The Japanese knew that carriers were fragile creatures, and believed that ground-based bombers were effective against them. This belief echoed their own concept of operations for the defense of their home waters, a layered defense with land-based air operating from island airfields, concentrating in successive barriers to wear down the advancing U.S fleet. Their confidence that their own land-based air could sink carriers would naturally translate into a fear that the enemy's could do the same, another manifestation of mirror imaging.

The US Army Air Corps (AAC) had 57 medium and heavy bombers on Oahu. Few were cutting edge in aviation technology, but they still represented a creditable threat. In addition to AAC aircraft, any US carriers in port would have flown off their air groups to various Oahu airfields, and were a threat. The Japanese carriers might be hit by as many as 165 AAC and Navy bombers carrying as many as 300 bombs and 36 torpedoes, escorted by F4F Wildcat and F2-A Buffalo fighters.

The Japanese would have to divide their fighters, some to accompany the strike and some to remain with the carriers. This allocation represented a difficult decision. If surprise was achieved, more fighters with the strike would mean more enemy aircraft destroyed on the ground by strafing, and less chance of a counterattack. In that case the ships' CAP would not contribute any damage to the enemy and would effectively be wasted. If surprise was not achieved, more fighters with the CAP would provide a better chance that the carriers would survive any counterattacks.

Forty-eight A6M Zeros, about one-third, were retained for fleet defense. Of those, one-third to one-half could be expected to be airborne and available to oppose a counterattack at a given time. With the Japanese predilection for the offensive, retaining even those was probably a struggle.

To place this in context, using the NWC wargaming rules, 24 fighters engaging 57 medium bombers would shoot down eight bombers prior to dropping their bombs, leaving 49 bombers to deliver their ordnance. With three bombs apiece and 5% hits there would be seven hits, enough to cripple or sink two carriers. Using Japanese expectations for level bombers, 16% accuracy would give 24 hits, sufficient for a Japanese disaster.

The Japanese needed an OCA effort to limit, disrupt, or prevent a counterattack on the carriers. Consequently, the first-wave dive-bombers were primarily assigned to airfield attack, followed by level bombers in the second wave.

Another reason to send some first-wave aircraft against airfields was to prevent congestion over the harbor. Dive-bombers, level bombers and torpedo bombers attacking the fleet simultaneously held the potential for mutual interference. At best, bomb runs would be aborted or disrupted, reducing the accuracy of weapons delivery; at worst, there could be mid-air collisions and weapons jettisoned.

A little over half the 250kg bombs and all the 60kg bombs allocated to OCA were carried by the B5N Kate carrier attack planes of the second wave. These bombers were trained to fly in formation and release their bombs when the lead plane released so the bombs would strike in a pattern over the footprint of the formation. This type of bombing was effective against area targets such as hangars, fuel tanks, and maintenance and administrative areas, but would be largely wasted against point targets such as individual aircraft in revetments.

The 250kg bombs on the D3A Val dive-bombers would best go against point targets, such as aircraft in revetments and on parking pads. The D3A Val was the "precision" delivery system and the B5N Kate the "area" system, with many more "precision" targets than there were Vals. The aircraft targets on the ground were expected to be widely dispersed. Those not destroyed by bombs would be the target of strafing fighters.

Why attack hangars and administrative buildings? The reason centered on the number of bombers versus the number of aircraft targets. It was unlikely that the dive-bombers would be able to eliminate all the American bombers. The Army at Wheeler had 85 revetments capable of protecting 109 aircraft. With only 54 D3A Vals assigned, there weren't enough OCA dive-bombers to be able to put one on each revetment.[24]

Revetments greatly reduce aircraft vulnerability by blocking the spray of fragments from ground burst bombs (air burst bombs had not yet been developed), requiring the bomb to hit inside the revetment or in line with the entrance to be effective. Revetments also provided partial protection from strafing attacks. The fighter revetments were mostly sized to contain only one aircraft and were not much wider than the P-40 fighter's wingspan of about 38 feet. The Japanese would expect that any aircraft parked outside of revetments would be dispersed. The metric for proper dispersal was to ensure that a single bomb would not be able to destroy more than one aircraft.

Considering that dive-bomber accuracy historically was on the order of 50 to 210 feet circular error probability (CEP),[25] a good performance by the dive bombers would destroy or critically damage one aircraft for every three bombs against aircraft in revetments, or one aircraft per one or two bombs for targets in the open. The 54 dive-bombers might be expected to eliminate 18 to 54 aircraft, out of the estimated 550 on Oahu, depending upon the mix of targets attacked. Something else had to be done to disrupt the enemy's response.

Consequently, level bombers had to reinforce the OCA effort. Fifty-four B5N Kate carrier attack planes were armed with GP bombs and assigned to airfield attack. However, every Kate so assigned was one less delivering battleship-killing ordnance.

One could argue with the wisdom of hindsight that the Japanese made good decisions in their allocation of the B5N Kates between warship and OCA targets, since the attack met their overall mission objective. But there were so many more fleet targets than battleships alone. The Japanese could have used additional torpedoes profitably, for example, against the four cruisers outside the Navy Yard, the nests of destroyers, and the fleet's tenders and auxiliaries; or, the B5N Kates with 250kg bombs could have profitably hit the shipyard piers, where four modern 10,000-ton cruisers were tied up.

The carrier attack plane aircrews on the two newest Japanese carriers were judged by the planners as insufficiently skilled to deliver torpedo attacks. According to Japanese sources, most training for these aviators was centered on basic flying—things like take-offs, landings, carrier qualifications, and flying in formation. Hangars and aircraft parking area targets did not require the precision flying required for a torpedo attack and were more tolerant of sloppy flying. So, all the bombers on *Shokaku* and *Zuikaku*, dive-bombers and carrier attack planes alike, were assigned to OCA. The aviators on the senior carriers would attack the fleet.

Ironically, the young aviators from *Shokaku* and *Zuikaku* would turn in a sterling performance, greatly exceeding expectations and outshining the dive-bombers from the more experienced carriers.

Level bombers were inefficient against dispersed aircraft and aircraft revetments. However, administrative buildings, hangars, and refueling and rearming facilities were large area targets, the destruction of which could do much to delay and disrupt the dispatch of a retaliatory strike. While the effects of destroying these targets are more difficult to quantify, they are real. Bomb damage would cause confusion, disrupt communications, and interrupt vital functions, as well as inflict personnel casualties. Little details could have huge ramifications—for example, the ammunition for many of the Army fighter squadrons was locked in their hangars and could not be retrieved when the hangars were on fire. If the administrative areas were destroyed and sufficient support personnel casualties inflicted, the process of organizing a strike, loading and fueling bombers, coordinating bombers and fighters, briefing crews, and dispatching an attack to the right location could be disrupted.

The level bombers might also be directed against aircraft on the tarmac and parking areas, but if the American aircraft were properly dispersed it would be a very inefficient use of the bombs. Aircraft near hangars were at risk of being destroyed when the hangars were attacked, but those aircraft would mostly be undergoing maintenance and not ready to fly.

Fighters could also contribute to the OCA effort. A rule of thumb used by combat modelers in the 1950's and 1960's was that strafing aircraft would destroy between 0.25 and .50 aircraft per sortie. This would add another 20 to 40 aircraft to those killed by the dive-bombers, for a total of 38 to 94 aircraft destroyed on the ground.

The Japanese optimistically expected more—they typically rated their A6M Zero fighters as three times as effective as an Allied fighter in their wargames.[26] Scaling off their wargame results, it appears that the Japanese would have expected 195 US aircraft to be destroyed in the air and on the ground. The calculations indicate that the Japanese expected a large contribution from their fighters.

The Army Air Corps had 57 bombers and 152 fighters on the island. The Navy had 301 aircraft, mostly utility types at Ford Island in maintenance or storage, but there were 61 combat-capable fighters and scout bombers. The Japanese would therefore need to direct attention to the Navy airfield at Ford Island and the Marine field at Ewa. They could reasonably expect to destroy only a fraction of the aircraft on the island. Even an outstanding success would leave 350 aircraft.

These calculations apparently agree with the Japanese assessments since, in their wargames, even when they achieved surprise the US forces mustered a counterattack. This explains why the Japanese allocated so many aircraft to the offensive counter-air mission. It explains the very real need to include strafing fighters against the airfields to hit the many aircraft expected to survive the bombing.

In retrospect, it is hard to predict if an AAC counterattack would have been as effective as the Japanese feared. Attacking ships underway was a specialized skill that required considerable practice. The AAC aviators had certainly demonstrated flashes of brilliance. In an exercise in August 1937, Army bombers attacked the target ship *Utah*, and on one day hit with 23% of their bombs from altitudes from 8,000 to 18,000 feet. Over the entire exercise they scored 11.9% hits.[27] If those hit percentages were duplicated, Pearl Harbor's 57 medium and heavy bombers carrying four bombs per aircraft had the potential to score 27 (average) or 52 (best) hits, sufficient to destroy all the Japanese carriers.

Once the war began, however, the AAC did not live up to expectations. From 7 December through the Battle of Midway, AAC bombers managed exactly one hit on a warship, on the heavy cruiser *Myoko* at anchor off Davao in the Philippines, on 4 January 1942.

The Potential Air-to-Air Battle
The Defender's Aircraft

With warning, a large portion of the 152 AAC fighters could have been airborne to meet the attack. The first wave of the Japanese attack included 45 fighters- 1 to 3.4 would have been steep odds for the Japanese to overcome.

However, there are additional considerations.

Only 99 of the US fighters were the latest generation P-40 aircraft, the rest being P-36's and P-26's.

The Curtiss P-36 Hawk was a fairly recent aircraft, first delivered in 1938. It had a decent combat record when flown by the French against the Messerschmitt Bf-109 in the Battle of France, so its combat capabilities were creditable.

The Boeing P-26's performance and armament was two generations behind the A6M Zero. The P-26 "Peashooter" an insignificant speed advantage over the D3A Val or B5N Kate[28] and was armed with only two 0.30-cal machine guns. But they were fighters, and could be dangerous to the lightly constructed, flammable Japanese bombers, particularly if they caught a torpedo-laden Kate lumbering low and slow towards the harbor.

Aircraft Availability

Many of the fighters would be undergoing maintenance or repair. In the Hawaiian Islands on 6 December 1941, 37% of the fighters overall, and 55% of the P-40s, were unavailable. This was an unusually high number of aircraft out of commission for maintenance.

To place these percentages in context, during peacetime a force that is able to stop flight operations and concentrate on "peaking and tweaking" its aircraft for maximum availability in advance of an important operation could be expected to have 80 to 90% of its aircraft FMC (full mission capable). In spite of every effort, though, there were the "hangar queens," aircraft that required a part that was not available locally or which otherwise defied repair. Supply systems are notorious for running out of parts.

At least one fighter squadron took its aircraft out of service every weekend to remove and clean the guns.[29] In early December many more aircraft were out of service than usual because the 14th Pursuit Wing had just come down from a lengthy period of heightened alert on the 27th of November. Aircraft were taken out of service to address the backup in routine maintenance and engine overhauls that such an alert leaves in its wake. Of the 12 B-17s on Oahu, half were out of service, mostly cannibalized for parts.[30]

During the war availability rates would plummet, reduced by battle-damaged aircraft that required more difficult repairs, lack of parts at forward locations, and lack of maintenance facilities. Availability percentages of 50–70% were not unusual for US forces, 30% or less for Japanese forward forces. The environment was a significant factor. Jungle heat, humidity, and desert sand were particularly hard on airframes and engines. Early in the war in the Pacific or North Africa theaters, 50% availability rates were a noteworthy accomplishment.

At the beginning of the war Japanese maintenance crews were good and well supported from their jumping-off bases. They also had the luxury of knowing when the war would start. Most Japanese units were 90% FMC or greater. Spare aircraft were assigned both to land-based squadrons and on board the carriers, so most Japanese squadrons went into early battles at full strength.

Japanese carriers could carry three aircraft of each type disassembled on board to replace battle-damaged aircraft. American carriers also often had spare aircraft in a partially disassembled state, either broken down and boxed or partially disassembled and triced up into the overhead of the hangar.

Later in the war the Japanese grappled with shortages in maintenance personnel to replace those killed and those isolated in bypassed bases. They did not have the pool of mechanically adept young men used to working with automobiles and machinery as did the Americans, so their maintenance personnel were more difficult to replace. Aircraft availability rates plummeted.

Sunday

The Japanese specifically chose Sunday for the attack because this day usually had the most ships in port. As a side benefit, many of the American pilots and other officers and men would be expected to be away from their bases, at their homes or on liberty at the hotels at Waikiki. Even though officially living in the Bachelor Officers' Quarters (BOQ), many officers would band together and rent an apartment on the "civi-side" of the island. Sunday, if the island was not on alert, would have the fewest number of immediately available fighter pilots.

Fighter Employment Doctrine

The first-wave fighters had one mission: to destroy enemy aircraft in the air and on the ground.[31] Several air-doctrine factors are conspicuously absent.

Missing was any statement that the fighters were to protect the bombers. This is a substantive omission, not just an order-writing oversight. The Japanese fighters were to seek out and destroy the enemy with the freedom to leave the bombers to do this. Just like in China, the bombers were to be protected by having their own fighters killing enemy fighters, rather than chasing US fighters away from the bombers.

This might sound like splitting hairs, but it reflected a significant difference in fighter employment. Nothing told the fighters to stay with the bombers in an escort role, or to maintain a CAP over airfields to prevent enemy planes from getting aloft, or to find and cover the bombers after they dropped their bombs. They were to destroy enemy fighters, not just deflect enemy attacks. They were offensive platforms like the bombers, only with different targets.

If surprise was not achieved, the fighters were not obligated to cover the bombers.

Employment of the Fighters in the Attack
Fighter Sweep

If *Kido Butai* was detected any time within 24 hours before the scheduled time of the attack, the fleet was still to press on and deliver the attack. However, the composition of the waves would change. All the fighters would be dispatched in an initial first-wave attack. The bombers would only be launched after the fighters had achieved "command of the air."[32] This operation, called a "fighter sweep" in the West, was used in China and by both sides in the unfolding European war and the Battle of Britain.

The objective was to destroy American fighter opposition. Nothing was planned against the AA defenses. The effectiveness of the US AA is explored in detail in a subsequent chapter, but in summary, there was enough AA to make for a Japanese disaster. In addition, with the Japanese samurais chasing air-to-air kills, few would have strafed bombers, so a counterattack could have been expected.

With warning of the attack, the American carriers in the area would have been notified. Halsey undoubtedly would have engaged. It is likely that a full-blown air-sea-land battle would have resulted, with results very different from what was seen historically.

Fighters to the Front

If *Kido Butai* had not been spotted in advance, a possible course of action would have been to launch a first-wave mixed strike of fighters and bombers, but have the fighters forge ahead and attack ahead of the bombers. Fighters were launched first, because they required less deck length to get airborne. They also had a faster cruising speed than the heavily laden bombers. They could fly directly to the enemy airfields, strafe, and then fly continuous cover keeping enemy aircraft from getting off the ground. If surprise was not achieved, they would engage fighters to clear the way for the bombers.

There were problems with this concept. The first is mass. The Japanese only had 45 fighters in the first wave. These aircraft would have to cover seven airfields, plus accompany seven different formations of bombers.[33] This would spread the fighters thin and make them vulnerable to concentrations of enemy fighters, a serious possibility considering that their intelligence expected 200 American fighters.[34] Some defending fighters would undoubtedly evade the A6M Zeros and get to the bombers.

One might think that the bombers would be adequately protected by sending the fighters directly against the airfields, especially if surprise was attained. What better way to protect the bombers then by preventing the fighters from ever getting off the ground? But if the enemy fighters were already airborne, the Japanese fighters might miss seeing them and go on to strafe empty bases. With poor radio communications the bombers would not be able to recall the fighters, allowing the defenders the opportunity to attack unescorted bombers

There simply were too few fighters for the first wave to employ fighter sweep tactics.

Close Escort

A second option would be to have the fighters remain with the bombers in a close escort role. In China, Japanese fighter pilots preferred to range freely and dogfight with the enemy, rather than to stick with a bomber formation. Close escort was simply not available in their doctrine or their mindset.

The Plan

The decision was to have the fighters accompany groups of bombers en route to the targets. The fighters would engage enemy fighters in the air or, in the absence of aerial opposition, strafe enemy airfields.

As the first wave flew south, groups would break off and head to their individual objectives.

- 25 D3A Vals and six A6M Zeros would break into two groups to hit Wheeler Field from the east and west;
- 26 D3A Vals and nine A6M Zeros would attack the Ford Island and Hickam airfields;
- 50 B5N Kate high-altitude bombers accompanied by nine A6M Zeros would head for Pearl Harbor;
- 40 torpedo-carrying B5N Kate carrier attack planes would drop down to low altitude and split into two groups to approach Pearl Harbor from the west and the east; nine Zero fighters would accompany the torpedo bombers until they were about 10nm from the harbor, where they would split off to attack Ewa Field.
- 12 Zeros would attack Kaneohe Field.[35]

Target	Torpedo Bombers	Level Bombers	Dive Bombers	Fighters	Notes
Wheeler			25	6	
Ford / Hickam			26	9	
Fleet		50		9	
Fleet	40				
Ewa				9	Ingress with TB group
Kaneohe				12	

The specific orders for the fighters are particularly noteworthy: "The targets of Fighter Combat Units will be enemy aircraft in the air and on the ground." That wording reflects the Japanese belief in the superiority of the offensive. The order did not say, "Protect the bombers from enemy fighters." Indeed, it directed the opposite: "In the event that no enemy aircraft are encountered in the air, the (Fighter Combat) units will immediately shift to the strafing of parked aircraft . . ."[36]

The fundamental Japanese fighter organization was a *shotai* of three aircraft, with three *shotais* combining into a *chutai* of nine aircraft. All the fighter formations assigned to each of the groups were from a single carrier, with the exception of the Kaneohe Field strike group that consisted of a mixture of *Shokaku* and *Zuikaku* fighters. This allocation preserved unit integrity, but maintaining unit integrity imposed a nearly even distribution of fighters across the formations that were disproportionate to the value of each formation.

For example, the torpedo bombers were expected to deliver 27 torpedo hits, enough to sink six battleships. The B5N Kates carrying AP bombs expected eight hits and perhaps to cripple one or two battleships. In other words, the torpedo bombers were three to six times as valuable as the high-altitude bombers. In addition, the torpedo bombers would be the most vulnerable. During their final run to target they would be flying singly, low and slow, in four long strings of bombers with each aircraft separated by hundreds of yards, beyond where their defensive machine guns could provide mutual support. The level bombers would be in five-ship elements with some degree of mutual protection.

These considerations should have caught the attention of the planners. Fighter cover should have been allocated to the torpedo bombers in proportion to their vulnerability and value. The torpedo bombers should have been wrapped in cotton wool and protected at all costs. Instead, the torpedo bombers, with 85% of the killing power, were protected by 20% of the fighters.

Even more inexplicably, the fighter *chutai* accompanying the torpedo bombers was to split off to attack the Marine Corps Air Field at Ewa, seven miles from Pearl Harbor. The torpedo bombers would make their final approach and attack *without any fighter protection over the harbor whatsoever*. While the Zeros were absent strafing airfields, the torpedo bombers could have been slaughtered.

This all was exacerbated by the fact that the fighters trained independently. They had not practiced with the bombers, so coordinated support was impossible.

The largest fighter unit was assigned to attack Kaneohe Field. This is inexplicable. Twelve of the available first-wave fighters (27%) were sent against an airfield fifteen miles from Pearl Harbor, to attack a PBY patrol wing. Granted, the "B" in PBY stood for "bomber," and pre-war aviation theorists actually thought these large, slow, poorly defended aircraft could be a threat to surface ships. Even if they constituted a threat, the PBYs at Kaneohe were not an *immediate* threat. It would have taken hours to locate the Japanese carriers and load bombs for an attack. A first-wave attack on Kaneohe could not be considered as an anti-reconnaissance measure, since the Japanese fighters were to arrive well after the Americans' dawn reconnaissance patrols were in the air. This target could have been deferred to the second wave. The primary concern of the first-wave fighters ought to have been enemy fighters, not reconnaissance aircraft.

In a plan featuring many unusual decisions, the most bizarre was that *more fighters were assigned to strike a wing of seaplanes than were assigned to ensure that the torpedo bombers reached their target*.

The primary mission of the fighters ought to have been to escort the B5N Kate torpedo bombers to the target and provide cover against enemy fighters, along with suppression of enemy air defense (SEAD) if the AA proved formidable (as it did). This was Japanese doctrine for attacking a fleet at sea—there is no reason why it should not have applied to attacking a fleet in port. After the torpedo bombers had successfully attacked, a process of only a few minutes if executed as planned, the fighters could have shifted to strafing airfields. But Japanese offensive propensities, along with their experiences in China, blinded them to the need to provide direct fighter support to the torpedo bombers.

The air groups from *Zuikaku* and *Shokaku* assigned to the Kaneohe strike were not held in high regard. Their air groups had only been recently formed out of the scrapings of available A6M Zero pilots. Much of their training in the months before the attack was in flying fundamentals, such as formation flying. It could be that they were shuffled off to the side and trusted to do little more than create some confusion, and delay the American reconnaissance effort.

No fighters (or bombers) were allocated for SEAD. It was as if the concept did not exist, or that the fighters had their own missions and would not be bothered to help the bombers along the way. "Combined arms" and "mutual support" were concepts absent from the Japanese lexicon.

The planners spread the available fighters nearly evenly over all the formations, regardless of the numbers or importance of those planes in the mission plan. The military proverb, "He who protects everything, protects nothing," applies. If the American forces at Hawaii had been in their usual readiness and detected the approach of the strike, and if the US fighters had massed over Pearl Harbor to protect the fleet (as was their responsibility), it is likely that the torpedo bombers' attack would have been thwarted.

One capability of their new fighter that the Japanese did not exploit was its incredible endurance. In the months before the beginning of the war the Japanese developed techniques to stretch the range of the A6M Zero to unheard-of lengths. Cruising at 115 knots at 12,000 feet, an A6M Zero with an average pilot at the controls could consume as little as 18 gallons per hour out of a normal fuel load of 182 gallons, giving ten hours in the air.[37] First-wave fighters launched at 0600 could have remained over Oahu for hours after the second wave had departed, if asked to do so. First-wave fighters could have been posted over each of the airfields and remained for the duration of the attack, ensuring that nothing got off the ground until after the second wave had come and gone. On US carriers this was known as "double cycling," and was usually done only with scout bombers on inner and outer AS patrols. US Fighters could be double-cycled after drop tanks were developed.

Evidently no thought was given to taking advantage of the A6M Zero's endurance. Instead, the fighters went in to the attack, expended their ammunition immediately, and joined up at the strike rendezvous point so the bombers could navigate them back to the carriers. The plan allowed the Americans a hiatus in the attack, time to recuperate from the effects of the first wave, recover and rearm what fighters they had gotten aloft, and prepare for the next wave.

Bomber Allocation for the Main Effort
The Intelligence Foundation

The Japanese were blessed with extraordinarily good intelligence for their attack. The Japanese Navy assigned a reserve naval officer, Yoshikawa Takeo, a graduate of the Japanese naval academy who had been medically disqualified from active duty, as a member of the Japanese legation on Oahu. While posing as a diplomat, his true role was kept secret from the legation staff. His neglecting of his "duties" at the legation scandalized the regular diplomatic staff, as he traveled about Oahu under the guise of a gadabout.

Almost daily he traveled to a tourist overlook surveying the beauties of Pearl Harbor and counted the fleet, noting mooring locations. He recorded the fleet's operating patterns. He determined the day of the week when most ships would be in port. He took tourist flights over the harbor, one on the 5th of December accompanied by two young ladies of questionable repute, a rather ingenious and amiable way to conceal intelligence activities. He attended open house events staged at the various bases, where he was allowed to wander about unsupervised. He worked in the kitchen at the Pearl Harbor Officer's Club, with access to the base and the officers' gossip. Attending a "Galaday" at Wheeler Field in August when the airdrome was dedicated, he inspected the facilities thoroughly.

Planners from the Naval General Staff also traveled to Hawaii aboard the civilian liner *Taiyo Maru*. This ship traveled along *Kido Butai's* intended route to take weather observations, gauge the density of traffic (no ships sighted), and observe American reconnaissance (ineffective). At Honolulu they delivered an extensive list of questions to Yoshikawa regarding Pearl Harbor and its defenses.

Yoshikawa divided Pearl Harbor into numbered squares and transmitted the locations of ships. Periodic messages to the Naval General

Staff in Tokyo, sent through diplomatic channels, included the specific anchorages and moorings occupied by the ships, along with listings of daily arrivals and departures. *Kido Butai* received one of these messages the day before that attack, with the information a day late due to being retransmitted from Tokyo. As *Kido Butai* approached Hawaii, Yoshikawa provided last minute tactical intelligence on anti-submarine nets at the entrance to the harbor (yes), anti-torpedo nets around the battleships (no), and barrage balloons (no).

The aviators had nearly exact information on the locations of moorings and berths and, more importantly, which normally hosted battleships and carriers. Each pilot was provided a map with the locations of their targets and the location of ground AA positions. They also were given aerial "Souvenir of Honolulu" photographs of the naval base. Copies would be found in aircraft shot down during the battle.[38]

The Japanese had a firm intelligence foundation upon which to plan and execute the attack.[39]

Operational Approach

Some of the most important decisions involved the overall concept of how the operation was to be executed, including the manner in which targets would be allocated to specific attackers, the attack order and timing, ingress and egress routes, and coordination.

Targets could be allocated in several ways. Under one option, specific aircraft could have been directed to hit specific targets. Alternately, a prioritization scheme could be used where the pilots were given general instructions regarding the types of targets to hit and in what order, with the aviators selecting their specific targets upon arrival. A compromise between the two would be for attackers to select specific targets out of an assigned area.

Each method has advantages and disadvantages.

Assigning aircraft to specific targets would give a better distribution of weapons over the intended targets, and would not require the aviators to make difficult target selection decisions when stress would be high. However, weapons could be wasted and confusion could result if the intelligence was inaccurate or if ships had moved since the last update. Pilots would still be required to recognize appropriate targets and avoid wasting weapons on inappropriate targets, something more difficult to achieve under combat conditions than might be suspected. Alternate targets could be pre-assigned, or the aviators could be given the freedom to independently find a target, or they could be directed to a marshalling area to serve as a reserve to be directed to a new target by the strike commander.

In contrast, a prioritization scheme would be most flexible to changes and conditions, but would require the aviators to make critical decisions under difficult conditions. Excellent visibility would be needed. And, somehow, the decisions of all the individual aircrews would need to be coordinated *in the absence of radio communication* to get the best performance out of the group as a whole, or else the possibility that all the aircraft would concentrate on a single high-priority target would have to be accepted.

Prioritization works best when targets are hit one at a time, so when the priority 1 target was destroyed the attackers could move on to the priority 2 target, and so on. But if the attack was to be simultaneous, or if individual pilots could not see the results of previous attacks, they would not have sufficient information for good decisions.

The Japanese combined features of both of these approaches. One group would go after carriers, one after battleships, and if anything unanticipated happened, the pilots were to find and attack anything suitable.

Prioritization

Three distinguished historians have recorded that the torpedo bombers used a prioritization scheme for assigning targets, as recorded in the Japanese official history of the war:

> Japanese operational priorities were defined as battleships and aircraft carriers, in that order, and the Kates of the first attack formation were given the task of dealing with American battleships. Because of the efficiency of their intelligence sources, the Japanese basically knew where individual battleships would be found and had listed them in numerical order of priority from one to eight. The Kates were under instructions to attack the first four American battleships in order of priority and there [after]; if carriers were in the anchorage, they were then to direct their attention against these. If carriers were absent, the Kates would be free to attack the battleships listed five to eight. The Vals, which were equipped with 250-kilogram bombs, were given the

task of dealing with American carriers. If these were absent, or in the event of the first attack formation having accounted for them, the priority of the Vals was to be American cruisers, and only after the cruisers had been destroyed was priority to be afforded to the battle line.[40]

This account does not square with the operations orders, the testimony of the pilots, and the actual organization and execution of the attack.

According to the Combined Fleet Operation Order No. 1, the "Targets for attack are land-based air power, aircraft carriers, battleships, cruisers, other warships, merchant shipping, port facilities, land installations," presumably in that order.[41] According to the Carrier Striking Task Force Operations Order No. 3, "The targets of the first group will be limited to about four battleships and four aircraft carriers; the order of targets will be battleships and then aircraft carriers."[42]

There was a gap between what the planners put on paper and what the warfighters were told to do. When interviewed postwar, many of the torpedo bomber aircrew specified that they were assigned to attack carriers as their first priority.

It appears that there were different official prioritization orders, apparently meant to placate different audiences. The Naval General Staff, anxious that Kido Butai be preserved, were told that enemy's means to mount a counterattack was first on the strike list; Yamamoto was told his battleships would have top priority. The aviators actually executing the attacks had the final say, and consistent with their belief that battleships were not as important as carriers, they were focused on taking out the carriers first.

As in most organizations, there are the official instructions, the real instructions given to the troops, and the instructions they actually execute. The torpedo bombers, with Murata in overall command, were organized into two groups, one to attack carriers at the carrier anchorage west of Ford Island (16 Soryu and Hiryu bombers under Lieutenant Matsumura Hirata), and one to go against Battleship Row (Murata's 24 bombers from Akagi and Kaga).

If targets were missing or destroyed by previous aircraft they were instructed to go find another target. The priority for alternative targets was carriers, battleships, and cruisers for the Soryu and Hiryu aviators, battleships for the *Akagi* and *Kaga* aircraft.

The prioritization scheme contained in the Japanese official history is overly complex and would be impossible to execute in combat, especially in the absence of excellent inter-aircraft communications, in an operation where pilots were scrambling to get in their attack before the AA defenses woke up. Aircraft were expected to attack "nearly simultaneously" in four long streams of bombers with planes at seven-second intervals. In the absence of reliable radio communications, in this formation leaders could exert only the most rudimentary "follow-me" leadership. Down on the deck, the rearmost planes in the string of attackers would not have the information to be able to make a reasonable decision regarding how far along the priority list the attack had progressed in order to properly allocate their own attack. To expect junior aviators to make such decisions while under fire for the first time, while flying 60 feet over the water in a wallowing torpedo bomber was unrealistic.

The official history prioritization scheme was more likely the story that was briefed to senior officers and the Naval Staff. The organization and actual execution of the attack indicate that Genda and Fuchida, on the cutting edge, considered things differently. Forty percent of the available torpedo bombers were to immediately attack the carrier moorings. This group would not wait to see if battleships one through four were hit. They were after carriers, pure and simple.

The choices available to the Japanese were constrained by their air-to-air communications. There are no reports that they used radiotelephones for tactical command and control. Their decision was to give guidance to the aircrews on target selection and the authority to choose their own targets. They then selected an attack formation for the torpedo bombers—a long string of aircraft one at a time separated by 500 meters—that eliminated any possibility of meaningful command by their formation leaders. Considering that most of the aircrews were young and inexperienced, these decisions effectively abrogated any possibility that the more mature leaders could influence the course of the torpedo attack.

Torpedo Bombers
Initial Calculations

Yamamoto himself wanted battleships sunk. One would expect that battleships would be allocated the bulk of the ordnance. There were also the carriers, a major risk to *Kido Butai* that had to be hit to prevent them from counterattacking. Any remaining torpedoes could be directed against cruisers. The Japanese operations order also listed auxiliaries and merchant shipping as potential torpedo targets, but they were at the bottom of the priority list, and there were no torpedoes to spare.

There are several ways the Japanese might have calculated their allocations. One of the most revealing methods is as follows. Assume that maximum firepower was wanted against the battleships. Allocate the *minimum* forces against the carriers, and send the rest against the battleships.

Two torpedo hits would cripple a carrier and prevent it from getting underway. Two carriers were operating out of Pearl Harbor; if they were both in port, four hits would be required. Assigning one additional attacker against each carrier to account for misses would result in six torpedo bombers allocated against the carriers, leaving 34 to go against battleships.

The Pacific Fleet had eight battleships. This would result in potentially as few as 4 torpedoes per battleship as a lower limit. If ships were double-berthed or in drydock there might be as few as four battleships accessible to torpedoes, giving an allocation of 8 torpedoes per battleship.

Battleship Row Attack Group

Akagi's and *Kaga*'s 24 bombers would approach the battleship anchorages and engage from the east. If moored singly there could be six battleship targets accessible to torpedoes, but more likely four.

In addition, across from Battleship Row was the flagship *Pennsylvania*'s usual berth along 1010 Dock. Attackers would have to approach this target from the southwest. It was not occupied by a battleship on the day of the attack, but rather by an antique minelayer moored outboard of a modern 10,000-ton cruiser. *Pennsylvania* was in drydock.

The torpedo bombers would attack first. There were good reasons for this: the torpedo planes had a very narrow launch envelope. Pearl Harbor was too shallow for standard aerial torpedo approaches.

Torpedoes dropped from the B5N Kate in their normal delivery profile would generally dive down to at least 100 feet and sometimes as deep as 150–300 feet before rising to their running depth. This technical problem was overcome by modifying the torpedoes with wooden vanes on their tail to slow their entry into the water and provide an immediate nose-up pitch, and by modifying the delivery profile of the aircraft so that the torpedo bomber at weapons release would be "low and slow"— 20 meters altitude, 140 to 150 knots, level attitude, gear and flaps up, as opposed to more usual drop parameters of 200 knots from 100 to 300 foot altitude. [43] At 20 meters, the pilots had to estimate altitude by comparing the aircraft's wing length to the distance above the water, a rather harrowing process that would keep the pilot's head out of the cockpit (away from monitoring airspeed and attitude) and looking to the side of the aircraft (away from the target). Too high, and the torpedo would dive too steeply and hit the harbor bottom; too low, and the torpedo might broach or skip on the surface and break up.[44]

The slow speed and low altitude would make the torpedo bombers easy targets for AA fire or fighters. Thus, the torpedo attack had to be launched before the enemy was fully alert. The warhead was also modified to arm after only a short distance through the water, about 650 feet.

Three of the specially modified torpedoes were dropped for tests. Two ran successfully; the third hit bottom at 39.3 feet. "On that basis the Japanese estimated that, out of 40 drops planned for Pearl Harbor, 27 would hit home."[45]

The best of the practice runs occurred in early November, days before the end of training. The torpedo bombers achieved 82.5% hits. With this percentage, 19 hits could be expected from the 24 bombers allocated to attack the battleline. If the attack was distributed evenly over six battleships, that would give three hits per battleship, which according to Japanese thinking was sufficient to cripple them all.

The torpedo bombers were allocated months before the attack, before the shallow water problem was solved. As late as 4 November, during what has been referred to as "the dress rehearsal,"[46] only 40% of the torpedoes leveled off at the correct depth. At this rate only 10 torpedoes would hit the battleline, perhaps two per battleship, which was sufficient to damage, and perhaps to cripple, but not to sink. Using Fuchida's original guesstimate, there would be 16 torpedo hits on the battleline, two or three per target if evenly distributed. And again, that was enough to cripple, but not to sink.

If 80% hits could be expected, then each B5N Kate with a torpedo would be worth 0.16 of a capital ship. Twenty-four torpedo bombers, cumulatively, would be worth 3.8 battleships sunk out of six potential targets.

The planners originally allocated only crippling power against the battleships, not killing power.

Carrier Moorings Attack Group

The other 16 torpedo-carrying bombers, two groups of eight, were assigned to attack the carrier anchorages on the northwest side of Ford Island. The Japanese formal estimate was that three of the carriers were operating out of Pearl Harbor,[47] although their intelligence agent's reports would attest that rarely were all three in port together.

Three carriers were assigned to the Pacific Fleet, *Enterprise*, *Lexington*, and *Saratoga*. *Saratoga* was at San Diego. She had not been operating out of Pearl Harbor while in drydock at Bremerton. The intelligence officer's reports would not have mentioned her presence since October.

The attack against the carrier moorings would involve a fairly easy approach along the length of the loch past Pearl City, with plenty of room to set up the attack and establish the proper release conditions. The approach would be at an angle so the targets would be foreshortened, reducing the target cross section by about 30%. The approach would pass several nests of destroyers, so surprise would be needed to avoid AA fire.

These 16 bombers represented 40% of the torpedo-armed bombers. The maximum number of carriers the Japanese could expect to find in port would be three, two more likely, fewer still considering the carriers spent a lot of time underway. At 40% hits, this group would be expected to score six hits, enough to sink two carriers; at 68%, ten hits, which could account for all three carriers or gut two; 82% would give thirteen hits, over four hits for each carrier assigned to the Pacific Fleet.

This allocation provided killing firepower against the carriers.

Weighting the Attack

The battleship anchorages might expose six battleships along battleship row. The Japanese assigned 24 aircraft to attack this group, four per potential target. The other group of 16 bombers would be attacking, at most, three carriers, more likely only two, for five to eight torpedo bombers per potential target. They maintained this overweight even after they received an intelligence report that none of the carriers were in port, in the hopes that the carriers might return.

Target	# Potential Targets	Torpedoes Allocated	Torpedoes per Target
Battleships	6	24	4
Carriers	2 or 3	16	8 or 5.33

Carriers did not have the built-in anti-torpedo protection of a battleship, and could sustain fewer hits before sinking. The Japanese felt that three to four torpedo hits were enough to sink a carrier compared to four to five for a battleship. The Japanese plan sent sixteen torpedo bombers to achieve the eight hits needed to guarantee the sinking of two carriers (two bombers per needed hit), but only 24 bombers to get the 30 hits needed to guarantee the sinking of six battleships (0.8 of a bomber per needed hit).

The D3A Val dive-bombers added more firepower against the carriers. Eighty-one Vals were to be sent against fleet targets in the second wave, and their first priority was aircraft carriers. If the carriers had been sunk or capsized by the torpedo attack, the dive-bombers were instructed to bomb the hulks. The planners added suspenders to their belt to ensure that the carriers would never sail again.

This was likely the aviation commander Genda's work. Genda had previously made clear his views that battleships were obsolete and that carriers were the most important objectives of the attack. In initial estimates for Yamamoto in February of 1941, Genda made carriers the attack's first priority, but was overruled.

Genda gave voice to his opinions the day before the attack. Aboard *Akagi*, he learned there were no carriers in Pearl Harbor. However, another staff officer pointed out that the carriers might return. Genda cheered up, saying, "If that happened, I don't care if all eight battleships are away."[48]

Another thing that suggests that the weighting was intentional was the numbers involved. The carrier attack moorings were attacked by two groups of eight carrier attack planes. Eight is an unusual number in Japanese air doctrine—it is not a multiple of the usual 3-plane *shotai*. This indicates that the number of planes sent against the carrier moorings was not a product of doctrine but a conscious decision.

Additional evidence comes from Abe Zenji, a dive-bomber pilot in the second wave, who stated, "If we could not find the carriers, our secondary targets would be cruisers." Speaking of the attack as a whole, he went on to say, "We missed *our main objective, the aircraft carriers,* since they were at sea."[49]

Genda and his aviators had their own priorities, and killing carriers was at the top of the list. They would go for battleships, but they were doubly interested in pulverizing their own US counterparts.

Did Genda slip this allocation into the plan, or was it made with Yamamoto's knowledge and consent? It is hard to say, because Japanese staffs had a much different culture from Western staffs. The Japanese military vested an unusual amount of independence to middle grade officers, to the extent that some started wars or initiated invasions or even assassinated political leaders on their own initiative. The planning environment allowed little interplay between seniors and juniors. Criticism would imply that the work was inadequate, a failure by the junior officer. Failure was anathema, a shame that in some cases might only be expunged by ritual suicide.

So, whether the firepower distribution was as Yamamoto wanted, or as Genda slipped in, is hard to discern. It likely was Genda's. After all, with an opportunity to assign additional firepower to targets when he granted the midget submarines a place in the attack, Yamamoto assigned them to strike battleships. Yamamoto wanted more hits on battleships; Genda wanted more on carriers.

It is never good when the objectives of the boss and his chief planner are not aligned.

There is another consideration. The torpedo bomber allocations were made early in the planning process. Some Japanese documents refer to the possibility that there might be four American carriers in port. If that was their expectation, then the Japanese were sending four torpedo bombers per carrier, the same as what they allocated against the battleships. This is still an overweight against the carriers, since carriers were more vulnerable than battleships. But if this was the case, it demonstrated again the incredible inflexibility in Japanese planning. They knew from latest intelligence reports that there were only two carriers operating out of Pearl Harbor, and should have adjusted their allocations accordingly. Their failure to do so would have tactical implications—as will be seen, it contributed to much of the confusion of the torpedo attack.

Attack Routes and Sequencing

The torpedo units were to attack in single file, a decision that Fuchida claimed to have made. This was a remarkable choice. Line abreast was the usual torpedo attack formation against warships, to make it more difficult for ships to maneuver and avoid several torpedoes dropped simultaneously, and to spread the defensive AA fire. Fuchida claimed that the formation was chosen because it was thought that "the long thin line [was] especially well suited to Pearl Harbor with its narrow channel and many obstacles."[50]

(6) Torpedo Bomber Planned Attack Routes

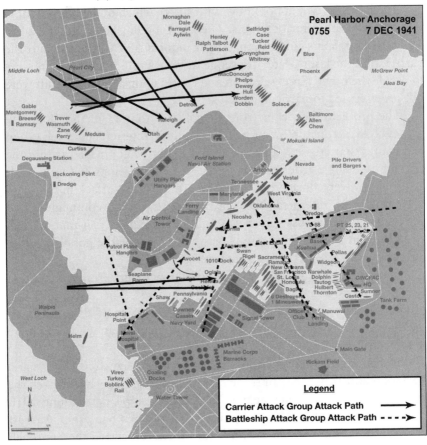

Gordon Prange's *At Dawn We Slept* contains a chart giving Fuchida's representation of the planned lines of approach for the torpedo bombers. The dotted lines show the attack paths assigned to the Battleship Row attack, while the solid lines were the routes assigned those attacking the carrier anchorage.

There were 18 different attack paths, six against Battleship Row, two against potential battleship moorings along 1010 Dock, and five against potential carrier moorings northwest of Ford Island. Five were directed against potential cruiser locations. This scheme was likely formulated by Murata, a torpedo expert, who had been delegated responsibility for much of the planning for the torpedo bombers.

The Japanese would not know with surety which of the berths would be occupied with priority targets. Their last intelligence would be 24 to 48 hours late. Ships could change their moorings or enter or depart the harbor after the last update. Consequently, the aircraft commanders were to decide their own target selection and routes upon arrival. Aircraft were not pre-assigned to particular routes.

The problem that leaps from the chart is that 11 of the 18 attack routes cross, setting up the potential of mutual interference. Each group had routes that crossed, a problem that might be controlled within the aircraft of a single group through good communications and tight leadership. However, considering that each group was to attack in two lines with aircraft at 500 meter intervals, that each aircraft commander had the authority to choose whichever route he felt best, and that aircraft would be out of communications with their leaders, the possibility that aircraft would select crossing routes remained.

The greater potential for mutual interference came from the fact that routes belonging to different groups also crossed. This potentially sets up mid-air collisions or air-to-air near misses that could disrupt the attack—in modern terminology, the torpedo bombers' attack routes were not deconflicted.

The most significant crossing route was one assigned to *Hiryu*'s and *Soryu*'s bombers going against the carrier moorings. They were given the option to deliver an attack against the fleet flagship's berth along 1010 dock, which might be occupied by either a carrier or a battleship. Aircraft choosing this route would recover from their run across the approach paths of bombers going against Battleship Row.

Crossing attack routes can be deconflicted by altitude or by time.

Altitude was obviously impossible, as the torpedoes had to be released from the same low altitude. The Japanese intended to feed bombers into the attack one at a time from each of the four groups, each sending in an aircraft at about seven-second intervals. But while each aircraft in a group would be separated by time, there was no way to prevent different groups from interfering with each other. Aircraft that were searching for alternate targets or repeating aborted runs would also be a hazard as they tried to re-insert themselves into the attack pattern. The aircraft were too far apart to communicate by hand signals, and the use of voice radios was apparently not considered.

This formation was a command and control nightmare. Once the attack began, the leaders could not exert any control, and the potential for mutual interference was great. None of this was practiced during the two rehearsals, with the Japanese taking the position that none of this type of interference would occur. Here, as throughout the war, Japanese planning generally assumed that events would be executed as planned, with little consideration for what might go wrong, and no contingency planning.

While Fuchida's drawing might suggest many aircraft attacking simultaneously, the natural result of using long strings of aircraft was that only a few routes would be used. Aircraft attacking one at a time in "follow the leader" style would be naturally drawn to select the easiest approaches. For the *Akagi* and *Kaga* torpedo bombers going against Battleship Row, the attack would concentrate, as a natural result of a form of self-organizing agent-based behavior, on the southern end of Battleship Row.

The Japanese noted this propensity during their November "rehearsal." Nothing positive was done to correct the problem.

The attack CONOPS (concept of operations) required the torpedo bombers to come into AA range one at a time at seven second intervals, sufficient time for a .50-cal AA machine gun to shift targets. Each bomber would in turn face the concentrated fire of all the automatic weapons along that path, without other aircraft to spread the defenders' fire.

The planners' scheme rejected the usual method of delivering a torpedo attack, with planes approaching in line abreast. Several modern attack aviators examined this aspect of the plan and believed that line-abreast attacks in waves of four against Battleship Row would have been possible, especially if they were echeloned at 50-yard intervals. Each bomber in a wave would attack a different target. The formation would allow the trailing aircraft in each echelon to see the aim point of the aircraft ahead of it, allowing it to select a different target. This would spread rather than concentrate the attack. In this way the attack against Battleship Row could have been completed in under a minute, with better control over the distribution of fire, fewer chances for mutual interference, and greater dispersion of the defensive fire.

Torpedo Nets

Torpedo nets had the potential to thwart the torpedo attack. The Americans considered using torpedo nets, particularly after Taranto in November 1940, where British torpedo bombers sank several Italian battleships in port. The idea was rejected by Admiral Kimmel. Kimmel may have felt the harbor was too shallow for torpedoes, although he knew of the successful British torpedo attacks in Taranto harbor and had been warned by the CNO that the depths of water at Pearl Harbor did not make a torpedo attack impossible.[51] Kimmel rejected torpedo nets because he believed they would interfere with an emergency sortie.

While Japanese intelligence indicated that torpedo nets were not being used in Pearl Harbor, they had to consider the possibility that the Americans would install them as the threat of war increased. Tokyo sent a message to the Consul General at Honolulu, received on 2 December, asking that information on torpedo nets be wired on a daily basis.[52]

In the days underway while steaming towards Hawaii, the torpedo bomber aircrews considered ways to defeat torpedo nets. They talked of dropping their torpedoes between the nets and the ships, which was impossible for a number of technical reasons. Their final solution was to have aircraft intentionally crash into the nets, a bizarre expedient with little chance of success, but a very Japanese course of action. Pilots were selected for the task.

One potential solution was to use 250kg bombs from D3A Val dive-bombers to blow the nets apart. Photographs show that the line of floats buoying the nets would be visible, yet as an option it was never mentioned.[53] This was another example of Japanese stovepipe thinking. Instead of using the different types of aircraft cooperatively, one type helping the other, the torpedo nets were considered to be a torpedo bomber problem for the torpedo bomber aircrews to solve, even if it required the most extreme expedients.

Alternately, a B5N Kate could have been loaded with a large number of 60kg GP bombs. It could have dropped a string of them across the nets from low altitude, giving a high probability of blasting holes in the nets. This was another solution evidently not considered.

It is curious that the aircrews were forced to consider the problem at all. A counter to torpedo nets ought to have been worked out earlier by the planners. As it was, it became a nagging worry hanging over the heads of the aviators for the duration of the 13-day transit to the target. Those selected to crash the nets must have been relieved when they learned, a bare four hours prior to launch, that the Japanese Hawaiian Consulate reported that the harbor had no torpedo nets.[54]

Level Bombers

The payload allocation of B5N Kate carrier attack planes was the key planning decision. If seven Kates with torpedoes were likely to cause the same damage against battleships as 50 to 100 planes with AP bombs, why were so many of the Kates armed with bombs?

At the time of the allocation decision, torpedoes still had significant uncertainties, and the technical problems had not been solved. The shallow water problem was resolved only a week before the end of training, torpedo nets were only confirmed as absent a day before the attack, and the double-berthing problem remained. The Japanese had to consider the possibility that the battleships might be vulnerable only to AP bombs.

After intensive training, the Japanese expected exceptional performance from their level bombers, anticipating "4 out of 5 salvoes to hit."

In American aviation terminology, a group of bombs dropped simultaneously on a target by a formation of level bombers was called a "salvo." In the gunnery terminology of the United States and Great Britain, a salvo was considered to have hit if one of the shells hit; it did not imply that all hit. This interpretation is confirmed by Lieutenant Takayoshi Morinaga, who said, "If one plane out of five bombers hit the target their attack would be successful."[55]

A Japanese post-attack evaluation entitled *Lessons (air operation) of the Sea Battle off Hawaii* (hereafter referred to as *Lessons*) was written perhaps in late August 1942 by the Battle-Lessons Investigation Committee. Fuchida probably served on the committee.[56] *Lessons* cited two numbers for the level bombers' expected results, based on a practice attack conducted on 24 October 1941: "Probabilities of hitting targets,

10% (Max. 17)," and "Probability of striking targets, 50% (Max. 75)."[57] "Probabilities of hitting targets" was likely the hit percentage per bomber, which would translate into five hits with a maximum of seven. "Probabilities of striking targets" was likely the probability of the salvo hitting. Fifty percent would equate to five hits; 75% to eight. Thus, the Japanese expected five to eight hits with AP bombs against inboard battleships, with additional hits possible on outboard battleships that might be caught within accurate bomb patterns.

Lieutenant Commander Sadao Chigusa's diary, in an entry ten days after the attack, said "The power of the No. 80-5 [AP] bombs . . . is enormous and sufficient to deal any battleships in existence a mortal blow if hit by 5–6 bombs . . ."[58] If this coincided with the planner's expectations for the attack, they might have expected enough hits to inflict sufficient cumulative damage to sink one battleship, if the hits were concentrated against one target. Since the comment was made after the attack, *Arizona*'s fate might have biased Sadao's opinion.

There were two different models of ship damage used in this period: a deterministic model and a stochastic model. Which model is chosen is critical to how the potential results of an attack would be calculated.

In the deterministic model, an estimate is made of the average number of hits that are required to sink a battleship. Damage is cumulative. Ships are sunk by the cumulative effect of many bombs. If 18 hits are thought to be needed to sink a battleship, one hit is worth 5.6% of a battleship. A ship would be considered crippled after 50% cumulative damage (9 hits).

The Japanese ascribed to the deterministic methodology, as did the US Navy in 1941. The US Naval War College's "Fighting Strength" methodology assessed the "Life" of a battleship to be about 18 penetrating 14-inch (680-kg) shell hits. The Japanese 800kg armor piercing bombs would be valued at 1.08 equivalent 14-inch hits. They were considered to be able to penetrate 150mm (5.91 inches) of armor when dropped from 8,200 feet, more when dropped from the planned delivery altitude of 3,000 meters (9,843 feet), so the American battleships' deck and turret top armor was vulnerable to penetration.

If 15% hits were expected, each AP bomb carried into the battle would have an expected value of one to two percent of a battleship, determined by multiplying the value of a hit by the hit probability. By this methodology, if all the hits were concentrated on a single battleship and no aircraft shot down before bomb release, the Japanese would need 50 to 100 bombers to sink a battleship.

The other model is stochastic. It assumes that a battleship is sunk or crippled by AP bombs not through cumulative damage, but by a catastrophic event such as a hit in a magazine or an engine room. Under this model each bomb has a chance to sink the ship. If luck is against the bombers, it is possible that the ship might take more than 18 hits without being sunk or crippled.

A stochastic model was developed by the US Navy Bureau of Ordnance during the war. A hit in an engineering space by an 800kg AP bomb could disable a battleship. If the expected hit percentage was 15%, and the engineering spaces constituted 20% of the target cross-section, then a single B5N Kate level bomber had a 3% chance of crippling a battleship. A hit in a main or secondary magazine or main battery turret could cause the magazine to explode and destroy the ship. Magazines constituted 23% of the target cross-section. Each bomber would have a 4% chance of hitting a magazine.

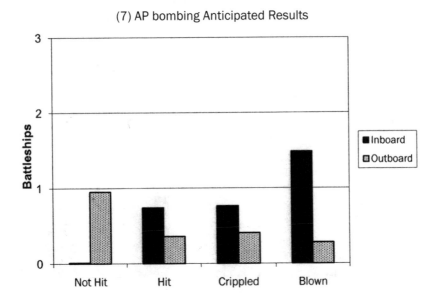

(7) AP bombing Anticipated Results

The chart above shows the result of a simulation of the AP bomb attack using the Bureau of Ordnance's stochastic model, along with factors shown in the actual attack. In the simulation, ten groups of five bombers attack the three inboard battleships, three each against *Maryland* and *Arizona* and four against *Tennessee*. Each group has an 80% chance of scoring one hit on their target. If a salvo hit the inboard target, there was a 25% chance of also scoring a hit on the outboard battleship, based on historical results. Each hit had a 23% chance of detonating a magazine and a 20% chance of hitting an engineering space.

The results shown are an average over 1,000 repetitions of the attack. An average of 1.5 battleships were destroyed by magazine explosions (meaning that in about half the trials, one battleship blew up, and in the other half, two blew up, with a small number of cases where none or all three were blown up).

The number of crippled battleships might seem low considering the bombs had nearly an equal chance of hitting an engineering space as a magazine. The reason is that if a ship had both an engineering hit and a blown magazine, it was shown as blown up.

There was also about a 70% chance that one of the outboard battleships would be crippled or destroyed, important if the torpedo attack totally failed, and of little additional importance if the torpedoes were successfully delivered.

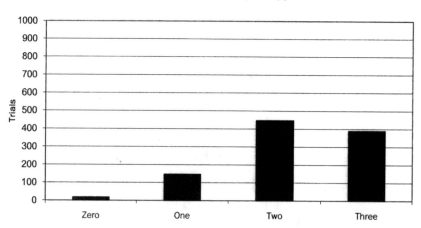

(8) Number of Inboard Battleships Crippled or Sunk

The chart above shows the data from the same 1,000 trials, this time showing the number of runs in which zero, one, two, or three inboard battleships were either crippled or sunk. Outboard or single-moored battleships are not included.

The chances that the level bombers would totally fail are vanishingly small. In over 80% of the trials, either two or three inboard battleships were either crippled or sunk.

The marginal value of an aircraft group in each role is revealing. A single group of five level bombers would have an expected return of one hit (80% hit on the target battleships, and if the salvo hits, another 25% chance of a hit on an outboard battleship). Each group would have a potential value of 0.43 of a battleship crippled or sunk.

The Japanese planners expected 67.5% hits with torpedoes, so five bombers would be expected to score 3.375 hits, sufficient to cripple or sink a battleship, or an expected value of 1.0.

So, even using the stochastic model, the expected return from a group armed with torpedoes was 2.3 times that of the same aircraft armed with bombs. The Japanese could have achieved better results if they had shifted several groups of level bombers to carry torpedoes, though this presupposes they had known that their technical solutions to the problem of launching torpedoes in shallow water would be successful.

Looking at the extreme case, the Japanese would have expected an additional 34 torpedo hits if they had armed all 50 of their level bombers with torpedoes. The three battleships double berthed would have been untouched, along with the one in drydock. In the actual battle, only one of these ships (*Arizona*) was crippled or sunk by AP bombs. In exchange, they would have had sufficient torpedoes to make all four outboard battleships nearly unsalvageable, with perhaps another 20 torpedo hits to distribute amongst cruisers and other fleet units. The damage to the fleet *as a balanced force* would have been much more extensive had those 50 Kate carrier attack bombers carried torpedoes, and if the Japanese were willing to expand their vision beyond battleships. An additional 20 hits could have sunk four cruisers and eight to twelve destroyers, sufficient ships to constitute a screen for a carrier task force in the early days of 1942.

In other words, the planners valued the chance of getting one or two inboard battleships over a higher probability of getting many cruisers, destroyers, and auxiliaries.

Attacking other ships was not in the Japanese mindset. They were not attacking the Pacific Fleet as a material force, but as a symbol of

American naval power. Their audience was not the Pacific Fleet Staff, but the American people. They were taking a spiritual approach toward attacking the enemy's morale and will to fight. The Japanese did not think in terms of maximizing the physical damage to the Pacific Fleet as a whole, but maximizing the damage against the popular symbols of American naval power.

Arguments could be made to either decrease or increase the allocation of level bombers. A decrease would free more bombers to carry the more lethal torpedoes. An increase would give the level bombers the potential to cripple or sink four battleships (the three inboard battleships and the one in drydock), thus accomplishing Yamamoto's objective without requiring any contribution from the torpedo bombers. The level bomber attack was less uncertain than launching torpedoes in terms of weapons delivery and the effects of AA fire, or the possible interference from enemy fighters.

Shifting carrier attack plane allocation between AP bombs and torpedoes was not an option available to the Japanese on 7 December 1941. The allocations had already been made and the crews trained in one role and one role only. There was no flexibility to change crews from one mission to the other.

The allocation decision, made in late September, represented Japanese expectations at that snapshot in time. As the training process unfolded, at times the Japanese seemed to expect that they could sink every capital ship in the harbor with the combined level bomber and torpedo bomber attack, and that everything would go well; at other times, if Fuchida is to be believed, they worried that they might not sink even one battleship, and that the torpedo attacks would achieve nothing.

These bipolar mood swings were apparently communicated to the aviators, and could have affected their decision making during the attack.

A Shortage of Torpedoes?

The decision to include level bombers was not made because of any shortages of the specially modified shallow water torpedoes. It was not recognized until late in the training process that the torpedoes needed modification, well after the aircraft weapon allocations had been made.

On 17 November 1941, *Kaga* loaded 100 shallow-water torpedoes at Saeki Bay, before departing for the rendezvous at the Kurile Islands. There the torpedoes were distributed. The striking force departed for

Pearl Harbor on 26 November. There were sufficient extra torpedoes to arm the 50 level bombers, if desired. But this was not a planned contingency, or even possible, since the 50 carrier attack planes assigned as level bombers had not trained for the tricky release conditions needed for a successful launch in the shallow, confined waters of Pearl Harbor.

Planning Inflexibility

The Japanese committed to their distribution of torpedo and level bombers very early in the process. It would have seemed logical to allocate weapons to the carrier attack bombers only after there was a better idea of the hit percentages that could be expected.

Most of the B5N Kates could have initially trained in the torpedo attack role, the most difficult method. Sufficient lead bombardiers could have been trained separately to accommodate an expansion of the level bombing group. If the numbers indicated that fewer torpedo bombers and more level bombers were needed, torpedo bombers could have been shifted to the level bombing role as wingmen, since all the wingmen had to do was maintain formation and release their bomb when the leader dropped, a skill that did not require extensive training. A last minute allocation of weapons could have been possible, had the planners made such a provision. The Japanese had the intelligence support, but they elected not to use it to its full potential.

If the aircrews were capable of delivering either torpedoes or high-altitude bombs, the proper allocation decision point would have been the day before the attack, based on last-minute intelligence on torpedo nets, the number of battleships and carriers in port, and the number of double-berthed battleships. Instead, the Japanese made their major allocation decisions three months prior to the attack and held to them, regardless of emergent information that ought to have prompted changes in their plan. This could be another manifestation of Japanese inflexibility, or it could be because Genda thought the aviators could not become sufficiently skilled in both roles to allow last-minute shifts.

Whichever the case, the result was inflexibility, and that inflexibility limited what the plan could achieve.

The Japanese did show some flexibility with their level bombers. Their doctrine was to employ level bombers in a formation of nine aircraft (a *chutai*), dropping a pattern of bombs that could compensate for target motion when attacking an underway target. They broke doctrine by going to a smaller formation of five bombers. This was a vote of confidence in the bombardiers, that they could hit a stationary target without needing the larger bomb pattern. Since the distribution of the bombs in the pattern allow for only one hit per group per target, doubling the number of groups provided twice the chances to hit. By breaking doctrine the Japanese went from five salvoes (five *chotai* with a total of 45 aircraft) to ten salvoes (ten formations with 50 aircraft).

Breaking up the established *chutai* organization shows that the planners were not totally enslaved by doctrine. At the same time it raises the question why such flexibility was not demonstrated elsewhere.

Dive-Bombers

Eighty-one D3A Vals of the second wave were assigned to strike fleet targets. Most histories imply that this force was to finish the destruction of ships only damaged in the first wave. This is incorrect.

The dive-bombers' first objective was the carriers. They were to sink them if they survived the torpedoes delivered by the first wave; if they were sunk they were still to bomb the hulks to make them unsalvageable. Lieutenant Commander Abe Zenji confirmed postwar that "the original plan for the dive-bombers was to attack the carriers."

Next they were to go after cruisers. Only after the cruisers were destroyed were they to direct attention to battleships.[59] This conformed with the capabilities of the 250kg GP bomb.

The dive-bombers trained to attack as a *shotai* or *chutai*. The lead bomber would attack in a 55-degree dive directed at a predetermined aimpoint, usually the ship's mast. The other aircraft would follow in 20- to 30-second intervals. If the leader hit, the following aircraft would maintain the predetermined aim point; if he missed (likely deflected by the wind or target motion), his followers would adjust their aimpoints, just as a ship would adjust its gunfire based on the fall of shot. In practice runs against the battleship-sized target ship *Settsu*, an attack by a *shotai* of three dive-bombers "almost always guaranteed at least one successful hit on target."[60]

The 1941 Combined Fleet Exercises saw dive-bomber hit rates improve to 55%.[61] For the Pearl Harbor attack, the lead dive-bomber pilot, Lieutenant Commander Egusa Takashige, trained his crews. The release altitude was reduced from 600 meters to 400 meters for better accuracy. Lives were lost during training when aircraft did not recover from their dives in time. At 55% accuracy, the 81 dive-bombers going against the fleet would expect 44 hits.

The wargames provide an indication of Japanese expectations for 250kg GP bombs against carriers and cruisers. In the September wargame, air groups from four Japanese carriers sank two carriers and severely damaged one, and sank three cruisers and severely damaged three others. If we assume that the carriers and cruisers were all the targets of the dive-bombers, and that each carrier was hit by at least four bombs and each cruiser by three, that would yield a total of 30 bomb hits, or approximately what would be expected from four carriers' dive bombers—if six carriers would score 44 hits, 4 carriers would score 29.

This corresponds to 1941 National War College lethality estimates. A carrier had a life of 6.8 equivalent penetrating 14-inch shell hits; cruisers 4.2 to 4.6. A 500-pound bomb had a value of 2.0, requiring four hits to sink a carrier and three to sink a cruiser. Given these assumptions, Egusa's dive-bombers would be expected to have the firepower to sink up to 14 cruisers, or three carriers and ten cruisers. There were eight cruisers in Pearl Harbor at the time of the attack. The dive-bomber allocation appeared to be a good match for what would be required to kill the Pacific Fleet's carriers and cruisers, with some overkill (as most military planners prefer). In the event, with no carriers in port, there would be extra dive-bombers available for other targets.

The calculations seem to confirm that the Japanese expected approximately 55% hits, matching their training results. This was optimistic. Over all of World War II in the Pacific, dive-bombers averaged about 20% hits against stationary battleship-size targets.[62]

Japanese dive-bombers delivered some of the very best and worst performances of the war. There were cases where every bomb from a *chutai* missed slow-moving merchantmen.[63] On the other hand there is the case of the heavy cruisers *Cornwall* and *Dorsetshire*, caught in the Indian Ocean by a strike of D3A Vals that scored on the order of 90% hits and damaging near misses (DNM), sinking both ships in short order. The success against *Cornwall* and *Dorsetshire* did much to establish the D3A Val's fearsome reputation in the history books.

The root reason for the wide variation in results is the Japanese dive-bombing technique. Wingmen followed as nearly as possible in the path of the leader, and corrected their bomb aim point based on the striking location of the leader's bomb. If the leader had a good sight picture and good aim and a steady release, there was a good likelihood that the wingmen would hit. If the leader was off, then the following aircraft would be adjusting their aim point based off the results of a bad attack, making it very unlikely that following aircraft in the *chutai* would hit. If the leader's aim was good but the wind strong it could be difficult for the wingmen to judge large corrections and apply them in the course of their dive. Any problem with the leader's attack and the entire formation could end up scattering their bombs over the ocean. In analytic terms, each Japanese dive-bomber was not an independent event with a 55% probability of hit, but had their probability of hit dependent upon the (improved or degraded) skill of the lead bomber. The Japanese technique could be devastating, or it could be ineffective, with little middle ground.

Airspace control and target selection also were issues. With so many bombers from different formations going after targets in a restricted airspace, the likelihood of mutual interference was high unless tight controls were maintained. The dive-bombers had the same targeting problem as the torpedo bombers—concentrate to sink as many cruisers as possible, but with a minimum of overkill.

The Japanese plan metered the bombers in to the attack, with each *shotai* attacking only when the previous *shotai* completed their runs. With nine *chutai* in the attack, one *chutai* should have been allocated per cruiser, with one spare. The attack ought to have been a process of the nine *chutai* leaders coordinating their target selection, and the rest of the aviators just following their leaders down. Problems could arise with smoke from fires caused by the first wave, especially where targets were close together, such as the four cruisers tied up at the shipyard piers—an early hit on one might obscure all four.

Nine aircraft at 20-second intervals would make for a three-minute attack. If four *chutai* went in one at a time against the four shipyard targets (the longest queue, the other cruiser targets being far enough apart that they could be attacked simultaneously), the attack would have lasted 12 minutes. This would mean a relatively drawn-out attack, and would allow the defenders to concentrate their defensive fire against each succeeding attacker, but it would minimize mutual interference in the bomb runs and allow some command and control over the distribution of aircraft to each target.

Approach: Time on Target (TOT)

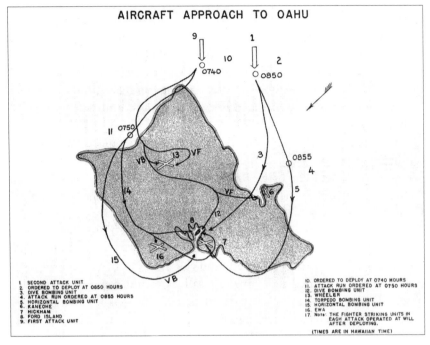

(9) Japanese Aircraft Approach Routes, From *Campaigns of the Pacific War*

The first and most elementary planning consideration ought to have been simultaneity. In the first wave, while torpedo bombers were attacking the fleet at Pearl Harbor, dive-bombers and fighters were to attack Hickam, Wheeler, and Ewa Fields. It was within the technology of the time for the first-wave aircraft to arrive over every target area simultaneously, called a Time on Target (TOT) strike. This would eliminate any chance that one defending area could flash a warning to other areas.

If simultaneous arrival over all the target areas could not be achieved, the attackers would want the Pearl Harbor group to go in first to allow the torpedo bombers to attack before the defenses were manned.

The approach was planned to come down the center of the island. North of Pearl Harbor the two torpedo groups would split to go to their initial points (IP) east and west of the harbor. The distance to their IPs would be nearly identical, so a "nearly simultaneous" attack by the two torpedo groups was planned.

A simultaneous TOT for all formations would not have been hard to plan or achieve. There were several prominent geographic points on the northern coast of Oahu that could have provided navigational starting points. The formations that had the furthest to go would fly directly to their target, while the other formations could orbit in place and depart timed so that all the formations would arrive at their targets simultaneously. This "time and distance" exercise is one routinely inflicted on pilot and navigator trainees on the way to their wings, and was within the technology of the period.

To place this in perspective, General Quarters could be set on a US battleship, with all AA guns manned and ready, in eight to ten minutes. "Ready" guns could be firing in less than one minute. To qualify as "all in the same instant," the attacks should all be initiated before General Quarters could be set.

There is a clue as to why the Japanese neglected to provide for TOT attacks. Many Japanese aviators commented on the speed with which the American defenses responded, and the intensity of the anti-aircraft fire. One pilot testified that Japanese sailors would never have been so quick. The Japanese mirror-imaged their expectations for the speed of the Americans' defensive response based on how they would expect their own forces to react. They simply did not believe that their enemies would respond so promptly, and consequently saw no need to time their arrivals with any precision.

Overall Impression of the Plan

The plan had significant shortfalls. It was not state of the art for the period, did not employ all the available tactics and techniques, and failed to anticipate what should have been obvious problems. It did not employ the combined arms approach that these same air groups practiced in attacks against battleships at sea. Either the plan or the planners themselves were remarkably inflexible, as there were no built-in decision points to respond to changing conditions or developing intelligence. As will be seen, the plan was not adjusted to address the problems revealed in rehearsals. The allocation decisions and target prioritization for all three types of aircraft are questionable. If the Americans had been in their usual level of readiness and reacted to the detection of the Japanese strike while it was inbound, it is likely that the torpedo attacks would have been a complete failure.

Overall, as a plan touted as "brilliantly conceived and meticulously planned," the attack on Pearl Harbor does not stand up well under close examination. Additional problems were revealed when the plan was executed.

Planning Deficiencies vs. Doctrinal Deficiencies

Planners are guided by the doctrine under which their forces are trained and operate. It is difficult at times to determine if deficiencies in the planning were due to planning oversights or doctrinal constraints. Certainly in a plan that matured over a ten-month period there was ample time to adjust and train to a new doctrine, if that was needed.

The Japanese planning process cannot be held to modern standards. Pre-war staffs were not capable of the same kind of structured planning that modern military forces employ. It would have taken a particularly brilliant planner to make the conceptual leap to, for instance, break the stovepipe structure of planning by aircraft type and take on a combined arms approach. Failures that came from a deficient planning structure ought not to be considered a failing of the officers involved in the planning.

There were cases where the planners recognized a need and adjusted doctrine—for example, they reduced the level bomber formations from nine to five bombers. In other cases, doctrine or the unique Japanese way of war blinded them to things that were needed, such as the failure to use the fleet's combined-arms SEAD aircraft tactics in the torpedo attack against the battleships. Another example is the failure to restrain the fighters from their independent attack role in order to have them provide cover for the torpedo bombers all the way to the target.

Doctrine is a good and necessary thing, but it should be a tool, not a set of blinders inhibiting planners from creative measures to solve problems. The Japanese did not have a reputation through the war of applying creative solutions to problems. They adjusted doctrine rarely, and then reluctantly, usually only after a significant defeat forced deficiencies to their attention. This study can only note where doctrine led to poor decisions or succeeded in providing good decisions, and where the planners were able to overcome their conditioning to arrive at creative solutions for the unique problems associated with the Pearl Harbor attack.

CHAPTER FIVE

PRE-ATTACK: TRAINING, REHEARSALS, BRIEFINGS AND CONTINGENCY PLANNING

Training

The Japanese dispersed their aircraft to many different airfields for their training. They were concentrated by type at each field, so there was no cross-pollination between dive-bombers, level bombers, torpedo bombers and fighters. Torpedo bombers, for example, were split between Kanoya and Omura air bases. Their training started on 31 September 1941. Six weeks lay ahead of them before the first of the carriers, *Hiryu*, departed Kyushu on 18 November en route to *Kido Butai's* marshalling rendezvous in the Kuriles.

The *Hikotaicho* (air group commanders) were responsible for training the units. Fuchida had the responsibility for the level bombers attacking the fleet, Shimazaki the OCA (offensive counter-air) level bombers, Lieutenant Commander Takahashi Kakuichi the OCA dive-bombers, Egusa the dive-bombers going after fleet targets, Murata the torpedo bombers, and Lieutenant Commander Itaya Shageru the fighters. [1]

The training was intensive, sometimes extending to several flights a day. Some of the dive-bombers' training was made more difficult by remote bombing ranges, requiring long flights which wasted time and fuel. The newer aircrews, of whom there were many, spent a lot of time in basic training and getting qualified to operate off carriers.

Time was spent in night training. Early plans were for the first wave of the strike to launch prior to dawn. This idea was cancelled when the *Zuikaku* and *Shokaku* aircrews did not attain the needed proficiency. The night training time was wasted.

Fighter training consisted mostly of fundamental airmanship skills such as formation flying. Postwar, veterans did not mention training in strafing techniques; evidently the fighters expended little ammunition at gunnery ranges.

Conspicuously absent was any combined training. Fighters did not train with the bombers to learn how to escort their approach or to protect them during their bombing runs. The attack was decomposed into a set of individual missions that were to be executed discretely, without reference to what other aircraft were doing. Combined arms and mutual support was not in the Japanese mindset.

Rehearsals

When possible, preparations for any large or complex military operation include a rehearsal. Rehearsals provide practice for the participants and an opportunity to test the plan. In the best rehearsals, all of the participants are informed of their role, and a time and location is selected that best emulates the expected conditions, geography, and terrain. Afterwards, a critique is held and adjustments are made to the plan.

The first rehearsal was held on 4 November. The carriers were positioned 200nm off Kyushu, and launched their attack against the naval air station at Saeki and the Combined Fleet at anchor. There was no attempt to emulate the geography or the restricted lines of approach the torpedo bombers would encounter at Pearl Harbor. The torpedo bombers went in first, followed by the level bombers. In a second wave, level bombers simulated striking Saeki Field and dive-bombers attacked anchored fleet targets, particularly the carriers *Akagi* and *Soryu*.

Afterwards, notes from Genda, Fuchida, and other staff officers were collected and reviewed. The approach to the target and the general deployment was faulted, as was the time required for rendezvous. Only 40% of the torpedoes leveled off at the correct depth, some dipping below 60 feet.

Another rehearsal was held the following day. This time a group of defending fighters intercepted the attackers about 80nm north of the target, resulting in an air-to-air battle. Afterwards, Genda faulted the accuracy of the level bombers, and Fuchida became concerned that the battleships closest to the attackers received the brunt of the attack.[2]

Rehearsals must be gauged more by the problems they expose rather than their successes. Many deficiencies were likely corrected but not placed in the historical record. It is impossible to judge the significance of the resulting changes. However, significant problems slipped by that were to have a considerable impact on the course of the attack.

The problem of the crossing torpedo attack routes was not revealed. There is no evidence that the target ships were anchored in any arrangement simulating that to be encountered in Pearl Harbor, so issues of deconfliction could not be explored. The problem of simultaneity for the torpedo attack was not exposed. The Combined Fleet was anchored at Ariake Bay, which is a wide anchorage without the restricted approach routes found at Pearl Harbor. Likely the torpedo bombers went in waves, as was doctrine in a normal attack, and so this problem was not exposed. Moving from the approach formation into the torpedo bombers' long "string" formations was not tested.

The fact that only 40% of the torpedoes functioned as desired was worrisome, and it appears that the planners concentrated their attention on this worrisome development. An equivalent rate during the actual attack would result in only 16 torpedoes with normal runs, and likely fewer hits than that. That this problem should be revealed so late in the process is remarkable, particularly considering that the shallow water problem was known from the outset of planning ten months before. This stimulated a flurry of corrective actions. Over the next few days the torpedo bombers tried out new techniques and raised their hit rate to 82 percent, a cause for jubilation.

But the distraction of the torpedo bombers' problem likely overshadowed other corrective measures that were not addressed. For example, the problem of poor attack distribution was not corrected.

There appeared to be no feedback from the troops—the aviators who were actually to deliver the attack—to the decision makers. At least, there was no mention in the standard accounts that the fleet aviators provided feedback to Fuchida and Genda. At this point the *chutai* leaders had been informed of the objective, but the rank-and-file aviators had not. How much useful feedback was lost by continued secrecy? This was likely a systemic problem with the Japanese system. Most Japanese aviators, including most of their pilots, were not officers but enlisted personnel. Culturally there was not a great deal of communications up the chain of command—officers decided, and enlisted men executed.

From training through rehearsal there were several noteworthy deficiencies. Each of the aircraft types had trained separately for their individual missions, flying out of separate air bases. There appeared to be little desire for combined-arms training. Types were not coordinated in any way other than in the attack sequence. There was no mention of wringing out command and control and communications problems—perhaps such problems did not surface because doctrine levied no real command and control and communications requirements on the attackers. The aviators likely were so accustomed to seeing themselves as individual samurai warriors that they felt no need for a higher level of control. Security was closely maintained—prior to departure only one group of fighter pilots and the senior bomber command aviators were informed of their objective.

A better rehearsal might also have surfaced two other issues. There was the potential problem of the rising sun in the eyes of *Soryu* and *Hiryu* torpedo bombers assigned west-to-east attack routes. Aircrews would need to classify their targets before committing to their run, but sun glare could interfere.

Rehearsals should illuminate contingencies—the "what if" issues. Some important and specific "what ifs" were: what if the carriers were not in port, what if surprise was not achieved, and what should the fighters do under various situations? The loss of surprise, the presence of torpedo nets, and whether the carriers would be in port were discussed during the transit, but discussions do not have the problem-illuminating potential of actual practice.

All contingencies for the bombers were "solved" by assuming that the aircraft commanders would be able to choose their targets carefully and accurately. This was a great deal of responsibility to place on the shoulders of the many junior aviators.

Up until this point the plans all assumed that surprise would be achieved. Curiously, even a rehearsal with defending fighters intercepting the strike force did not prompt any thoughts that the real attack might have to go in without the cover of surprise. It is perhaps a measure of the work overload on Fuchida and Genda that these thoughts were not triggered until several days later, by Yamamoto himself.

Overall, the rehearsals proved their worth by revealing the shortfall in torpedo delivery technique, and the last-minute solution of the torpedo delivery problem saved the operation. However, in other areas, the critique and corrective actions that ought to have come from the rehearsals were sadly deficient.

Briefings

After *Kido Butai* departed, Japan the aircrews were briefed. A large-scale model of Pearl Harbor was used, constructed on the same scale as the harbor would be seen from 10,000 feet. It was appreciated as a beautiful work of craftsmanship. Fuchida briefed large groups and met with smaller sections to brief their particular roles, and afterwards was hoarse after a day of talking. Likely he flew from carrier to carrier to speak to all the aviators.

Before the attack Fuchida claimed that he had a case of the nerves. He feared his level bombers would not be successful. And the presence of anti-torpedo nets would leave the responsibility for a successful raid in their hands. So, in his briefings to the aircrews, Fuchida "stressed the importance of mass concentration against a single target." He emphasized that minor damage, even to every enemy ship, would add up to an unsuccessful mission.[3]

However, on another chart that he constructed for Gordon Prange, Fuchida showed four lines of approach that were briefed to the level bombers, with the weight of the attack evenly distributed. Three of the mooring points were those occupied by *Arizona, Tennessee*, and *Maryland* on the day of the attack. The fourth was *Pennsylvania's* usual berth along 1010 dock. The bombers were to attack one group at a time, aiming at ships in the order listed on the chart. After the first four groups attacked ships one through four, the next four groups would repeat against the same four ships. Only double-berthed ships were to be attacked. If these instructions were followed in the actual attack, three groups would have attacked *Maryland* and *Arizona*, and four against *Tennessee*.

Including Pennsylvania's berth at 1010 dock is curious, because the flagship rarely double berthed with another ship and thus ought to have been accessible to torpedoes. It could be that the prestige of sinking the fleet's flagship played a role in this decision.

Fuchida's instructions are inherently contradictory, a point that has eluded most historians. How could Fuchida give instructions for an even distribution of attacks and at the same time "stress the importance of mass concentration on a single target?"

Which approach was correct? It depends upon the model of bomb damage that is used. If it is believed that damage is cumulative, that each hit contributes a quantum of damage, and crippling damage is the result of cumulative damage from each hit, then concentration is the proper approach. If it is believed that damage is stochastic, that each bomb has a certain percentage chance of hitting an engineering space or a magazine, and a single such hit can cripple or sink the ship, then distribution is the proper approach.

Fuchida likely never directed his level bombers to concentrate on a single target. He made this statement postwar. Claiming that he directed a concentration of bombers on a single battleship might have been a way for him to garner some reflected glory from the explosion that destroyed *Arizona*, along the lines, "I was afraid the level bombers would not sink anything, so I directed them to concentrate on a single battleship, and as a result of my good advice the *Arizona* blew up."

Fuchida had a personal stake in the performance of the level bombers. He was a level bombing specialist at a time when many Japanese aviators considered eliminating that technique from the carriers' repertoire due to low hit percentages. He also participated in the attack in a level bomber. There is no conclusive evidence on one side or the other to confirm Fuchida's testimony—only the recognition that his statements are contradictory.

The torpedo bomber aviators were also briefed on their group's targets, either along the carrier moorings or Battleship Row. They were given considerable latitude to choose their targets. One torpedo pilot in a postwar interview related how he flew over the harbor "looking for a target"—not looking for *his* target.

The 16 carrier attack aircraft assigned to the carrier moorings were warned that the carriers might not be in port. Had a single carrier been present, it is very likely that one full string of eight bombers, and perhaps all 16, would have attacked her. They were also warned that the demilitarized battleship *Utah* occasionally used the carrier moorings. They were instructed not to waste a torpedo on her.

In the briefings, Fuchida emphasized that aircrews were to take the initiative in selecting alternative targets, and were to break off attacks on ships that were obviously destroyed.

The briefings sent a number of mixed signals to the aircrews and had several inconsistencies.

- The aircrews were told that light damage against all of the ships was unacceptable. At the same time, they were responsible for shifting away from targets that were destroyed. In other words, they were to concentrate their attacks, but don't concentrate too much. Such instructions are easily said in briefings but hard to achieve on a battlefield obscured by smoke and livened by anti-aircraft fire.
- Yamamoto wanted to sink battleships. The planners were airmen who believed that carriers were the most vital targets.
- The aviators were to prioritize their attacks, but at the same time go in nearly simultaneously.

Fuchida "hoped that some ships would try to escape, thus giving the Japanese the opportunity to cork up the channel."[4] This could only be done by the dive-bombers of the second wave, as the channel was not wide enough to launch a torpedo against an underway ship. The dive-bombers were supposed to go after targets matching the capabilities of their bombs—carriers first, then cruisers. One wonders if a question was asked as to what to do if a battleship was in the channel.

Thus, the aircrews were to distribute their fire, concentrate their fire, strike nearly simultaneously while adhering to a prioritization scheme, watching out for crossing aircraft, pull back from inappropriate targets, sink at least one battleship, sink all the battleships, shift fire away from ships already sunk except for carriers, which were to be pulverized; on top of all this, target prioritizations might be overridden if a ship was in the channel. A higher-fidelity rehearsal might have been able to ferret out and resolve some of these contradictions, or clarify how the aviators were to deal with them. Overall, the aviators had to contend with a Gordian Knot of conflicting demands.

Surprise! A Contingency Plan is Created

Remarkably, when the Japanese fleet units departed Japan the plan was entirely predicated on surprise.[5] Quite by accident, another vision struck the planners.

In Seaki Bay on 17 November 1941, Yamamoto, his chief of staff Ugaki, and other staff officers met on *Akagi* with about 100 key members of the First Air Fleet. Yamamoto, uncharacteristically without a drafted speech, spoke of the quality of their opponent and the snare of overconfidence. "Although we hope to achieve surprise, everyone should be prepared for terrific American resistance in this operation."[6]

With a jolt of recognition, Fuchida and Genda realized that their plan did not consider the possibility of terrific American resistance.

Genda and Fuchida met with Murata, the leader of the torpedo bombers, to discuss what to do if surprise was not achieved. Prange relates the discussion as follows:

> They decided that if the attacking aircraft flew into a blast of anti-aircraft fire, Murata's slow-moving torpedo planes must not approach the target first, as they had been practicing. The other bombers must precede them to cause as much confusion as possible and draw fire upward and away from the torpedo aircraft. In this way Murata's men might still be able to do considerable damage. Murata objected, not relishing the idea of following a trail which others had blazed for him, but Genda and Fuchida stood firm. More was at stake than Murata's amour-propre.[7]

This account delivers two body blows to those convinced of the brilliance of the Pearl Harbor planning.

Almost a year after the attack was first contemplated, and weeks after training was commenced, the attack planning covered only the most favorable scenario, based on the assumption that surprise would be achieved.[8] This was remarkable when one considers that the operational plan specified that the attack would proceed even if *Kido Butai* was detected by American reconnaissance up to 24 hours prior to the scheduled attack time. So, Yamamoto would accept attacking against an alerted opponent, but the attack planners did not consider this possibility until it was too late to prepare for the contingency.

Yamamoto has to be considered culpable. He signed an attack order that directed *Kido Butai* to fight their way in to their target without verifying that his planners were ready to execute such an attack.

Not until Yamamoto's chance remark on the eve of departure did the planners consider the possibility that the attack might not be a surprise. This is a harbinger of what was to come throughout the war—Japanese planning was often deficient in considering alternative situations, a characteristic that was to particularly handicap them during the Guadalcanal campaign.

It is remarkable how little these men changed the plan to accommodate the possibility of heavier enemy resistance. In the original plan, assuming surprise, the torpedo planes were to assault Pearl Harbor in four lines of attackers "nearly simultaneously," while the rest of the force orbited until their attack was complete. If surprise was lost, they could have considered simultaneity of attacks, or, as a minimum, reallocating the targets of the dive-bombers and fighters to provide SEAD and DEAD along the approach route of the torpedo bombers, recognizing that a few less aircraft destroyed in OCA was worth ensuring that the torpedo attack went home. Fighters might have been reassigned to strafe the defenses along the torpedo bombers' attack routes—they had intelligence showing the AA emplacements around Pearl Harbor.

Instead, the only measure they employed was to have the dive-bombers surge ahead to deliver their attacks against the same targets as before, but a few minutes before the torpedo bombers were to attack.

If surprise was achieved, Fuchida was to fire one flare, and the attack would go as planned. If surprise was not achieved, Fuchida was to fire two flares.

This scheme required recognition of the situation and a positive order by the strike leader. Rather than have a default plan, and a signal to change to the backup plan, the Japanese chose to give an order directing the strike to assume one plan or the other. If there was a problem with communications, or the signal was not seen or recognized, the force would go into the attack without the entire team acting on the same plan.

Second, it involved a visual signal rather than a radio transmission, and the visual signal was not backed up by a radio signal. This could reflect the fact that all the attacking aircraft did not yet have radio equipment installed, or that the radio equipment was not trusted, or that the relative newness of the equipment indicated that the Japanese were not sufficiently familiar with it to feel comfortable relying on it in a critical situation. The signal to attack (*"To To To"*) was sent over keyed CW to initiate the attack, but for some reason radio was not used to communicate which attack plan was in force, probably because fighters did not have CW radio sets.

But why was the order not given also over voice radio, or at least backed up on that circuit? If surprise was lost, it made no sense to maintain radio silence, if that was their concern. It could be that, in the short meeting where the alternate plan was devised, it was just not considered.

It was an oversight. Japanese radios were notoriously unreliable, and had been in the fleet such a short time that their use may not have been instilled in the planners' mindset. However, radio communications ought not to have been totally ignored. Even a 50% chance of connectivity was better than nothing.

Prange attributed Murata's objection to removing his torpedo bombers from the lead to *amour-propre*—self-love or self-respect—a rather curious motive to ascribe to a combat commandeer under the circumstances. Presumably he was trying to infer that Murata's objections were based on the honor of being the first to attack, rather than any sound tactical reasons. Prange characteristically attributed decisions to the personalities of those involved, a propensity that has injected serious distortions into the historical record. He felt comfortable attributing decisions to personal quirks, an area in which he evidently felt comfortable, instead of to tactical, doctrinal, or material considerations, areas where he was largely unschooled. He did not have the knowledge of aviation tactics to understand that Murata's objection was well founded tactically and did not spring from egotistical concerns. He implies criticism of Murata, when in fact the blame for a remarkably bad decision lies squarely in the laps of Genda and Fuchida.

The last remarkable thing about this meeting is its small size. Only the head planner, strike leader, and torpedo bomber leader were included. Why were there not also representatives from the dive-bombers and the fighters? What good ideas were lost by the failure to consult a broader slice of the available leadership?

Last Minute Intelligence

A day before the attack the Japanese received an intelligence update. The battleships were in harbor, but none of the carriers.

The Japanese discussed this report, particularly with regards to Matsumura's torpedo attack against the carrier moorings. With advance word that the carriers were gone, the Japanese could have taken action to allocate these torpedo bombers to alternate targets. Instead, the planners decided to leave the attack plan unmodified, hoping that the carriers might return.

This decision is illuminating. First, it confirms that the group of 16 torpedo bombers was indeed intended for carriers as their first priority, and confirms the importance the planners attached to the objective of killing carriers. Second, it shows remarkable intransigence in planning not to take advantage of timely intelligence to change a plan obviously overtaken by events. This is not an unusual human reaction—there is a psychological propensity to cling to the original plan in which so much effort and training has been invested. The Japanese were not the only ones to suffer from this defect. For example, prior to Operation Market Garden, Allied intelligence noted that several German divisions had moved close to the area of the offensive, including at least one armored division. These decision makers also chose to ignore the intelligence, and made no changes to their plans.

Whether due to human psychology or Japanese psychology, the plan, inappropriately, remained unchanged.

A captured photograph showing columns of water from torpedo explostions. The tallest plume is about 25 seconds old, one is six seconds and the other is one second, an indication of the intervals between torpedo bombers at the outset of the attack. *Source: Naval Archives, Washington, DC*

CHAPTER SIX

EXECUTION OF THE ATTACK

In the dark of night *Kido Butai*, a flock of knife-edged hulls cutting through troubled seas, turned their bows south and worked up to 24 knots. They would make their final run to the launch point sheltered by darkness and unseen by enemy patrols.

This night was the culmination of a massive movement. Over 90% of the Japanese fleet was underway, positioning for attacks spread over a 6,000 nm front. The movement of ships directed against Pearl Harbor had begun as early as 11 November, when nine long-range submarines departed the Empire from Saeki Bay en route a refueling stop at Kwajalein, then on to Hawaiian waters. Now, 23 Japanese fleet submarines, five of which carried midget submarines clamped to their decks, patrolled the waters around Oahu, performed reconnaissance, and awaited the air strike, expecting an opportunity to sink the remnants of the American Pacific Fleet as it bolted out of Pearl Harbor to escape the aviators' bombs.

To the submariners, not the aviators, was given the honor of making the initial moves in the actual attack.

Midget Submarines

Japan's midget submarines, commanded by young officers none more senior than lieutenant, were released from their transport submarines in the hours of darkness before the aviators' attack. They attempted first to find and then to penetrate past the submarine net guarding the entrance to the harbor.

One or more were detected outside the harbor by patrolling destroyers and aircraft. One submarine, surprisingly, did make it past the entrance, only to be detected inside the harbor during the attack. It fired its torpedoes at a tender and a destroyer. Both missed and exploded against the shore. The destroyer *Monaghan* rammed and sank the submarine.

Three of the submarines definitely did not penetrate the harbor. One was sunk by the destroyer *Ward* a few hours before the arrival of the bombers. The surprise of the main Japanese attack was saved by a small miracle of US Navy bureaucratic indecisiveness. Blending into the background "noise" of the many false alarms and submarine alerts of the previous weeks, the new warning was not assessed as anything particularly unusual or threatening. Instead of issuing an alert, an order was sent for the stand-by destroyer to sortie.

Considering that a submarine had been detected trying to enter the harbor, and considering the history of the British battleship *Royal Oak* (which was sunk in October 1939 by a German submarine that penetrated into Scapa Flow), the harbor should have been placed on alert to a submarine threat. All ships should have been required to set material condition Zed, their maximum state of watertight integrity (today called material condition Zebra). Had Zed been set before the bombers arrived, *California* would have remained afloat and *Oklahoma* might not have capsized.

Two submarines ran out of battery power and did not deliver any attacks. Both were eventually discovered by the Americans with their torpedoes aboard. One was found beached off Bellows Field, the second 15 years later in a small cove. (The fate of the fifth midget submarine will be discussed in Chapter 11.)

The attack by the midget submarines could be seen as an allegory for the entire concept, execution, and spirituality of the attack. A flawed strategic concept was executed with incredibly bravery by men who certainly knew that the odds of their success was slim; warning that should have giving the defenders sufficient time to man their defenses and prepare their ships for attack instead became another instantiation of Yamamoto's life-long string of incredible good fortune. The fleet and its defenders continued to sleep.

Reconnaissance

Yoshikawa Takeo, the Japanese intelligence officer working out of Japan's Pearl Harbor legation, kept a stream of information on its way to *Kido Butai*. The striking force received intelligence communiqués on 3, 4, and 7 December (Tokyo time) updating the situation through 6 December. He reported that no balloons or torpedo defense nets were protecting the battleships. In a message received on 4 December, six battleships, eleven cruisers, and one aircraft carrier were in harbor. Updates reported the departure of *Lexington*. The day before the strike, the Naval General Staff transmitted to Nagumo that the harbor contained nine battleships, three light cruisers and seventeen destroyers, with four light cruisers and three destroyers in drydock.[1] There were no carriers in port, but that disappointment was balanced by the information that the US military on Oahu was not in any unusual state of alert.

As *Kido Butai* steamed south at high speed en route to the launch point, the fleet submarine *I-72* nosed into Lahaina Roads off Maui. She transmitted, "The enemy is not in Lahaina anchorage."[2]

In the pre-dawn darkness, the cruisers *Chikuma* and *Tone* launched reconnaissance floatplanes. One headed to Lahaina Roads and one to Pearl Harbor, scheduled to arrive after first light.

The first wave was launched. Of the 189 total aircraft planned, there were 6 aborts: one B5N Kate carrying an AP bomb, three D3A Vals, and two A6M Zeros. One hundred and eighty-three aircraft executed the attack.

Chikuma's scout radioed that nine battleships, one heavy cruiser and six light cruisers were in the harbor, and excellent weather conditions existed for the attack. No carriers were observed. This information was received before the second wave was launched. It is not known if the message was copied by the first-wave aircraft; Fuchida, the strike commander, does not mention it in his accounts of the attack.

Due to remarkably speedy aircraft handling, the second wave was ready 15 minutes ahead of schedule. With the first wave still north of Oahu, the second wave launched. One A6M Zero and three D3A Vals aborted. One hundred and sixty-seven aircraft formed for the attack, of which 78 were D3A Vals allocated to go against warships.

As they droned on their nervous course to Pearl Harbor, the aircrews watched a spectacular sunrise, prophetically similar in appearance to Japan's national symbol, radiating beams from a rising sun, an apparent mark of favor of the gods that raised the spirits of many of the approaching aviators. With careful tuning they could pick up an Oahu radio station playing Hawaiian music, welcoming visitors to the islands. The radio station provided a local weather forecast: visibility clear, a steady tropical breeze out of the northeast, and a heavy cloud layer floating in at 3,500 feet.

Transit

Fuchida claimed that the torpedo bombers were to attack "at almost the same instant." As Gordon Prange related:

> According to this scheme, on receiving Fuchida's deployment order, Murata would lead his planes in a sweep over the western side of Oahu. Just as they reached a point almost due west of Pearl Harbor, they would divide into two sections and strike the target from two directions at once.[3]

This statement is very deceptive. It implies that the movement down the western side of Oahu was planned, and that the point where the torpedo bombers would separate into two groups was planned to occur west of Pearl Harbor.

The planned route was actually down the center of the island, not "the western side of Oahu." The separation of the torpedo bombers into two groups was also logically planned to occur north of Pearl Harbor, so as the two groups swung around to attack from the east and the west each would have to travel approximately the same distance to reach their attack IP, allowing for a "nearly simultaneous" attack.

However, upon landfall, Fuchida noted heavy clouds over the Ko'olau Mountains. He decided to skirt the cloud bank, turning the formation to fly in clear air down the western coast. Fuchida's statement about reaching a point "due west of Pearl Harbor" reflected what actually occurred and not what was planned.

Fuchida's chosen track effectively eliminated any possibility that the two torpedo bomber groups would attack simultaneously. The Battleship Row attackers would now have to fly south of the harbor, turn east over the ocean, turn inland, and skirt Hickam Field before reaching their IP for the turn to their attack course, while those attacking the carrier moorings would have a straight run in to their targets. Battleship Row would have perhaps five minutes advance warning before *Akagi*'s and *Kaga*'s torpedo bombers were in position to attack.

This problem had not been anticipated by the planners. There was no provision to coordinate the two attacks in the event that a different approach course was required. Evidently Fuchida did not see this as a problem, as he took no action as Strike Commander to address it; alternately, he saw the problem, but did not have the means to exert any control.

Fuchida's Fumble with the Flares

Fuchida was responsible for determining which attack plan would be used and communicating his decision to the attack force, firing one flare for "surprise achieved" or two for "surprise not achieved." At 0740, off the northwest coast of Oahu, Fuchida made his decision. An account based on interviews with Fuchida related:

> Almost sure that the strike would come as a surprise, he fired a single Black Dragon rocket. Murata saw it and swung low toward the target [with his torpedo bombers]. But Lieutenant Masaharu Suginami, a fighter group leader, kept his aircraft in cruise position. Thinking he had missed the first rocket, Fuchida fired another. Then he groaned—Takahashi, mistaking the second rocket for the double signal meaning the enemy was on the alert, swooped in with his dive-bombers. Fuchida ground his teeth in rage. Soon, however, he realized that the error made no practical difference.[4]

Takahashi, the leader of the dive-bomber formation—Fuchida characterized him as "that fool Takahashi, he was a bit soft in the head"[5]— firewalled his throttles and put his nose down, picking up speed. Assuming that it was now his role to immediately attack and distract the enemy defenses, the dive-bombers forged ahead without climbing to their normal bombing altitude. Murata, confronted by this unexpected development, had his torpedo bombers accelerate, trying to get in his attack before the defenses were fully aroused, but his heavily-laden torpedo bombers inexorably were left further and further behind.

Approach

Out of position and at cross purposes, the first-wave formation broke up as the subordinate formations scattered to their assigned targets. There was no attempt to attack the various bases with any simultaneity, and no concern that an attack by one group might prematurely announce the attack to other locations. The attacker's first shots were fired by a *Soryu* B5N Kate gunner. Lieutenant Nagai Tsuyoshi, anxious to quicken the attack pace, forged ahead of the *Hiryu* torpedo bombers and cut across the island, passing so close by Wheeler Field that his gunner cut loose on some parked P-40 fighters.

The Japanese fighters searched the skies for defending fighters. They saw none. Then they looked for anything flying, anything to kill. A US Navy patrol plane spotted the incoming marauders and transmitted a warned, which went unheeded—unable to do more, the aircraft found the clouds and slipped away. But there were other aircraft aloft, mostly civilian pleasure aircraft and private pilot instructors with their students. Some of the more alert fighter pilots recognized these aircraft as a waste of ammunition, but others, anxious for an air-to-air kill befitting a true samurai, broke formation and went for the kills. Several civilian aircraft were shot out of the sky, a few winged away to safety.

The first bombs hit Wheeler at 0751, six minutes before the first torpedo was dropped into Pearl Harbor. The bulk of the defenders' fighters, modern P-40s and P-36s leavened with obsolete P-26s, were lined up next to the hangars. The base commander had requested permission to keeps the fighters in their revetments, but he was told that would alarm civilians.

Twenty-five D3A Vals hit the base hard. Bombs accurately hit among the lines of densely-packed parked aircraft, smashing many, and igniting tremendous fires fed by aviation gasoline from leaking fuel tanks. Bombs exploded within hangars, which burned gushing dense clouds of smoke. The fire house went up in flames, along with administrative buildings and the Post Exchange. The smoke angled off in the steady breeze, obscuring parts of the flight light and much of the ground facilities, but after the dive bombers' 550-kg bombs were expended there still were aircraft undamaged, at least 22 that were unobscured by smoke at the upwind end of the fight line. Then, nine A6M Zeros, accompanied by many of the D3A Vals, began to methodically strafe the undamaged aircraft. Wheeler was out of the fight.

Kaneohe was attacked at 0748 (or possibly 0753—in a world without digital clocks absolute precision is not possible). Attempts to warn

Bellows and Hickam fields by telephone were disbelieved.[6] Eleven A6M Zeros delivered an eight-minute attack against the base and her 33 PBY-5 patrol planes. The initial slashing attack caused considerable damage and confusion, but the damage was not complete—a movie taken from a second-wave B5N Kate shows many of the PBY-5s by the hangars apparently undamaged. A second wave of level bombers completed the job—in the end, all the American aircraft were either damaged or destroyed.

At Hickam, home of the AAF's B-17, B-18, and A-20 bombers, nine dive bombers attacked the hangars and administrative buildings while eight others hit the hangars. Nine A6M Zeros strafed the parked planes. Personnel casualties were particularly heavy, with 35 killed when a bomb exploded among the men breakfasting in the mess hall.

As the dive and torpedo bombers approached Pearl Harbor, the fighters that accompanied them peeled off to attack Ewa Marine Corps Air Station, ten miles short of the harbor. Additional fighters, looking for targets for their remaining ammunition before heading for their rallying point, took Ewa as a target of opportunity. By 0815 over two-thirds of Ewa's aircraft were destroyed or damaged.

The fighters searched for their primary target, enemy defensive fighters in the air. After fifteen minutes of futile search most had given up hope of aerial opposition and instead transitioned into strafing attacks on any reasonable ground target, and some unreasonable ones. While there were some reports of inexpert pilots and inaccurate machine gun attacks, on the aggregate they were highly effective. Considering that many of the bombers were assigned to hit hangars and administrative buildings, it is likely that most of the American aircraft were actually destroyed and damaged by strafing fighters. Inexpert or not, the American aircraft parked in orderly, compact rows were targets that could hardly be missed.

The dive-bombers beat the torpedo bombers to Pearl Harbor. The first bomb was aimed at the southern tip of Ford Island, where there was an amphibious seaplane ramp, an aircraft hangar, and parked aircraft. Various accounts claim that it either destroyed a PBY-5 Catalina seaplane or missed the island entirely. Additional bombs followed, blasting the seaplane and the hangars, and generating a black column of smoke visible for twenty miles. Some ships immediately called away General Quarters. One, still very much in a peacetime mindset, called away their Rescue and Assistance Party thinking that a terrible accident had occurred.

The torpedo bombers were in two groups of two formations each. Murata, commander of *Akagi*'s air group, led 12 *Kaga* and 12 *Akagi* Kates assigned to attack the battleships moored on the east side of Ford Island. Second in overall command was Lieutenant Matsumara Hirata, the torpedo squadron leader off *Hiryu*, who led eight *Soryu* and eight *Hiryu* torpedo bombers against the carrier moorings. As the torpedo bombers approached Oahu, Murata wagged his wings to signal the shift into attack formation.

The two forces separated, with Matsumara flying down the east side of the Waianae Range and Murata down the west side. The *Hiryu* and *Soryu* carrier attack planes moved into two strings of eight, while the *Akagi* and *Kaga* torpedo bombers tried to form into a single long line of 24 aircraft at 400-meter intervals.

The formation change was poorly executed. Contributing factors were the speed change, the confusion over the flares, and the unplanned location of the formation change, all coupled with the lack of a meaningful rehearsal. Some intervals between aircraft opened out to 1,500 to 1,800 meters, about 25 seconds between aircraft.[7] Followers could not keep track of their leaders, and it was impossible for leaders to exert control over their formations. Some aircraft missed turns and ended up orbiting, searching for their comrades, and falling behind the rest of the attack groups.

The distances prevented communication with hand signals, and radio silence was maintained, even well after it made sense to do so – the Japanese totally ignored the potential of the voice radios that had been installed over the previous year. Japanese aviators later remarked that their radios were unreliable, and considered them of little use. Only the most basic "follow me" leadership was possible in the approach, none for the attack.

Each *shotai* (for this attack, increased to four aircraft instead of the normal three) would normally remain together, but each plane commander (who could be the pilot, navigator, or radioman/gunner, depending upon who was senior) had the authority to alter the target. Some overruled the decision of their *shotai* leaders.

Matsumura and his radioman searched the northwest side of Ford Island with binoculars trying to identify targets. The rising sun made determining ship types impossible. Nagai, leading the *Soryu* eight, became impatient. Matsumura related that Nagai drew up alongside and "urged me by hand signal to quicken the attack pace." Perhaps thinking it better to allow Nagai to get in his attack before the dive-bombers thoroughly woke up the island, Matsumura assented. Nagai banked left and, followed by the seven other *Soryu* torpedo bombers, descended to 150 feet and headed directly for the harbor.

Matsumura turned south, delaying his approach while trying to identify the ships at the carrier moorings. Six of the eight aircraft in his formation missed his turn and ended up orbiting Ewa Town trying to get their bearings.

Torpedo Attacks: *Soryu* and *Hiryu* Bombers

Nagai approached the carrier anchorages from the northwest. Nagai's observer tried to classify targets using binoculars, but glare from the rising sun reflecting off the water interfered with his view. Nagai, however, was able to identify *Utah*, and rejected her as a target. He saw what he thought to be a battleship moored alongside 1010 Dock, where he had been briefed that the Pacific Fleet flagship *Pennsylvania* often moored. He turned to pass south of Ford Island to get into position for an attack run, followed by Petty Officer First Class Mori Juzo. But Lieutenant (junior grade) Nakajima Tatsumi, leading the trailing half of the formation, broke away, banked left, and led three others against *Utah*.[8] Nakajima saw a battleship and went for it, not recognizing that the shapes over the barbettes were not turrets, but boxes covering empty holes.

Mori, following behind Nagai, could not see a target along the carrier moorings worth a torpedo. Observing Nakajima begin his attack, he thought, "How silly. Can't they see that two of the ships are nothing but cruisers?"[9] Then the two trailing torpedo bombers in his own group of four broke off to join Nakajima, leaving him to follow his leader alone of the eight *Soryu* torpedo bombers.

Six of the eight *Soryu* torpedo bombers went for *Utah*, flying closely past nests of destroyers to execute their attack against targets foreshortened by the angle of approach. They attacked while the American defenses still slept. Six torpedoes hit the water, but only two hit their target, slamming into *Utah* just before its colors were to be raised at 0800. One of the first torpedoes missed *Utah* so badly it hit the adjacent cruiser *Raleigh*, according to her executive officer, at about 0755.

The other ten torpedo bombers assigned to attack the carrier moorings, spurning further waste of ordnance against a target ship and aged small cruisers, went looking for battleships.

Nagai, followed by Mori, lined up to make his run against the ships berthed along 1010 Dock, only to discover there was no battleship. *Pennsylvania* was in drydock; her prestigious berth was occupied instead by the light cruiser *Helena* with the WWI minelayer *Oglala*, flagship of the Pacific Fleet Mine Force, moored outboard. In accordance with the attack prioritization scheme, *Helena* was a valid target, a modern 10,000-ton cruiser barely two years in commission. However, Nagai wasn't after anything as small as a cruiser. He was deceived by the backlit superimposed silhouettes of the two ships and took the pair to be a battleship. His torpedo scored, passing under *Oglala's* keel to slam into one of *Helena's* engine rooms. *Helena's* engine room clock stopped at 0757.[10]

Mori, next behind him, was close to releasing his torpedo:

> We had closed to less than 600 meters when it suddenly struck me that this was an odd-looking battleship. Then I realized that it wasn't a battleship at all, but a cruiser. Nagai was as bad as Nakajima wasting his torpedo on such a small target.[11]

Mori broke off his attack.

Meanwhile, Lieutenant Kadono Hiroharu, who had missed Matsumura's turn and ended up orbiting over Ewa, observed Nagai's torpedo hit *Helena*. He decided to go for the same target. He led five other *Hiryu* torpedo bombers towards *Helena*.

When Kadono saw Mori abort his run he also pulled off, followed by Petty Officer First Class Sugimoto. But the other four pressed their attack. More ominously for the Japanese, the defenses awakened: they had to press their attacks into the face of AA fire from *Helena*, *Oglala*, and *Shaw*. AA fire caused at least one out-of-envelope drop. One torpedo missed, destroying a power transformer station on the pier next to Helena; the others buried themselves in the mud. Four torpedoes, no hits.

Kadono's bomber was hit by AA—a bullet nicked a fuel line, spraying gasoline into the cockpit. Kadono's navigator wrapped a rag around the leak and held it in place by hand until they regained the carrier.

As the *Helena* attackers came out of their runs they cut across the attack route of the *Akagi* and *Kaga* bombers going against Battleship Row.

Torpedo Attacks: *Akagi* and *Kaga* Bombers from the East

Matsumura, leading 24 torpedo bombers from *Akagi* and *Kaga*, passed Ewa, ten miles west of Pearl Harbor, heading southeast. The *Akagi* and *Kaga* torpedo bombers trailed him at 500 meters altitude, trying to attain a spacing of 500 meters between aircraft with 100 meters offset to the left rear. Their formation was ragged and they were obviously having difficulty establishing their assigned intervals. Smoke from a fire on the south tip of Ford Island blocked Matsumura's view of the harbor. He turned east to gain a position to attack Battleship Row. The aircraft following him, distracted by Nagai's attack, missed the turn. Thus, the leader of all the torpedo bombers found himself with no one to lead.

The bulk of the formations continued south until they were over the ocean, turned left to skirt the coast, then turned left again to approach Hickam Field from the southwest while dropping to 50 meters altitude. Past the field and the Naval Shipyard, they pulled a sharp left turn to head down the Southeast Loch past the Submarine Base, dropping to 20 meters. Murata, at the head of the line, was immediately greeted by machine gun fire.

The timing of the attack can be determined from testimony of the aviators and by time-and-distance calculations tracing their route. As they passed southwest of Pearl Harbor, their view of Battleship Row was blocked by the column of smoke rising from the first dive-bomber attacks, indicating they passed after the first bombs exploded and the smoke cloud had developed. They headed south to the ocean, turned left, passed Hickam Field, and then left again to line up with the Southeast Loch, a total distance of four to eight miles. Cruising at 140 knots, the first torpedo attack against Battleship Row was delivered four minutes after the first bomb hit, and four to eight minutes after the first torpedo was dropped against the carrier moorings. Nagai made his attack run almost the same time as Murata dropped the first torpedo against *Oklahoma*.

The times can be calculated using *Helena*'s engine room clock as a benchmark. *Helena* was hit at 0757. Using relative motion, speeds, and distances traveled by Nagai and Nakajima, *Helena* was attacked probably two minutes after the first attack against *Utah* and *Raleigh*, making *Raleigh*'s XO's report of being hit at 0755 accurate. This would time the first torpedo hit on Battleship Row at just before colors (0800).

Of the *Hiryu* and *Soryu* torpedo bombers, Matsumura, Shira, Petty Officer Third Class Oku Yasumi, and Kadono and his wingman Sugimoto, all headed to join the attackers against Battleship Row, taking different routes. They intermixed with *Akagi* and *Kaga* bombers, disrupting approaches. Some of the Battleship Row attackers were forced to abort and go around for second attempts. The torpedo bombers' attacks would last for 11 to 15 minutes, though the majority managed to release their weapons during the first ten minutes.

The first torpedo hit a battleship as early as 0757, possibly as late as 0759.[12] The defenders took advantage of the precious minutes' warning afforded by the Ford Island bomb blasts, so that when the first torpedo plane sped past the Navy Yard to hit *Oklahoma*, many AA gunners were ready. As related in the destroyer *Bagley*'s AR:

> Immediately, general quarters was sounded. One of the forward machine guns was manned by the Chief Gunner's Mate, SKINNER, . . . who started firing at the third torpedo plane, and hit the fourth plane to come in. This plane was seen to crash in the channel off the Officer's Landing.
>
> Machine gun fire on about the eighth plane was so heavy that it swerved to the left in front of the *Bagley*. This swerving caused the torpedo to drop and it exploded in the bank about thirty feet ahead of the *Bagley*. The plane crossed the bow of the *Bagley* and turned to recross. At this point JOHNSON . . . fired at the plane from No. 1 .50-caliber machine gun and downed it in the Navy Yard channel.
>
> The third torpedo plane to be hit by the *Bagley* was shot down by PETERSON . . . who was not a machine gunner but who volunteered to assist at No. 3 machine gun. The plane, swerving under the fire of the forward machine guns, headed for the light cruisers, *Honolulu* and *St. Louis*, moored in the slip astern of the *Bagley*. As PETERSON's shot hit it, it went out of control, dropped its torpedo and seemed to hit the L head crane in the Navy Yard. The machine gunner was seen to fall out. This was probably about the eleventh plane to come in.
>
> WILLIAMS, . . . regular machine gunner on the after machine guns shot down the next plane to be hit by the *Bagley*. This plane came down over the dock, evidently thinking it would

escape the *Bagley*'s fire which was very well placed. WILLIAMS, an excellent machine gunner, downed it with one short burst. The torpedo was dropped in the lumber pile on the dock and the plane is believed to have crashed on the dock.

The *Bagley*'s fifth plane was brought down by WILLIAMS and PETERSON together. This plane came down on the starboard side to the *Bagley*, having crossed over from the port side. As the bullets hit the plane smoke came out of the plane, it nosed directly up into the air and spun into a crash losing its torpedo.

Bagley's four .50-caliber AA machine guns contributed to the destruction of four of the five B5N Kate torpedo bombers that were shot down. It is a measure of the fleet's rapid initiation of AA fire that many other ships had a hand in their destruction—*Arizona* claimed two kills, *Maryland* two, and *Nevada* two. Most of the battleships' reports acknowledged that multiple ships were firing on each kill. Nearly all of the torpedo bombers were hit, some suffering killed or wounded aircrew.

The third torpedo plane hit by *Bagley* was approximately the 11th plane to follow that same attack route. Perhaps 28 aircraft used this path to attack Battleship Row, avoiding the more technically challenging routes over the supply depot or over the main shipyard. *Kaga*'s string of 12 bombers lagged *Akagi*'s by three miles, a 70 second gap. Twenty-eight aircraft at approximately twenty to twenty-five second intervals comes out to nearly ten minutes, but this should be compared with some of the Japanese pilots' estimates that the torpedo attack took fifteen to twenty minutes, reflecting the confusion of the attack and the degree to which torpedo bombers had to abort runs and go around. The decision to employ "one at a time" attacks turned the Southeast Lock into a shooting gallery.

One Japanese aerial photograph taken early in the attack gives a clue regarding their success in maintaining intervals. The photograph shows Battleship Row, with three torpedo plumes rising from hits on *West Virginia* and *Oklahoma*. The age of these plumes can be estimated by wind drift and height calculations. The oldest is 30 seconds, one six seconds, and the last, one second. Assuming no great variation in torpedo run times, that would make for an interval of 24 seconds between the first and the second hits, and five seconds between the second and the third.

Fuchida's error with the flares provided precious minutes warning for the US gun crews to break out their ready service ammunition and prepare to receive the torpedo bombers. The smoke from the bomb hits interfered with the planned traffic pattern over the harbor, adding a further disruptive element.

But most significant was the response of the defenders. The Japanese, mirror-imaging the expected response, took from their contempt for the defensive and their estimation that the typical Japanese response to a surprise attack would be slow to develop, expected that their torpedo bombers could execute their attack before significant opposition could be mustered. Instead, defensive machine guns were firing within seconds after the first torpedo hits on *Utah*, and within minutes the approaches to Battleship Row would verge on impenetrable.

Crossing Routes for the Torpedo Bombers
The saga of Petty Officer First Class Mori, in Nagai's group assigned to the carrier moorings, illustrates the lack of any semblance of control exerted by the strike leadership:

> Mori, who had swept directly across Oahu, was still looking for a target [after rejecting an attack against *Utah*]. He hedgehopped over Ford Island, but finding only a cruiser on the other side [i.e. *Helena*], made a semicircle and came back just above the waves toward *California* at the southern end of Battleship Row. At the last moment a breakwater[13] loomed between him and the target. He climbed, circling over *Utah*, which looked as if it had twisted in two, again went down to 15 feet and came at *California* from a different angle. His radioman-gunner took a picture of the torpedo explosion as Mori prepared to make his left circle to the assembly point. But his path was barred by a heavy pillar of smoke at the end of Ford Island and he was forced to bank right directly into the oncoming torpedo planes from *Akagi* and *Kaga*; he narrowly missed collision and his plane rocked from the turbulence.[14]

Mori dropped against *California*. "It's running straight!" screamed one of his crew. "It's a hit! Banzai!"[15]

Five B5N Kates from *Soryu* and *Hiryu* intermingled with the two dozen *Akagi* and *Kaga* torpedo bombers heading for Battleship Row. Intervals were irregular and extended. Petty Officer First Class Yasue Tomoe and Petty Officer First Class Katsuki Sadasuke lined up for attacks on *Oklahoma*. They were in what looked to be good runs when Katsuki veered into Yasue's path. One of the bombers, likely Yasue's, nearly lost control. To avoid crashing it jettisoned its torpedo.[16]

The *Akagi* aircraft heading for *Oklahoma* were interrupted by two *Hiryu* aircraft.

We cut in the row of an *Akagi* unit to release the torpedo. Then we were caught in heavy turbulence by the preceding attacker. Our plane bumped so wildly we could not aim at a target. Therefore we made a right turn to retry.[17]

Two of the aircraft attempting runs against *Helena,* using the route that crossed those of the aircraft attacking Battleship Row, were forced to abort their runs and go around and make another approach.

Lieutenant Suzuki Mimori was heading for Battleship Row, down the Southeast Loch, when his B5N Kate took a hit that detonated his torpedo warhead. The blast knocked sailors at the Submarine Base off their feet. *Nevada* claimed this kill for her 5-inch battery, a direct hit that caused the "disintegration of the plane in midair."[18]

In spite of the increasingly heavy fire, the Japanese aviators bore in to their targets resolutely. Some of the bombers, taking damage as they passed the naval shipyard, went for the target that was most directly lined up with their approach path along the loch, *Oklahoma* or *West Virginia*, hoping to get their torpedo in the water before their aircraft became unmanageable. Many found the narrow release envelope too challenging. Torpedoes rammed into the harbor bottom and stuck, their motors sending a cascade of bubbles to the surface.[19]

Most aviators wanted the honor of skewering a battleship—how else would a true samurai react but to go against the biggest and heaviest of their enemies? In the face of unexpectedly heavy AA fire, most picked the most prominent targets, *Oklahoma* or *West Virginia*.

The approach to the southern end of Battleship Row was a fairly long run that passed the shipyard, the easiest of the routes, one that gave the bombers a run of a thousand yards over the water to stabilize on their precise release parameters (airspeed, altitude, and attitude) before dropping their torpedoes. Still, this was only a 15-second run, and the pilot would have to be very skilled to get inside the launch envelop in such a short time after making a hard left turn on the deck. Given the choice between a difficult approach that might be unsuccessful, but against a battleship that was not damaged, or an easier approach that more likely ensured a hit, most of the Japanese pilots chose the easiest approach, much to the detriment of *Oklahoma* and *West Virginia*.

Success

The torpedo bombers quickly achieved the planners' hopes to sink at least one battleship. *Oklahoma* capsized. *West Virginia*, with a more advanced internal torpedo defense system and benefiting from prompt counterflooding by alert junior officers and petty officers, was saved from a similar fate, eventually settling on the bottom on an even keel. *California's* torpedo defense system resisted the torpedoes, but she was undone by ten or twelve access covers to her torpedo defense voids that had been removed for a material inspection, and another dozen that had their securing nuts loosened.[20] *Nevada* was torpedoed on the forward port side, which should have been sustainable. However, the flooding of her forward magazine due to the proximity of a fire, the flooding of her after magazine due to a communications misunderstanding, and with additional damage forward from bomb hits, poor watertight integrity and a severe design flaw that contributed to progressive flooding, she was eventually intentionally grounded. With four sunken battleships just from the torpedo attacks, Yamamoto's criterion for a successful attack was fulfilled.

Level Bombers' Attack

The level bombers formed up in ten "V" formations of five aircraft each, with the lead bombardier at the point of the formation. One American observed, "The formation was perfect . . . and the timing on the dropping of the bombs was so perfect that I could follow them down in V formation right to the ground, right to impact."[21]

All ten formations lined up to pass over the targets one formation at a time. Even though they initiated their attack only minutes after the first torpedoes hit the water, they were surprised by a heavy volume of AA fire. Fuchida later remarked, "It was not wise to have deployed in this long single-column formation. The whole level bomber group could be destroyed like ducks in a shooting gallery."[22] Fuchida recognized too late the value of simultaneity.

The formation's lead bombardier—again, curiously, not in Fuchida's aircraft—had difficulty obtaining a clear sight picture due to smoke and clouds. Perfect alignment was a necessity—as examples of what errors could do, from 6,000 feet and 90 knots, a pitch error of 2 degrees would result in a 200-foot error in the impact point, and a roll error of 2 degrees from 10,000 feet would mean a 350-foot error—and the Japanese bombers were flying higher and faster, magnifying these potential errors.

Their initial target was *Nevada*, a curious choice since she was not double berthed and was accessible to torpedo attack. The run was aborted when *Arizona*'s powder magazine blew. Another run, and possibly two more, had to be aborted due to smoke. Eventually they lined up against *Maryland*.

One of the formation's aircraft had prematurely lost its bomb due to a material failure caused by AA damage. Sometime between 0820 and 0840 Fuchida's formation dropped their remaining four bombs. As Fuchida related:

> Pilots, observers, and the radiomen all shouted, "Release!" on seeing the bomb drop from the lead plane, and all the others let go their bombs. I immediately lay flat on the floor to watch the fall of bombs through a peephole. Four bombs in perfect pattern plummeted like devils of doom. The target was so far away that I wondered for a moment if they would reach it. The bombs grew smaller and smaller until I was holding my breath for fear of losing them. I forgot everything in the thrill of watching the fall toward the target. They became small as poppy seeds and finally disappeared just as tiny white flashes of smoke appeared on and near the ship.
>
> From a great altitude, near-misses are much more obvious than direct hits because they create wave rings in the water which are plain to see. Observing only two such rings plus two tiny flashes, I shouted, "Two hits!" and rose from the floor of the plane. These minute flashes were the only evidence we had of hits at that time, but I felt sure that they had done considerable damage.[23]

David Aiken[24] has determined that Fuchida's formation did not score a hit. There were no "tiny flashes" on *Maryland* other than those from her AA battery. Apparently Fuchida inferred from the two misses that there were two hits, or his mind willed itself to see flashes. What he did not see—or chose not to report—or rejected as irrelevant—were two clouds of dirt from two bombs that drilled deep into Ford Island.

Of the ten groups of level bombers, two groups missed. Besides Fuchidas', the other miss was an attack directed against *California*, who recorded that at 0825 a salvo of bombs hit the lagoon off her starboard bow.

Two of the formations attacking *Arizona* scored, each with a hit on the battleship and one on the repair ship *Vestal* moored alongside. The remaining six formations all apparently scored single hits.

Overall, the level bombers showed great coolness and precision. They were surprised by the fierce anti-aircraft fire, but were not deterred from making repeated runs until their sight picture was perfect.

Fighter Opposition Develops

The first wave attack arrived unopposed. The first defending fighters got aloft from Haleiwa Auxiliary Field at about 0830, and were directed to Ewa, where Japanese fighters continued to strafe the air station. The Japanese attackers were in a long line, breaking off into strafing attacks one at a time, totally fixated on the ground targets. Two American fighters jumped into the line and got two quick kills. Low on fuel and ammunition, they returned to Wheeler Field to replenish.

Four P-36 fighters got aloft from Wheeler Field at about 0850, just in advance of the arrival of the Japanese second wave. They engaged Japanese aircraft over Kaneohe, which was targeted by 18 B5N Kate level bombers and 18 A6M Zeros. In the fight the US fighters claimed three kills and one probable at the cost of one P-36.

Back at Wheeler, the two rearmed P-40s managed to get aloft during a lull in the second-wave attack. They claimed another kill and a probable over Wheeler, and a kill over Ewa.

At Bellows Field, two fighters attempted to take off but were shot down by A6M Zeros seconds after clearing the runway.

Other fighters took off from Haliewa and Wheeler and engaged Japanese aircraft as they joined up to return to their carriers.

Overall, during the attack fourteen American fighter sorties were able to get aloft. Two other aircraft attempted to take off, but were acquired by Zeros while in their takeoff roll and shot down seconds after they cleared the end of the runway before they could attain fighting airspeed or altitude.

Of the fourteen sorties, two American fighters were lost. The survivors submitted claims for ten kills and four probables. The AAF awarded official credit for nine kills; a close analysis indicated that the actual score might have been as low as eight kills and as high as eleven. That represents a four-to-one (or 5.5 to one) kill ratio in favor of the American fighters.

Just as significantly, twelve of the fourteen American fighters, outnumbered in the air by 36 of the vaunted A6M Zeros, survived and returned to their bases.

In spite of an overwhelming aerial superiority in numbers and aircraft performance, the Japanese fighters did not sweep the skies of defending fighters. This was a disappointing performance by the Japanese fighters, and certainly a failure to achieve their primary mission.

The performance of the Japanese fighters will be further examined in Chapter 9.

The Second-Wave Dive-Bomber Attack

Before taking off, the dive-bomber aircrews were told there were no carriers in port. With their primary target absent, one aviator reported that they "were told to attack the same targets as the first wave,"[25] meaning battleships. Another recorded they were to "finish off ships damaged in the first attack, preferably the battleships."[26]

These oral instructions contradicted the prioritization plans, which directed the dive-bombers to attack cruisers before hitting battleships. It meant using GP bombs against battleships, in spite of the fact that the Japanese recognized that these bombs could be expected to do only superficial damage. Why the targeting instructions were changed at this last minute is unknown.

The dive-bombers' strike leader, Lieutenant Commander Shimazaki Shigekazu, signaled the attack at 0854 as they approached Kaneohe Naval Air Station on their path to Pearl Harbor. They were greeted by a tremendous volume of AA fire, something never before seen in their combat experience over China, a stunning development. A massive column of smoke rose from Battleships Row and drifted over Ford Island, obscuring any chances for an up-wind attack against the battleships. An almost solid layer of clouds covered the harbor at 3,500 to 5,000 foot altitude, interposing between their usual pitch-over altitude of 10,000 feet. Shimazaki could not have been happy with the conditions.

Fuchida, orbiting the harbor, watched as the dive-bombers approached. *Nevada* had slipped her moorings and was underway heading south between Ford Island and the shipyard. He saw this as a great opportunity to sink a ship in the channel and bottle up the entire Pacific Fleet. He had instructed his aviators in the pre-strike briefings to be alert for such a chance. He said that he considered assuming command of the dive-bombers, but demurred when he saw the leader of the dive-bombers lining up against the *Nevada*.

A large oiler backed into the channel as *Nevada* passed. The *Neosho* was nearly as massive as a battleship, 25,000 tons at full load. It would have been easier for the dive-bombers to sink her in the channel rather than a heavily armored battleship. The oiler was mostly ignored.

Lieutenant Makino Saburo, leader of *Kaga*'s dive-bombers, headed for *Nevada*. Other bombers moved into position. As *Nevada* pulled abreast of 1010 Dock they attacked from two directions, into the wind from the southwest and crosswind from the southeast.[27]

The dive-bombers were handicapped by environmental conditions. When using their 55-degree dives initiated from 2,000 meters (6,561 feet) altitude, the planes had to start a half-mile from their target. However, huge pillars of smoke were rising from Ford Island, Battleship Row, and Hickam Field, and clouds had moved in creating a nearly solid cloud base from 2,000 to 3,500 feet, obscuring targets except for fleeting glances. It was hard to identify targets, and hard to establish a path to attack the targets.

About 14 dive-bombers attacked *Nevada*.

Many of the American ships had awnings mounted to shade their living compartments from the tropical sun. The awnings broke up the normal profiles on the ships' identification cards with which the aviators had trained, making differentiating battleships from large auxiliaries difficult.

The attack dragged as the bombers sorted out targets. Bombers were metered into the airspace, as they customarily would attack in order of each *shotai* in each ship's formation of bombers, with units waiting until the previous attackers had completed their dives.

American observers noted some strange behavior on the part of the dive-bombers. Sometimes they appeared to just dive through a hole in the smoke, and then set up to attack whatever they found below them.

Some of the dive-bombers were observed on an attack path toward one target, only to divert in mid-dive to a different target. Some attacked in dives steeper than the customary 55 degrees, while others glide-bombed under the cloud cover at angles of 20 to 40 degrees, an attack technique outside their normal training and beyond the settings of their bomb telescopes. The customary tactical unit of a *shotai,* consisting of three bombers, was sometimes broken up, with perhaps a third of the planes attacking individually or in pairs. Some opted for easier targets away from the maelstrom over the harbor. There was no central command and little localized control, forcing individual decisions onto stressed *shotai* leaders and individual pilots.

Defensive fire was intense. Of the 78 dive-bombers, 14 were shot down (18%) and another 14 so damaged they were written off on their return to the carriers.

While the 78 D3A Val dive bombers in the second wave gave their attentions to the ships in the harbor, 54 B5N Kate bombers loaded with 250kg GP bombs from the green aircraft carriers *Shokaku* and *Zuikaku* headed for Oahu's airfields. Their primary targets were hangars and administrative areas. While it is impossible to separate out the damage that they inflicted from that of the previous wave's dive bombers and strafing fighters, their attack was evidently effective. Only one salvo was a clear "miss," a set of bombs that hit a baseball field near one of the air bases. This was a location that had been planned for an installation of underground fuel tanks, igniting a historical rumor that the Japanese had somehow obtained the Americans' airbase building plans.

Of the 94 operational American fighters, only fourteen sorties got aloft, with two other aircraft shot down as they attempted to take off. Those fourteen sorties scored eight to eleven kills, some by interjecting themselves unnoticed into the holding patterns of Japanese aircraft waiting their turn to dive in on strafing runs against the airfields. None of the American fighters appeared over Pearl Harbor or contributed to the defense of the fleet, their primary mission.

The second wave attack began at 0854. The fleet's defenders reckoned the attack was over around 0930.

Finally, over the harbor, the sky was clear of aircraft.

The attack left behind 2,403 people dead or dying and another 1,178 wounded. Of the dead, 1,177 were assigned to *Arizona* and 429 assigned to *Oklahoma*. Three battleships were sunk and two sinking. Two cruisers were torpedoed and three destroyers wrecked. The majority of the Army Air Force and Navy aircraft were either destroyed or damaged.

The Japanese left behind 29 aircraft with their crews, and five sunken midget submarines.

CHAPTER SEVEN

ASSESSMENT OF THE ATTACK

The Pre-Dawn Reconnaissance

Just prior to the day of the attack the Japanese had received accurate information that the fleet was in port and not off Maui, that no carriers were present, and there were no torpedo nets. This was important information, needed to allow the plan to be changed if necessary before the strike was launched. The submarine accomplished its mission without being detected.

Why, then, were additional floatplanes launched on the morning of the attack to repeat the reconnaissance? The chances that the fleet would move out of Pearl Harbor to Lahaina Roads on a Saturday night were miniscule—the Japanese had months of reports and knew the Americans' operating patterns. Lahaina Roads had not been used as a fleet anchorage for almost a year due to its vulnerability to submarine attack.

The reconnaissance seaplanes might be spotted and identified. The most probable American reaction would be to launch additional fighters, in addition to the usual dawn patrol, to investigate. The air defenses might also be placed on alert, as the presence of a Japanese floatplane required the presence of warships. As it was, two radar stations on Oahu detected these aircraft at 0645.

Planning an aircraft reconnaissance of Lahaina was appropriate, in case the submarine did not accomplish its mission. However, after the submarine reported, this flight ought to have been cancelled. This is another example of the lack of flexibility demonstrated by Japanese decision makers, and another place where alert defenses could have changed the course of history.

A second floatplane was to overfly Pearl Harbor to report the number of ships and the weather conditions. Again, this was an unnecessary report. The first-wave strike would receive this information en route, about 40 minutes before the attack, with no real opportunity to act on it due to a lack of communications between leaders and the strike aircraft. At this point the information had no real tactical significance. It accurately reported that there were no carriers in the harbor, but the Japanese did not use the information, and the information did not prevent the mistaken attack on *Utah*. The weather report was not particularly useful, since the attacker would be able to see the weather for themselves in a few minutes, and the report was not needed for any decisions. Even then, a more accurate report was intercepted from a commercial Oahu radio broadcast. There simply wasn't time (or communications paths or command and control) to react to any unique information the reconnaissance flight might discover.

Both of these sorties risked the success of the strike for very little return. Had the Army's Air Information Center been active, a full alert could have been triggered. But the Japanese plan assumed that their scouts would not be detected, and that was the end of the matter.

Updating the Plan for the Updated Intelligence

Two different sources confirmed that the carriers were not in port. There were no changes made to the attack plan to reflect this intelligence—the planners clung to the hope that a carrier would arrive in time for the attack.

Hope is not strategy. This intolerance to dynamic circumstances was an early manifestation of the inflexibility that would dog Japanese planners throughout the war. Matsumura's 16 torpedo bombers remained assigned to the carrier anchorages in spite of the knowledge that the carriers were absent, a stunning decision (or lack of one). Either the carriers were so important in Genda and Fuchida's minds that they could not bear to re-allocate the aircraft, or alternately, after working on their plan for so many months they were psychologically wedded to it in all its details. Both, perhaps. Certainly the second factor was there, considering that when earlier they needed to provide a contingency plan for the case where surprise was not achieved, their response was to only make minimal changes to their established plan. This reflects a fundamental lack of flexibility in Japanese staff processes.

The meeting between Genda, Fuchida, and Murata, where they considered what to do if surprise was not achieved, was a very curious meeting. It only involved the three of them, the chief planner, the strike commander, and the commander of the torpedo bombers. Absent were the commander of the fighters and the commander of the dive-bombers, the commanders of the OCA strikes and, most significantly, any flag officers. One would think that such a momentous decision would need to be coordinated with all elements of the attack, and would warrant flag interest and review.

The torpedo bombers who were to attack the carrier anchorages were, if the carriers were missing, to seek out other targets. The attack routes available to Murata's formations included routes against nests of destroyers and tenders, targets low on the priority list. Were these actually intended to be considered as targets, considering that only "crippling power" was allocated against the battleships? How could Murata's aviators be expected to allocate their attacks down a priority list without information on the damage inflicted to higher priority targets by other torpedo bombers that they might not see?

The failure to react when circumstances were different from those assumed in the plan meant that 16 carrier attack planes were buzzing about Pearl Harbor looking for targets, an air traffic control horror story.

Fuchida's Fumble with the Flares

The process of communicating using flares was not well thought out. Fuchida fired two flares, which was interpreted both as signaling the "surprise" and "no surprise" contingency plans by different elements of the force. The attack went into the attack with the same level of organization as the Kentucky Derby after the horses are turned loose. Everyone was racing for their target, the dive-bombers under the assumption that the defenders had been alerted, and the torpedo bombers realizing that surprise had been achieved and wanting to get their attack in before the defenders woke up. According to one of the observers on a torpedo-carrying Kate, "Due to miscommunication between our pilots the attack sequence was utter confusion. All of our aircraft were trying to attack at the same time."[1]

The planners failed to provide a clear and reliable means of communicating which attack plan was to be used. They also failed to provide a plan that could be executed in an organized manner should the enemy defenses be alert. "Surprise," and then "no surprise" was signaled, resulting in disarray. The communications problem could have been easily solved, either by designating different colored flares for each plan, or by specifying an interval between two flares as the signal, or by having the flares fired only to signal a change in plan away from a default plan.

Radio was not used, either as a primary or backup means of signaling. It is not known why the Japanese would signal the initiation of the attack ("*To, to, to,*" for "charge") and not use that same means to signal which plan was to be employed. Tactically, apparently no attempt was made to use the radio by the leaders of the torpedo bombers to prevent the attack on *Utah*, or to sort out and allocate targets. Although as we have seen, the IJN's radio equipment at the time was flawed, the Japanese had not yet come to terms with radio's command and coordination potential.

Fuchida's attitude towards his error with the flares is remarkable. Rather than taking responsibility for the error, he disingenuously attempted to convince a historian that his blunder was of no import. This claim was accepted for 65 years, but more thorough analysis indicates that Fuchida's blunder was significant. It cost lives and wasted weapons.

The mistimed wake-up call to Pearl Harbor came as bombs detonated on Ford Island a short distance from Battleship Row. A more effective reveille cannot be imagined. In exchange, the Japanese destroyed an aircraft and a hangar, targets that were not time-critical and could have no impact on the early part of the battle. If surprise had indeed been lost, the first bombs ought to have been targeted as SEAD to support the torpedo bombers' attack—but the Japanese did not think in those terms.

Most of the ships in Pearl Harbor were in Condition Three, an alert status that required 25% of the anti-aircraft battery to be manned, with ammunition adjacent to the guns but locked in ready service lockers. These explosions triggered a frantic search for the keys, which in most cases were held by the senior duty officer, the duty gunnery officer, or the duty gunners mate. Many impatient gun crews smashed the locks off. The minutes required to get the "ready" guns firing were provided through Fuchida's error.

The average time to get the ship's anti-aircraft batteries into operation was five minutes for the battleships, four minutes for the cruisers, and seven minutes for the destroyers.[2] The first bomb landed about two minutes before the first torpedo detonated against *Utah*, which in turn was several minutes before the attack developed against Battleship Row. The bomb explosions preceded the torpedo attack against Battleship Row by about four to five minutes, compared to the four to seven minutes needed to get AA batteries in operation.

The first torpedo planes to attack Battleship Row took fire, led by Murata and Lieutenant (junior grade) Goto Jinichi. Goto reported, "In spite of the surprise attack early on a Sunday morning Murata and I saw machine-gun bullets coming onto us before we launched our torpedoes! . . . We were under a curtain of machine-gun fire."[3]

The premature warning allowed American machine gunners on *Bagley* critical seconds to get their weapons in operation. *Bagley* reported that she was able to engage the third torpedo bomber in the stream of attackers.

Fuchida's blunder cost lives and aircraft.

A British study of low-level aircraft bombing attacks against merchant ships in the Mediterranean found that when ships fired back during an aircraft attack, 10% of the ships were sunk, while 25% were sunk when they did not. The AA only shot down 4% of the attacking aircraft, but reduced the rate of ships being sunk by two thirds. At Pearl Harbor, the defensive fire caused torpedoes to be launched outside the release envelope, disrupted their aim, and contributed to poor target selection as the torpedo bomber crews hurried to drop against the easiest available target. Of the 40 torpedoes brought to the battle, 35 were dropped, 19 hit a ship and perhaps 4 ran but missed their targets. Probably a total of 12 torpedoes (34% of those dropped) were delivered out-of-envelope or had technical failures and ended up stuck in the bottom mud of the harbor. Two of the 12 were dropped against *Utah*, three against *Helena*, and seven against Battleship Row.

The poor approach tactics handicapped the attackers. Most of those that attacked Battleship Row flew directly past the Navy Yard, one at a time, allowing the gunners on *Bagley* and other ships to practice, learn, adjust, and hit.

Fuchida's fumble with the flares contributed to the loss of five torpedo bombers and precious torpedoes that were shot down or jettisoned before launch, and probably also contributed to the improper delivery of 12 others.

Assessment: Torpedo Attack

One of the ideas pounded home during the aviators' briefings was that heavy damage on one battleship would be better than slight damage on many battleships. This was one of Genda's initial planning principles. Yamamoto, too, wanted battleships crippled or sunk. How many torpedo hits are required to sink a battleship?

The US Naval War College assessed that the Treaty classes present at Pearl Harbor could take six to seven Japanese aerial torpedo hits before sinking. If the hits were scored within a fifteen minute period they could only take four to five, as the ships' counterflooding capability would be overwhelmed and the ship would capsize.[4] A postwar study conducted by the US Navy's Operations Evaluation Group derived similar numbers.[5]

American battleships sacrificed speed in favor of sturdy construction, heavy armor and better torpedo protection. The damage-resistance capability of their hulls was demonstrated when the *Colorado*-class hull of the battleship *Washington* (BB-47) had to be expended under the terms of the Washington Naval Treaty, and so was used for damage-resistance tests.[6] Two 400-pound torpedo warheads and three 1,000-pound bombs were detonated against the torpedo defense system. The hull remained afloat for three days, even without a crew to perform damage control.

The best condition to resist damage is where the ship is at sea, with General Quarters set, fuel levels and tank closures in combat condition, the firemain split and pressurized,[7] dewatering systems manned and ready, and with the ship buttoned up with all watertight doors secured. This was known as "Material Condition Zed," or, more familiarly, Zed.

Zed was not maintained in harbor. Maintenance, repairs, and resupply had to be performed, watertight doors were open for access and ventilation, and at times tanks and voids and other unmanned compartments were opened for corrosion inspections or maintenance. Open doors, hatches and access ports allowed progressive flooding, where water can spread far beyond the immediate vicinity of the hit.

The effects of reduced watertight integrity on ships in port were demonstrated earlier in the European war. The Japanese were aware of them via information from their Axis partners.[8] On 14 October 1939, the British battleship *Royal Oak* was sunk by three German submarine torpedoes in Scapa Flow. At Taranto on 12 November 1940, the Italian battleships *Conte di Cavour* and *Caio Duilio* were each hit by one aerial torpedo and sunk, and *Littorio* (a modern ship completed in 1940) was intentionally grounded after three aerial torpedo hits. In November of 1941 the British battleship *Barham* was sunk by three German submarine torpedoes when she was underway, though not at Action Stations.

Royal Oak was an old ship, an "R" class laid down in 1914 under lesser standards for anti-torpedo protection. Italian Navy crews did not have a good reputation for damage control. From these examples the Japanese would have concluded that four hits on a battleship would be sufficient to achieve their objective. With potentially eight battleship targets, and assuming 80% hits, five aircraft should attack each battleship. This would require all 40 torpedo bombers.

The Japanese received specific reports on where the battleships were moored, and knew that only four battleships were positioned where they could be hit by torpedoes. There were four additional ships within their targeting instructions and accessible to torpedoes. *Phoenix*, a modern 10,000 ton cruiser, was anchored in the East Loch astern of *Nevada*; a sister ship, *Helena*, was moored at 1010 Dock; *Raleigh* and *Detroit* were at the carrier moorings. Four other cruisers were at the Navy Yard piers, but *New Orleans*, *San Francisco*, *St. Louis*, and *Honolulu* were inaccessible to torpedo attack.

Adding the accessible cruisers to the four outboard battleships gives eight valid torpedo targets within the Japanese prioritization instructions. An even distribution would have put five torpedo bombers against each target; a better distribution would be four against each cruiser and six against each battleship. A 50% hit rate would have likely sunk the four cruisers and sunk or crippled all the battleships. This would have more than doubled the returns for the torpedo bombers over what was actually achieved.

The original Japanese plan had 24 torpedo bombers directed against Battleship Row. Evenly distributed, this would allocate 6 bombers against each vulnerable battleship; an 82.5% hit rate (as achieved in the last practice session) would give five hits per battleship.

The second group of 16 bombers had 13 potential attack paths against ships at the carrier moorings northwest of Ford Island, cruisers anchored in the East Loch, and two potential paths of approach directed against ships pierside at 1010 dock at the Navy Yard.[9] Had they gone for the cruisers, as would be logical under their prioritization scheme, there would have been four torpedo bombers per cruiser, enough to sink them all even with a 50% hit rate.

Mental Errors and Physical Errors

In sports such as football and baseball there are mental errors and physical errors. The same holds true in battle: there are bad decisions, mental errors, and physical errors, such as poor execution in aiming and firing. The torpedo bombers committed both types of errors.

The first significant mental error was committed by the torpedo bombers assigned to attack the carrier moorings. These moorings were occupied by *Utah*, an aged demilitarized battleship serving as a target ship, two early-'20s-era cruisers *Raleigh* and *Detroit*, and *Tangier*, a former cargo ship converted to an 11,760-ton seaplane tender. The obsolescent cruisers were legitimate targets on the priority list, although not very glamorous; *Utah* was a clear waste of ordnance.

John Toland relates the story of Lieutenant Matsumura, leading *Hiryu's* torpedo group, as he approached Pearl Harbor:

> "Look for carriers!" he called through the voice tube to his observer. . . . Half a dozen planes converged on a big ship that looked like a carrier on the northwest side of Ford Island. "Damn fools," he repeated, "Who can they be?" Before takeoff he had warned his men to leave this one alone. It was merely the thirty-three-year-old target ship *Utah*, her stripped decks covered with planks.[10]

Mori, flying on Nagai's wing, also observed this attack. "Can't they see that two of the ships are nothing but cruisers? It would be a crime to waste torpedoes on them when the battleships are right there in sight a bit further on." Mori was determined to use his torpedo on nothing less than a battleship,[11] an attitude shared by all the Japanese aviators.

Regardless of warnings, six of the torpedo bombers attacked *Utah*, four of them after breaking away from their *shotai* leader. One torpedo missed so badly it hit *Raleigh*. *Raleigh* nearly capsized, forestalled by prompt damage control.[12]

This waste of torpedoes can fundamentally be blamed on the planners. Word had been received that there were no carriers in Pearl Harbor. They let stand the attack on the carrier moorings hoping a carrier might return, a hope that ended up wasting six torpedoes.

Their hope did come close to being fulfilled; *Enterprise* would have arrived on Saturday but was held up by bad weather. But a bad decision should not be considered good just because fortune intervenes. The fact remains that the planners left no provision to change the plan to react to updated intelligence.

Toland stated that *Utah* was misidentified as a carrier, an assertion that has been echoed by other historians.[13] Comparing the silhouettes of *Utah* with *Enterprise* (or any other carrier) makes this hard to accept. Photographs of *Utah* capsizing show that her decks "stripped and covered with planks" did not make for a carrier silhouette. Japanese veterans stated that *Utah* was actually misidentified as an operational battleship.

The first physical errors are apparent. Of six torpedoes launched against *Utah*, only two hit their target. One hit *Raleigh* in the adjacent berth. One torpedo slid up a muddy beach onto Ford Island. The other two are buried in the harbor bottom. These bombers were unopposed by AA fire and had an easy approach path to their targets, virtually training conditions. They should have achieved the training level of success, five hits instead of two.

In the absence of carriers, *Soryu*'s and *Hiryu*'s torpedo bombers were to search out and strike alternate targets. Matsumura related:

> My assignment was to find and attack a carrier in the harbor, so I tried very hard to locate one. But I could not find a carrier, so I hit a battleship. . . . I saw smoke coming from Ford Island but didn't go into it. Instead, I took a detour and flew in the airspace off Hickam Field, but I didn't plan to do this. During my initial attempt to drop my torpedo, I was too close to another aircraft. Because of this, my Type 97 [Kate] was rocked by this plane's 'prop wash,' so I had to turn around and come back again. . . . [M]y torpedo hit the *West Virginia*.

Another five aircraft attacked the 1010 Dock mooring occupied by an antiquated minelayer outboard of a modern light cruiser, a puzzling silhouette when backlit by the rising sun. The light cruiser *Helena* was a legitimate target on the priority list; however, it was not so important a target as to justify five torpedoes. The attackers saw in the confused silhouette what they wanted to see, a battleship, a common occurrence under the stress of combat.

One torpedo passed under minelayer *Oglala* to explode against *Helena*. The blast split the seams of the WWI-era minelayer, which slowly filled with water and eventually capsized. *Oglala* was eventually salvaged, but with difficulty—she was raised and sank three times before she could be towed into drydock. This was done not because she was a valuable ship, but because her sunken hull blocked one of the most valuable berths in the harbor.

Three of the torpedoes hit bottom. A photograph shows what might be the froth from the engines of two torpedoes stuck in the mud near the channel dredge, along the attack path leading to *Helena*.[14]

The remainder of *Soryu's* and *Hiryu's* torpedo bombers attacked battleships; most went for *Oklahoma* or *West Virginia*, the recipients of more than their fair share of torpedoes.

The reason why *Oklahoma* and *West Virginia* were disproportionately targeted is apparent from the chart. The approach to these ships was the easiest, a straight 1,000-yard run, flying along the Southeast Loch past the Navy Yard waterfront. In contrast, the approaches to *Nevada* and *Arizona*, shown on Fuchida's chart, involved skimming over the Kuahua Supply Base. After clearing the turbulence generated off the fuel tanks, and the alternating sink and lift generated by alternating bands of land and water followed by another band of turbulence from the supply base buildings, the pilot would have about 6 seconds to throttle back, descend, establish launch parameters in speed, altitude, and attitude, and release their torpedo. These routes were impossible, and all the pilots had the good sense to avoid them.

The alternative was to take the same route down the Southeast Loch on a course of about 300 degrees, and then, when near the junction with the main channel, rack the aircraft into an 80-degree right turn and release the torpedo on a course of about 020 degrees. That turn, at slow speed in a heavily loaded aircraft at an altitude of less than 60 feet, would be dangerous. The aim would have to be precise, as the targets would be foreshortened by the angle on the bow.

This approach was selected by probably only one or two aircraft: *Lessons* praises those aircraft that, "realizing just prior to charging [firing] torpedoes that they were aiming at the wrong target, made bold turnings to the right targets amid fierce gunfire."[15] It is no wonder that *Nevada* was hit by only one torpedo, and *Arizona* none.

The attack approach against *California* would be easier, but from the drop point the target angle against the ship was about 45 degrees off the port quarter, presenting a foreshortened target. One torpedo bomber, in a spectacular display of airmanship, approached from the south along the main channel, cleared the Navy Yard, angled to the left to line up the attack and dropped off the ship's bow, scoring a hit.

Attack Routes and Deconfliction

An orderly attack was not achieved. The deconfliction plan, to have all aircraft make a left turn after dropping, was not always executed. Routes were blocked by AA fire and smoke. Formations became intermixed, runs were aborted, re-run, aborted again.

In postwar interviews the aviators did not mention target prioritization; rather, they spoke of unexpectedly heavy AA fire, the difficulty of identifying targets, and their desire to get their torpedo into a battleship, any battleship. Only the most experienced and steady aviators thought of spreading the attack. What the planners saw as a simple task just could not happen under combat conditions. The fact that an attack planned to take two minutes actually took 11 to 15 is an indication of the severity of the problem.

Overkill

Fuchida's 27 December 1941 map used to brief Emperor Hirohito shows 36 torpedo hits. Twenty-one were on *Oklahoma* and *West Virginia*, twice as many as needed. Five were on *Helena*, over 100% overkill, and six on *Utah*, all a waste. Thus, from Fuchida's own report, 19 of 36 torpedoes (53%) were either overkill or wasted. Fuchida's expressed desire to concentrate and bag at least one battleship may have been reflected in the concentration of fire, if only subconsciously.

Another consideration comes from the viewpoint of the torpedo bomber pilots. Attacking at 20- to 30-second intervals, aircraft might only see a few previous torpedo plumes, if they registered any at all due to target fixation and tunnel vision. They would not have information regarding the total number of hits a given battleship had absorbed prior to their attack. The photographs attest that after a plume subsided, there were few clues to guide the later torpedo bomber pilots to facilitate a weapons distribution decision. An aircraft, seeing plumes on *Oklahoma,* would shift to the next easiest target, *West Virginia.* After a few hits on *West Virginia,* the plumes on *Oklahoma* would have subsided, inviting additional torpedoes to be directed at *Oklahoma.* The 70-second gap between the *Akagi* and *Kaga* attackers made the problem harder.

To properly distribute their torpedoes under a prioritization scheme, the aircrews needed more information beyond that which they could collect with their own eyes. Otherwise, the harrowing approach would invite repeated hits on the easiest target. This occurred in the rehearsals and was not corrected.

Lessons acknowledged "there were over concentrations of attacks and also some gaps which had not been damaged." They attributed this to a number of reasons, including "errors in identifying ships in the aircraft reconnaissance report," a somewhat odd notion, and perhaps a typically oblique Japanese reference to the torpedoes wasted against *Utah. Lessons* also blamed poor visibility caused by the smoke from burning aircraft on Ford Island. This could be attributed to Fuchida's error with the flare guns if it were true; however, the wind blew the smoke from Ford Island to the southwest, away from all the torpedo attack routes, so it is hard to see how smoke would have interfered with the attacks on Battleship Row. Photographs show Battleship Row clear of smoke until *Arizona* exploded, which occurred after the torpedo attacks had been delivered.

Lessons also mentions that pilots could not evaluate the damage done by preceding torpedoes before launching theirs, and a concern that aircraft might run into the water columns from exploding torpedoes.

The last reason cited in *Lessons* was most significant: "It is human nature to seek an easy-to-attack objective." Twenty-one torpedoes were launched at *Oklahoma* and *West Virginia,* over half the available torpedoes, because the attack planning and briefing failed to give workable guidance on target selection. Over half the 40 pilots, anxious to be individually successful, took the easiest approach. Some reported that they aimed at *Oklahoma* or *West Virginia* because they were taking heavy fire and they wanted to get their weapon in the water before they were shot down. The geography of the approach would naturally funnel the attack towards the southern end of Battleship Row. The aviators should not be faulted, but rather the planners indicted for their failure to anticipate the problem, particularly after the problem of overconcentration was revealed to them during the rehearsals.

Chart 11 shows the attack paths actually used by the torpedo bombers. The circled numbers show the number of hits and the number of torpedoes that were launched on each route. Most of the Japanese pilots opted for the less technically demanding approach, down the loch past the shipyard to establish altitude and airspeed, and a final turn to line up on the target. There are no eyewitness accounts indicating that the near-impossible hop over the supply base to hit the northeastern part of Battleship Row was even attempted. The route taken by one pilot over the Navy Yard to hit *California* from the south is from the pilot's testimony and American witnesses.

These problems were an early demonstration of the inflexibility in planning and execution that was to bedevil the Japanese throughout the war. Ugaki, Yamamoto's chief of staff, saw this when his staff would present him with plans that did not provide alternative courses of action. "I can't help feeling that they are considering the war too rigidly," he recorded in his diary. "They don't seem to know that [war, combat operations] depends largely upon momentum and chance."[16]

The whole idea of a prioritization scheme was counter to Japanese psychology. What young Japanese warrior, filled with the spirit of *Bushido*, in this most important battle in Japan's 2,600 years, would want to come home and report, "I attacked a secondary target"? *Not one Japanese pilot dropped a torpedo against what he believed to be a secondary target.*

Torpedo hits on battleships

The attack against Battleship Row resulted in a skewed distribution of hits. Twelve hits were scored on only two of the battleships. The remaining three torpedo hits were scored on *California* (two hits) and *Nevada* (one hit).

There was a bogus report of an additional hit reported on *Arizona's* bow, first reported at the time of the attack and recently repeated in the television program *Killer Subs in Pearl Harbor*. This claim is not substantiated by any material evidence. When divers inspected *Arizona's* hull they found no evidence of a torpedo explosion, or even a dent from the impact of a dud. This was reported in *Arizona's* War Damage Report,[17] and verified by many subsequent inspection dives, including a detailed mapping of the hull after the war and periodic hull inspections by the National Park Service interested in containing oil leaks. The official final analysis of the loss of the battleship unequivocally stated, "It therefore can be accepted as a fact that a torpedo did not hit *Arizona*."[18]

If a torpedo had exploded against *Arizona*, the repair ship *Vestal* would have suffered the same underwater damage as did *Oglala* when *Helena* was torpedoed. She did not.

In addition, an aerial photograph of Battleship Row just prior to *Arizona's* magazine detonation does not show any oil leaking from *Arizona* (the outboard fuel tanks were filled to 95% capacity in the area of the alleged hit), or any of the characteristic ripple of shock waves in the water associated with torpedo hits. Finally, no torpedo bomber claimed to have attacked *Arizona*.

Surprisingly, this has become an issue in another historical question, the theory that a midget submarine penetrated the harbor. This will be discussed further in Chapter 11.

The reported torpedo hit on *Arizona* was actually the plume from an 800kg AP bomb dropped by a *Hiryu* level bomber.[19]

Surprise

Surprise magnified the results of the attack. If the US ships had not been surprised, and had simply been in a proper condition of material readiness with Zed set and damage control teams manned and ready, *California* and perhaps *Nevada* could have shrugged off their torpedo hits and remained afloat; fire damage to *Tennessee* and *West Virginia* might have been better contained; *Oklahoma* might have had a shot at counterflooding, and might have remained upright if the void covers on her torpedo defense compartments had been properly closed.

Lack of Reserves

The uneven distribution of hits points to another flaw in the plan: a lack of reserves. The plan's concept was to have all the torpedo bombers attack "nearly simultaneously." By executing the attack in strings the leaders had no way to control the distribution of weapons. If a few torpedo bombers had been held in reserve, the commanders could have directed them against targets needing additional attention. Some of the overkill on *Oklahoma* and *West Virginia* could have been sent against *Nevada* and *California*, or against cruisers. An attack by a reserve group of torpedo bombers could have been covered by a SEAD group of dive-bombers and fighters, or even strafing runs by D3A Val dive bombers that had expended their bombs against Ford Island.

Success Achieved by Eleven Torpedo Bombers

With better execution the results would have been considerably worse for the Pacific Fleet. Against the 82.5% torpedo hit rate achieved by the Japanese at the end of their training program they achieved only 19 hits (48%).

Discounting the overkill on *Oklahoma* and *West Virginia*, and the torpedoes wasted on *Utah*, there were only thirteen torpedo hits that contributed to achieving the attack's mission—*Raleigh* (1), *Helena* (1), *Nevada* (1), *Oklahoma* (4), *West Virginia* (4), and *California* (2). That is an effectiveness rate of 33%, a figure well under Japanese expectations, and less than half the rate achieved by the British at Taranto in an attack executed at night in a harbor festooned with balloons and torpedo nets. Considering that *Raleigh* was hit by a torpedo aimed at another ship, and *Helena* was attacked under the assumption she was a battleship, the number of accurate attacks is reduced to eleven. The effectiveness of the aircrews in recognizing and attacking appropriate targets and accurately delivering their ordnance is reduced to 28%.

Calling this "brilliant" is a clear overstatement.

However, all four battleships hit by torpedoes were out of the war six months or more, so it can also be said that those eleven aircrews fulfilled the Japanese hopes for the Pearl Harbor attack.

The shortfalls in the torpedo attack can be mostly attributed to the planners and their unrealistic prioritization scheme and awkward attack formation, and the lack of a realistic rehearsal. Near-collisions caused aborted attacks. An attack that should have taken less than 90 seconds stretched out over 11 minutes from first run to last.[20] All the bombers that were going against the primary targets, the battleships, attacked after the defenders' ready machine guns were firing.

The greatest indictment of the planners' prioritization scheme is that not one torpedo bomber intentionally attacked anything other than what they thought was a battleship.

The Torpedo Attack: Plans v. Reality

The following two flow diagrams illustrate the difference between plans and reality in combat. It puts to question those who believe that "the attack was almost textbook perfect."

(10) Timeline of Planned Torpedo Attacks on Carriers and Battleship Row

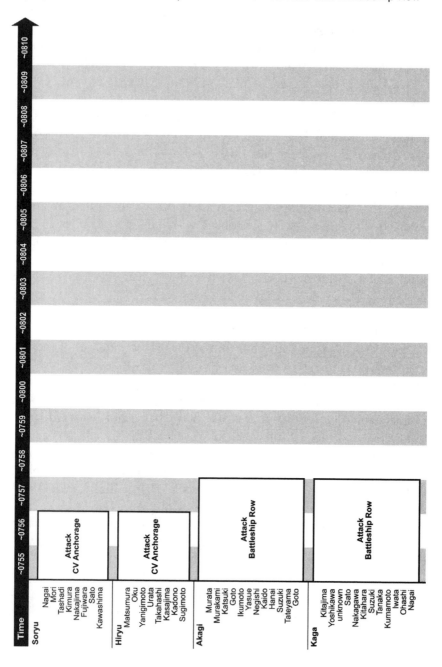

(11) Actual Development of Torpedo Attacks on Carriers and Battleship Row

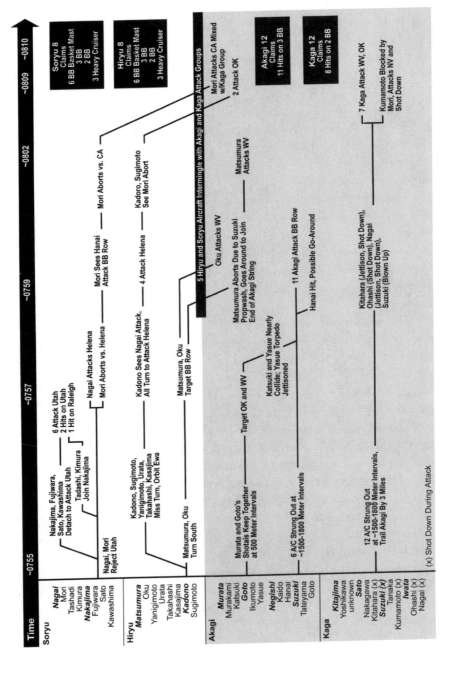

The first chart shows what the Japanese planned. The time scale is shown across the top. The *Hiryu* and *Soryu* groups of eight torpedo bombers each were to attack the carrier anchorages at seven-second intervals. With two targets, the two formations could attack simultaneously, separated laterally. The attack should have been concluded, from first drop to last, in under a minute.

The *Akagi* and *Kaga* groups of 12 torpedo bombers each would simultaneously attack the other side of Ford Island, going after the ships at Battleship Row. There was adequate room for the two groups to attack together, separated laterally, even if they all chose to attack down the length of the Southeast Loch. Their attack should have been executed in under 90 seconds.

The second flow chart shows a reconstruction of the events of the torpedo attack based on post-war interviews with veterans and official reports. The blocks on the left show the formation groups and the pilots in their order of attack. An "x" indicates those shot down. The dotted lines show events that are interrelated (such as one pilot observing another group's attack), which helps to establish the order of occurrence of the events.

The times of the events, shown in boxes following the "approximate" sign ("~") provide an estimate of the time certain events were initiated, based on records and reports, and plotting out the time and distance of the tracks of the various groups. The initiation of the attack against the carrier anchorage is established by US witnesses, as well as the logged time when ships sounded the air raid alarm along Battleship Row.[21] The torpedo hit on *Helena* is marked by her engine room clock, which stopped at 0757. The attack against the carrier anchorage occurred before that. The beginning of the attack on Battleship Row is approximated by testimony that it was after Prep but before Colors, and the time and distance required by the groups to get in position. The end of the attack, at approximately 0810, is established by Stillwell's assessment of when *Arizona* blew up,[22] coupled with the testimony of sailors on the *Vestal* that a torpedo was seen heading in their direction seconds before *Arizona* detonated. This torpedo was likely launched by Petty Officer Second Class Kumamoto Kenichi against *Nevada*, and was the next-to-last torpedo dropped. Log entries from various ships place *Arizona's* magazine explosion as early as 0806. *Vestal*, alongside *Arizona*, logged it at 0820.

The flow chart provides an altogether different impression of the attack. Rather than a smooth, "textbook" operation, there were significant problems with visual identification of targets, command and control, and mutual interference.

The groups targeting the carrier anchorages demonstrated the faulty principles upon which the attack was based. The idea of a prioritization scheme that the aviators were to follow based on ship identifications made "on the fly," plus the authority given to individual aircraft to break off targets at their discretion, meant that the *Soryu* and *Hiryu* torpedo attack aircraft scattered, wasted most of their torpedoes on poor targets, and disrupted the *Kaga* and *Akagi* groups' attack on Battleship Row. Of the 16 bombers assigned to the carrier anchorage, only five attacked battleships. *Utah* and *Helena* were both attacked under the supposition that they were operational battleships.

The differences in the flow charts show the gap between planning and reality. What could have been a smooth attack was marred by considerable confusion. The second chart is based on the testimony of the Japanese aviators who survived the war. It is likely, given the timing, that there were many more cases of mutual interference and aborted attacks than are recorded.

All of the B5N Kate losses were from *Kaga*'s air group, which attacked last—five of the last seven torpedo bombers were shot down, four before they could deliver their weapon. But for the premature warning caused by Fuchida's failure to communicate the correct attack plan, the attackers might have gotten in and out without losses.

The black boxes in the chart show the immediate post-battle Japanese assessment of the attack. *Soryu* and *Hiryu* together reported 11 hits distributed over three battleships, and three hits on a heavy cruiser (14 hits out of 16 aircraft). *Akagi* reported 11 hits distributed over three battleships (11 hits out of 12) and *Kaga* eight hits on two battleships (eight hits out of 12). Thirty-three hits were claimed. Four aircraft were shot down before they could launch their torpedoes, and one torpedo was jettisoned due to a near-collision with another plane, leaving 35 torpedoes launched for a claimed 94% hits.

Overall Assessment of the Torpedo Bombers

The effort of the torpedo bombers must be seen from two viewpoints.

First, they accomplished Yamamoto's objective to sink four battleships. Mission accomplished, well done; for such a daring attack there is no higher accolade.

Second, their efforts could have accomplished so much more. Eleven torpedoes accomplished their objective out of 40 brought to the battle. The rest were wasted in overkill, against improperly identified targets, or simply missed hitting a ship. A large degree of the blame can be attributed to the planners' ideas of how the attack should be conducted. There were shortfalls in target distribution instructions, designated attack profiles, and command and control. Blame must also go to the strike commander for fouling up the ordered attack plan, which resulted in premature warning for the defenders.

The Japanese did not appear to use radio communications for tactical control, which effectively meant their commanders had no control after battle was joined. Fuchida himself was in a level bomber attacking from 3,000 meters altitude while the heavy-hitters, the torpedo bombers, upon whose shoulders the fate of the attack rested, went in at 20 meters. Fuchida could exert no control over the torpedo attack while he was busy dropping his bomb. He was in no position to exert control for the entire duration of the first wave's attack. He transmitted the order, "Charge!" and command and control went by the board.

The torpedo bomber leaders had limited ability to control their own subordinates. Their aircraft were strung out in lines miles long, out of reach of anything other than the most basic "follow me" leadership. There is no evidence that any torpedo leader attempted to re-direct any portion of the attack against more appropriate targets other than by leading their own wingmen, that is, in those cases where the wingmen decided to follow.

Subordinates were given the authority to pick their own targets, a necessary principle when applying a prioritization scheme. However, this also allowed very junior airmen to make mistakes without a way for the more experienced leaders to exercise effective supervision. Aircraft missed turns, lost sight of their leaders, and had near-collisions and aborted runs as aircraft milled about looking for targets while trying to get in and out as rapidly as possible. Many of the torpedo bombers effectively made their attack decisions independent of their leadership.

The inflexibility of the planning and training efforts must also be faulted. The large number of B5N Kates allocated to high-altitude bombing with AP bombs was excessive once it was known that there were no torpedo nets protecting the battleships in the harbor. Trading in 20 AP bombs for 20 torpedoes would have been like trading three AP bomb hits for 12 torpedo hits. Granted, the torpedo hits would likely have been directed against cruisers and destroyers, but most would argue that sinking three or four cruisers and some destroyers in exchange for a small chance of crippling an additional battleship was a worthwhile trade.

The prioritization scheme for the attack was useless, and mostly ignored. Not one torpedo was intentionally launched at a cruiser.

Looking at the torpedo attack as a whole, the planners' efforts merit no praise. The torpedo bomber aircrews, hampered by a poor approach plan and an unworkable prioritization scheme, had a lot to overcome. Poor delivery techniques and target selection limited the effective torpedoes to less than one third, an unimpressive result.

Lack of SEAD in the "No Surprise" Scenario

The volume of AA fire undoubtedly contributed to the below-expectations performance of the torpedo attack. The total of 19 confirmed torpedo hits[23] was well under the 82.5% hits recorded in the last practice session (a projected score of 33 hits out of 40 torpedoes), and also under the planners' earlier expectation of 27 hits. While fewer hits ought to be expected under combat conditions, the hit percentage compares unfavorably with the performance of the British at Taranto, where 9 of 12 torpedoes (75%) scored hits in a night attack under more trying conditions.[24]

The problem of American AA fire could have been mitigated by better strike planning. The only difference between the "surprise" and "no surprise" plans was in the order in which the strike aircraft would approach their targets. There were no changes in the assigned targets. In the "no surprise" plan, the assumption was that the bombers "would create so much confusion and draw such heavy fire upward that the torpedo bombers could sneak in virtually unseen, securing a high percentage of direct hits and suffering little damage in exchange."[25] But all of these dive-bombers were to attack airfields, not ships or AA positions. Guns on the ships that would be firing on the torpedo bombers could generally not bear in the direction of the dive-bombers attacking Ford Island, and were out of range of the ones attacking Hickam Field. The "no surprise" plan did not, *could not*, divert any fire away from the torpedo bombers.

Genda and Fuchida's move to change the order of the attack if surprise was not achieved was less than useless—it instead provided warning so that the defenders could prepare to receive the torpedo bombers' attack. There were no provisions to directly suppress or divert those AA batteries most likely to interfere with the torpedo bombers' runs, that is, the harbor-side batteries of the battleships and the guns of the ships moored at the Navy Yard.

The first wave included 54 dive-bombers assigned to hit airfields. Some of these could have been reasonably employed in clearing the way for the torpedo bombers, particularly considering that in the "no surprise" situation, many of the defending fighters could already be airborne and past the ministrations of dive bombers. The first bombs, instead of hitting a hanger and reconnaissance aircraft at the south tip of Ford Island, ought to have been used to suppress AA fire. There were also 45 A6M Zeros in the first wave, all of which were assigned to attack airfields. Remarkably, the nine fighters—only nine!—accompanying the torpedo bombers departed ten miles short of the harbor to strafe the Marine Corps Air Station at Ewa. Considering the value and vulnerability of the torpedo bombers, these fighters ought to have escorted the torpedo bombers all the way to the target, and maintained top cover for the duration of their attack. Some of them could have provided SEAD support—a single strafing run against *Bagley* could have gone far towards saving several torpedo bombers, which might have resulted in another two or three hits. In other words, a single strafing run might have been worth half a battleship.

The idea that the torpedo bombers were to attack "at almost the same instant" applied only to the initiation of the attacks which, remarkably enough, they nearly achieved—torpedoes were in the water against targets at the west and east sides of Ford Island within minutes. However, there was enough time, between the following aircraft, that ships were able to sequentially engage them as they arrived (according to US witness reports) in clusters of three to five aircraft with pauses between clusters. Within each cluster witnesses reported the aircraft attacked with between six to twenty-five seconds separation between aircraft. The attack stretched out over at least eleven minutes and possibly longer, hardly a "simultaneous" attack.

Suppression of a target ship's AA fire was a concept established in the 1930's, and employed by the Japanese in their "massed attack" doctrine.[26] The tactic consisted of fighters strafing the AA batteries of the target ships, or bombers delivering contact-fused bombs, just prior to or at the same time as the torpedo planes' attack. The intent was to kill the gun crews or have them hiding under cover while the slow, vulnerable torpedo planes made their runs. Such measures could have been highly effective against the American battleships, which had many of their heavy AA guns (5"/25s and 3"/50s) in exposed mountings without splinter vprotection.[27] This tactic was in the Japanese kit bag. It should have been employed.

Assessment: Level Bombers of the First Wave

Of the 50 800kg bombs assigned against inboard battleships, eight scored direct hits on battleships—six on inboard and two on an outboard ship.

The distribution of the 800kg bomb hits was effective. All inboard battleships were hit: two hits on *Tennessee*, two on *Maryland*, and two on *Arizona*, including the hit that caused the spectacular detonation of the ship's forward magazine. Two bombs hit an outboard battleship, *West Virginia*. There were two additional "collateral damage" hits on the repair ship *Vestal*, moored outboard of *Arizona*. *Vestal* suffered severe flooding and had to be beached.

Fuchida claimed that he instructed the level bombers to concentrate on one battleship to ensure its destruction. This statement does not match with what happened in the attack. The table shows Fuchida's possible briefed instructions to concentrate on a single battleship, the best possible distribution of attacks, the distribution actually achieved during the battle, and hits achieved.

Group Attacks on Battleship Row and Hits

	California	*Maryland*	*Tennessee*	*Arizona*
Briefed by Fuchida			10	
Best distribution		3	4	3
Actual distribution	1	1	5	3
Number of Hits	0	2	2	2

Of the ten salvoes, six salvoes scored hits for 60%, two less than the 80% expected. Usually, as a rule of thumb, combat results are a third less than training results, which appear to be a good approximation in this case. Four of the hitting salvoes also put bombs into outboard ships, boosting the overall hit percentage to 10 hits out of the 50 bombs carried by the level bombers.

This was a phenomenally good performance for level bombers. The pattern mean point of impact (MPI) CEPs were likely on the order of 100 to 150 feet, compared to US heavy bombers which typically had a MPI CEP on the order of 2,000 feet. Japanese level bombers at the start of the war were very effective—they devastated Clark Field in a fatal blow to US air power in the Philippines, burned Cavite Naval Shipyard to the ground, and sank the aircraft transport *Langley* while she was underway during the Java campaign. In contrast, USAAC aircraft employing the celebrated Norden bombsight during the Battle of Midway dropped 291 bombs from altitudes between 4,000 to 25,000 feet for zero hits.[28]

The Japanese level bombers' efforts were sabotaged by faulty weapons. Six of the ten bombs failed, seven if a bomb that passed entirely through *Vestal* before exploding is included. A dud rate of 5% is the norm, but 60% is outrageously high. In spite of having two independent fuzes, two of the bombs completely failed to explode, and four others had low order detonations that delivered only a small fraction of their destructive potential. The modifications that removed weight to convert the shells into bombs weakened them so that some shattered on impact.

The two bombs that penetrated the 4-inch Class "B" armor covering the turret roofs on *Tennessee* and *West Virginia* hit a joint between two armor plates and squeezed between the overlapping edges, a process which shattered the weakened bomb casing and cracked open the explosive cavity, scattering the explosive. The resulting low order detonations did only minor damage, as the turrets were empty of powder. Both turrets were repaired and their turret top armor replaced and thickened.[29]

Overall, it was a totally unsatisfactory performance by the Japanese weapons establishment.

The simulation was re-run to examine the potential of the attack under various conditions. The hit rate per salvo was changed to 60%. A 60% dud rate was used on bombs that hit engineering spaces. A 50% dud rate was used for magazine hits, assuming that some low order detonations might be enough to ignite powder that was broken open by the bomb's impact. Since the magazines were shielded by gun turrets empty of powder, the probability of hitting a magazine was cut in half.

(12) AP Bombing Under Actual and Expected Conditions

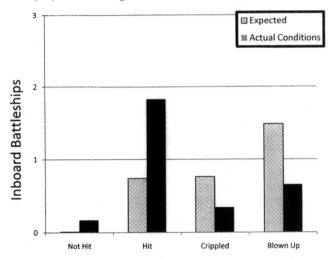

The shaded bars show the original expected performance of the attack. The black bars show the results under the attack conditions. As would be expected, the expectations for blown up and crippled ships are reduced significantly. Over the 1,000 trials, 650 battleships were destroyed by magazine explosions.

(13) Distribution of Number of Inboard Battleships Sunk or Crippled

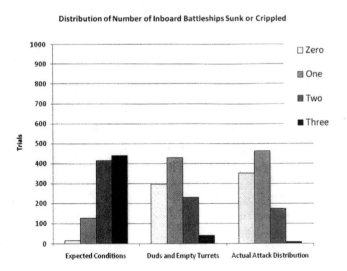

Distribution of Number of Inboard Battleships Sunk or Crippled

The second chart shows the numbers of battleships crippled or sunk under three sets of conditions. The "expected conditions" used the original hit rate assumptions as shown earlier. "Duds and Empty Turrets" uses the historical 60% hit rate and includes the historical dud rate, shielding of the magazines by the empty turrets, and distributes the attacks evenly over the targets. "Actual Attack Distribution" adds the actual attack distribution to the "Duds and Empty Turrets" conditions. Each bar shows the number of times out of 1,000 runs that zero, one, two, or three battleships were crippled or sunk.

The leftmost results ("Expected Conditions") were shown earlier and are included for comparison. In about 85% of the trials either two or three battleships were crippled or sunk.

In the center set of bars ("Duds and Empty Turrets") the most likely result is that one battleship would be crippled or destroyed, with only a 27% chance that two or three would be crippled or destroyed, down from 85%. The chance that no battleships would be crippled or sunk has risen from nearly zero to 30%, a significant risk that the entire level bombing effort could have come to naught.

The last set of bars ("Actual Attack Distribution") shows the additional effect of the maldistribution of attacks as they occurred historically, where five groups targeted *Tennessee*, three groups targeted *Arizona*, and one group apiece attacked *California* and *Maryland*. The probability that none of the inboard battleships would be crippled or sunk increases to 35%. The expected value of the attack (the weighted average number of inboard battleships destroyed) drops from 1.02 battleships to .845 battleships, indicating that the actual attack distribution reduced the potential performance of the level bombers' effort by about 18%.

The "surprise" plan called for the first wave D3A Val dive-bombers to wait until after the level bombers delivered their attacks. Instead they hit Ford Island early, generating clouds of smoke that interfered with the level bombers' sight picture. Some of the level bombers aborted several passes and ended up dropping on whatever battleship was visible at the time. Thus, the 18% reduction in attack potential can partially be attributed to Fuchida's communications error with the flare guns.

The most dramatic difference is in comparing the chances for a clean sweep (destroying or crippling all three inboard battleships) under expected conditions versus the actual conditions. The chances drop from over 40% to less than 2%. The chances of getting two or three battleships drops from 85% of the trials to under 20%. Under historical conditions, the most likely result is that one battleship would be crippled or destroyed. So, the faulty bombs reduced the level bombers' damage potential by one to two battleships.

The level bombers destroyed one battleship, meeting Japanese hopes.

The hit on the *Arizona* has often been represented as a "one in a million" or "lucky" hit. The simulation shows that the battleships were more vulnerable to the high level bombers than previously believed, and the loss of at least one battleship to AP bombs would be expected.

Overall, the performance of the level bombers was very good under trying circumstances. Compared to the performance of high-level bombers throughout the war, their effort was outstanding.

Assessment: Dive-Bombers of the Second Wave

Seventy-eight D3A Val dive-bombers arrived over the harbor to hit ships.[30] With the 250kg GP bomb expected to be ineffective against battleships, and no carriers present, under the original prioritization scheme the dive-bombers' assignment was to sink cruisers. Either just before or just after launch their assignment was changed. They were told to finish off ships damaged in the first wave attacks.

The second wave dive bombers had a difficult task trying to identify targets with the anchorage filled with smoke and a cloud layer at 3,500 feet, between their pitch-over attitude and their targets. They had to deliver their attacks through heavy AA fire from an awakened defense.

A Tactical Error? The Attack on *Nevada*

The second wave arrived to see *Nevada* underway and heading towards the entrance channel. The Japanese had hoped for an opportunity to sink a ship and block the channel.

Fuchida claimed that he considered taking command of the dive-bombers, but noticed Egusa setting up to attack *Nevada*. Fuchida had his pilot bank to give him a better look, and related that he thought, "Ah, good! Now just sink that ship right there."[31] This has to rank as one of the more foolish thoughts to come out of the battle.

There are several issues regarding this decision, and the conduct of the second wave dive-bombers in general:

1) Was the decision to attack *Nevada* appropriate?
2) Were their other target selections appropriate?
3) Was their bombing accurate?
4) Was it possible to block the channel?

Target Assignment

According to the planned prioritization of targets, the second-wave dive-bombers were to attack carriers first, followed by cruisers, then followed by battleships. Veterans recount that their targets were carriers. The 250kg GP bombs were capable of sinking carriers, possibly with as few as four hits.

If the torpedo bombers capsized any of the carriers, the dive-bombers were directed to hit the overturned hulls and reduce the ships to scrap. This was a bad decision. A sunken carrier would take more than six months to raise and recondition. If the war lasted longer than that, any bomb damage inflicted on a capsized hull would not add to the repair time. Such hits would require additional repair facility man-hours, but would not necessary extend the duration of the repair work. If Genda did not think of the idea, he surely approved.

The idea that dive-bombers were to attack sunken carriers was a bad planning decision that would not have contributed to achieving the mission of the attack. It is another reflection of the disparity between Yamamoto's and Genda's goals.

According to some testimonies, the second wave was on deck and preparing to launch when the aircrews received the word that the reconnaissance aircraft reported no carriers in Pearl Harbor. According to the prioritization scheme they should then have considered cruisers as their primary target; however, at least some of the aircrews were told just before launching to "hit the targets left over from the first wave," meaning battleships. Forty percent did go after battleships, an inappropriate weapons-target match that did not contribute to accomplishing the attack's objectives.

Targeting Decision Making and Bombing Accuracy

The second-wave dive-bombers' target selection was miserable. GP bomb hits and significant DNMs (damaging near miss)[32] tell a part of the story of what the dive-bombers attacked:

	Target location	GP Hits	DNM
Priority 1 targets:			
Carriers	none available		
Priority 2 targets:			
Honolulu (CL-48)	Navy Yard		1
Raleigh (CL-7)	CV moorings	1	
Priority 3 targets:			
Nevada (BB-36)	underway	5	
Pennsylvania (BB-38)	drydock	1	1
California (BB-44)	Battleship Row	1	
Not on target list:			
Shaw (DD-)	drydock	3	
Cassin (DD-372)	drydock	2	
Downes (DD-375)	drydock	1	
Curtiss (AV-4)	Middle Loch	1	
Helm (DD-388)	Outside Channel		2
		15	4

Only one hit and one DNM were achieved on the dive-bombers' highest priority targets. None of these cruisers were sunk, and the other six were untouched. Seven hits and one DNM were achieved on battleships, 10% of the 78 bombs.[33] Including all ships that were attacked (no matter how inappropriate), 15 bombs hit something of value, raising the hit percentage to 19%; the percentage improves to 24% if four DNMs are included.

Destroyers *Cassin* and *Downes* were in the same dry dock as *Pennsylvania*; the bombs that hit these destroyers were aimed at the battleship. This would reduce the "hit what was aimed at" percentage to 15%, with three hits in the category of "collateral damage."

Why aircraft attacked the destroyer *Shaw* is unknown. It is possible that the destroyer and floating drydock combination was misidentified as a cruiser or battleship. Recall that the Japanese dive-bombers were to attack at about a 55-degree dive angle beginning about a half-mile from the target. At that angle, visually the sides of the floating drydock would merge with the sides of the ship, particularly in the dramatic shadows of early morning light. With both painted grey, the pair would very much have the bulky look of a battleship when viewed through cloudy skies.

It is also possible that the bombs that hit *Shaw* were actually aimed at *Nevada* as she passed by the floating drydock in her sortie down the channel.

Studies of German dive-bombing accuracy by Ju-87 Stukas (an aircraft very much like the D3A Val) under combat conditions found a circular error probable (CEP) on the order of 30 meters, or about 90 feet. Battleships were on the order of 600 feet long by 90 feet in beam, while the Americans' larger 10,000-ton cruisers were approximately 600 feet long with a 65-foot beam. A 50–60% hit rate ought to be expected if the Japanese dive-bombers' accuracy were comparable to that achieved by the Germans. In practice sessions the Japanese had scored 50–60% hits on a target the size of a small battleship underway at 14 knots.[34]

The 1941 edition of the NWC Maneuver Rules specifies that dive-bombers against a stationary, battleship size target would obtain 16% hits, close to what the Japanese actually achieved. A 1951 OEG study changed that rate to 20%, using a CEP under "ideal combat conditions" of 175 feet, based on the wartime performance of US dive-bombers.

At Pearl Harbor, the dive-bombers' accuracy was well below Japanese expectations, in fact, below the historical performance of dive-bombers in the Pacific over the entire war, and their target selection was poor. From the hits and near misses that were observed, it is likely that approximately 31 of the dive bombers assigned to ship targets went after the battleships *Pennsylvania*, *California*, and *Nevada*, rather than cruisers—40% of the dive-bombers wasted their weapons in inappropriate weapon-target matches.

The ultimate ignominy was that the dive-bombers were out-scored in hit percentage by the level bombers, who before the battle were expected to get a hit rate about a quarter of that expected of the dive-bombers.

Level of Effort Against *Nevada*

Egusa's decision to use dive-bombers to attack *Nevada* was an inappropriate weapon-target match. The 250kg GP bomb was not a battleship killer. It did not have the penetration to breach the citadel or reach the magazines or engineering spaces, and was not a direct challenge to the ship's watertight integrity. The chances that these weapons would sink a battleship in the channel were exceptionally low.

If the basic decision to attack the *Nevada* was bad, it was made worse by the level of effort that the flight commanders allocated. Approximately 14 D3A Vals (possibly as many as 18) attacked *Nevada*. Under training conditions this might get eight hits. The dive-bomber commanders would have no way of knowing that *Nevada* had been previously hit by a torpedo, so they had to expect to sink the ship on their own. Were eight 250kg bomb hits sufficient to sink a battleship?

The answer is a resounding "no." The Japanese knew that GP bombs had no chance of sinking the ship, and the Americans' assessment was the same. *Striking Power of Air-Borne Weapons*, a US Naval Intelligence document, makes this assessment of GP bombs v. battleships: "Even though fires and extensive structural damage above the armored deck result from the employment of G.P. bombs, sinking is not to be expected except when a comparatively large number of such hits are received."[35] In the NWC Maneuver Rules of June 1940, 64 500-pound GP bomb hits would be needed to sink *Nevada*, 55 in combination with a single aerial torpedo hit. In this case the deterministic model of ship damage is appropriate, since the bombs did not have the penetration to get into magazines or engine rooms.

The Japanese expected that it would take 18 dive-bombers to sink a fragile carrier.[36] How, then, could they expect to sink a tough battleship using only 14?

The Japanese dive-bombing attack on *Nevada* was a wasteful half-measure. Even if all the bombs had hit, 14 hits were well short of what they must have known was needed. The attempt to sink *Nevada* in the channel was a waste of ordnance that could have been better employed against targets more vulnerable to their effects.

A charge of negligence has to be directed against the authors of this hare-brained idea—Fuchida (who briefed the idea), Genda (who allowed the idea to be briefed), and doubly again against Fuchida who, as the on-the-spot strike commander, allowed it to proceed.[37] Fuchida should either have cancelled the effort, or poured on sufficient dive-bombers to have at least a chance of sinking the ship. The dive-bomber crews or commanders ought not be blamed—they operated as briefed, although they should have known that the numbers committed were inadequate.

The very idea that sinking a ship in the channel would bottle up the Pacific Fleet was a shocking miscalculation. This myth will be more fully explored in Chapter 10.

But, how can the decision to attack *Nevada* be considered poor when the damage inflicted by the dive bombers directly contributed to sinking the ship?

Sinking *Nevada*

The Japanese benefited from an extraordinary chain of circumstances in their attack on the *Nevada*.

Two GP bomb hits contributed flooding, something that ordinarily would not be expected. One passed through the forecastle and out the hull to explode directly alongside, punching in side plates and leaving two wide cracks, one 25 feet long and the other 18 feet long. While this seems dramatic, flooding from this hit was limited to the outermost torpedo defense void. A second bomb passed through the forecastle and out through the bottom to explode under the hull, creating a hole six feet in diameter.[38] This caused more flooding, but it was flooding outside the ship's armored, watertight citadel, and as such should not have been lethal. This was the extent of the flooding directly caused by the 14 GP bombs. It was not enough to sink the ship. Many, many more hits like this would have been required to give the immediate, large scale flooding needed to sink a battleship in the channel.

The ship would have remained afloat had not three other factors come into play. *Nevada* succumbed not to Japanese bombs but to poor material condition, critical design flaws, and a massively significant damage control mistake.

Starting from the initial attack, *Nevada* was hit by a single torpedo forward port side between the two forward main battery turrets. The innermost torpedo bulkhead held, but leakage at the seams and butts caused flooding below the first platform. At this point the poor material condition factor came into play. Manhole covers to the torpedo defense voids and some fuel tanks were either loose or were sprung by the torpedo hit, allowing oil and water to flood the third deck. As the ship settled oil began shooting up out of the fuel tank sounding tubes, past caps that ought to have been sealed with effective gaskets. An initial five degree list was corrected by counterflooding. But the flooding was being contained, and this hit would not have sunk the ship.

After getting underway the ship was hit by five 250kg GP bombs. Two of the hits caused additional flooding forward, as mentioned above. The other bombs started a large fire in the forward superstructure. One bomb passed the forward gasoline storage tank to explode just under the bottom of the hull, opening a six foot hole in her plates. Gasoline leakage and vapors almost immediately ignited in the forward part of the ship near the magazines. The forward superstructure was engulfed in flames, and by the end of the battle the foremast structure containing the bridge was destroyed.

Because of this fire, the forward magazine was ordered to be flooded. Then the next factor came into play. Somehow the word was passed to flood the after magazine as well. These two flooded magazines put a huge tonnage of water inside the armored citadel, and the ship settled deep in the water.

Then the last factor came into play, two design flaws. The first was that the second deck was not watertight. As portions of the non-watertight second deck were submerged the flooding became progressive and compartments were flooded from above. The efforts of the damage control team were then stymied by the ship's poor material condition. According to the ship's war damage report, the crew was in a "losing fight against water spreading through boundaries and fittings which should have been watertight but actually were not."[39]

For example, the Main Battery Plotting Room was one of the most protected spaces in the ship, five decks below the main deck at the bottom of the armored conning tower tube and inside the citadel. It escaped damage during the attack. Five hours after the last bomb had been dropped water started to enter through a watertight door and began streaming down from the overhead, and the compartment flooded.

Many similar deficiencies caused inexorable progressive flooding. For instance, sounding tubes in some crew spaces led down into fuel tanks. These tubes were capped with a threaded plug seated against a gasket. Many of the gaskets were either cracked or missing, or the cap missing altogether. When the fuel tanks were flooded by torpedo hits and pressurized as the ship settled in the water, the result was a fountain of fuel oil gushing out of the sounding tubes.

Throughout the ship watertight doors were not watertight and stuffing tubes for cable and piping runs leaked.

Then, the second significant design flaw frustrated all attempts to keep the ship afloat. The ship had a centralized ventilation system called the "Bull Ring" where the main ventilation air intakes were located. Air from the Bull Ring was distributed throughout the ship, with ventilation ducting piercing many watertight compartments. There were inadequate closures in the ventilation systems, so when the Bull Ring flooded, it distributed water throughout the ship, outside and inside the armored citadel.

Flooding progressively compartment by compartment, the ship eventually settled onto the mud.[40]

The Japanese objective of disabling *Nevada* for at least six months was thus achieved. *Nevada* was drydocked on 14 February 1942, and afterwards sailed under her own power to the Puget Sound Naval Shipyard on 22 April 1942. She was revamped and modernized, her old superstructure stripped off and an entirely new superstructure built, along with a greatly augmented AA battery and changes to correct the ship's poor internal watertight integrity.

Nevada could have been repaired and returned to service in only a few months, albeit without many of the modernizations. The modernization took longer because her return to service was given a low priority, as the shipyard was directed to concentrate on new construction, battle damage repair, and modernizations for cruisers and destroyers. Plus, the battleships were not expected to be needed for some time. American pre-war planning had always expected the decisive battleline engagements to occur near the Philippines or the island chains close to Japan. This was not anticipated to happen in 1942. Forward deployment of battleships would also require a robust logistics chain, again something that would not be established in 1942. So, repairs to *Nevada* could wait.

Nevada was back to sea in December 1942, one year after the attack.

Was the decision to attack *Nevada* with dive-bombers a good decision? A superficial analysis, based on the result – one sunken battleship – would intimate that it was. *Nevada* would not have sunk if she had not been hit by those five GP bombs, which caused the fire, which caused the magazines to be flooded, which caused the ship to settle and flood the second deck and the Bull Ring, which caused the progressive flooding which sank the ship.

However, the Japanese had no way of knowing that such a progression was possible. There was no way they could incorporate those factors in their decision process. The dive bombers' attack, under any reasonable military criteria, ought to have been inadequate to sink the ship, by criteria used by both the Japanese and the Americans. The fact that the bomb hits triggered a chain of event that inflicted damage far out of proportion to any reasonable expectation was a result of factors that the Japanese could not reasonably predict.

Consider a man who wanted to start a farm, and so he decided to buy a piece of desert land. He should have known that he could not grow crops on parched land. Was it a good decision? Then, while plowing the ground to plant his first crop he strikes gold. The unexpected event does not make the original decision to start a farm in the desert a good decision.

The dive bomber's success against *Nevada*, however unexpected, was the second wave dive bombers' shining moment. It achieved success by a remarkable string of unlikely occurrences. Lefty Gomez once said, "I'd rather be lucky than good," a sentiment in this case seconded by the Japanese dive bomber pilots.

Similarly, the other dive bomber attacks against other battleships were also bad decisions. Absent the factors that made the attack on the *Nevada* successful, those other attacks achieved what would be expected, that is, they achieved almost nothing, little more than nuisance damage to the heavily-armored ships. Superstructure damage such as was inflicted upon *Nevada* made for spectacular photographs, but essentially could be repaired with new sheet-metal and replacement electrical wiring. It was damage that could not be expected to put a ship out of the war for any significant period, and did little to contribute to the objective of the attack.

In *Nevada*'s case, there was effectively no chance that the ship could have been sunk in the channel and zero chance that the ship could have been sunk by five or even fourteen 250kg GP bombs. It was the design flaws, poor material condition and damage control errors that sank *Nevada*, not the Japanese dive bombers. The proper decision would have been to put those five hits on two cruisers which, with only a smidgeon of good fortune, would have put two cruisers on the bottom of the harbor.

Cruiser Targets

Cruisers were vulnerable to GP bombs. During World War II, nine Allied cruisers were sunk by GP bombs. A single bomb hit on a cruiser would, on average, require six to seven weeks of shipyard repair; one 500kg (1,102-pound) bomb hit on the British cruiser *Suffolk* forced the ship to be beached, and she was out of action for eight months.

There was a very lucrative grouping of cruiser targets available. In the Navy Yard, *New Orleans, San Francisco, St. Louis*, and *Honolulu*, all modern, powerful 10,000-ton cruisers, were crammed into a very restricted space. Bombs dropped into the Navy Yard piers area could hardly miss hitting something of value—a ship, a pier, quays, tugs or yard craft, floating cranes, or the industrial facilities. In the face of this crowding, the number of 250kg bombs that splashed in the water causing no damage was remarkable.

Hits on ships in the yard could be particularly devastating. When undergoing what is known as "shipyard availability," material condition Zed cannot be set. Electrical power cables, welding leads, and high and low pressure air hoses are strung through watertight hatches from their sources on the pier down into the depths of the ship, making it impossible to close hatches to contain either flooding or fire. One cruiser had a large access port cut into her side to remove machinery. Portions of a ship's fire-main system might be isolated and drained for valve maintenance. Lots of flammable materials—oils, grease, oil-based paints, wooden staging— would be scattered throughout the ship, a damage control nightmare.

A bomb hit on a ship in this condition could cause fires and flooding that could not be isolated, and could potentially spread progressively throughout the ship. A bomb hit could be expected to cause much more damage than under normal combat conditions. This should have been recognized by the Japanese before the attack. These were lucrative targets in a very vulnerable condition.

The *Chronology* estimated that 30 dive-bombers attacked the Navy Yard area (including those that attacked *Pennsylvania*). These attacks were inaccurate. Only two hits were achieved, one each on *Honolulu* and *Pennsylvania*. Most made thundering splashes that almost swamped yard craft. One bomb did shatter a ship's boat, wounding three men with bomb fragments.

The dive-bomber pilots were instructed to dive into the wind, in order to better maintain their dive angle and so the wind would not push their bomb off line. To make this approach, they had to pass close to the cloud of smoke billowing out of Battleship Row up to an altitude of 8,000 feet, a column of turbulence that without doubt disturbed their attempts to get lined up on their targets during the critical initial part of their dive. Some of the pilots ignored this instruction, as American observers noted dive-bombers coming in from both the west and the east.

The story could have had a happier outcome for the Japanese had they followed their target prioritization scheme and hit the cruisers in the Navy Yard with more bombers more accurately. In the first year of the war, with many of the battleships knocked out and with insufficient tankers to keep the remainder in fuel in forward areas, cruisers became the "heavy units" of the surface war in the Pacific, and were constantly in demand and short in supply. By employing dive-bombers against battleships, more of these critical cruisers survived. The bombers diverted by Egusa to the more spectacular, but less logical and less appropriate battleship target, could have had a greater impact on the war than they did.

Striking *Nevada* was an emotional, Japanese-logic decision that backfired. It provided the most memorable inspirational event that cheered the defenders on, rather than another nail in their intended coffin of despair.

Blocking the Channel by Other Means

Had the planners really wanted to sink a ship in the channel, there was *Neosho*, one of the largest tankers in the world. *Neosho* pulled out of her mooring at the Ford Island Fuel Pier just after *Nevada* passed by. She was 50% to 75% full of volatile aviation fuel. She would have been easier to put on the bottom than *Nevada,* but even then it would have been no easy thing, with her large tanks holding a cargo that was lighter than water. At the Battle of the Coral Sea, *Neosho* was hit by seven bombs and one suicide aircraft and at one point was abandoned due to fires, yet remained afloat for four days.

Photographs show *Neosho* in the channel and lining up to enter the Southeast Loch past the Navy Yard as the dive-bomber attacks began. If the Japanese wanted to sink a ship in the channel, *Neosho* was the better choice. But, even against her, more than 14 bombers would be needed.

Two dive bomber pilots made an attempt. *Neosho's* AR reported that "several bombs fell close to the stern jarring the ship appreciably." Otherwise, *Neosho's* crew was more than pleased to be ignored.

The most appropriate method to block the channel would have been with mines. Considering that cruisers *Phoenix* and *St. Louis* and several destroyers sortied in spite of reports that there were mines in the channel, the chances were high that a well placed mine would score before any minesweeping effort could be organized. However, aerial mining was not in the Japanese mindset. The Japanese considered mines to be defensive weapons. They did not have an effective air-delivered mine until the Type 3 was developed in 1943.

Overall, the Japanese second-wave dive-bombers expended 18 weapons (14 against *Nevada*, and two against *Dale* while she was steaming out of the harbor in the channel, and two against *Neosho*), nearly 1/4th of their available bombs, in attempts to block the channel. Five additional weapons were expended against the destroyers *Dale* and *Helm* when they were beyond the channel and outside the entrance buoy—evidently five of the dive-bomber pilots found the AA fire in the harbor too hot for their taste. Twenty-one of the available 78 weapons were wasted on inappropriate targets.

Dive-Bomber Targeting

Gauged against the objectives of the attack, none of the dive-bombers' attacks directed against battleships accomplished anything significant. They put a hit and a near miss on *Pennsylvania* in drydock, which did not affect the ship's long-term combat readiness, and put five hits on a battleship that was already out of the war for at least six months due to a torpedo hit. They seriously damaged three destroyers (two probably by accident, with bombs likely aimed at battleships). Other dive-bombers hit a seaplane tender (misidentified as a cruiser) that required four days in the shipyard at San Diego to mend.

Many of the dive-bombers misidentified destroyer tenders as cruisers. The Imperial Navy did not employ destroyer tenders as did the Americans. Instead, they assigned their 5,200-ton light cruisers (such as their *Kuma* and *Nagara*-class ships) to serve as flotilla leaders, and Japanese destroyers normally nested with them. Attacking a nest of destroyers, the aviators reported what their experience told them was a cruiser nested with destroyers.

A few dive-bombers that somehow found themselves miles south of the objective attacked the destroyer *Helm* south of the entrance channel buoy. Two near misses flooded her forward peak tank and put severe cracks into the fire control tube supporting the massive Mk 37 main director. A few weeks later a marine railway hauled *Helm* out of the water. Temporary repairs were made to the bow, and the fire control tube was re-welded. Permanent repairs were performed seven months later in drydock at Sydney, Australia.[41]

Ineffective attacks were scattered about. In all, five dive-bombers went after destroyers that were underway departing the harbor (misidentified as cruisers), two went against a destroyer outside the harbor (misidentified as a cruiser), several bombers went after tenders on the west side of Ford Island, and one attacked an ammunition ship pierside in the West Loch. There was even a report of bombs dropped on the armed Dutch liner *Jagersfontein* off Honolulu, an attack that the Dutch reportedly resisted with spirited AA fire.[42]

The full distribution of attacks will be analyzed in the next chapter, but it is enough to observe that about one third of the dive-bombers attacked targets at the bottom of the priority list when higher priority targets were undamaged.

One bomb did wonders for some American sailors' morale. It blasted open a mobile Gedunk Wagon[43] on 1010 Dock. Men from the *Helena* and everywhere within shouting distance raced to gather pies, ice cream and candy bars, their fast reaction ensuring that the Japanese could not claim credit for the destruction of vital supplies.

250kg Bomb Malfunctions

Many of the 250kg GP bombs malfunctioned. Some, such as a bomb that landed off *Pennsylvania*'s bow, caused so little damage that they might have been low-order detonations. Two which landed ahead and behind *Rigel* at the Navy Yard piers were duds. Another four duds were reported by *Avocet* south of Ford Island as she observed the attacks on *Nevada*. *Cachalot* reported a dud bomb that landed 20 feet off her starboard quarter, possibly one directed at *Neosho* during her transit to Merry Point.

Of eleven GP bombs that hit Ford Island, two were duds and one a low-order detonation which scattered a "yellow sulfuric powder" that caused skin burns.[44] These eleven bombs exhibited a 27% malfunction rate.

Some of the reported duds that landed in the water could have been splashes caused by AA shells. The reports listed above correlate to dive-bombing attacks and were likely accurately identified as bombs. It is also likely that there were other duds or low-order detonations that went unrecorded.

The 0.2 second delay fuze, appropriate for finishing off carriers, was less effective against smaller ships. Many bombs that missed buried themselves in the bottom of the harbor before exploding, delivering up only a torrent of mud. Bombs passed entirely through *Nevada* and *California* to explode in the water. Yet, many bombs also exploded on the surface inflicting fragmentation damage, indicating that the fuze delay function was inconsistent.

Bombs reported as "incendiaries" were weapons with quality control problems. Poor detonation could occur if the explosive filler was loaded haphazardly with air gaps and irregularities, so that some of the explosive underwent a prolonged low-order partial detonation or deflagration that would spread dramatically colored burning fragments. This could give the red signature mentioned in the reports.[45]

The 250kg GP bombs with their long delay fuzes were also inefficient against ground targets. One of these weapons hit in the Ford Island dispensary courtyard. The resulting crater was about 10 feet deep with a diameter of 25 feet. The bomb did little beyond that. All the force of the explosion was spent in digging the crater and blasting the debris almost straight up: the walls of the dispensary, some directly adjacent to the crater, were hardly damaged, with only a few scratches and score marks; some windows at the lip of the crater retained some of their glass.

As in the case of the 800kg AP bombs, the 250kg GP bombs were deficient. The Japanese aviators were let down by their ordnance establishment, twice over.

Dive-Bombers' Attack: Summary

Overall, the dive-bombers' most significant contributions towards achieving the objective of the attack were a hit on the cruiser *Raleigh* and a DNM on *Honolulu*. The bomb hit on *Raleigh*, along with a torpedo hit amidships, almost capsized the ship. After drydocking she was seaworthy enough to escort a convoy to the West Coast in February 1942. The hits kept her out of the war for eight months. The DNM on *Honolulu* dished in her hull about five or six feet over a 40-foot length, causing flooding. She was put to rights before the end of December and was out of the war less than a month.

By a combination of bad decisions, bad bombing, and bad ordnance, *the 78 dive bombers in the second wave made **no substantive contributions*** to the attack.

Assessment: Fighter and OCA Performance
Fighter Doctrine

The Japanese considered fighters to be an offensive strike asset. They were to engage enemy fighters in the air or strafe aircraft on the ground. They were not given formal responsibility for the safety of the bombers. This was a philosophical orientation that both limited the fighters' accomplishments and made their OCA (offensive counter-air) effort a huge success.

The planners did not assign fighters as top cover. When the approach to the target was made the entire fighter force shifted to the attack, going after either aircraft in the air or aircraft on the ground. They were not responsible for the safety of the bombers with which they flew. Most became "target fixated" in their ground attacks and lost situational awareness, so much so that several US fighters were ignored until they started shooting down bombers.

With only 45 fighters in the first wave and 36 in the second wave over a 600-square-mile island, it ought to have been expected that some enemy aircraft could get aloft even if complete surprise was achieved. Second Lieutenants Welsh and Taylor took off from Haleiwa Airfield and were vectored to intercept aircraft strafing Ewa Airfield. They hooked on to the tail of a long line of aircraft and scored two confirmed kills apiece.[46] Other US fighters reported a similar situation. Most of the US kills were against Japanese planes that did not see them.

This is not unexpected: after the Vietnam War, several US Air Force studies (most notably, the *Red Baron* study) found that 80% of the pilots killed did not know they were being targeted until their attacker opened fire. This is just what happened over Pearl Harbor, and exactly what top cover aircraft were supposed to prevent.

Japanese fighters were never particularly effective as escorts. During the war in China:

> . . . one of the real problems of fighter tactics was the tradition of personal combat that went back to Japan's middle ages. In aerial warfare, this tradition was manifested in the Japanese penchant for dogfighting. It was difficult for Japanese navy pilots to forgo the opportunity for personal glory in the individual dogfight for the sake of the teamwork demanded by formation flying. . . . There were other reasons for the failure of Japanese close fighter support for bomber formations, of course. One was the lack of oxygen equipment in the A5M fighters. Even more critical was the absence of adequate aircraft-to-aircraft communication.[47]

The war in China forced Japanese naval fighter pilots to reconsider their role in escorting bombers, as unescorted bombers were taking horrendous losses. Any resulting change in mindset was lost after the Japanese naval participation in long-range bombing missions was withdrawn. Formation flying and group tactics came to be ignored, and naval fighter pilots "reverted to their predilection for the individual heroics of dog-fighting."[48]

The Japanese Operations Order assigned specific groups of fighters to attack specific airfields, but not to provide persistent top cover. Even then, the fighters often ignored their geographic assignments. Many Japanese fighters, after hitting the obvious targets at their assigned location, flew off looking to expend the rest of their ammunition in more exotic locales. Not being held down by top cover, a few US fighters did manage to get into the fight. US Naval War College figures estimated that fighters attacking bombers would shoot down four bombers for every ten fighter sorties. At Pearl Harbor, the US fighters shot down eight to 11 aircraft in 14 sorties, or 1.5 to 2 times the predicted rate.

The lack of provision for top cover was a by-product of the Japanese single-minded concentration on offensive action at all costs. At one time in the mid-1930's, the Japanese seriously considered giving over carrier flight decks entirely to bombers. "When Lt. Comdr. Shibata Takeo, a leading fighter pilot, tried to point out to a Navy General Staff officer the importance of fighters in defending the fleet, the latter shot back a stinging rebuke against defensive tactics: 'And you claim to be a Japanese!'"[49]

Attackers tend to become fixated on their target, excluding from their attention peripheral vision, sounds, or other considerations. Defending bombers requires wide area situational awareness, with the pilots' "head on a swivel" instead of watching the fireworks. It takes a great deal of discipline to stay with the bombers and not hare off chasing individual glory. Unless fighters are specifically designated to stay and defend the bombers, aggressive fighter pilots will go roving, leaving behind gaps for enemy fighters to exploit.

Comparative Attrition

It could be argued that the loss of 8 to 11 bombers was small compared to the damage that the strafing fighters caused. However, it is not known what the Japanese expected from their strafing fighters. A thumb rule used by analysts is to expect between 2.5 to 5 aircraft destroyed on the ground for every 10 fighters employed in airfield strafing missions. With 45 fighters assigned to strafing in the first wave, this would give an expectation of 11 to 23 aircraft destroyed. Combined with the expectations from the dive-bombing attacks, this would give a Japanese expectation of destroying 47 to 77 aircraft on the ground in a surprise attack. This calculation is on the same order of magnitude as the results in one of the Japanese wargames, where they expected 80 aircraft to be destroyed on the ground (albeit with a smaller number of carriers in the attack).

The performance of the fighters in their strafing mission is hard to evaluate. American aircraft were destroyed on the ground by D3A Val dive-bombers, and some Vals also strafed the airfields. It is impossible to determine how many US aircraft were destroyed by bombs, how many by strafing, and how many by being caught in gasoline fires while crowded together in their "anti-sabotage" parking arrangement. Instead of strafing individual aircraft the Americans' parking scheme transformed difficult "point" targets to easier "area" targets. Planes were so crowded together that nearly every machine gun bullet and ricochet caused damage.

In areas where the aircraft were not parked wingtip-to-wingtip the fighters performed less well. For example, the fighters that attacked Kaneohe likely put in only an average performance. Movie film taken by a second wave B5N Kate level bomber shows seven seaplanes parked near the hangars, only two of which appear to have been damaged by the first wave fighters.[50] After the second wave bombers departed, of the 33 PBY's on the ground and floating offshore, 27 were destroyed and six damaged.[51]

Prior to the actual attack, the Army Air Corps had 143 operational aircraft on Oahu, with an additional 88 under repair, a total of 231 aircraft. After the attack there were 87 operational USAAF aircraft, 79 repairable or under repair, and 65 destroyed, for a net loss of 56 operational aircraft and 9 aircraft under repair, a net change in status of 65 aircraft. Of the 301 US Navy aircraft, before the attack 202 were operational, 52 in storage, 31 in overhaul, and 16 under repair. Of these aircraft, 80 were destroyed and 169 damaged, a net change in status of 249 aircraft. This totaled 314 aircraft hit by 189 aircraft allocated to OCA, or a return of 1.66 aircraft destroyed per aircraft committed, three to six times higher than the historical rate of .25 to .50 aircraft per sortie. The primary factors were the lack of air opposition and the fact that the American aircraft were not dispersed and not in revetments.

The consequences of General Short's decision to declare a holiday and park his aircraft wingtip to wingtip can be quantified: it cost between 215 and 252 aircraft damaged and destroyed over and above what would normally be expected to fall victim to that level of effort.

As to the employment of the fighters: with target aircraft parked wingtip-to-wingtip, the rate of kill for the strafing fighters would likely be on the order of 1 to 2 kills per sortie, with the A6M Zero's small ammunition supply the dominant constraint. This would give 43 to 86 destroyed or damaged aircraft due to the efforts of the strafing A6M Zeros in the first wave. Assuming that the 43 fighters would have been able to stop the 14 Army fighter sorties from shooting down any bombers, this means that 43 to 86 ground kills were achieved at a cost of 8 to 11 Japanese aircraft shot down, a loss ratio of between 4 and 8 to 1.

As it was, the Japanese estimate of damage was inflated. They estimated that approximately 500 American planes were "wiped out."[52]

Was it worth it? On a macro scale, during 1943 the United States produced 85,433 planes compared to 16,693 by the Japanese, a ratio of 5.1 to 1. If you consider that at least two-thirds of American aircraft were earmarked for the European war, then the production ratio would be 1.7 to 1. Thus, the 4 or 8 to 1 loss ratio could be considered an excellent return for the Japanese.

However, the importance of destroying American aircraft had to be balanced by the potential losses of Japanese pilots and aircrew. At the beginning of the war, the Japanese Navy had about 3,500 pilots, with about 600 assigned to the carrier groups and the majority of the remaining assigned to land-based squadrons. In 1943, the US trained 89,714 pilots compared to 5,400 Japanese pilots, a 16.6 to 1 ratio.[53] Japan's core of trained air crew at the beginning of the war represented Japan's best chance for victory. Losing 8–11 aircrew that could have been prevented by better discipline by the fighters would not contribute favorably to the 16.6:1 ratio they would need in pilot losses just to break even, particularly considering that destruction of an American aircraft on the ground did not imply loss of its aircrew. The Japanese could not afford to trade their aviators for unmanned American aircraft. Japan's initial cadre was precious—the decimation of these trained aviators during 1942 and 1943 was one of the primary reasons why Japan lost the war.

Doctrinal Shortfalls

The Japanese eventually recognized the need for top cover. *Lessons* recorded:

> It is quite necessary to retain elements of the forces as guards in the air even if there is no enemy interceptor in the air, while ground strafing. Fighters which, after strafing Bellows Field, were about to strike Kaneohe airfield, circling at an altitude of 2,000 meters, were surprised by nine enemy interceptors. This was attributed to the lack of attention to the air. In any case, close attention to the air is unavoidable.[54]

Missing also was coordination of the efforts of the bombers and the fighters. The plan did not provide for what is identified today as SEAD, or Suppression of Enemy Air Defenses. SEAD is generally provided when the level of enemy air defenses could potentially interfere with the bombers' delivery of their payloads, or even to shoot down the attacking bombers. SEAD was a recognized mission for fighters at sea in 1941, although it was not called by that name. It consisted of either strafing air defense positions or bombing them. Fighters were provided with hard points to carry a number of light bombs for this purpose. The AA positions to be suppressed could be ashore, on the decks of the target ship(s), or their escorts.

Employment of this kind of SEAD in support of torpedo attacks was known and practiced by the Japanese. In such a coordinated attack, fighters would strafe the decks of target ships, killing the crews of light AA guns or forcing their crews to take cover and otherwise drawing AA fire away from the torpedo bombers. This form of support was suggested from previous experience against the Chinese since the inception of the Sino-Japanese War in 1937,[55] and against the Russians during the Nomonhan incident in 1939.

Fighter Performance

Overall, there were elements of the Japanese fighters' actions that were questionable. They attacked private planes on recreational trips, shooting down two. They strafed civilian automobiles as far as three miles from the bases[56] on the roads outside Wheeler and Pearl Harbor. Pictures of machine-gunned private automobiles appeared in the Honolulu newspapers, triggering outrage in the population. At Wahiawa, a small town next to Wheeler and Schofield Barracks, aircraft strafed the residential area. A plane flying up the road from Pearl Harbor gunned down an old Chinese hired man.[57] A telephone lineman along a civilian road was chased off his pole by machine gun bullets. Chartered fishing boats were strafed outside the harbor. A non-commissioned officers' housing area was strafed.[58] For some reason the fighters put concentrations of fire into private cars in an outlying parking lot at Ewa Field. All that ammunition could have been better employed against targets more relevant to the objectives of the attack.[59]

Their aggressiveness was not matched with good judgment. A single aircraft at 0830 strafed Bellows Field, which was not scheduled for attention until the second wave. "That lone strafer did Bellows a favor, for the warning gave . . . about an hour's grace to disperse the planes."[60]

A similar lack of discipline was noted later in the war.

Observers on the ground testified to the fighters' aggressiveness. One fighter strafed so low that its propeller struck sparks off the runway, another scraped its belly tank—aggressive strafing runs, or alternately, inexperienced pilots, target fixation, and a too-low pullout.

The lack of forethought in planning, integrated training and rehearsal was evident. *Lessons* assessed that:

> At Wheeler and Barbers Point airfields, ground strafings were made from the beginning without any control, so that flames and smoke arose elsewhere prevented continued attacks on un-damaged planes. When many planes attempted to make simul-taneous strafing attacks from other directions through poor visibility, there was much danger of colliding with each other. Therefore, a plan should be made to control strafing attacks in such cases.

Probably their most portentous event was the failure to shoot down 13 B-17s that appeared over the island after a trans-oceanic flight from California. These aircraft were important targets, especially considering that they had the range and speed to be an immediate threat to the Japanese carriers. The bombers were flying without ammunition and with their defensive armament in cosmoline, so there was no opposing fire. Yet, none of the B-17s were shot down. They all made safe landings at various places throughout the islands, one on a golf course. Only one was destroyed, burned in half on a runway when Japanese bullets ignited flares stored in the aircraft. The B-17 was a tough plane, as the Japanese would learn again in the Philippines. The fact that these huge bombers escaped has to be scored as a black mark against the fighters.

Some of the A6M Zero pilots displayed poor skills. An American noted that one Japanese strafer

> ... pulled awful hard on the stick, not as any regular pilot would do, and I might say he was an awful poor pilot, because the way he was following in on his gunnery line, why, he tried to fire—to follow me straight in, and to correct fire, why, he gave it too much rudder from one side and then too much rudder on the other side, and he completely missed his target.[61]

Overall, the fighters that took advantage of the concentration of closely parked aircraft did their job effectively. Theirs was the best performance of the raid, delivered by the aviators that the Japanese believed to be the least skilled.

One shadow of the future can be illustrated by the actions of one fighter pilot, although it applies to all Japanese aviators. A rescue submarine was stationed off a small island to the west of Oahu to provide a haven for damaged aircraft. An A6M Zero fighter sustained damage while strafing and was leaking fuel. It would not be able to return to the carrier. Rather than heading to the rescue submarine, the pilot chose to intentionally crash himself and his aircraft into the enemy, ending his service as an Imperial Japanese Navy fighter pilot rather than attempting to go for the rescue submarine. There were other cases where damaged aircraft might have taken similar action—two dive-bombers crashed into tenders, and at least one other dove into a hangar.

This was very much in line with Japanese fighting spirit and their ethos of self-sacrifice. However, in the long run, the losses of trained aircrew in these incidents and in the hundreds of more to come would be one of the most significant factors in Japan's defeat.

The greatest aspect of the fighters' performance that has been unrecognized over the years is their failure to execute their primary mission. They did not sweep the sky of American fighters and maintain air superiority for the duration of the attack. Where American fighters could get aloft they scored over a four to one kill ratio, and suffered only 14% attrition in an environment where they were outnumbered by about four to one by the higher-performance Japanese fighters.

In China the A6M Zero dominated the skies and destroyed the Chinese Air Force. Over Pearl Harbor, the few American fighters that got aloft more than held their own.

Assessment: Command and Control

Japanese command and control during the attack was nearly nonexistent and totally unsatisfactory.

First there was the fumble with the flares.

Then the commanders lost control of the torpedo attack. Torpedo bombers went crisscrossing hither and yon, runs were aborted, torpedoes wasted on unsuitable targets, planes nearly collided, and ordnance was poorly distributed over the targets.

The second wave dive-bombers command and control was also poor. First, they had their instructions changed at the last minute while they were on the carriers' decks, something inexcusable for an attack following ten months of planning. Their weapons could not achieve the desired effects on their new targets. The last-minute change was triggered by a reconnaissance report that there were no carriers in the harbor. This contingency ought to have been anticipated, and planned for accordingly. This was the first of a series of command gaffes that contributed to making the dive-bombers' attack ineffective.

Over the targets the dive-bombers' leadership made a number of questionable decisions. They tried to sink *Nevada* in the channel with unsuitable weapons and an inadequate level of effort. Attacks were delivered against destroyers in the channel misidentified as cruisers. Attacks were wasted on tenders misidentified as battleships. Attacks were wasted on destroyers outside the harbor, and an auxiliary several miles from Battleship Row.

As for the commanders of the fighters, there was no evidence of positive control at greater than the *shotai* level. Rather, it looked like a bunch of teenage samurais on a bust-'em-up spree. Pilots went swanning off independently looking for what they could find, wasting ammunition and fuel on many inappropriate targets. After carting ammunition 3,000 miles from Japan to Pearl Harbor, it is easy to imagine admirals grinding their teeth to have it wasted on pot shots at telephone linemen and pleasure aircraft and yachts. Had it not been for the fact that the aircraft on the airfields were lined up like clay pigeons on a firing range, in bunches hard for even the most inept pilot to miss, the results of the fighters' efforts could have been greatly reduced. The fighters showed little discipline and their commanders little inclination to enforce any.

Much of this absence of control stemmed from Japanese doctrine. The commander of the strike was really not expected to exert control once the battle was joined. The strike commander, Fuchida, was in a level bomber at 10,000 feet trying to deliver his own attack at the same time the torpedo bombers were trying to complete theirs. Fuchida's attack was one of the last; he dropped after the torpedo bombers had all completed their runs. The strike commander was not in a position to sort out the confused torpedo attack.

Neither was he in a position to observe and count the torpedo hits, a critical bit of information needed if he were to be able to direct the second-wave bombers to the most effective distribution of their attacks, since underwater damage might not be observable from 10,000 feet an hour after the torpedoes hit. Instead, Fuchida passively looked on as the dive-bombers wasted most of their bombs.

The Japanese command and control failed. The commanders had little control and did little to contribute to the success of the attack beyond the ordnance that they personally delivered. Some of their decisions reduced the effectiveness of the attack.

Target Vulnerability

The Japanese had the advantage of delivering the first attack in the Pacific War. They were inflicting damage on a fleet still largely in a peacetime configuration. During peacetime, habitability and maintenance and "spit and polish" take precedence over combat considerations. Ships had layers of flammable oil-based paint on their bulkheads, sometimes an inch thick. Attractive linoleum was on the decks, which burned and released toxic gasses. Flammable materials were everywhere, paint, oils, fuel for the ships' boats. The living spaces had everything from wooden furniture to pianos. Stuffing tubes for wire and pipe runs had their sealant material dried and cracked, so boundaries thought to be watertight were not. Gaskets around relatively inaccessible closures, such as those in ventilation ducts, leaked copiously, contributing to problems with progressive flooding.

Many of the ships in the fleet had yet to recover from a decade of depression-era underfunded maintenance and repair. For ships constantly hogging and sagging and working in the seas, the stresses caused metal embrittlement, loose rivets, watertight doors with dried and cracked gaskets that would not seal and were warped beyond a tight fit, decks that leaked and machinery foundations brittle and vulnerable to shock damage.

Vestal was hit by an AP bomb that passed through her stern and exploded beneath the ship. The flooding forced her commanding officer to put her aground.

> The lesson to be learned from *Vestal's* experience is that watertight integrity cannot be counted on in the case of older vessels. This ship was about thirty-three years old at the time, and it was found that flooding was progressive through the bulkhead and deck boundaries which supposedly were watertight.[62]

At Pearl Harbor, the entire battle line consisted of "older vessels"— the oldest was 27 years old and the youngest 20, in an age when the Washington Naval Treaty specified that a battleship's life was 20 years with replacement construction beginning after the ship's 17th year.[63] Little money was allocated to maintain the older battleships in anticipation of their retirement, and some ships had seriously deteriorated. Even the youngest of the Treaty battleships, better maintained, had their problems. Ensign Victor Delano in *West Virginia*'s Central Station related how he saw water that "spouted through the cracks around the edges [of a watertight door] and shooting like a hose through an air-test opening." This was a telling statement on the ship's material condition, considering that Central Station was the ship's damage control center, responsible for maintaining the ship's watertight integrity.

After the attack, US ships would be stripped of linoleum, bulkheads chipped to bare metal to remove flammable paint, wooden furniture was offloaded, paints, oils, and fuels better stored and better controlled, watertight integrity corrected and verified, and other measures taken— damage control quickly took precedence over habitability, comfort, or convenience. The susceptibility of ships to bombs and torpedoes would be greatly reduced as the war progressed.

Assessment: The Japanese Fleet Submarine Effort

Twenty three large fleet submarines were sent to Hawaiian waters. On 7 December they were deployed in three layers around the harbor, at choke points, and along expected shipping lines of approach.

Five were "special attack force" submarines carrying midget submarines. They departed the area on 12 December 1941, leaving 18 submarines to blockade the islands.

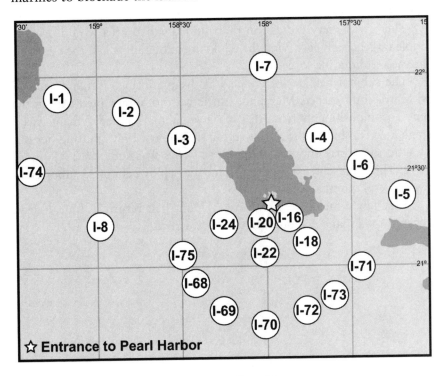

(14) Submarine Patrol Areas

Yamamoto expected the air attack to flush the fleet out of the harbor. Damaged ships would be sent to the mainland for repairs. Those ships underway at the time of the attack would need to return to Pearl Harbor for fuel. The submarines were to sink these ships. At one time Yamamoto mentioned that he expected better results from the submarines than from the aerial assault.

In fact, both US carriers were out on missions, and there were a large number of cruisers, destroyers, and minesweepers in the exercise areas—44 Pacific Fleet combatants were out of the harbor at the time of the attack.

Merchant shipping was also a target. The Hawaiian Islands themselves were not self-sufficient: in 1941 imports required approximately 25 shiploads per month to bring in food and manufactured goods and take away export products (mostly sugar and pineapple).[64] This traffic was also to be sunk.

There was every indication that the Hawaiian area would provide ample targets, fully justifying the deployment of almost half the available Japanese submarine force.

The submarines' performance was disappointing. Warships moved with little interference. Merchant traffic was not interrupted. About the only accomplishments from this massive submarine deployment was a single torpedo hit on the Saratoga on 11 January 1942, putting her out of action for three months. The oiler Neches was sunk on 23 January 1942. This represented a slim return for the deployment of 23 submarines over several months.

Very few attacks were executed. Upon their return, Admiral Ueda accused the Japanese submariners of cowardice.[65]

CHAPTER EIGHT

BATTLE DAMAGE ASSESSMENT

The initial damage assessment was reported to Admiral Nagumo by Commander Fuchida. He had lingered over the harbor until after the departure of the second wave to evaluate the results. He returned to *Akagi* and made a quick round of the other aviators, comparing observations prior to going to the flag bridge. His initial estimate was two battleships sunk, four battleships with severe damage, and four cruisers greatly damaged.

A Japanese submarine reported a tremendous explosion in the harbor after dark. Later the Naval General Staff received a report through diplomatic channels that a battleship had been sunk by midget submarines after the air attack, a report that was accepted happily and uncritically.

After Fuchida's initial report, the aircrews were individually debriefed, recording their assessments as to what they attacked and their results. Admiral Kusaka, "a man of the highest integrity who would scorn to embroider,"[1] relates how "on each carrier a minute examination was conducted against the claimed result of the attacks, gathering the returned fliers. Its results were successively sent to the *Akagi*."[2]

On *Akagi*,

Fuchida instructed all officers to develop their attack photographs at once for study in preparing a final assessment of damage inflicted. Courier planes from the other five carriers landed aboard *Akagi*, bringing data and photographic film from the attack units. By late afternoon he had all the prints. The flight leaders studied them most of the night, and the next morning Fuchida turned in his battle report.[3]

On 17 December, while still at sea, Nagumo transmitted a preliminary Action Report. Torpedo hits were estimated at "over 35 out of 40."[4] The report estimated four battleships, two heavy cruisers, and one tanker sunk; "one type uncertain (sunk by torpedoes)";[5] two battleships, two light cruisers, and two destroyers with "heavy damage;" and two battleships and four light cruisers with "small damage."[6] The biggest change over Fuchida's initial verbal report was that the number of battleships sunk was doubled.

Eight cruisers were claimed hit. Two were reported sunk by a combination of torpedoes and 250kg GP bombs; the other six were assessed as damaged by a total of nine 250kg GP bomb hits.

A total of 26 250kg bomb hits are mentioned specifically, along with "several" 250kg hits against a *Maryland*-class battleship.

The report would go straight to the top:

> Most signal honor of all, the Pearl Harbor raiders learned that the Emperor wished to hear the account of the operation directly from those who had led the attack. ... Fuchida and Shimazaki [the leader of the second wave] worked together on their reports. Fuchida would relate to His Majesty the story of the strike on the United States ships; then Shimazaki would brief Hirohito about the attack on the air bases. Because Shimazaki was far handier with the controls of an aircraft than with brush and paper, Fuchida had to write both reports.[7]

Four days after returning to Japan, on 27 December Commander Fuchida briefed the Emperor. He used a top-secret map with beautiful brush-strokes and vivid colors, which showed in detail the position of the ships, the number of torpedoes hitting each ship, and the numbers of AP and GP bomb hits. The chart identified the ships by type or class, but not specifically by name. This will be referred to as the BDA Report.[8]

On the chart, damaged ships were classified either as "sunk" (symbolized as "X" on the chart); "serious" damage ("///"), meaning impossible or very difficult to repair; "moderate" damage (//), meaning possible to repair; and "minor" damage ("/"). Symbols identified the location of each torpedo, AP or GP bomb hit.

Destroyers *Dale* and *Helm* were misidentified as class "B" cruisers, repair ship *Vestal* was misidentified as an oiler, and tender *Dobbin* was misidentified as either an "A" or "B" class cruiser. The movements of *Nevada* and *Oglala* were shown, but the escape of *Neosho* was not. Otherwise, the depiction of the ships and their locations was remarkably accurate.

The left portion of the next table contains a summary of the information contained on Fuchida's BDA report. The right portion shows the actual damage inflicted taken from official reports and two published accounts of the salvage efforts.

Torpedo BDA

Fuchida's BDA briefing chart shows an arrow symbol representing "torpedoes." There are 36 torpedo symbols shown on the chart.

In *Lessons*, the Japanese stated that 40 torpedoes were launched, of which 39 ran and 36 hit for 90% hits.[9] The initial assessment made at sea claimed "over 35" hits. The torpedo hit percentage claimed was greater than the best hit percentage (82.5%) achieved during pre-attack training.

According to Kusaka, the battle reports from the individual carriers claimed 33 torpedo hits (*Akagi* 11, *Kaga* 8, *Soryu* and *Hiryu* combined for 14). How Fuchida and his assessment team arrived at 36 hits is unknown. 36 torpedoes were not launched—four aircraft were shot down before dropping, and one jettisoned its torpedo. Three hits were reported against cruisers, while Fuchida's report claimed five, all on *Helena*.

Chart 15 shows the hits claimed in the BDA report, shown in the dark circles v. the actual hits, shown in the light circles.

The BDA Report assessed 25 torpedo hits against four battleships. Of them, 21 (84%) were concentrated against only two, *Oklahoma* and *West Virginia*. The report honestly records the six torpedoes wasted against *Utah*, and the BDA chart identifies her by name. All six are assessed as hits. The torpedo that hit *Raleigh* was evidently unobserved.

JAPANESE BATTLE DAMAGE ASSESSMENT

Target	Torpedo	AP Bomb	GP Bomb	Damage
BATTLESHIPS:				
BB-36 Nevada (outboard)	1		8	Moderate
BB-37 Oklahoma (outboard)	12			Sunk
BB-44 California (outboard)	3		5	Moderate
BB-48 West Virginia (outboard)	9	3	1	Sunk
BB-38 Pennsylvania (DDock)			1	Minor
BB-39 Arizona (inboard)		4		Serious
BB-43 Tennessee (inboard)		3		Sunk
BB-46 Maryland (inboard)		2	12	Serious
AUXILIARIES:				
AO-23 Neosho			3	Sunk
AG-16 Utah	6			Sunk
IDed as CA or CL (Dale)			2	Moderate
AV-4 Curtiss				
IDed as Oiler (AR-4 Vestal)		1		Sunk
AR-4 Vestal				
CM-4 Oglala				Minor
IDed as Oiler (AR-11 Rigel)			3	Serious
IDed as CL (AD-3 Dobbin)			2	Moderate
AD-3 Dobbin				
CRUISERS:				
CL-7 Raleigh			1	Minor
CL-48 Honolulu			1	Minor
CL-50 Helena	5		6	Sunk
CA-32 New Orleans			1	Minor
DESTROYERS:				
DD-388 Helm				
DD-372 Cassin			1	Serious
DD-373 Shaw			1	Minor
DD-375 Downes			1	Serious
	36	13	49	
	90%	26%	63%	

ACTUAL DAMAGE INFLICTED

Target	Torpedo	AP Bomb	GP Bomb	DNM	Damage
BATTLESHIPS:					
BB-36 Nevada (outboard)	1		5		Beached
BB-37 Oklahoma (outboard)	5				Sunk
BB-44 California (outboard)	2		1	1 AP	Sunk
BB-48 West Virginia (outboard)	7	2			Sunk
BB-38 Pennsylvania (DDock)			1	1 GP	Minor
BB-39 Arizona (inboard)		2			Sunk
BB-43 Tennessee (inboard)		2			Minor
BB-46 Maryland (inboard)		2			Minor
AUXILIARIES:					
AO-23 Neosho					Undamaged
AG-16 Utah	2				Sunk
IDed as CA or CL (Dale)					
AV-4 Curtiss			1		Minor
IDed as Oiler (AR-4 Vestal)					
AR-4 Vestal		2			Beached
CM-4 Oglala					Sunk
IDed as Oiler (AR-11 Rigel)					Splinters
IDed as CL (AD-3 Dobbin)					
AD-3 Dobbin					Undamaged
CRUISERS:					
CL-7 Raleigh	1		1		Serious
CL-48 Honolulu				1 GP	Moderate
CL-50 Helena	1				Serious
CA-32 New Orleans					Splinters
DESTROYERS:					
DD-388 Helm				2 GP	
DD-372 Cassin			2		Scrapped
DD-373 Shaw			3		Serious
DD-375 Downes			1		Scrapped
	19	10	15		
	48%	**20%**	**19%**		

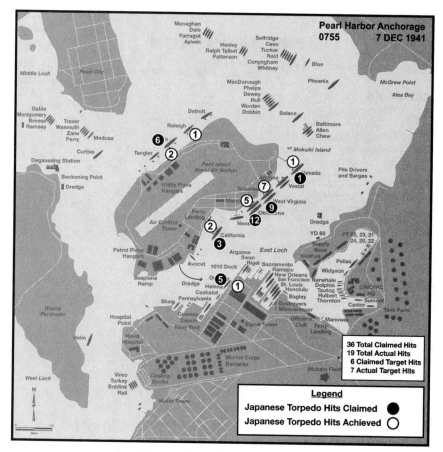

(15) Torpedo Hits: Claimed and Actual

The actual number of hits is uncertain. For *Oklahoma*, the whole side of the ship was nearly completely blown open, making it difficult to pinpoint individual detonations. Explosion effects overlapped. Some have asserted that additional torpedoes must have entered the ship through holes blasted by previous torpedoes. This did not occur. If a torpedo had penetrated into the ship though a hole blown by a previous torpedo, then the entire force of the explosion would have been contained inside the ship. The expanding gas bubble would have caused massive internal damage, to include lifting up the armored deck directly above the explosion, and warping belt armor plates out away from the ship instead of in an inward direction. No evidence of such damage was evident.

Witnesses reported nine torpedo hits on *West Virginia*. The salvage engineers reduced this to seven: four deep hits amidships, two that hit above the ship's belt armor as the ship listed, and a hit on the rudder.[10]

Allegations of a hit on *Arizona* are unsubstantiated. The Japanese did not claim any torpedo hits on *Arizona*.

The minimum number of hits shown in the chart, 19, is likely accurate.

The BDA Report indicates that torpedoes were directed at only six ships: four battleships, one cruiser, and *Utah*. Four battleships and four cruisers were located in positions vulnerable to torpedo attack. Torpedoes were directed at four of the eight (50%) susceptible priority targets. Five (63%) of the eight were hit, including *Raleigh* hit by a torpedo aimed at *Utah*. Attacking only half the accessible priority targets was not a good performance.

Fuchida overestimated the number of hits on *California* (three claimed, two actual), *Oklahoma* (12 claimed, five actual), *West Virginia* (nine claimed, seven actual), *Helena* (five claimed, one actual), and *Utah* (six claimed, two actual). But these errors did not result in an overestimation of the net damage in the final assessment. The differences in the BDA report and the actual results could be attributed to unanticipated vulnerability of the ships and some external events.

California would not have sunk except for many Zed closures that were still open. General Quarters and Material Condition Zed had not yet been fully set when she was hit. She had open and loose manhole covers to various voids, with six covers on her double bottom removed and 12 loosened.[11] In addition, burning oil swept down on her after *Arizona's* explosion, and she was temporarily abandoned, interrupting damage control efforts at a critical time.

Nevada sank from only one torpedo hit and five GP bomb hits due to poor material condition, design flaws, and a significant damage control blunder.

The BDA report overestimated the number of torpedo hits but underestimated the number of battleships sunk.

A significant error was the assessment of hits on *Helena*: five torpedo hits were claimed, which would have gutted any cruiser. *Helena* took only one torpedo hit in the forward engine room. Excellent damage control minimized the flooding. She was out of the war for six months under repair at California's Mare Island Naval Shipyard.

The report of 36 torpedo hits exceeded their pre-attack expectation of 27 hits (67%), and also their best score during training, 82.5%. The individual carriers claimed only 33 hits based on aircrew reports. It is difficult to imagine how a post-attack evaluation team justified increasing the claim—they mainly would be working off photographs, which might indicate that a ship was torpedoed, but not how many times, as the damage would be underwater, invisible to post-strike photographs. It might have reflected a simple decision to credit all the surviving torpedo bomber aircrews with hits, along with one to a crew that was shot down. In this way no stigma of failure would be attached to any of the surviving aircrews, a very Japanese behavior.

More significantly, this shows that the BDA team was willing to adjust the combat results away from what was reported by the aviators, and adjust it in a positive direction. Later in the war it was recognized that aviators' reports generally overestimated the results of their attacks, and on the Allied side it was usual for post-action assessments to discount claims by 50% or more. Here, the staff gave the aviators credit for more than they claimed.

The Japanese post-war official history claimed 23 torpedo hits on battleships, eight more than occurred. It assessed one hit on *Nevada* (one actual), two hits on *Arizona* (zero actual), two hits on *California* (two actual), and nine hits each on *West Virginia* and *Oklahoma* (seven and five hits, respectively).[12] With the combined 11 hits on *Utah* and *Helena*, the official history only reduced the total hits claimed by two.

AP Bombing BDA

The BDA report gave the horizontal bombers credit for 13 hits with 800kg AP bombs, or a hit rate of 26%. This is well above the eight hits expected. All of the hits were assessed against battleships but for one hit on a ship, identified as an oiler, in the location of the repair ship *Vestal*.

American ARs and post-battle damage inspections suggest ten confirmed AP bomb hits, eight against battleships and two against *Vestal*.

Arizona

Some sources assert that eight AP bombs hit *Arizona*. These claims draw from variety of sources, including crewmembers and officers of the *Vestal* and official Navy reports. Most of these hits supposedly landed amidships and forward, where the extensive damage from the magazine

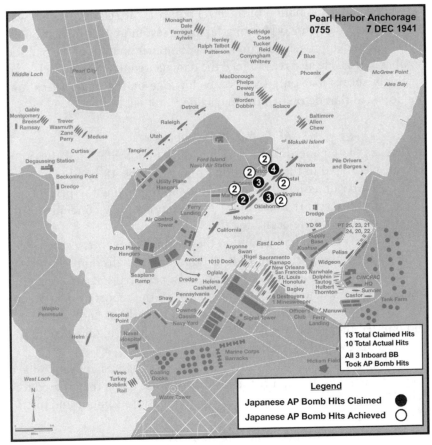

(16) AP Bomb Hits: Claimed and Actual

explosion and fire precluded confirmation.

Human testimony on the number of hits observed during a battle is notoriously inaccurate. Hits might be double counted, or secondary explosions counted as additional hits.

Either two or three formations dropped 10 or 15 bombs on *Arizona*. With the spread of the formations exceeding the dimensions of the target, multiple hits by the same formation on the same part of the target would have been nearly impossible.

The BDA report claimed four hits on *Arizona*, assessing "serious damage." The ship forward of her, *Tennessee*, was assessed as "sunk" from three AP bomb hits. Both ships were shown on fire.

A detailed examination of the level bombers' attack on *Arizona* was made by De Virgilio incorporating Japanese testimony, the formation dimensions, and approach direction into a computer analysis of the ballistic bomb patterns. He also reexamined the damage reports. His analysis convincingly shows that only two bombs hit, one on the quarterdeck and one forward that detonated the magazine.[13]

AP Bomb Hit Percentages

In *Lessons* the Japanese claimed 13 hits out of 35 bombs (37% hits). 35 aircraft were used in the calculation rather than the 48 bombs dropped or the 50 aircraft assigned to level bombing, improving the percentage. The post-battle report notes that "These figures were concluded only from those which were accurate."[14]

If Fuchida indeed had a hand in the writing the report, as the leader of the level bombing effort and a level bombing specialist himself, he was psychologically disposed towards, and had a personal stake in seeing the results put in a favorable light. The author of the report evidently considered the bombs from three formations (15 aircraft) as "not observed," and omitted them from the calculation, thereby lowering the denominator and improving the percentage.

This is the second place in the report where figures appear to have been manipulated to magnify the results (the first being the inflated torpedo hit percentage). In this case, the manipulation is minor and justifiable.

The number of hits claimed in the BDA Report was overstated by over 60%—13 hits claimed on battleships, eight hits actually achieved. Four battleships were claimed hit, and four battleships were actually hit. All three inboard battleships were hit.

Overall, the level bombers delivered a superb bombing performance, and the subsequent assessment was creditable.

Effectiveness of the 800kg Bombs

Except for the hit that detonated *Arizona's* magazine, the AP bombs inflicted remarkably little damage. When the lower body of the bomb was shaved down to lighten the weapon, it weakened the bomb such that impact at an angle could crack open or deform the projectile. Six of the ten hits were either duds or low-order detonations.

A bomb that hit *Maryland* detonated on an awning strung above the forecastle; one that hit *Vestal* penetrated entirely through the ship and detonated on the bottom of the harbor. These hits indicate that the delay fuze functioned irregularly.[15]

Other than the hit on *Arizona*, the most serious hit was on the top of main battery turret 3 on *Tennessee*. The bomb hit the turret top armor at an overlapping joint between armor plates. The plates were forced apart and the bomb was deflected. The aft section of the bomb slapped against the overlapping roof plates, crushing the lower body and breaking it apart. The base plug containing the fuzes probably separated. The impact ignited (rather than detonating) the explosive. Damage was limited to a rammer in one of the turret's three gun chambers.

West Virginia took a similar hit, penetrating the six-inch roof armor. "The nature of the penetration indicated defective material," according to the Navy damage report. This bomb, too, was a dud, only damaging a loading slide.[16]

As for *Arizona's* magazine explosion, the US Navy investigation was predicated on the belief that the bomb did not have the capability to penetrate into the magazine.[17] Instead, they theorized that the bomb exploded on the second deck and ignited something flammable inside the ship such as powder left outside the magazine. The hot gasses were believed to have flashed through an open armored hatch leading to the black powder magazine, which then detonated.

This sequence is highly unlikely. For it to work, black powder had to be left out in an unsecured passageway outside the magazine, and a hatch to the magazine left open. In a safety-conscious Navy, doors to magazines were just not carelessly left open over a weekend. Magazine doors were shut and locked unless absolutely necessary. All ships had Sounding and Security Patrols that checked magazine spaces hourly, recording temperatures and ensuring that all hatches are locked and that bulkheads of locked compartments are not warm to the touch, a possible indication of a smoldering fire. Magazine temperatures are taken hourly. Having a magazine door open and powder scattered about on a Sunday morning before colors (before the beginning of normal working hours) would have been inconceivable. The evidence throughout the fleet that day testifies that sailors were forced to break open locked magazines to get the flow of ammunition started.

This explanation was unchallenged by ship's personnel because the gunnery department personnel responsible for the forward turrets and magazines were wiped out in the explosion.

Even if a hatch had been open before the attack, there was between eight to 13 minutes from the beginning of the attack for the ship to set General Quarters and Material Condition Zed before the bomb hit. All the turrets had reported manned and ready with Zed set prior to the explosion, as had the after magazine.

A much more likely scenario has been developed independently by three analysts, De Virgilio, Okun, and Aiken. Their assessment is that the bomb did have sufficient armor penetration capability to penetrate into the forward powder magazines. A movie camera recording the *Arizona* at the time of the explosion records a seven second delay from when the bomb hit and the magazine exploded. The sequence of events on the film suggest that the powder in one of the starboard magazine spaces began to burn and explode, building up pressure and spreading hot gasses to the other starboard powder rooms, then crossing to the port side, and eventually detonating the port powder rooms. Physical evidence on the sunken hull is consistent with this scenario.[18]

The Navy investigation team, largely made up from Bureau of Construction and Repair naval architects, looked for an explanation that would be consistent with their assumptions. They were predisposed to believe their original design calculations that the magazine was sufficiently protected and that AP bombs could not penetrate to the magazines, so they looked for how else the explosion could have occurred. They settled on an explanation based on operator error rather than a design error. Admitting that the bomb penetrated into the magazine would be an admission that the magazine was inadequately protected, something that they simply did not believe from the outset. They also explained the penetration of *West Virginia's* turret top as due to defective armor. This was not a cover-up or conspiracy, but rather another example where incorrect initial assumptions and an inflexible mindset biased an investigation.

Assessment: Level Bombers' BDA

The most serious disconnect between the BDA and the actual results were in the assessed fate of two of the three inboard battleships. The BDA had one battleship sunk and two with serious damage.

Arizona was indeed sunk, but *Tennessee* and *Maryland* suffered only minor damage. The BDA indicated that all three battleships would likely be unavailable for six months. *Tennessee* and *Maryland* were available within weeks, sooner if necessary.

This appears to be a case where Fuchida overrepresented the damage attributed to his level bombers. He could have assumed that a lack of bomb detonation signature meant that the AP bombs had penetrated deeply into the target, making crippling damage likely. Considering that he claimed that he was the one who insisted that level bombers be included in the attack, and that he himself led the level bombers, he was certainly psychologically predisposed to see crippled battleships as a result of his personal efforts.

Had it not been for the one fortuitous hit, the level bombers would have given a very poor return on their investment.

The postwar Japanese Official History downgraded the claimed hits to eight: one on *California* (none actual), one on *Maryland* (two actual), two on *Tennessee* (two actual), and four on *Arizona* (two actual).[19]

Assessment:
Dive-Bombing Against Fleet Units BDA
Hits Claimed and Target Classification Accuracy

The individual reports from the carriers submitted to the flagship immediately after the attack complained that most of the second-wave dive-bomber attacks could not be properly assessed due to smoke obscuration. *Akagi* claimed an unspecified number of hits on a battleship and one hit on an *Omaha*-class cruiser. *Kaga* claimed that "most" bombs hit *California* and two other battleships. *Soryu* and *Hiryu* submitted a combined report[20] claiming five hits on two light cruisers and one on a destroyer in drydock. The reports suggest a combined total of 20 to 30 hits.

The BDA Report claimed 49 hits for 63%. Almost a year later, *Lessons* changed this to 38 hits out of 65 bombs (59%). These percentages were in line with expectations from training: 60% hits from 78 bombers gave an expectation of 43 hits.

The air groups' performances were very uneven: flagship *Akagi* was credited with one hit out of 15 or 18 bombs (6%), *Kaga* with 8 definite hits and 13 probables out of 27 (78%), *Soryu* 14 hits out of 17 (82%), and *Hiryu* a remarkable 15 hits out of 16 bombs (94%). This totaled 38 hits (49%) with 13 probables. In Fuchida's BDA report to the Emperor, probables were not reported—11 probables were converted into hits, and two dropped.

Akagi was credited with a very low performance compared to the other carriers. *Akagi* was the flagship. This is extraordinary.

Flagships characteristically were the best performing ships in the fleet, the "Battle E" winners, the best of the best. While some of this elevated reputation can be attributed to flag staff members who give inflated grades in exercises to the ship in which they live and serve, it also can be attributed to the fact that flagships are "high profile" ships that get their pick of high-performing officers and men. Flagships were under constant scrutiny from the flag and his staff, and so were motivated to maintain top performance. This represents a cultural characteristic in all the major navies—flagships generally are the shiniest, and the best performers.

Assigning *Akagi*'s aviators a miserable hit percentage was a seismic turnabout. Experienced naval officers would note this with shock. The best dive-bomber aircrews were given the lowest scores. They were on the ship where the assessment was being formulated, and so were available for questioning. It would be hard to misrepresent their results. The huge gap between *Akagi*'s results and those attributed to the others is a huge anomaly.

In this context it should be noted that *Akagi*'s torpedo bombers were the ones that likely scored the majority of the 11 effective hits on Battleship Row, confirming that flagship aviators generally perform well.

The BDA Report claimed a target selection biased against battleships. No hits were claimed against priority 1 targets, carriers (granted, there were none in port, but at least *Utah* was not claimed to be a carrier). 14 hits were assessed against seven different cruisers (priority 2), 27 hits against five battleships (priority 3), and 8 hits against auxiliaries and smaller ships (priority 4 and lower). The chart shows how these hits were distributed, along with the number of aircraft reportedly attacking each target.[21]

The BDA Report has flaws in target identification. *Dobbin*, a 12,650-ton destroyer tender, was identified as a cruiser, as were destroyers *Dale* and *Shaw*. *Shaw* was correctly identified in the flyers' report as a destroyer in drydock, but the BDA report promoted her to a cruiser.

Overall, only five of the claimed hits (10%) had their targets misclassified. While photographs were being taken by the attackers, they probably did not get 100% coverage of all the targets that were attacked, and had to rely to some extent on aviators' reports.

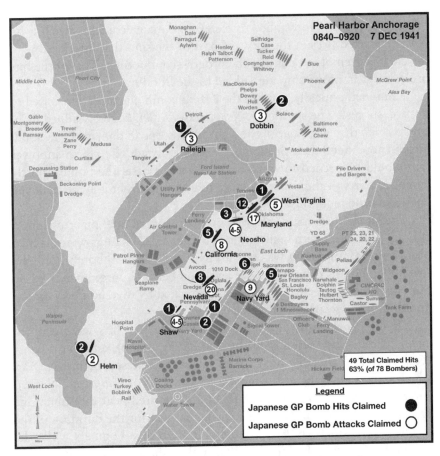

(17) GP Bombs: Hits Claimed and Attacks Claimed

Actual Hits

US War Damage Reports (WDR) and ARs document 15 hits, 19% of 78 bombs, less than one-third of the hits claimed. Seven of the hits, against destroyers *Shaw*, *Cassin*, and *Downes*, and tender *Curtiss*, were on low priority targets that did not materially contribute to the objective of the attack.[22]

One hit on *Pennsylvania* resulted in minor damage that was put to rights in a few weeks, while a hit on *California* did not lengthen the time the ship would be out of commission to repair the damage from her two torpedo hits.

A hit on *Raleigh* added damage to a torpedo hit and nearly caused the ship to capsize, forestalled by excellent damage control. Five hits on *Nevada* started fires in the forward part of the ship that interfered with the crew's attempts to contain the progressive flooding. Two of the hits broke the skin of the ship and added to the flooding.

Examined critically, *none* of the 250kg bomb hits hits contributed to mission success. The six hits on *Nevada* and *Raleigh* merely added damage to ships that were out of the fight from torpedo damage. The bomb hits did not extend their time out of service, only added to the manpower that would be needed for repairs. In *Nevada's* case, the bombs mostly damaged parts of the superstructure that would eventually be removed anyway in the modernization effort.

The hit claims Fuchida showed on the report to the Emperor show a curious disconnect with reality. For example, 12 250kg hits were claimed on *Maryland*. *Maryland* was not hit by any 250kg GP bombs, only by two 800kg bombs from first wave level bombers at approximately 0810. *Maryland* did not record that she was attacked by dive-bombers for the duration of the second wave attacks.

Of the other ships along Battleship Row, five hits were claimed against *California* (actually hit by one 250kg bomb), and one against *West Virginia* (no 250kg hits). Three hits were assessed against *Neosho* which supposedly sank at the fuel transfer pier aft of *California*. *Neosho* had actually gotten underway at 0842 and moored near the submarine base at Merry Point at 0930. She was underway for the duration of the second wave attack, and was targeted by two dive-bombers while she was in the channel. The Japanese BDA report shows *Neosho* sunk at her Ford Island pier, her location at the beginning of the attack.

Matching Claims with Hits

The next chart shows the hits claimed by the Japanese and the hits and DNMs recorded in ships' damage reports and ARs.

Hit Claims Away From Battleship Row

Five hits were claimed on three different cruisers at the shipyard piers. Only one bomb was an actual DNM. Six hits were claimed on *Helena* moored along 1010 dock, with no hits actually achieved. Two hits were claimed on *Dobbin* with no actual hits, two against *Dale* with no actual hits, and five against *California* with one hit actually scored. 14 hits were claimed vs. one hit and one DNM actually achieved.

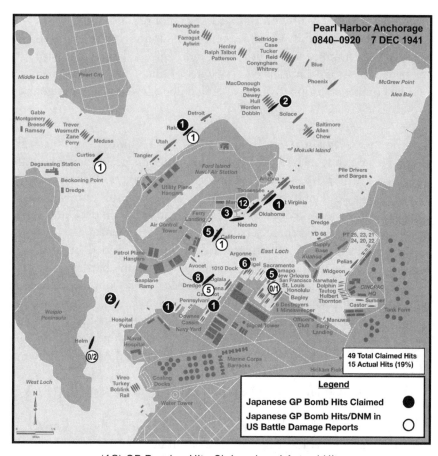

(18) GP Bombs: Hits Claimed and Actual Hits

Hit Claims Along Battleship Row

Five hits were claimed on *California*, one on *West Virginia*, three on *Neosho*, and a rather remarkable 12 on *Maryland*, 21 hits at all. Applying the claimed overall hit percentage (63%) to these attacks would imply that 33 dive-bombers attacked Battleship Row targets, almost half of the total dive bombing effort. Such a significant level of effort ought to have merited entries in the American logs and accounts of the attack.

However, there are few references to second-wave dive-bomber attacks against Battleship Row, by either Japanese or Americans. In one veteran's account:

Ofuchi swooped down on a battleship moored along the south end of Ford Island. "When we went into our attack dive, my feelings were numbed and, truthfully, I didn't give a damn what happened. I just gave myself over to Fate," Ofuchi said, "But when the bomb was dropped, and we pulled up to level off, I really got scared."[23]

The "we" Ofuchi refers to apparently means himself and his rear-seater. He does not relate how many other bombers accompanied his attack, but it was probably his *shotai* of three bombers. *California* was damaged by a 250kg GP bomb that hit her starboard side amidships and exploded on the second deck, blowing a hole in the main deck and starting a fire that engulfed three secondary battery casements.

In another account, Lieutenant (j.g.) Furuta claimed he attacked *Maryland*. He remembers that he "aimed at the enemy battleship's mast using my scope. . . . I identified the ship as *Maryland* from its position in the battleship formation." According to *Hawaii Sakusen*, Furuta's target was the fleet oiler *Neosho*."[24] *Neosho* had nothing that looked like a battleship mast, and she was well away from the "battleship formation" before the arrival of the second wave. *Maryland's* log and AR do not record anything corresponding to Furuta's claimed attack.

Lieutenant Commander Abe reported he attacked Battleship Row:

> I believe I attacked the *Arizona*, but at the time I didn't know what ship I was attacking. All I was thinking about was the two paired-up ships on the east side of the island that I had heard about. I was looking at the ship from above and didn't know that it was the *Arizona*, but I clearly remember seeing the shape of the *Vestal*, which was anchored near the outer side of the *Arizona*. However, when I attacked the ship was sinking, because it was attacked by the first wave. I confirmed an outline of a huge ship prior to dropping my bomb; however, I didn't see any upper structures, flames, or smoke.[25]

Vestal had cut her mooring lines and was clear of *Arizona* ten minutes before the second wave arrived. *Arizona* at that time was totally obscured by smoke. There were no reports of bombs impacting at the northern end of Battleship Row to correlate with this claimed attack. Abe probably actually attacked *Dobbin* and her nested destroyers.

Assessment

Aviators during WWII generally overestimate the number of their hits, sometimes by as much as 100%. Overestimating by a factor of seven is unusually poor reporting. Considering that this was a "set piece" battle with targets at anchor, the aircrew had trained for months for this specific attack, and that the strike leader was flying over the area doing nothing but observing, it is unusually bad reporting. The 78 dive-bombers attacked over about a 36-minute period, an average of 2 per minute. From US witness reports, nearly all of these attacks were well clear of the smoke cloud rising from *Arizona*.

Claims Distribution

Twenty-seven of the 49 claimed GP bomb hits were against battleships—along Battleship Row, *Pennsylvania* in drydock, and *Nevada* underway. This was a poor weapon-target match, particularly considering there were four modern 10,000 ton cruisers tightly packed into the shipyard area, undamaged and clear of smoke, and four others at anchor. In the absence of the carriers, cruisers were the dive-bombers' top priority. Only two cruisers sustained damage from 250kg bombs, rather than the seven claimed.

The GP bomb hits on battleships caused mostly superficial damage which would not have kept them out of the war for six months. The Japanese BDA report is an admission of poor weapon-target matching, poor target selection, and poor target identification—if it actually happened that way.

The *Chronology* estimated that 30 dive-bombers from the second wave attacked the Navy Yard area, which included the cruisers at the Naval Shipyard piers, *Pennsylvania* in drydock, and *Shaw* in the floating drydock. If that were true, then only two of these 30 bombers (7%) damaged targets on their priority list: a hit on *Pennsylvania*, and a DNM on *Honolulu*. If bombs that struck *Cassin* and *Downes* are included (bombs that missed their intended target, *Pennsylvania*), along with the hit on the *Shaw*, then six of the 30 bombs (20%) were useful.

Estimating the Japanese Attack Distribution from US Reports

The Japanese claims and US damage reports conflict. Ideally a combination of Japanese records of the debriefings of their aircrew combined with American ARs could be used to ferret out an accurate account. Detailed Japanese records did not survive the war, and the surviving dive-bomber aviators have left only a few anecdotal testimonies. The Japanese attack must be reconstructed largely from American records.

The most important records are the ARs submitted by the ships and the *Chronology* put together by the CinCPAC staff to support the Congressional Investigation of the attack. Care must be taken in using these sources. AR times were recorded inconsistently. They were mostly based on ships' logs which, understandably, might not have been the Officer of the Deck's first concern during the battle. Some entries record when an event started, some when it finished, and some might just indicate the time the Officer of the Deck glanced at his watch before writing the entry, which might be many minutes after an event. Some time shifts in the logs were as great as 20 minutes.

Many of the logs recorded "attacks" by dive-bombers. "Attacks" could have been bomb runs, strafing attacks, or even dummy bomb runs to draw fire away from other bombers, or just a bomber flying by as it recovered from its dive on a different target. The Japanese dive-bomber gunners sprayed machine gun rounds at whatever came into sight, making a log entry of an "attack" understandable.

The American logs are remarkably specific in recording bombs. They recorded how many were dropped, where they landed, and what they did. Cases were encountered where several ships in close proximity all would claim that a given bomb was actually aimed at them—a rather human propensity—but such entries could be correlated and helped reconstruct the Japanese expenditure of bombs. Consequently, this analysis relied on bomb counts to reconstruct the dive-bombers' attack.

The next chart adds where 250kg GP bombs were dropped. The list of these attacks and sources are provided in Appendix A, with a summary provided in the table.

The analysis accounts for 76 of the 78 bombs. The "Possible" column adds up to 85 because the entries in that column represent the maximum number reported in each attack—when several maximums reported from different observers are combined there was some double counting, which was eliminated in the summary count.

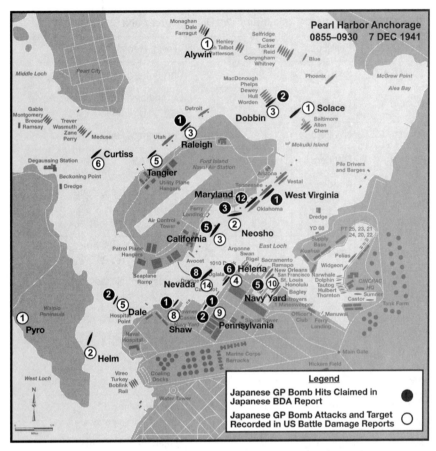

(19) GP Bombs: Hits Claimed and US Records of Attacks

For instance, Egusa's biographer states that the 18 bombers he led attacked *Nevada*. However, the ARs recorded that a portion of the group attacking *Nevada* broke off and instead attacked *Shaw* in the floating drydock. This could reflect either a shift of targets or bombs that were so inaccurate they landed closer to *Shaw* than *Nevada*. One ship's log recorded that one-third of the attackers diverted. Another offered a count of 21 bombers that went after the Navy Yard area, some of which diverted to attack *Nevada*.

Fourteen D3A Val dive-bombers from the second wave were shot down. The missing two bombs could have been on aircraft that were shot down before they released their weapon.

Ship & Type	Location	Minimum	Possible	Sources and Comments
Aylwin DD	East Loch	1	1	*Aylwin, Henley* ARs
Solace AH	East Loch	1	1	Chronology, *Allen* AR, *Infamy* 136
Dobbin AD	East Loch	3	3	Chronology, *Dobbin, Breeze, Dewey, Hull* ARs
Raleigh CL	NW Ford Is	3	5	Chronology, *Raleigh* AR
Tangier AV	NW Ford Is	5	5	*Tangier* AR
Curtiss AV	Middle Loch	6	6	*Curtiss, Medusa, Zane* ARs
California DD	BB Row	1	3	Prange—Ofuchi's attack
Repair Basin	Navy Yard	10	10	*Honolulu, Rigel, Tautog, Sumner, Ramapo, Pyro, Preble* ARs
Pennsylvania BB	Drydock 1	9	9	*Pennsylvania, Cassin, Downes, Tracey* ARs; Lord 132, Wallin
Helena CL	1010 Dock	4	4	Lord 119, *Helena* AR, Wallin
Shaw DD	Floating Drydock	8	8	NAVSHIPS A (374), *Shaw* AR, Chronology, Wallin 205
Nevada BB	Channel	14	18	Smith, Chronology, many ARs
Dale DD	Underway	5	6	*Dale* AR, Olson
Helm DD	Underway	1	2	*Helm* AR
Neosho AO	Underway	2	3	*Neosho, Cachalot* AR
Pyro AE	West Loch	1	1	*Pyro* AR
	Totals	**74**	**85**	Some double counting in *Nevada*–Navy Yard–Drydock totals
	Most Likely		**76**	Eliminating double counting

Comparing Claims, Hits, and Attacks

Although the Japanese claimed 21 hits against Battleship Row targets, the Americans recorded only Ofuchi's *shotai* attacking *California*. The Americans do not record any major dive-bombing attack against Battleship Row.[26]

Explaining the Mystery

There are several possible explanations for this mystery.

1) *The Japanese dive-bombers did indeed make a major effort attacking Battleship Row that was not recorded in US logs.*

This is very unlikely. First, there were many, many observers. The likelihood that all observers would have missed reporting an attack of 20 to 30 aircraft is diminishingly small.

Even if the dive-bombers did not score hits, the misses would have been sufficiently traumatic to be recorded. Between 0854 and 0930 there were men in the water all around Battleship Row, from the capsized *Oklahoma*, blown off *Arizona*, and driven off other ships by fires. Small boats and yard craft were picking up survivors. Firefighting craft were attacking the fires. One photograph (#24) shows over 20 boats and craft in the water.

"Tugs, lighters, gigs, and small craft of every kind rushed across the waters of Pearl Harbor rescuing swimmers." Boatswain's Mate First Class Thomas Miechurski, master of yard tug YT-129, approached Battleship Row but boats "were so thick around *Arizona* that YT-129 could not get close enough to help."[27] While standing by off *Arizona* Miechurski watched the dive-bombers' attack *Nevada* in the channel. He does not mention any attacks against Battleship Row.

A bomb thrown into that maelstrom would have killed people, sunk rescue boats and scattered flaming oil. It would have been recorded as part of the Battleship Row disaster. There are no such records.

In addition, the analysis of American records account for all but two of the bombs. There are no "missing" bombs that could have been dropped on Battleship Row and not recorded.

It appears that the major dive-bombing attack against Battleship Row claimed in the Japanese BDA report did not occur.

2) *The US accounts of attacks are inaccurate.*

Exact accuracy cannot be expected. However, the alignment between recorded attacks and physical damage is good. Reports of individual bomb detonations were recorded, sometimes by multiple independent sources which correlated well in the ARs. There are sufficient clues to allow a good recreation of the targets actually attacked.

3) *The Japanese aircrews were mistaken regarding where they attacked and what they hit.*

Aircrew ARs were notoriously inaccurate during the war, having a very bad record of claiming more damage than actually occurred. Sometimes the aircrews were overoptimistic, and sometimes the aviators saw what they wanted to see. Ensign Honma Hideo, flying a B5N Kate level bomber, relates how later in the war 18 level bombers attacked an airfield at Lae. He felt that only a few bombs actually hit the airfield, "But after the mission, our commander said that we had a 100% hit rate."[28]

There were two witnesses in each dive-bomber (pilot and gunner/radioman). Doctrine had the dive-bombers attack as a *shotai* giving six aircrews to testify on the target location. In addition, the attack commander, Fuchida, observed the progress of the attack as the individual unit commanders selected their targets.

These factors suggest that the Japanese aircrew should have been able to give a decent report as to where their target was located. But that leaves the fact that there is a significant disconnect between what was shown in the BDA report and the distribution of the attack effort extracted from the US records.

Two additional factors would have prevented dive-bomber attacks against Battleship Row. First, there was the huge amount of smoke covering the area. The prevailing wind blew the smoke from *Arizona*'s raging fires and the oil fires around *Tennessee* and *West Virginia* down the length of Battleship Row. Flaming oil eventually drifted down upon *California*, the southernmost battleship on Battleship Row, forcing her to be temporarily abandoned.

Photographs taken from Japanese aircraft show heavy cloud cover over the harbor, as do American photographs taken just before the arrival of the second wave and during the dive-bombers' attack. The dive-bombers would have to either find holes through the clouds or dive through them to make their attacks, a very difficult situation. Some approached their targets under the cloud base, which gave them insufficient altitude to execute attacks as they had been trained.

The Japanese trained to execute a standard dive-bombing attack. The attack would begin with an approach to the target area at 10,000 to 12,000 feet. As they approached the target they would go into a gentle glide to increase airspeed and head for a point downwind of the target. They would arrive at the pitch-over point about a half-mile from the target at between 6,400 to 9,600 feet altitude. They attacked in a 55 to 60 degree dive with 20 to 30 second intervals between aircraft in the *shotai*. The intervals were longer than in American doctrine, allowing following aircraft to correct for wind drift based on the splash of the previous bomb. Bomb release could be as low as 300 to 400 meters.

This technique required good visibility. Smoke and clouds like those over the harbor would prevent a conventional attack. If the dive-bombers wanted to attack Battleship Row they had to come in crosswind or with the wind, reducing bombing accuracy. With 80 to 90% cloud cover between 2,000 to 3,500 feet the dive-bombers had to either find a hole in the clouds or begin their attack from under the cloud layer, another departure from their usual practice. Witnesses noted that some dive-bombers appeared to shift targets in the middle of their dive. A lower pitch-over altitude also meant less time for target identification and aiming before weapon release.

The smoke boiling out of Battleship Row would also have suggested that those targets were already destroyed. The aircrews had been briefed to pass up such targets.

Possible Misidentification of Targets

Photographs show that many of the battleships rigged canvas awnings over their decks, shielding them from the radiant heat of the tropical sun. Tenders and auxiliaries also rigged awnings. This, coupled with the smoke and low cloud cover, could have confused target identification. American reports indicate that eleven D3A Vals released bombs against the tenders *Tangier* and *Curtiss*. They might have believed them to be battleships. If the attacks on *Shaw*, *Curtiss*, and *Tangier* were added to those attacking *Pennsylvania*, *California*, and *Nevada*, there would be a total of 45 dive-bombers reporting they had attacked battleships.

The Japanese aviators' reports could have been sufficiently vague that the BDA team had to apply their own judgment. The concentration of hits reported on Battleship Row targets could have just been a consequence of smoke, a low ceiling, and vague reporting.

If this were the case, the magnitude of the errors was breathtaking.

A Purposefully Inflated BDA Report?

Three times as many GP bomb hits were claimed than actually achieved. The BDA Report claims more hits than were reported by the carriers.

The officers on the flagship assessing the results increased the number of hits over what was reported by the aviators.

Those officers might have assumed that the dive-bombers would duplicate their training performance, and so "promoted" hits reported as "probable" to definite hits. This is a common occurrence documented in psychological studies of decision making: people tend to see what they expect to see. If the reports were not specific regarding the target's location an assessors might have attempted to place the expected hits against specific targets based on smoke, fires, or photographic evidence. With a process like that, some additional bomb hits could have been assigned to Battleship Row. But the aviators reported only 13 probable hits, of which 11 appear to have been promoted by the assessors to definite hits. This is much less than the 21 hits assigned to Battleship Row targets.

It could be that aircrews were vague about where their targets lay. Bombers that attacked the tenders west of Ford Island might have misidentified them as battleships, and if in the rush to get an initial assessment to the command, reported target locations in an imprecise manner, giving the BDA team the flexibility to assign them to Battleship Row. But there were only 16 aircraft that attacked tenders, insufficient for 21 hits to be assigned to Battleship Row even assuming all were hits.

The last possibility is that the hits claimed in the BDA report were intentionally inflated to attribute an excellent performance to the dive-bombers.

Organizational Theory would suggest that such an action would require three kinds of authority: the authority of rank, the authority of position, and the authority of knowledge.

The man in charge of the BDA was the strike commander, Fuchida. He had the "authority of rank," the senior man assigned to the damage assessment effort. He also had the "authority of position" as head of the strike and leader of the assessment group.

After delivering his attack as part of the first wave, Fuchida remained over the harbor. Fuchida observed the entire course of the attack by the second wave, and was not distracted by a requirement to make an attack of his own. He stated he was the last to leave Pearl Harbor after making a tour to note the results. He had the "authority of knowledge" as the one that could be expected to have the best overall picture of the results of the second-wave bombing attacks.

The combination of these three authorities would make his judgments the ruling authority in the BDA process. He was the one responsible for accepting an inflated number of torpedo hits, an overestimated number of AP bomb hits, and he had the authority and opportunity to do what he wished with the dive-bomber results. If he did not do it personally, he could have guided and influenced the group performing the assessment towards inflated results, something not hard to do, as this group would have been prone to see the results of their efforts in the best possible light.

The Japanese practice of having the strike commander responsible for collecting and collating the BDA assessment was faulty. In the US Navy, intelligence officers interviewed returning aviators and assembled a consolidated report. The process characteristically would result in a reduction in claims, as an individual aircraft's results had to be corroborated by other aircraft. If a pilot claimed a hit and his attack was not observed by others, the claim was generally downgraded to a "probable."

A process like this was not in place in the Imperial Japanese Navy. The strike aviators submitted their own claims, and the strike leaders consolidated the reports and made judgments under the supervision and guidance of the strike commander. They were not impartial observers.

Fuchida was responsible for the effort to collate all the data from the attack units. The reports and photographs from all the carriers were flown over to *Akagi* for the net assessment. He had assistance from *Akagi*'s senior flyers, and perhaps some of the bomber leaders flew over from the other carriers, although this last is not mentioned in the accounts of the post-battle evaluation. Fuchida headed the effort overall and personally was in charge of appraising the attack against the fleet, while the second-wave flight leader assessed the OCA effort against the airfields.

There were several psychological pressures on Fuchida.

Fuchida had personal interests in the D3A Vals' performance. He was a "special friend" of LCDR Egusa,[29] the leader of the second-wave dive-bombers. Naturally he would want to see his friend succeed. Egusa's reputation was at stake. He would be embarrassed by a poor performance by the dive-bombers, as their leader and as the man responsible for their training.

Egusa could also be embarrassed by the poor target selection command decisions made by the dive-bombers' leadership. He was directly involved in the decision to attempt to sink ships in the channel, which resulted in the attacks on *Nevada* (a poor weapons-target match and inadequate level of effort), and on what were identified as class "B" cruisers that were actually destroyers *Dale*[30] and *Helm*. Class "B" cruisers, similar to the *Omaha* class, were not high on the target priority list.[31] All of these attacks were poor weapon-target matches or poor target identification. If the final assessment reported a poor dive-bombing hit percentage, it would open the door to inquiries, and Egusa might be held responsible for using valuable bombs on targets too tough for the weapon, or targets too small to be worthwhile.

A poor performance by the dive-bombers might open up the floodgates of criticism. Genda and Fuchida might have a share of the blame thrown in their direction in their role as attack planners. Genda was Fuchida's friend. Fuchida had assisted him in formulating the attack plan. Fuchida had also briefed the dive-bombers to be alert to an opportunity to sink a battleship in the channel, an effort that failed.

Lastly, a poor performance by the dive-bombers would also reflect poorly on the performance of *Kido Butai* as an offensive weapon system, something an air power advocate like Fuchida would deplore. Dive-bombers were one-third the aircraft and half the offensive punch of the fleet carriers. Aviators were still sensitive to the competition between carrier advocates and battleship gunnery specialists for leadership in the Imperial Navy, and were in competition with them for resource. To have half of the offensive punch of the carriers perform in an unsatisfactory manner would not have promoted the aviators' cause. This is especially the case when it is considered that the torpedo bombers' attack could be represented as a fluke that could not be repeated against a forewarned enemy at sea and free to maneuver and evade torpedoes.

Torpedo bombers were already assumed to be, in some aviation circles, ineffective. The Americans questioned their viability, at one period considering abolishing torpedo bombers. The carrier *Ranger* was built without facilities for torpedo bombers and was to carry only fighters and dive-bombers. If aviators expected the torpedo bombers would score few hits and suffer debilitating attrition from enemy AA fire, and if the dive-bombers were also found to be ineffective, then the carriers would have their credibility questioned in the Imperial Japanese Navy as well. Carriers' effectiveness in anything but a surprise attack might be questioned. The Imperial Navy might look to build more battleships like

Yamato and fewer carriers like *Shokaku*.

There was also another possible motive, an institutional motive. A poor showing by the dive-bombers would put that aviation sub-community under scrutiny. Careers could be threatened. The Imperial Navy's commitment to dive-bombing might be questioned.

All these factors point to very serious consequences if the BDA Report stated that the dive-bombers did not perform as expected. Fuchida might have taken it upon himself, or he might have been directed by some higher authority, to change the hit numbers to forestall internal conflicts within the aviation communities and to make all the carrier aviation branches look good. Such an order might not be made explicitly, but in conversations and other ways such demands could clearly be made or implied.

These are all potential motives. There is no evidence to support or challenge these observations. They are only possibilities—but strong possibilities.

Fuchida had potential personal, social, professional, and institutional motivations for seeing the dive-bombers perform well. Fuchida was in position, through manipulating a few numbers, to help his friends, protect himself, protect the dive-bomber community, protect the concept of carrier striking forces, and protect naval aviation in general.

These problems could have been solved by "padding the returns." Twelve GP bomb hits were assigned to *Maryland*, eight to *California*, three to an oil tanker that Fuchida assessed as "sunk," and six to a cruiser, all hits that had not occurred. Other bogus hits were scattered about among targets at the naval shipyard. Two hits and "moderate damage" was also assigned to a "Class B Cruiser" that was actually the undamaged destroyer *Dale*. These inflated returns brought the score for the dive-bombers up to a hit percentage in line with their performance during training, and gave Egusa's men justification to take pride in "their share" of the destruction of several targets.

These bogus hits were not arbitrarily assigned. It appears that they were assigned after careful consideration to ensure that the deception could be concealed to the largest extent possible.

Additional hits against ships on battleship row could be assigned because:

1) battleships were on the priority list for Egusa's men, regardless

of how inappropriate the weapons-target match;

2) there was so much smoke over Battleship Row, and the second wave dive bombers' attacks so geographically scattered, that no one else could really have a full picture that might contradict Fuchida's word;

3) the smoke along Battleship Row could be attributed to the effects of the additional GP bomb hits;

4) the dive-bombers attacked so many scattered and diverse targets over such a duration that, when seeing all the hits claimed against Battleship Row, the dive-bomber aircrews would probably just assume that aircraft from one of the other ships were responsible for those hits;

5) many dive-bomber pilots who attacked tenders or the floating drydock might have reported that they attacked battleships. Abe's and Furuta's accounts serve as examples. If their location report was vague, Fuchida would have taken the responsibility of assigning the attacks to likely battleship targets.

Dive-bombing attacks on Battleship Row would have been nearly impossible. There was dense smoke boiling out of *Arizona*, along with the burning oil on the water that caused the evacuation of the after part of *Tennessee* and of *West Virginia* and *California*. Photographs show that area to be totally obscured by smoke as high as 8,000 feet. Only *California*, on the extreme southern end of Battleship Row, peeked out from under the smoke clouds; apparently only *California* was actually attacked by one *shotai* of dive-bombers.

The disparate performance between the various carriers' can also be explained. *Akagi*'s dive-bombers were given credit for 6% hits, while the other carriers were given credit for hit percentages between 78% and 94%. Fuchida was on board *Akagi* and had direct access to *Akagi*'s airmen, and they undoubtedly knew what they achieved and could be interviewed directly to provide reports of what they attacked and if their bombs hit. The leaders of *Akagi's* dive-bombers likely assisted in formulating the BDA Report. It would be very difficult to manipulate the results of *Akagi*'s airmen, as they were literally looking over his shoulder. Fuchida would have little flexibility regarding *Akagi*'s reported results. However, the other carriers' aviators could not immediately review the work. If hits were to be added to improve the D3A Vals' overall score, they would have to be credited to the other carriers.

The number of torpedo hits credited in the BDA Report was larger than the aviators' claimed. It was inflated apparently to give a hit for every torpedo dropped and one for every aircrew that returned, sparing anyone the embarrassment of failure, a critical consideration in Japanese society. This establishes in principle that the final BDA report numbers were manipulated, as it would be impossible to count torpedo hits from post-action photographs. Similarly, the results reported for the level bombers exceeded practice scores and exceeded the aviators' own claims, indicating that someone on the flagship upped those numbers, too.

Aviators had a tendency to see hits where no hits occurred, or hits that were not their own, and report results that were serious exaggerations. Fuchida himself claimed two hits for his formation that did not occur. This is not an indictment of dishonesty, but rather recognition that in high-stress environments the mind's eye tends to see what it expects to see. The Japanese aviators at the end of the war suffered badly from this syndrome. According to their reports, Halsey's Fifth Fleet was sunk several times over.

However, what is being extracted now is different. The question is not only the hit percentage, but the location of the claimed hits compared to the truth on the ground of what they actually attacked.

Either about half the second-wave dive-bombers' aircrews misrepresented or mistook the targets in which they attacked and claimed hits that did not occur, or Fuchida signed a report that misrepresented their targets and results. Occam's razor might come into consideration: "All other things being equal, the simplest answer is the most likely." What is simpler, a collusion authored by a large group of unassociated personnel, or a few tweaks to the report under the authority of one individual?

If Fuchida saw the need to report some 30 additional 250kg GP bomb hits, how could it be done? Hits could not be claimed where photographs did not show damage. Some hits could be assigned to targets that were actually attacked, but the battle damage assessment photographs would not support too many hits since the damage simply was not there. Some hits could be assigned to the tanker that disappeared off the photographs and could be claimed as sunk at its moorings when the mooring area became totally obscured by fires, and to the "cruisers" *Dale* and *Helm* attacked in the channel.

But even with extra hits assigned to these targets, the photographic evidence would still not support 30 additional hits. The hits had to be assigned to something that had been destroyed, could likely be thought of as absorbing many hits to prevent accusations that bombs were wasted on destroyed ships, and to targets that were on the priority list to prevent investigations on why inappropriate targets were attacked, and to targets that were obscured in the photographs so that individual smoking holes could not be counted.

The only targets that filled all these requirements were the ships on Battleship Row. There were valid targets there and too much smoke to allow a detailed count of bomb hits.

Additional Questionable Claims

Fuchida reported a tanker sunk at the location occupied by the *Neosho* at the beginning of the attack. *Neosho* was underway just before the arrival of the second wave. The conventional explanation is that, observing an empty mooring, Fuchida believed *Neosho* disappeared under the water the fueling dock. This reasoning does not stand up.

When built in 1939 *Neosho* was the largest tanker in the world, displacing almost 25,000 tons when loaded. She was not much shorter than a battleship. She had a draft of 32 feet, comparable to battleships' draft of between 33 and 36 feet. In the photograph showing her beyond *California* and backing away from her berth, she is at about 75% load with about 15 feet of freeboard.

Another photograph shows *West Virginia* outboard of *Tennessee*. *West Virginia* is sunk and sits on the bottom. Her main deck is barely awash. There is only a six to ten foot draft difference between normal riding conditions and sitting on the bottom of the harbor. This documents the depth of the water at these mooring locations adjacent to where *Neosho* was located.

The depth of the channel at the battleship row moorings was 40 to 44 feet. The water just covered *West Virginia*'s main deck, leaving the entire superstructure above the water. Had *Neosho* been sunk at the fueling pier, she would have lowered only about eight to ten feet. Her main deck would have been barely awash and her amidships and after superstructure would remain above the water, along with her elevated forward gun tubs, her masts, and her kingposts.

Fuchida was acutely aware of depth of the water in the harbor, as were the other aviators involved in formulating the BDA Report. He would have known that the depth of water next to that pier could not conceal a sunken ship.

By claiming *Neosho* as sunk, Fuchida had a way to run up the dive-bombers' score by another three hits, and to credit them with a ship sunk solely by their bombs, a morale-building effort.

Neosho got underway at 0842. *Nevada* was underway two minutes earlier, at 0840. A photograph shows *Nevada* passing *California,* just before the beginning of the dive-bombers' attack, with *Neosho* in the background on a course to enter the loch past the shipyard.[32] Another panoramic photograph taken just after the beginning of the second-wave attack shows Neosho prominently in the center of the channel. None of the dive-bomber aviators would have reported attacking an oil tanker at the fueling pier off Ford Island because there was no ship there. The photographs clearly show that *California* and *Neosho* were not obscured by smoke.

Fuchida was over the harbor awaiting the arrival of the second-wave dive-bombers. He reported seeing *Nevada* underway. It is difficult to believe that he missed seeing *Neosho* get underway at the same time. Two dive-bombers attacked *Neosho* as she passed the naval shipyard. It was not as if she was stealthy.

Fuchida's report of an oil tanker sunk at berth F-4, the aviation fuel pier at Ford Island, as shown on his chart for the Emperor's briefing, is indefensible. There was no ship there to be sunk, as Fuchida knew.

The Threat from *Lessons*

The assessment that Fuchida presented to the Emperor claimed 49 hits by D3A Val dive-bombers.

Many months later, after the Battle of Midway, the Battle-Lessons Investigating Committee that studied the Pearl Harbor attack represented a significant threat to Fuchida's BDA report. There, presumably many more senior officers would have access to the data—the aviators' reports and strike photographs—rather than just Fuchida's small group of flight leaders on *Akagi,* with Fuchida the authority for the final decisions. The Investigating Committee could have made a major re-assessment of the hits claimed for the second wave dive-bombers, which would threaten the veracity of the claims Fuchida originally made to the Emperor.

Fuchida was probably a member of the Investigating Committee and there to defend his original assessments. Some of the pertinent records and witnesses were probably lost when *Akagi, Kaga, Soryu* and *Hiryu* were sunk at the Battle of Midway. The Committee did some digging, but went only so far: only 11 of the 36 bogus GP bomb hits were discarded. But by then nothing was to be gained by denigrating Japan's signal victory.

Failures, even minor ones within an overall successful operation, tend to generate investigations. Success generates congratulations. The Pearl Harbor attack was clearly a success. There was no reason to go digging for individual failures, a reason why the problems with Fuchida's BDA report to the Emperor have gone undetected.

Fuchida's Reputation

Fuchida's character must be a consideration. If Fuchida had a reputation for absolute veracity, any accusation that he intentionally misrepresented data in his report to the Emperor ought to be vigorously contested. However, Fuchida has been caught in other fabrications.

The Pearl Harbor Second Strike Story

On his return flight to the carrier after the Pearl Harbor attack Fuchida claimed he "mentally earmarked for destruction the fuel-tank farms, the vast repair and maintenance facilities, and perhaps a ship or two bypassed that morning for priority targets." After the war, he claimed he strongly recommended to Admiral Nagumo that additional attacks be launched against "the damaged battleships and the other vessels in the harbor, the dock yards, and the fuel tanks."[33] In another version, "He begged the admirals to launch another attack at once and this time concentrate on the oil tanks."[34]

Fuchida claimed that a heated argument ensued, with Genda supporting Fuchida. This exchange is depicted in the movie *Tora! Tora! Tora!* Fuchida was a technical advisor to the film.

No one else corroborates Fuchida's tale.

It is likely that Fuchida created the story to amplify his reputation as a strategist with foresight. The "Second Strike Myth" will be more comprehensively covered in Chapter 10.

Midway—only seconds away from victory

Fuchida claimed that during the Battle of Midway the Japanese had a strike on deck just beginning to be launched when the American SBD

Dauntless dive bombers attacked and destroyed three of the four Japanese carriers. In one account, "Throughout the torpedo attack, preparations continued for launching the *Akagi's* second wave. The first Zero
took wing. At that moment, Fuchida saw the approach of American Hell-
divers."[35]

In Fuchida's book *Midway: the Battle that Doomed Japan*, he described the scene:

> Preparations for a counter-strike against the enemy had contin-
> ued on board our four carriers throughout the enemy torpedo
> attacks. One after another, planes were hoisted from the hangar
> and quickly arranged on the flight deck. There was no time to
> lose. At 1020 Admiral Nagumo gave the order to launch when
> ready. On *Akagi's* flight deck all planes were in position with en-
> gines warming up. The big ship began turning into the wind.
> Within five minutes all her planes would be launched.
>
> Five minutes! Who would have dreamed that the tide of bat-
> tle would shift completely in that brief interval of time? . . . At
> 1024 the order to start launching came from the bridge by voice
> tube. The Air Officer flapped his white flag, and the first Zero
> fighter gathered speed and whizzed off the deck. At that instant
> a lookout screamed: 'Hell-divers!'[36]

According to Fuchida, "the dive bombers had caught the First Carrier
Division with flight decks full of armed and fueled aircraft, with others
in the same condition in the hangar decks waiting to be lifted."[37]

Fuchida was trying to establish that the Japanese carriers had been
defeated only by a whisper, "The Gods of War snatched it away from
us," an interpretation very acceptable in Japanese culture.[38] Given another five minutes, their strike would have been launched and their carrier decks clear of the flammable aircraft and ordnance that was to
destroy them. In Fuchida's vision, but for those few minutes the probable
result would have been several American carriers sunk with the Japanese
losses considerably lower.

The Midway volume of the Japanese official history of the war, *Sen-
shi Sosho*, contradicts Fuchida's assertion that the strike was on deck and
ready to be launched. It states there were no attack aircraft on the flight
decks. This agrees with the reports of the American dive bomber pilots.

Photographs taken during the dive bomber' attack show only a few A6M Zero fighters on deck. It was not a matter of minutes but likely an hour or more before the Japanese would have had their attack staged and ready to launch. Only recently, in Parshall and Tully's *Shattered Sword*, has the truth migrated across the ocean.[39]

In *Midway* Fuchida also criticizes Genda's search plan, claiming that he would have been more comfortable with a two-phase search plan. Two-phase search plans were not developed until after Midway, in reaction to the failure at Midway. Again, Fuchida tells a tale that tends to represent himself as more intelligent and with more foresight than his superiors, a pattern in his behavior.

Surrender on the *Missouri*

After the war Fuchida claimed that he was aboard *Missouri* for the surrender ceremony in Tokyo Bay. *God's Samurai*, Fuchida's biography based on interviews with Fuchida, tells the following tale:

> Fuchida prepared transportation for the Japanese delegation, but the launches he secured proved unnecessary. An American destroyer carried the official party to the battleship. Several liaison officers, army and navy, went out in a "big, beautiful launch" assigned to the Yokosuka commander. Fuchida was among them. These men ranked far down the echelon to rate a position on the surrender deck, but he could see the ceremony clearly from an upper deck.[40]

According to the Curator of the USS *Missouri* Memorial,

> It is our understanding based on all official sources we have gained access to that no other Japanese nationals were brought aboard *Missouri* other than the official surrender delegation and one, possibly two, Japanese News photographers whose names have not been recorded. . . .
>
> From the official oral history of *Missouri's* commanding officer, Admiral (then-Captain) Stuart Murray, the following description of arriving Japanese nationals can be considered authoritative: . . . The Japanese were allowed to have a news reel photographer. My recollection is only one, but there might have

been two. B[y] my orders, since they only had the limited number, he was assigned a position on the 40mm gun platform on the starboard wing of the verandah deck. Two Marines had been assigned him to keep an eye on him because I felt there was a possibility he might try to pull a fancy trick with his camera or something and be a hero or a kamikaze by taking with him some of the central people. So these two Marines each had a hand on his leg and put him in his place and told him to stay there. . . . they had their other hand on the butt of their Colt .45 . . . there was no question that (he) got the word . . .[41]

Fuchida's account lacks credibility from the outset. Why would an aviation staff officer be tasked to arrange small boat transportation instead of one of the port officer's staff? Why would an air staff officer from an outlying air base be involved with any aspect of the surrender ceremony at all?

Captain Murray's account makes it clear that there was no possibility that "several liaison officers, army and navy," including Fuchida, were allowed near *Missouri*. Accounts of the ceremony indicate that there was no "liaison" necessary, or even tolerated—the eleven Japanese representatives came on board looking, according to one commentator, "as if they all had swallowed a toad," signed where they were directed to sign, stood where they were directed to stand to watch the Allies sign, handed their copy, and hustled off. 30 minutes, no tea, no tour of the battleship, and certainly not something a Japanese patriot would want to voluntarily witness.

Security for this event was tight. All outside guests would have boarded under the scrutiny of the Officer of the Deck, who was responsible for ensuring that only authorized people were allowed aboard. Anyone who has participated in a naval ceremony would recognize that control of such events is obsessive. Officers put their careers on the line ensuring that nothing untoward occurs.

No Officer of the Deck on a flagship anchored in enemy territory would have allowed some random group of Japanese "liaison officers" access to his quarterdeck, much less release them to wander about unsupervised. The Japanese representatives were picked up by a US destroyer expressly to keep Japanese small boats away from the battleship. In a part of the world populated by 9,200 Japanese *Shinyo* suicide boats, there is no way a "big, beautiful launch" carrying Japanese naval personnel would be allowed anywhere near *Missouri*.

If Captain Murray was aware of, and took personal interest in the disposition and control of a news photographer, how much more would he have insisted that uniformed members of the Japanese armed services have their own escort? Why would "liaison officers" not be required to stand with the Japanese official delegation? This was a fleet that had been fighting off kamikazes for months. Japanese were not trusted to be rational actors. As an example, a Russian photographer—one of the Allies—tried to move to a different viewpoint and was physically tackled by a Marine guard and escorted back to his assigned position.

The curator of the Battleship Missouri Memorial has observed that had Fuchida been aboard "his presence would have been noted, and his placement would have been noted in the official records . . . and would have been strictly monitored and recorded."[42]

Fuchida evidently used the newsreel produced by the Japanese photographer to inform his descriptions of the event. He spoke as if he were on the "upper deck," the same location as the newsreel photographer. But it is hardly likely that the United States Navy would have given a courtesy pass to the surrender ceremony to any Japanese aviator, much less the leader of the Pearl Harbor attack.

For whatever reasons, Fuchida's moral compass and the cultural imperatives working on him did not require strict adherence to the truth in these four cases.[43] This reinforces the observation that the many questionable statements Fuchida made regarding his part in the planning, briefing, and execution of the Pearl Harbor attack did not strictly adhere to the truth.

Fuchida's initial report gave four battleships as sunk and four damaged.[44] After examining the photographs and the reports from the airmen on the carriers, the BDA Report that went to the Emperor claimed three battleships sunk, two seriously damaged, two moderately damaged, and one with minor damage.[45] The actual result was five sunk and three with minor damage. Considering the amount of smoke around Battleship Row, this assessment was remarkably good, especially considering that *Nevada* and *California* did not touch the harbor bottom until well after the attackers had departed, and should not have sunk from the damage inflicted but for *Nevada's* poor material condition and *California's* open inspection hatches. Fuchida's full BDA Report actually underestimated the damage inflicted against the battleships, a rare occurrence for aviators returning from a strike.

While it appears that Fuchida was not above manipulating reports to help himself, his friends, and the naval aviation community, he also gave the most accurate overall battle damage assessment possible to his commander and his Emperor, even though it meant reducing the numbers of battleships sunk from the number given in his original report.

In Fuchida's defense, his untruthful or questionable statements were made after the war. Fuchida had gone from being a celebrated senior aviator to a starving dirt farmer, a stunning reduction in fortunes. The postwar attention he received from American historians provided a needed boost to his self-esteem, which he apparently reinforced by all these statements where he claimed intelligence and prescience to exceed that of his comrades—"If only they had listened more to me. . . . "

The tale of the Pearl Harbor third-wave attack dispute, Midway, and the *Missouri* surrender ceremony story all point to a pattern of behavior, a character flaw that adds credibility to the questions put forth in this analysis regarding his various questionable statements, such as that he was the one to ensure that level bombers were included in the strike mix, that he ordered the level bombers to concentrate on one ship, that his error with the flares was inconsequential, that his level bomber formation scored two hits, that 36 torpedoes hit warships when only 33 were reported. The falsification of the dive-bombers' performance in Pearl Harbor is probably another. With a history of falsification one suspects more of the same, rather than come to a conclusion that the errors were the result of simple understandable mistakes or the "fog of war."

Fuchida had a complex set of personal and cultural imperatives acting on his decision processes. No simplistic labels fit, and none should be applied.

Two Alternative Explanations

The preceding analysis is based largely on circumstantial evidence and cannot be considered conclusive. There is no available surviving testimony as to what actually happened during the BDA reconstruction on the *Akagi*. Besides the possibility of deliberate falsification of the data, there are alternate explanations.

Fuchida could have instead been the victim of vague and unclear reports from the other carriers. *Akagi*'s aviators could have been given such low hit percentages perhaps because Fuchida had personal access to them to cross-examine and ferret out exaggerated claims. The other carriers were able to pass on exaggerated claims because their aviators were not immediately available for questioning by the assessors on the flagship.

The dive-bombers' attack on the fleet was made under difficult conditions, through heavy AA fire, ubiquitous smoke, and dense cloud cover. The aviators could have become disoriented as they circled looking for gaps in the clouds. Damage assessment photographs taken at the end of the attack might have shown *Neosho*'s berth obscured by smoke or covered with burning oil, suggesting that the oiler was sunk and burning. The reports sent to Fuchida might have required extensive interpretation, and Fuchida might have been working to represent the results of the attack as accurately as humanly possible. So, one alternative explanation is that *the additional GP bomb hits, and their locations on Battleship Row, could just have been an honest mistake.*

A second alternative is a middle ground between the two. Fuchida may have received reports that were vague and subject to interpretation. In the background, operating in his subconscious, were all the factors mentioned previously: the desire to support his ally, the dive-bombing community, and carrier aviation in general by making the dive-bombers' performance look good. There were also his expectations, conditioned by the long training period, which made him expect to see 40 to 50 hits by the dive-bombers. His inherent cultural bias was not to call down criticism on his fellow aviators or question claims. He did not want to cause the dive-bomber crews any embarrassment by suggesting that their performance was poor. Consequently, he was psychologically primed to see 50 hits. All the imperatives mentioned above would drive him to look hard for those 50 hits. A second explanation is that, with all the conditioning from the long days of training and planning, *his mind would make him willing to see the additional hits on the scantest of evidence.*

So, the exaggerated effectiveness of the second-wave dive-bombers recorded in the BDA report to the Emperor could have been the result of:

A) the fog of war,
B) a purposeful falsification of data, or
C) a subconscious predisposition to see hits where there were none.

In the absence of definitive evidence, readers must decide for themselves which case is the more compelling.

Other Comments on the Accuracy of the Japanese Battle Damage Assessment

The underestimated damage on *Nevada* is understandable. She was hit by only one torpedo, and sank well after the strike departed. Had the mistaken flooding of the magazine and the progressive flooding not occurred, the assessment of moderate damage would have been accurate.

The same held for *California*. Under normal combat circumstances two torpedo hits would not have been enough to sink her.

The assessment that *Tennessee* was sunk by three 800kg AP bomb hits is questionable. It might have been prompted by the burning oil released from *Arizona* that engulfed her at the end of the second-wave attacks. The heat from these external fires was so intense that fires were started in some of *Tennessee*'s internal compartments, and her magazines were flooded as a precautionary measure. The Japanese probably thought that *Arizona*'s magazine explosion was actually *Tennessee*, as the assessment of the ship in *Arizona*'s berth was that she was only "seriously" damaged.

Vestal was misidentified as an oiler and assessed as sunk by a single AP bomb. *Vestal* had moved during the lull between the attack waves. Presumably she was in photographs of the attack by the first wave, and absent from photographs made by the second wave, and this was used as justification for a claim she was sunk. Like *Neosho*, if she would have sunk much of her superstructure would have remained above the water, so this was a poor assessment.

The net assessment was remarkably accurate with respect to the battleline and poor with regards to cruisers and auxiliaries. Compared to some of the later battles when the Japanese pilots returned wildly optimistic reports on the damage they inflicted, the overall assessment of the Pearl Harbor attack against the mission-critical targets was good, even though some of the details were exaggerated.

Most of the opposition to the Japanese torpedo bombers came from .50-cal water-cooled machine guns. Shown is a battery mounted on *Enterprise* at the Battle of the Coral Sea. The gun sight is not mounted. The white liquid splashed on the gun mounting and catwalk is protein foam, used for firefighting. The loader, to the left of the gunner, has cans of ammunition reloads at his feet. Guns like this on destroyers and battleships were responsible for four of the five B5N Kate bombers shot down.
Source: Naval Archives, Washington DC

CHAPTER NINE

WHAT MIGHT HAVE BEEN: ALERTED PEARL HARBOR DEFENSES

Initial Conditions

The US Army was responsible for the defense of the Pearl Harbor area, and Oahu in general. On 7 December the Army air defenses were in a complete stand-down, totally unready. This contrasted with the previous weeks, where the defenses were at high alert, with pilots standing by their aircraft, fighter patrols aloft at daybreak, and AA guns in position with live ammunition.

As early as 14 June 1940 the Army was practicing alerts for the defense of the islands. Lieutenant General Herron wrote of it in a letter to the Army Chief of Staff, General Marshall:

> I have just come from seeing the dawn patrols take the air, and the anti-aircraft men roll out of the blankets at the first gray light at the sound of the Klaxon and stand at their guns. . . . I have been highly gratified with the promptness and precision with which the planes get off the ground every morning promptly at 4:30. It is further encouraging to see the discipline and quiet efficiency among the ground crews. It is my belief that the Air Corps here comes on well. . . . A week ago today I gave the command for a surprise alert, which went off smoothly and efficiently.[1]

In the months before the attack the Army had constructed an aircraft warning service system patterned after that used by the British during the Battle of Britain. The full system consisting of radar and human observers connected to an Aircraft Information Center (AIC), which would control the pursuit squadrons and air defenses. The AIC was successfully tested on 27 September 1941, more than two months before the raid. In that exercise, carrier aircraft playing the part of an enemy raiding force were detected 84 miles from Oahu, giving the defenders 40 minutes to react before the attacking planes went "feet dry," and another 10 minutes before they reached Pearl Harbor. Within six minutes Army pursuit aircraft were aloft. The raid was intercepted 30 miles offshore.[2]

This was not a fully realistic test. It was scripted and the participants alert and ready to fly at the beginning of the exercise. There were still deficiencies, such as the fact that the system lacked the ability to differentiate hostile from friendly tracks. But it was a system fully capable of detecting a major carrier-launched strike with enough warning to allow the defenders to be manned and ready to receive it.

With the excuse that they lacked officers to man the center, Lt. General Short and Admiral Kimmel decided to wait until after the war began to place the AIC in operation.

On 7 December one of the system's radars (operating beyond its scheduled time, for training) picked up the Japanese strike 136 miles north of Oahu. Before that, it had tracked the two Japanese reconnaissance floatplanes. Had the AIC been operational, the fleet and army forces would have had approximately 50 minutes warning. Additional sighting reports were called in by a ground observer and an aircraft, but the AIC was not in operation and had no authority to act on the information, so nothing happened.

However, what if the defenders had been alert and ready?

The Fleet

The fleet was in Condition Three. For the battleships, this specified that one-fourth of the heavy AA guns would be manned with 15 rounds of ready service ammunition on station per gun, along with two .50-caliber machine guns with 300 rounds each. The ready service ammunition was generally padlocked in ready service boxes in the immediate vicinity of each gun, with the keys under the control of the duty gunnery officer.

With a trained crew, the 5"/25 could fire up to 20 rounds per minute, so they had ready ammunition for about a minute's fire. The ready service ammunition was to be immediately supplemented by the regular ammunition supply from the main magazines. These magazines were also locked, usually with the keys in the custody of the commanding officer, the gunnery officer, or the senior duty officer. In most cases the crews did not wait but broke the locks. The ready service ammunition was fired, and then there were delays and interruptions in the ammunition supply until General Quarters was set.

Saturday offered shore leave for the officers and liberty for the sailors. With few accommodations available ashore and with personal budgets more attuned to provide drinking money than overnight room rental, most enlisted men returned to their ships after liberty, and were available Sunday morning—some with hangovers, but available. Overnight absences were mostly taken by the more senior officers and senior enlisted men, some of whom were married and had establishments ashore. Some ships had as many as 50% of their officers absent on Sunday morning. The most significant manpower gap would be in manning the gun directors, where junior officers and senior petty officers were often assigned to the AA battery directors.

The Army

The Army had a significant anti-aircraft capability on Oahu. The Coast Artillery forces which bore primary responsibility for air defense had 26 3-inch AA in fixed positions around Pearl Harbor, 60 mobile 3-inch AA, 20 37mm and 107 .50-cal.[3] Other .30 and .50-cal machine guns with ground forces units could be set up in the AA role. Of the 3-inch guns, only the fixed batteries of the seacoast regiment were in position when the first attack came. The mobile guns were miles from their designated firing positions. The joint Army-Navy exercises that had been held on Sunday mornings over preceding weeks were not scheduled on 7 Dec.[4]

The fixed AA positions had their own ammunition magazines at the gun positions, but they were not manned under Alert 1. The gun crews were billeted at Fort Shafter. The mobile 3-inch AA guns and support vehicles were parked at various Army stations about the island. For example, the mobile batteries that were assigned to defend Wheeler Field were parked at the adjacent Schofield Barracks. They were parked without ammunition. The 3-inch AA ammunition was located in a storage depot at Schofield Barracks and an ammunition storage bunker at Aliamanu

Crater, about three miles from Ft. Shafter.[5] The AA batteries were also undermanned, with many of their personnel new inductees or reservists with less than 90 days in the service. When properly emplaced the AA batteries would have been controlled by state-of-the-art directors, many with radar.

The antiaircraft detachment of Battery P, 55th Coast Artillery (CA) (155mm) came into action at 0815. They fired 89 rounds of 3-inch and were credited with two kills. HQ 2d Battalion, 97th CA (AA), opened fire with small arms at 0815. Battery F of the battalion fired 27 3-inch rounds beginning at 0900. With those bright exceptions, other than small arms and machine guns improvised as AA weapons at the airfields, Army AA was nonexistent.[6]

The Army Air Corps

The Army Air Corps had 64 P-40, 20 P-36, and 10 P-26 pursuit aircraft operational on Sunday, 6 December 1941, a total of 94 fighters. There were an additional 35 P-40, 19 P-36, and 4 P-26 aircraft in a maintenance status. The P-26 lacked the performance to engage the more modern Japanese aircraft. The P-40 and P-36 were capable, modern aircraft.

When in Alert 2, all available squadrons were on immediate alert, with aircraft dispersed among the 85 revetments capable of protecting 109 aircraft;[7] pilots wearing their flights suits were standing by their aircraft. Air patrols were launched at 0430 each morning.

Alert 2 was in place until 28 November. General Short then instituted Alert 1, which consisted of measures to defend against sabotage. Alert 1 assumed that there was no threat "from without." The pursuit wing was placed on 4-hour standby. Even then, pilots were restricted to the base and were available to fly on very short notice. That restriction was lifted on Saturday, 6 December 1941. All but the duty officers were given the weekend off. Ammunition was removed from the aircraft and locked in storage in accordance with peacetime procedures.

Historical Results

The Japanese lost 29 aircraft, nine out of the first wave and 20 out of the second. Of the 20 second-wave aircraft, between eight[8] and eleven were shot down by defending P-40 and P-36 aircraft. There were eight P-40 and six P-36 sorties during the attack, a total of fourteen, with at least two pilots flying two sorties.[9] The USAAF awarded nine official kills distributed among five different pilots.[10] Two to four kills could be attributed to ground fire from AA weapons defending the airfields.

Consequently, 14 to 19 kills can be attributed to ships' guns.

An additional 20 Japanese aircraft that managed to regain their carriers were damaged beyond repair, some pushed overboard immediately. In total, 111 recovered aircraft were damaged,[11] and 55 aviators were either killed or mortally wounded.

There have been several analyses that have looked at the effectiveness of World War II anti-aircraft fire. One study calculated rounds-per-kill for ships in the Pacific Theater firing at kamikaze and non-kamikaze targets over the duration of the war.[12] Another study broke down AA ammunition expenditures to "rounds per bird" (RPB), that is, rounds per aircraft shot down, on a year by year basis.[13] The lowest RPB was in 1942. This was likely because early in the war ammunition was scarce and there was a tendency to hold fire until the targets were well within range and most likely to be shot down. As the war progressed AA batteries tended to open fire earlier and be more willing to expend ammunition on crossing targets and other difficult shots; plus, there were more ships and more guns firing on each target.

The table provides rounds per kill for various AA weapons.

	Kamikaze	Non-Kamikaze	Rounds Per Bird 1942
5"/38 AA Common	1,162	960	252
3"/50 AA Common	710	752	183
40mm Bofors	2,272	3,361	2,788
1.1"/75	2,231		1,503
20mm	8,972	7,152	1,809
.50-cal MG	28,069	15,139	9,496
.30-cal MG			56,950

These numbers are not precise. For one thing, rarely was there only one type of weapon firing on a target. For a torpedo bomber attacking through a barrage put up by every weapon that could bear, it would be impossible to attribute a kill to a particular weapon—"shared kills" would be the norm. The figures provide an order of magnitude estimate connecting ammunition expenditure to kills.

The CinCPAC AR lists the ammunition expended during the attack. It obviously cannot be totally accurate, since some ships (such as *Arizona* and *Oklahoma*) could not provide figures. Using the highest and lowest estimated rounds-per-kill listed above, a first-order estimate of kills can be calculated:

	Expended	RPK–RPB	Estimated Kills
5"/51, 5"/38, 5"/25	3,188	1,162–252	2.7–12.7
3"/50, 3"/23	2,801	752–183	3.7–15.3
1.1"/75	5,770	2,231–1,503	2.6–3.8
50, .30-cal MG	270,037	56,950–9,496	4.7–28.4
Total			**13.7–60.2**

The Congressional Investigation was presented with different numbers for heavy AA, but included ammunition expenditure numbers for machine guns.[14]

	Expended	RPK–RPB	Estimated Kills
5"/51, 5"/38, 5"/25	4,929	1,162–252	4.2–19.6
Machine Guns	275,807	56,950–9,496	4.8–29.0
3-inch and 1.1-inch	(CinCPAC AR)		6.3–19.1
Total			**15.3–49.7**

The 14–19 kills actually shot down during the engagement by ships' guns are at the low end of the range of estimates of what they ought to have accomplished, half to one-third the average performance of ships' AA during 1942 but approximately the same order of effectiveness as the average performance over the duration of the war.[15] This below-average performance has been attributed to "impromptu American gun crews, faulty ammunition, and the cramped conditions in the moorings."[16] The

effects of surprise, interrupted ammunition supplies, interrupted fields of fire, and lack of 100% manning for the guns and directors contributed, with some of those effects offset by the high level of training and the skills of the long-service sailors in the fleet.

40 Minutes Notice for the Fleet

If the fleet had received 40 minutes of warning of the air attack, General Quarters (GQ) would have been set throughout the fleet. The usual time to set GQ at sea was eight to ten minutes; in port on a Sunday, the factors of "surprise," "peacetime," "men ashore," and "hangover" would cause delays, but not over 20 minutes. Battle stations would be manned, including AA gunnery for defense, engineering for reliable ship's electrical power, high and low pressure air for the guns, and firefighting water pressure. Damage control stations would be ready to fight fires, de-water spaces, control flooding, and counterflood if necessary.

On that Sunday morning 65% of the officers and 95% of the crew were on board, so battle stations would be sufficiently manned, the most serious potential deficiency being officer leadership in the AA gun directors. With 40 minutes of warning, all the AA gun directors would have been manned. This is significant, because the US Navy was the world's leader in accurate AA gun directors, which would be aiming the acknowledged world's best heavy naval AA gun, the 5"/38. The fleet had been training hard over the previous year, so the personnel were at a high state of readiness, with many cross-trained to fill different roles at their battle stations.

Material condition Zed would be set. This would put the ships in their maximum state of watertight integrity. In those ships that had inspection covers removed from their torpedo defense voids the engineers would get a start on replacing the covers, but there might not be time to get them all, unless local Damage Control parties doing their pre-battle tour of their spaces were clever enough to recognize the problem and pitch in.

Magazines and ready service lockers would be unlocked and ammunition passers on station to ensure an uninterrupted supply of ammunition. There would be some time to clear away objects interfering with the AA guns' fields of fire. Nests of destroyers might be able to separate, providing their guns with clear fields of fire.

Fire would be opened with the heavy AA guns as soon as the first wave Japanese formations were sighted, at 0750 or earlier, compared to 0805 as reported in many of the ARs. There would be an additional approximately 15 minutes of fire from all available AA guns, with a better supply of ammunition to the guns for the duration of the attack.

There are various counts of the number of heavy AA weapon. One records 353 3-inch and 5-inch AA guns on the ships in Pearl Harbor;[17] another gives the numbers as follows:

Type	Number
5"/38	136
5"/25	96
3"/50	121
3"/23	14
1.1" Quad mounts	16
.50-cal AA machine guns	397
.30-cal AA machine guns	14
37mm	1

Some of these weapons were broken down for maintenance, and many could not be brought to bear due to blocked fields of fire. The number able to engage can be estimated by examining the locations of the ships and their material readiness condition. For nested battleships, only 50% of the heavy batteries could engage (the outboard guns), and for nested destroyers, it was assumed that only eight 5-inch guns would come into operation per nest (the superstructure of adjoining ships would limit the arc of fire of some guns). For ships pierside at the Navy Yard with ammunition and functioning guns, only half their available guns were assumed to come into operation.

Rates of fire for the 5"/38 and 5"/25 is largely a function of crew skill, and can be anywhere from 10 to 20 rounds per minute (rpm) when on target. Later in the war, trained 5"/38 AA crews recorded 22 rpm over short durations of fire, and 15–17 rpm over a sustained 30-minute trial.

The average rate of fire was set at eight rpm, assuming that 50% of the time the guns would not have a target. This figure is taken from the average rate of fire of the 5"/38 guns aboard *North Carolina* (BB-55) during an air raid on 24 August 1942 in an environment that was similarly "target-rich." Over 10 minutes *North Carolina* fired at approximately 49 dive and torpedo bombers and 12 high-altitude bombers.

Similar assumptions were made for the 3-inch, 1.1-inch, and machine gun batteries. The automatic gun batteries were considered to fire only for ten minutes due to their shorter range.

Using rounds per kill figures consistent with the actual results during the attack allows a calculation of the estimated kills during this first 15-minute period.

	Rounds Expended	RPK	Kills
5"/51, 5"/38, 5"/25	13,000	1,000	13
3"/50, 3"/23	1,600	1,500	1
1.1"/75	24,000	2,000	12
.50, .30-cal MG	192,000	30,000	6
Total			32

Potentially, about 32 kills could have been achieved in the period 0750 to 0805, before the ships historically opened fire against the first wave.

Adding the five first wave kills attributable to ship's guns actually destroyed from 0805 to the end of the first wave and the total first wave losses over the fleet would then be approximately 37 aircraft. However, with warning the number of kills after 0805 would have been greater than achieved historically. In the battle there were interruptions in the continuity of fire while magazines were opened and the ammunition train established. For example, *California*'s commanding officer reported, "The shortage of ammunition immediately available at the guns was acute, and orders were issued to ammunition parties to expedite the service of it to the guns."[18] In the actual battle most of the guns had only two to three minutes worth of ammunition in their ready service lockers. For example, the battleships' 5"/25 gun ready service lockers held 15 rounds, or a little under two minute of fire at the assumed rate of eight rpm. If it took eight minutes to set GQ, the guns had a potential shortfall of six minutes' firing. With GQ set all of the guns would have been manned rather than just the "ready" guns. The guns would likely have expended four times the ammunition. These assumptions lead to an estimate of 20 kills from 0805 to 0813, 15 more than actually occurred, which can be added to the kills calculated for the period 0750 to 0805.

	Lower range of estimate	Higher range of estimate
AA Kills by Fleet v. 1st wave	41	52

With a better AA defense there would be fewer torpedo and bomb hits, and more of the ships' AA guns would have remained in action longer—for example, *Oklahoma* with material condition Zed set and damage control parties on station would likely not have capsized as quickly, if at all, adding her 5"/25 heavy AA and .50-caliber machine guns in the fight. So, the number of historical kills used as the starting point of the calculation—five kills—would likely have been larger.

The calculations indicate that the Japanese could have lost many more aircraft than they did. This is not particularly surprising—if anything, the estimate might be low, considering the number of guns that could be brought into action at Pearl Harbor compared to the volume of fire generated by the carrier task forces at Coral Sea and Midway and later carrier battles, where some attacks lost over 50% and sometimes over 75% of their aircraft.

The additional kills would likely be concentrated amongst the torpedo bombers. With warning, the calculations indicate that 20 to 34 torpedo bombers might be shot down, many before they could launch their torpedoes, leaving perhaps 20 to 28 torpedoes in the attack. Considering that five of the last seven torpedo bombers to attack were shot down when the full volume of defensive fire was developed, it is likely that more would have been shot down had the fleet been alerted.

The storm of fire opposing the torpedo bombers would have disrupted the delicate task of establishing the critical flight conditions for a successful drop. If the numbers from the British study of bombing in the Mediterranean apply, the hit percentage could be reduced by 60% from what could be achieved against undefended ships. Applying this reduction to the hit percentage actually accomplished in the raid results in a hit percentage of 19%. This is still greater than the average of 15% hits achieved by torpedo bombers throughout the war. If the fleet had 40 minutes of warning it is possible to justify only five total torpedo hits, perhaps four against battleships. Four hits could have sunk one battleship or damaged four.

In this scenario the second wave would have encountered more fire than the first wave due to fewer ship losses. A conservative estimate would be to credit the ships with the lower range of kills as occurred historically. The higher estimate would be the higher range of this kills that happened historically, with additional kills credited to the guns of Battleship Row.

	Lower range of estimate	Higher range of estimate
AA Kills by Fleet v. 2nd wave	14	25

Kills against the first wave were calculated to be significantly higher than those against the second wave. This can be attributed to several causes: first, the torpedo bombers were more vulnerable targets, and would have been engaged by at least twice as many machine guns than in the historical case, with a full volume of fire greeting the very first aircraft; second, the first wave attack was strung out, with aircraft coming in to attack almost one at a time, providing more sequential firing opportunities for the defenders.

	Lower range of estimate	Higher range of estimate
Kills by Army fixed 3"AA	6	30

40 Minutes Notice for the Army's 3-inch AA Batteries

With 40 minutes notice the Army AA batteries could have had time to man the 26 fixed 3-inch AA guns in emplacements around Pearl Harbor. The gun crews were quartered at Fort Shafter. There were ammunition magazines at each site.

In 1946 the General Headquarters, US Army Pacific issued a report, "Anti-aircraft Artillery Activities in the Pacific," which included rounds expended per kill figures for 90mm, 40mm, and .50-cal weapons. It credits the 90mm AA gun with about 400 RPK, the same order of magnitude as the 1942 Navy 5"/38 figures. The Army report had its data from official reports or accredited sources, and the numbers of kills cited are claimed to be conservative.[19]

Many of the Army's AA batteries were manned by young reservists with less than 90 days Regular Army experience.[20]

The CinCPAC AR identified three periods of attack:

0755-0825	torpedo and dive-bombers	(30 minutes)
0840-0915	horizontal bombers	(35 minutes)
0915-0945	dive-bombers	(30 minutes)

While the times are somewhat inaccurate—for example, a more accurate estimate of the second wave dive bomber attack on the fleet would give the attack lasting between 0854 to 0930—the overall duration of 95 minutes likely reflects how long AA guns were engaged fairly well.

Twenty six guns firing at a sustained rate of eight rounds per minute[21] would be expected to destroy 12 to 30 aircraft. At four rounds per minute (assume targets were in range only half the time), 6 to 15 aircraft would be downed. The figures serve as an upper and lower bound for the expected number of rounds fired. The lower rate of fire does not imply that the guns were fired slower, but rather account for times when the gun was not firing due to changing targets, or a lack of appropriate targets.

40-Minute Notice for AAC fighters

In Alert 2, which the Army maintained up until 28 November 1941, the AAC fighters were ready to fly.

The army fighters, for their part, were cocked and primed; they were the ones standing alerts in their bunkers about Wheeler Field. Ground crews virtually "lived" next to their assigned planes. Alert pilots, rotated by squadron, were dressed in flight suits and either sat in their cockpits or lounged in the under-wing shade.[22]

According to one pilot, "We were under virtual house arrest. It was tough to get your laundry done and get to the PX. We were in our flight suits for a week at a time and got pretty ripe."

Sunday, 7 December, was the first Sunday for months when the alert was relaxed. Unlike Alert 2, the controls in unattended planes were locked using a large metal collar that fit over the joystick, with four cables attached to the seat. They were difficult to remove even under normal circumstances.[23]

The Japanese had originally scheduled their attack for one of these alert periods, but the attack was delayed. According to Araki and Kuborn:

> During the week proceeding 7 December, the entire Hawaiian Department, by order of General Short, engaged in a full-scale exercise for seven consecutive days. Army units from Schofield Barracks deployed, antiaircraft units drew ammunition and set up stations all over the island, and the Hawaiian Air Force armed aircraft and dispersed them to protective revetments. The warning center was fully operational and launched aircraft against simulated attacking targets.[24]

There were 94 fighters operational on 7 December, lower than the norm. Many aircraft had been put out of service to catch up on maintenance deferred during the previous weeks of alert. One entire squadron was placed out of service to remove and clean their guns. Under normal circumstances, this work would probably have been done on a plane-by-plane basis during the overnight hours. Adding these aircraft into the total would give 106 available fighters.

Historically, the 14 fighter sorties that were able to get to altitude achieved 8 to 11 kills.[25] At that rate 106 defending fighters flying one sortie apiece would score 61 to 83 kills.

	Low estimate	High estimate
Historical kills / sortie rate	61	83

To those steeped in tales of the invincibility of the Zero, this will seem high. It is high, compared to the early war record of the P-40 in the Philippines and the record of the defenders of Java, Ceylon and Singapore.

A better metric might be the performance of the US fighters defending Midway the following June. The island's defenses were alert, and the incoming Japanese raid was spotted by a PBY and by ground radar. There were 28 fighters on the island, 21 F2-A Brewster Buffalos and seven F4-F Wildcats, with one of each unavailable due to engine problems. 26 fighters intercepted the Japanese strike of 72 bombers and 36 A6M Zeros. The A6M Zeros dominated the air-to-air engagement—only a few of the defending fighters were able to get through to the bombers, and all were quickly placed on the defensive trying to deal with "the swarm of Zeros, from one to five of which got on the tail of each Marine fighter."[26]

Of the 26, 10 returned, with only two in a flyable state. The US AR gave them credit for 33 kills.[27] In the Japanese AR, 5 to 8 aircraft losses were attributed to Midway's fighters.[28]

Applying these results to the defense of Pearl Harbor would give between 20 to 33 Japanese aircraft lost to defending fighters, compared to the 61 to 83 kills with the previous methodology.

	Low end estimate	High end estimate
Midway kills/sortie rate	20	33

The most probable result would have been somewhere between the extremes. At Midway there were factors that reduced the effectiveness of the fighters compared to the situation at Pearl Harbor:

1) The US fighters were outnumbered, 26 to 36.
2) The US fighters were a "pick-up team" with little experience and training as a team. Some of the pilots had few hours in type.
3) The US fighters were committed piecemeal, in an uncoordinated manner.
4) The F2-A Brewster Buffalo was seriously outclassed by the A6M Zero.

At Pearl Harbor, the US fighters could have outnumbered the first wave of Japanese fighters, 43 Japanese to 106 US. They were experienced flyers with lots of hours in type and training together as a team. The Japanese strike was fragmented, with the Japanese fighters scattered among their many ground targets in penny packets. And, the P-40 and P-36 fighters could be effectively flown against the A6M Zero with the appropriate tactics.

At Pearl Harbor the US fighters got aloft after the Japanese fighters had abandoned their covering mission and were concentrating on strafing. The American fighters were protected by the fact that they were so few among so many—by the time they got into action, most of the Zeros were "target fixated" on ground targets and had dismissed the possibility of seeing any defending fighters aloft. Some of the US sorties were initially unnoticed until they opened fire for their first kills.

The 14 fighter sorties that did get off were piloted by exceptionally aggressive and skilled aviators. One witness noted that when aviators recognized they were under attack there was a general scramble for available aircraft, but some of the pilots were not running as fast as others. The ones that got aloft really wanted to fly, leaving behind their less confident compatriots.

A study conducted of 800 Korean War fighter pilots found that half did not achieve any kills, while less than 10% of the pilots achieved over 50% of the kills. The pilots that did get aloft were more likely to be in this latter group, more aggressive and more skilled than the average pilot. If 106 aircraft had been airborne all of the pilots would not have achieved the same rate of kills as in those 14 sorties.

There are arguments for accepting the higher figure. It is known that the P-40 could be effective against the nimbler Japanese fighters. In China, Claire Chennault devised a set of tactics for the Flying Tigers that gave the advantage to the P-40s, and the American Volunteer Group racked up a confirmed 15:1 kill ratio.[29]

Several things contributed to the poor early showing of American fighters in the Pacific, particularly in the Philippines. There was a lack of intelligence information and appropriate tactics to counter the A6M Zero. Good intelligence would have driven them to the same conclusions as those reached by Chennault: American fighters should not dogfight with the Zero. Second, at the Philippines many of the US pilots were very junior, some just out of flight school and then with no flying time for months during their sea voyage to the islands. Many had only a few hours in type,[30] and were flying aircraft that sometimes literally had just been assembled, with engines not broken in for high-performance flying.

These conditions did not apply in Hawaii. "The pursuit squadron commanders and most flight leaders were all seasoned pilots with nearly 1,000 hours of flight time. Many of the junior pilots were from the Flying Class of 1940D but still logged 500 to 600 hours, half of it in fighters."[31]

This can be compared with the pilots of *Kido Butai*, who averaged 800 hours, with about 10% of the pilots with combat experience in China.[32] But the 800 hours figure was an average, and included all types of aircraft. There was a shortage of Zero pilots for the Pearl Harbor attack, and many of the very young and very inexperienced were prematurely transferred to carriers. Their training for the months before the attack concentrated on flying fundamentals—take-offs and landings, carrier qualification, navigation, and formation flying.

The 14th Pursuit Wing at Pearl Harbor did not lack information on how to properly kill the A6M Zero. Chennault had passed through Oahu in July of 1941 and took the time to make a presentation to the Army pilots. One of them recalled:

> The meeting was held at the Wheeler Field officers' club and was packed. Chennault was a spellbinder who spoke for nearly three hours. He told us his experiences in China and reviewed the quality of Japanese flyers and their new fighter, the Mitsubishi Zero. He said that we would be surprised at its agility and sharp-turning characteristics."[33]

This visit was reinforced by several documents that were distributed in Army and Navy aviation circles. Major James H. McHugh, USMC, the Assistant Naval Attaché for Air in China, filed a report based on an interrogation conducted by the Chinese of a captured Japanese pilot. It provided accurate information on the fighter's speed, armament, and rate of climb. Lieutenant Stephen Jurika, Jr., USN, the last pre-war US Navy Attaché for Air in Japan, attended an aviation exhibit in Tokyo and, in a monumental security lapse by the usually paranoid Japanese, was allowed to sit in an A6M Zero. He copied all the information on the aircraft's side plate and the labels inside the cockpit, and filed a report with the Office of Naval Intelligence. Another report on the A6M Zero's characteristics was filed by Major Ronald Boone, USMC, in the summer of 1941.[34] Chennault himself had written a report on the A6M Zero which he delivered to General George Marshall on 12 December 1940. A few days later Marshall told a conference about the new Japanese fighter which had effectively eliminated the Chinese Air Force. Marshall passed on the information in a letter to General Short in February of 1941.

The Army had good pilots in Hawaii who knew their aircraft and would not be surprised by the quality and performance of their enemy. The Zero pilots were not overwhelmingly skilled or experienced. Chennault undoubtedly passed on his tactical ideas that led to the 15:1 kill ratio for the Flying Tigers. Given all that, the kills-to-sorties ratio achieved at Pearl Harbor, 8 to 11 kills in 14 sorties (officially, 9 kills and 4 probables), is understandable. There is less reluctance to extend this ratio to a full battle with 100-odd defending fighters with a 2.5:1 advantage in numbers.

The Japanese expected high losses if the Americans were alert. In their first September 1941 wargame, an American scout reported the approach of the Japanese. The first wave

> encountered a swarm of interceptors which kept it so busy fighting its way to the targets that it could not bomb effectively. At the same time ship guns and shore batteries blazed away at the attacking planes, dropping them like ducks over a hunter's blind, . . . Half of Nagumo's aircraft scrambled back to their carriers, having inflicted only minor damage to the ships in Pearl Harbor and the military installations on Oahu. [35]

Aircraft combat losses can also be estimated using loss rates predicted in the Naval War College Maneuver Rules. Losses are calculated as a percentage of the attacking and defending numbers. Fighters were allowed two engagements per sortie.

For the first wave, 43 US fighters would be engaged by 43 Japanese A6M2 Zeros, while the remaining 63 US fighters went for the bombers. Losses would total 34 US fighters and 38 Japanese planes, 12 of them fighters and 26 bombers.

The NWC air-to-air combat formulas remained unchanged between 1941 and 1945. In the 1946 rules, the equations for air-to-air losses were revised to take into account wartime experience. Using these rules 8 US fighters and 50 Japanese aircraft, 12 fighters and 38 bombers, would be shot down.

The NWC rules allowed the surviving US fighters to return to their bases to be re-armed and re-fueled and sent up again. The P-40s were based at Wheeler airfield, about 8 miles northwest of Pearl Harbor, so flight time would be short. The NWC rules specified the required ground turnaround time. 60 fighters would be aloft to engage the second wave,

40 with two engagements and 20 with time for one. This likely overesti-mated the turnaround time at Wheeler, where most aircraft had individ-ual ground crews, revetments, and service equipment. Aircraft could also be serviced by outlying airfields, reducing the queue at Wheeler.

The Japanese second wave was to consist of 33 A6M2 Zero fighters, with bombers bringing the total up to 167 aircraft. Using the same as-sumptions as before, the 1941 NWC rules would result in 12 US fighters and 16 Japanese aircraft (nine fighters and seven bombers) lost. The 1946 rules give six US fighters lost, with nineteen Japanese (nine fighters and ten bombers) shot down.

	US Fighters Lost	Total Japanese Aircraft lost
NWC 1941 formula	46	54
NWC 1946 formula	14	69

The NWC rules have weaknesses.
- None of the tactical details of the encounter are considered, such as altitude advantage, cloud cover or the presence of AA. Bombers had the same chance of being shot down in forma-tion as they had when flying alone.
- The individual qualities of the fighters are not considered. A P-26 with two .30-caliber machine guns was given the same effectiveness as an F6F with six .50-caliber machine guns.
- The numbers of aircraft involved are not considered. Kill rates drop off in large encounters—fighters with a 30% chance of a kill in a 4 v. 4 encounter might have a 20% chance of a kill in a 50 v. 50 fight. With more aircraft in the "fur-ball," pilots had to spend more time evading enemy fighters and had to abort more attacks when other aircraft got on their tail.
- The odds are not considered. In the formula, four fighters would shoot down the same number of enemy aircraft if they were engaging four of the enemy or forty.
- Skill and training are not considered. Nuggets just out of train-ing achieve the same results as veterans.
- The NWC formula allowed for only two engagements by each fighter. This is low.

The NWC approach was designed as a "quick and easy" way to inject air combat losses into a wargame that was being executed with judges performing all the calculations with pencil and paper. It was designed to give expected value, approximate results on an operational level. It reflected the informed expectations of aviators during the interwar period; after the war, it was changed to reflect combat experience. The calculations provide a reasonable first-order estimate of losses in an air-to-air action.

The scenario calculated above does not include the 15 USMC F4F Wildcat fighters at Ewa Field, 14 of which were operational. If the AAC fighters engaged the first wave, Ewa would likely not have been strafed and these F4F Wildcats might have been able to join the battle. The Marines could have contributed an additional 16% to Japanese losses.

Full Army AA Alert

The Army conducted a full-scale seven-day exercise just prior to the attack. All AA guns were deployed and supplied with live ammunition. But, as related by a Provost Sergeant assigned to the defense of Bellows Airfield, "On Saturday, 6 December, we were told to take down all arms and lock [them] in [the] Armory and take our passes to Honolulu."[36]

The AA unit assigned to protect Ford Island was quartered 15 miles away at Camp Malakole. Daily the guns were trucked to Pearl Harbor, complete with ammunition. They arrived at Ford Island by ferry. 7 December was the first Sunday in months this task was not performed.[37]

If the Japanese had attacked during the Alert, 19 mobile 3-inch batteries totaling 76 guns would have been added to the defenses.[38] They could have accounted for an additional 12 to 48 aircraft destroyed. The combined Army three-inch AA batteries could have destroyed 18 to 78 aircraft.

Each of the airfields had an assortment of 20mm, .50-cal, and .30-cal machine guns available for perimeter and overhead defense, along with small arms. It is very difficult to make an estimate of enemy losses from these weapons, as it would require knowing how many aircraft came within range. These short-range weapons may have shot down as many as 4 aircraft in the attack. The contribution of these weapons can be included by adding the 4 historical kills to the estimates.

	Low end estimate	High end estimate
Full Army AA Alert	18	78

All the Defenses Combined

Adding together the potential Japanese losses from all sources gives the following low and high-end estimates.

	Low end estimate	High end estimate
Japanese aircraft losses	107	307
Of 350 attacking aircraft	31%	88%

This is a first-order estimate only. Calculating losses independently and then adding them will tend to overestimate losses—more aircraft shot down by fighters would mean fewer targets for the AA guns, and so on. The point of the calculation is to approximate the magnitude of Japanese losses to see if the American defenses were "inadequate" as claimed in many history books.

If the American defenses had been active as they should have been, the Japanese would have suffered stunning losses, and the damage to the Pacific Fleet would have been considerably less than what was actually experienced.

Losses most likely would have been on the order of 50% of the attacking force. This is in line with aircraft losses in the 1942 and 1943 aircraft vs. ship battles. At the Battle of the Coral Sea, the Japanese lost 30% of their aircraft, and the carriers *Shokaku* and *Zuikaku* were put out of the war for approximately a year working up replacement aircrews. At Midway, *Hiryu* launched two strikes against the US carriers that suffered 63% losses. The US torpedo bombers at Midway took 86% losses. On 20 February 1942, *Lexington* was attacked by 18 land-based twin-engine Betty bombers and 16 were shot down, for 89% losses. On 12 November 1942, 21 Betty bombers attacked an American task force off Guadalcanal and suffered 95% losses. The Japanese aircraft losses at Pearl Harbor could have been equally horrific.

The following table shows the Japanese fleet carriers and their active aircraft capacity. If the Japanese took any significant losses from their air groups in the Pearl Harbor attack, it is likely that they would consolidate their air groups, stripping some carriers to keep the others operational. The table shows what carriers might be forced out of service due to lack of aircrew:

	Aircraft complement	Low end estimate losses—107	High end estimate losses—307
Akagi	64	Out of Service	Out of Service
Kaga	72		Out of Service
Hiryu	54	Out of Service	
Soryu	54		
Shokaku	72		Out of Service
Zuikaku	72		Out of Service

In other words, the Japanese fleet would have had one-third to two-thirds of their fleet carrier force placed out of action, and might have had only two carriers with their smallest aircraft capacity remaining in service, with the others out until late 1942.

Japanese aircraft were also in short supply. In the above scenario an additional 50 to 75 aircraft might have been damaged beyond repair—in the actual battle 20 damaged aircraft were jettisoned as unserviceable. With those additional aircraft losses another carrier would have been out of service for some months awaiting replacement aircraft.

The Japanese were short on manufacturing capacity for naval aircraft, and had no reserve A6M Zeros. Two Japanese light carriers were not fitted with combat air groups in the early months of the war due to lack of aircraft and aircrew. Two active light carriers, *Hosho* and *Ryujo*, started the war with obsolescent A5M Claude fighters, aircraft with fixed landing gear, and continued to carry these aircraft for months.

Conclusion

If the Japanese had attacked just a few days earlier, while the Army defenses were in Alert 2, they would have lost enough aircraft and aviators to put one-third to two-thirds of their fleet carriers out of service. The Japanese could have conceivably lost more than half of their total stock of experienced carrier-qualified aviators. This would have had a significant effect on the course of the war in the Pacific.

Above: Wisconsin outboard of the salvaged *Oklahoma*. The Japanese could choose to fight *Oklahoma* on the open seas, or attack Pearl Harbor, delay a fleet encounter, and face *Wisconsin* later in the war. Either choice would likely have led to defeat. *Source: Naval Archives, Washington DC*

Below: Pearl Harbor, 30 October 1941, looking south, with the channel to the open sea at the top. This is the view that the Japanese should have seen from their planned IP north of the harbor. B5N Kate torpedo bombers would then have split east and west to attack Battleship Row and the carrier anchorage nearly simultaneously. *Source: Naval Archives, Washington DC*

Above: An A6M Zero fighter plane. This photograph is from a set of recognition photographs taken of a captured A6M Zero taken in 1943.
Source: Naval Archives, Washington DC

Below: A B5N Kate carrier attack bomber, from a series of recognition photographs of a captured plane taken in 1944. A torpedo or up to three 250kg bombs could be slung externally under the fuselage.
Source: Naval Archives, Washington DC

Above: Two Japanese B5N Kate carrier attack bombers in formation.
This is a Japanese photograph taken in 1939.
Source: Naval Archives, Washington DC

Below: A B5N Kate carrier attack bomber taking off from a carrier early in
the war. This photograph was taken from an early WWII Japanese newsreel.
Source: Naval Archives, Washington DC

Above: A pre-war photograph of Battleship Row (top right), the Supply Base (center, on the peninsula), and a portion of the Submarine Base (lower left), and the edge of the shipyard piers (upper left) along the Southeast Loch. All but a few attackers avoided hopping the Supply Base and instead followed the loch past the shipyard to attack the southern end of Battleship Row. *Source: Naval Archives, Washington DC*

Below: The attack route past the shipyard piers. The best approach would have been to arrive in echeloned waves with 50 yards between aircraft, with each aircraft attacking the ship to the right of that attacked by the previous aircraft. This would have better distributed the attack and split the defensive AA fire.

Echelon Attack
in Waves

Routes Over
Supply Base

Above: With a 10 to 15 knot crosswind, a bomber would encounter turbulence over the fuel storage tanks and an alternating zone of lift over the
warming ground and the relatively colder water. The warehouses had to be
cleared by only 20 feet. Past the warehouses the pilot would have 5 to 6 seconds to establish the right weapons delivery altitude, attitude, and airspeed.

Below: A late 1941 photograph showing Hickam Field, a fuel tank farm, and
the Naval Shipyard. To the right is the channel leading to the open sea at the
top of the photograph. The channel was 400 yards wide.
Source: Naval Archives, Washington DC

Above: A 600-foot plume of water is next to *Oklahoma*. A torpedo bomber is above *Neosho*. Another can be seen over the Naval Shipyard, in a left turn to line up for a run down the loch, possibly a *Hiryu* or *Soryu* bomber cutting into *Kaga* or *Akagi*'s stream of attackers. *Source: Naval Archives, Washington DC*

Below: Leaking black oil covers the water around *Oklahoma* and *West Virginia*. Note the two splashes in the water on *Arizona*'s starboard quarter, and one in line outboard of *Vestal*, from high-altitude AP bombs. Of the other two bombs from this formation, one hit *Vestal* and one hit *Arizona*. Note that there is no discernable signature from the hits. *Source: National Archives at College Park, MD*

Above: California after the first wave has departed. She is listing and near to settling onto the bottom. Note all the debris in the water, from the capsized *Oklahoma* and *Arizona*'s explosion. Flotsam like this, drifting with the current, was likely the source of many of the reported submarine and periscope sightings.
Source: Naval Archives, Washington DC

Below: California in drydock, showing the damage produced by one aerial torpedo. The explosion did not penetrate the ship's anti-torpedo defenses. *California*'s belt armor, 14 inches thick on top tapering down to 8 inches above the hole, does not appear to be damaged or deformed by the explosion. The bilge keel, lower left, is bent down in the vicinity of the hit. *Source: Naval Archives, Washington DC*

Pearl Harbor, ~0900. A more famous version of the scene telescopes in on the smoke pouring out of Battleship Row. Heavy cloud cover disrupted the dive-bombers' attack. *Neosho* is in the center of the channel and easily visible. Fuchida, overhead observing the attack, should have noted that ship's movement. *Source: Naval Archives, Washington DC*

Right: A photograph taken during the second wave attack on the fleet. Note the heavy cloud cover. The small black smudges are AA shell bursts. A dive-bomber can be seen to the left about two-thirds of the way up the photograph, silhouetted against the clouds. *Source: National Archives at College Park, MD*

Below: A D3A Val after releasing its bomb. The dive brakes under the wings are extended. The bomb release yoke or *bukadan-ka* (bomb rack) is extended under the fuselage. The yoke, called by Americans the "trapeze," guides the bomb away from the aircraft's propeller. *Source: Naval Archives, Washington DC*

Above: A captured Japanese photograph of Hickam Field and Pearl Harbor through a break in the clouds. In the upper left is the dark fuselage of a B5N Kate. Smoke is rising from Battleship Row, right, and from the *Shaw* in drydock, left. *Source: Naval Archives, Washington DC*

Below: Taken before the arrival of the second wave, this photograph shows *California* listing to port, with *Neosho* backing out into the channel. *Neosho* is at 75% load and is showing about 15 feet of freeboard amidships. *Neosho's* bottom was about eight to ten feet above the harbor bottom. If she was sunk, some of her main deck and all of her superstructure would have remained out of the water. *Source: National Archives at College Park, MD*

Above: A Japanese bomber, identified as one of *Kaga*'s D3A Val dive bombers, shot down over Pearl Harbor and in the process of salvage. The long tube above the fuselage forward of the cockpit is the bombsight telescope. The bomber's streamlining "spats" encasing the landing gear and tires have either been removed or were knocked off in the crash. *Source: National Archives at College Park, MD*

Below: Neosho departing from her Ford Island berth prior to the arrival of the second wave, showing how visible this movement would have been to newly arriving aircraft. Note also the very heavy layer of cloud cover arriving from over the mountains in the background. Smoke is coming out of *California* apparently due to a fire on the main deck starboard side. Many small boats and craft are near the battleships—over 20 boats and craft are visible. Had the dive-bombers attacked Battleship Row, bomb misses would have sunk many of these boats.
Source: Naval Archives, Washington DC

Above: This photograph shows *Neosho* nearing the center of the channel. The burning oil from Battleship Row that will eventually engulf *California* is beginning to move south with the current. The cloud cover is prominent.
Source: National Archives at College Park, MD

Below: Burning oil drifts toward *California*. The oil totally obscures *Neosho*'s former berth. Any Japanese photograph taken at this time might lead them to believe that the oiler had been sunk. *Source: Naval Archives, Washington DC*

Above: West Virginia, sunk, is sitting on the harbor bottom outboard of
Tennessee. Most of *West Virginia*'s main deck and all of her superstructure
remain above the water. Had *Neosho* been sunk, her superstructures would
have similarly remained visible. *Source: Naval Archives, Washington DC*

Below: The fuel oil storage tanks adjacent to the Submarine Base. Note the
tank dikes, sized to contain the entire contents should a tank rupture. Some of
the tanks have been camouflaged with simple paint patterns. One tank is
painted to look like a building. *Source: Naval Archives, Washington DC*

Above: A view of the Naval Shipyard during wartime. The piers are adjacent to the industrial area encompassing nearly 500 acres. To the upper right is the southern end of Battleship Row, with one berth occupied by an *Essex* class carrier. *Source: Naval Archives, Washington DC*

Opposite page: The controversial "midget submarine in the picture," shot from a Japanese bomber. The Japanese caption: "Thanks to the blessings of heaven and the will of the gods the sky opened up suddenly over the Hawaiian Naval Base of Pearl Harbor, and below our eyes were ranged in rows the enemy's capital ships." After describing the type and class of each ship in detail, the caption continued: "Our Sea Eagles' determined attack had already been opened, and a column of water from a direct torpedo hit on a Maryland Class is rising. On the surface of the water concentric waves are traced by the direct torpedo hits, while murky crude oil flows out. The three bright streaks between the waves are torpedo tracks." The Japanese examined the photograph closely and did not mention a midget submarine. American copies might be marred. Sailors in a launch caught in the photo near the splashes did not see a midget submarine. *Source: Naval Archives, Washington DC*

Utah in the process of capsizing after two torpedo hits. Toland's assertion that
Utah was attacked because she "looked like a carrier" is clearly wrong.
Japanese aviators stated that *Utah* was mistaken for an operational battleship.
Source: Naval Archives, Washington DC

CHAPTER TEN

ASSESSING THE FOLKLORE

A mass of folklore has developed concerning the attack on Pearl Harbor. Stories, assumptions, unverified witness reports and other tales have been passed from source to source with little critical examination.

1) *Japanese "Superpilots"*
Before the war most Westerners had little respect for Japanese aviators. Among many odd beliefs, Americans thought that the Japanese had defective vision (stereotypically, the Japanese in pre-war movies characteristically wore glasses, especially the bad guys), and a genetic predisposition towards defective balance, making them poor pilots. Many believed Japanese aviators were not capable of executing so complex a task as an attack on Pearl Harbor.[1]

From the depths of contempt, after Pearl Harbor the Japanese aviators were hoisted to the status of demigods. Reinforced by their successes in the first six months of the war, legends have developed around the pre-war trained core of Japanese carrier flyers, that they were super-aviators, masters of aerobatics, consummate warriors, and all seasoned veterans of the China Wars. One historian claimed that "many" of the Pearl Harbor attackers had "hundreds of hours of combat flying experience."[2] "Japanese aviation abilities, heavily downplayed by the United States and Great Britain before the war, were suddenly accorded almost mystical reverence."[3]

Some of the perpetrators of this myth have used statistics to bolster their claims. "The average flight time of a US Navy pilot in December 1941 was 305 hours against an average of 700 in the entire Japanese Navy and up to 2,000 in the Pearl Harbor strike force,"[4] intoned one source.

The aviators of the *Kido Butai*, the carriers of the Mobile Striking Force, averaged 800 hours at the time of Pearl Harbor. To place this in context, Japanese pilots received about 300 hours in basic training and 200 hours in advanced training before being assigned to a carrier. This took about two years, a year of ground school followed by a year of flight training. Even then, a pilot reporting to an aircraft carrier was not an "all-up round" ready for combat. Peattie found that "Japanese naval aviation, unlike the other branches of the service, mainly used its operational units as training facilities rather than training its personnel in specialized schools."[5] Aviators newly assigned to an operational carrier needed to qualify in their front-line aircraft, learn to land on a carrier, fly in formation, launch and marshal, and fight.

A "large-scale reshuffling" of the air groups occurred in early September 1941,[6] two months before the departure of the ships for the Pearl Harbor operation. Large numbers of junior aviators were introduced into the air groups. Among the critical torpedo bomber aircrews, many young, green fliers were initially assigned to the carrier groups from August throughout September. It was four to six weeks before the new arrivals completed their basic carrier qualifications.[7] This turnover was normal, similar to the spate of transfers and promotions that any large military organization goes through as senior people are transferred to training or administrative or command jobs, replaced by new junior personnel. In the memory of one Japanese aviator, "Usually people spent only one year on a carrier, because it was physically exhausting."[8]

As a result:

> Owing to comparatively large-scale reshuffling before the operation, there had been many fliers who were not familiar with landing-on-carriers practice. Moreover, efforts had to be made to have carriers available for that practice, for during that period carriers were engaged in one-by-one repairing.
>
> Most of the training time for young fliers was therefore used

in landing-on-carriers practice which was the fundamental technique.[9]

In September 1942 there were many new pilots ("nuggets" in modern US Navy slang) fresh to the Japanese carriers. There were also new ships to be manned, as escort carrier *Kasuga Maru* joined in September and fleet carriers *Zuikaku* and *Shokaku* were completed in October of 1941. This added an additional capacity of 171 carrier aircraft, up from 351, or a one-third increase.[10]

Ensign Honma Hideo, a B5N Kate pilot assigned to *Zuikaku*, relates:

> Frankly speaking, I feel that many of the aviators on the carriers *Zuikaku* and *Shokaku* were really "green" and had very little flying experience. For example, only three pilots (including myself) had experience doing torpedo attacks using a Type 97 [B5N Kate] carrier attack plane. So, compared to the aviators on our other carriers, most of our men were not that experienced as pilots. Hence, prior to Pearl Harbor, we did mostly basic flying maneuvers, such as take-offs, landings, and a little bit of formation flying. We also did some level bombing training with our Type 97s.... most of the men on our carrier were "rookie" pilots... [11]

Ensign Honma was 19 years old and one of the more experienced aviators on his ship. The two others in his crew were 16 or 17 years old. The aged Honma "felt they were still kids."

Genda, in a postwar analysis of the Pearl Harbor attack, admits that the "airplane units of the 5th Carrier Division [new carriers *Zuikaku* and *Shokaku*] could not keep up with the 1st and 2nd even to the end because the units were newly organized and were not trained sufficiently."[12]

One Japanese senior officer mentioned that when these ships joined the fleet skilled A6M Zero pilots were hard to find. Airmen were transferred from the light carriers *Ryuji* and *Shoho*,[13] while others were pulled from instructor duty and experimentation duty with the Yokosuka Air Group.[14] This provoked opposition from the Navy Ministry's Aeronautical Department and the Personnel Bureau. Yamamoto was risking his "seed corn;" if these experienced aircrew were lost, the lack of trained and experienced instructors would make it all the more difficult to reconstitute the air groups.

The converted former luxury liner *Kasuga Maru* joined the fleet as an escort carrier [later named *Taiyo*] three months before the Pearl Harbor attack. She was fitted for an aircraft complement of 27—nine A6M Zero fighters (with 2 spares) and 15 B5N Kate carrier attack bombers (with one spare). However, there were insufficient airmen to make up her air group,[15] and so she was classified as an auxiliary and relegated to duties as an aircraft ferry. She was reclassified as a warship on 31 August 1942, but performed ferrying duties for a considerable period thereafter, only participating in one operation in a combat role.

All the aircrews began an intensive period of training for the attack. For the B5N Kate carrier attack bombers assigned to carry torpedoes, it meant three sorties a day for many weeks. For the dive-bombers, Abe Zenji, commander of a group of nine dive-bombers on carrier *Akagi*, testified, "These practice missions continued over and over, on some occasions for five hours or more." According to the Japanese Navy's post-operation study, " . . . there had been many fliers who were not familiar with landing-on-carriers practice. . . . Most of the training time for young fliers was therefore used in landing-on-carriers practice."[16] Abe recalled that among the dive-bombers, "Accidents were common and some aircraft dived into the sea because the pilots were unable to withstand the G stresses in the face of the exhaustion brought on by the severe training schedule . . . we faced death every day."[17]

In other words, a large portion of the air groups were nuggets, and much of their training was devoted to fundamental flying skills. Weapon delivery practice came next. Integrated air group training, or rehearsals of the actual attack, was last, and never satisfactorily accomplished. There was no inter-type training, so the bombers never learned how to work with the fighters, and vice versa. This reflected the Japanese's "stove-pipe" attitude towards aircraft missions. Each type was independent with little cooperation envisioned.

Under intensive training the aviators would accumulate over 100 hours of flight time per month—Ensign Maeda Takeshi's flight log recorded 128 hours in October. This would have brought nuggets right out of flight school up to 700 to 800 hours total by November 1941. The sprinkling of second tour aircrew and leaders, most with over 1,500 hours, would bring the average flight hours up to the stated 800 hours average. So, the intimation by some historians that the Japanese aviators having an average of 800 hours denoted an unusually experienced and well-trained force is not correct. The statements in many histories intimating that the Japanese sent to Pearl Harbor a flock of super-pilots, seasoned veterans of the war in China, is a myth. This was a normal contingent of aviators, the majority in their first tour on a carrier. The major advantage was in the 26 flight leaders, of which a few had seen limited action—most of the naval aviators that saw action in China were land-based medium bomber aircrews, not carrier aviators. Only a few strikes, numbering in the single digits, were launched from carriers. The idea that "many" of the Japanese aviators had "hundreds of hours of combat experience" is wrong.

American pilots during the interwar period were given 500 hours before being sent to their squadron for advanced training. Just before the war began, to accommodate the rapid expansion of the fleet, training hours were cut back. Some pilots joined combat units with only 250 hours. They began arriving in the fleet in the autumn of 1942, well after Pearl Harbor.

"The [US] pilots in the service before World War II were an 'elite' group," according to a pilot who joined his first squadron in September of 1942.[18] The Japanese training program, in terms of flight hours, was not superior to that given to American pilots during the interwar years. In contrast, in 1939 Canadian recruits were given 100 hours of flight training before receiving their wings and being transferred to combat duty in Britain.[19]

The Japanese sent to Pearl Harbor airmen trained to typical interwar standards. Their primary advantage over their American opponents was a period of intensive training just prior to the operation, which got the newer airmen (including most of the aircrew on the two newly-commissioned carriers) up to the same operational level as new American pilots that were sent to operational units. The Japanese aviators that attacked Pearl Harbor were not the super-pilots that folklore would have us believe, particularly the A6M Zero fighter pilots, the subjects of particular veneration in the popular mind. Understanding this, it is easier to comprehend how the American fighter pilots at Pearl Harbor were able to rack up a kill ratio of between four : one to six : one, and lose only 15% of their numbers. When it came to their primary mission, to sweep the skies of American fighter opposition, the Japanese fighters failed. They shot down two fighters that were barely aloft after their takeoff run, but of the fourteen fighters that attained combat altitude they only disposed of two, a far cry from the Japanese fighter performances in China where the A6M Zero would typically shoot down 20 of 23 Chinese fighters. The Japanese fighter pilots were not as good as in China, and the American fighter pilots and their fighters outclassed what the Japanese had previously seen.

The quality of *Kido Butai's* fighter pilots would improve over the first six months of 1942, where they had the opportunity to gain more flying hours in attacks that were almost unopposed. They reached peak efficiency during the raid into the Indian Ocean and the attack on Darwin. Even so, they were not overwhelmingly dominant in the Battle of the Coral Sea, and their lack of flight disciple and command and control deficiencies directly led to the annihilation of the carrier striking force at Midway.

The Japanese training standards eroded dramatically during the war. The aviators at Pearl Harbor were much better than later flight school graduates, another contrast that accentuated their relative prowess.

A noteworthy point was that the Japanese planners decided upon the number of bombers to carry torpedoes before they resolved the technical problems of launching torpedoes in shallow waters, and before any reasonable percentage of hits could be estimated. The number of B5N Kate bombers allocated to level bombing attacks against the battleline was also determined in advance, when level bombing percentages were so abysmal that Genda had "almost given up on horizontal bombing."[20]

An alternate approach would have been to train all of the aircrews in both forms of attack, and then allocate weapons after the technical issues had been resolved and after a better estimate of hits with each weapon could be determined. This would have allowed the planners the flexibility to change weapon-target pairings at the last minute based on such factors as the accuracy displayed in training or the latest information on the composition of the American fleet in harbor. Instead, the weapons-target pairings and aircraft assignments were made months in advance, and not changed. One reason for this was the training required to get the aviators sufficiently skilled in just one form of attack. They were not sufficiently skilled to swap from one role to another. This limited the flexibility of the planners.

Shokaku and *Zuikaku* were operational just weeks before the Pearl Harbor raid. *Zuikaku* and *Shokaku's* B5N Kates were all allocated to level bombing attacks against airfields, targets demanding less accuracy than fleet targets.

In the end, the attack time was postponed from dawn to 0800 because a dawn attack would require launching in the dark, and *Zuikaku* and *Shokaku*'s air groups were not qualified for night operations. X Day was delayed from 20 November to 7 December because the skill level of the aviators was judged to be insufficient, and more training was needed.[21] Ironically, this served to their advantage: if the attack had gone down on 20 November the Americans would have been in Alert 2, with dawn patrols aloft, AA batteries in place, and the Japanese would have suffered.

2) *"Thank goodness the fleet was in port . . ."*
Attacking the Fleet Outside the Harbor

Some commentators believed it was fortunate that the US Pacific Fleet was in port, because if it had been attacked at sea, the defeat would have been much more serious. Ships sunk in deep water would have been unsalvageable.

In a scenario supporting this theme, Japan does not attack Pearl Harbor; instead the Pacific Fleet sallies forth to the immediate relief of the Philippines. It is destroyed in deep water by Japanese long-range torpedo bombers operating off island bases. Not only are the battleships all lost in deep water but so are their crews, decimating the experienced Regular Navy talent foundation that served as the cadre for a mass of new construction ships and delivered training to the masses of wartime volunteers and draftees.

While this discussion will explicitly analyze the first scenario, the second can be considered as a lesser and included case.

The "Fleet at sea off Pearl" scenario was tested in a wargame conducted under the auspices of a television program, featuring some of the luminaries of the wargaming world and with the combat results adjudicated by a "sophisticated computer program."[22] In the scenario the US fleet received warning of the attack at 0530, allowing sufficient time for the US commander to sortie the majority of the fleet and meet the air attack while underway in deep water, with the ability to maneuver at full speed, GQ and Zed set, and all AA batteries ready. The results were dramatically announced: four American battleships sunk in exchange for 75 Japanese aircraft shot down.

One of the participants in the game, a retired Rear Admiral, stated that he did not believe these results. He felt that the Americans suffered far too many losses in the game. A careful assessment would suggest that he is correct.

To sink four battleships at sea would have required a minimum of sixteen hits, or 40% of the available torpedoes, very close to the 48% hits the Japanese achieved against stationary targets in a surprise attack. At sea, ships would have been able to maneuver freely, and torpedo hits would have been harder to achieve. Over the last months the US Fleet had been training hard and sailing as if under wartime conditions, and their training and readiness was considered to be excellent. Material Condition Zed would have been set, so the progressive flooding that was so damaging to ships moored in Pearl Harbor under holiday routine would not have occurred as readily.

Compare this situation with that of the attack on the *Prince of Wales* and *Repulse*. There, 51 torpedo bombers took off on the mission and 49 torpedoes were launched achieving 6 to 8 hits, or a hit percentage of 12 to 16%.

In that engagement, the two battleships were escorted by destroyers with no area air defense capability. Most of the AA capability was vested in the *Prince of Wales*. A single devastating torpedo hit, the first to hit the ship, disabled most of the *Prince of Wales'* AA capability. A torpedo exploded on the port side aft; it dislocated a port shaft, which thrashed about in the shaft alley smashing the surrounding bulkheads and destroying the watertight integrity of compartments all the way from aft to amidships. Several major engineering spaces flooded, some so fast that the crews could not shut watertight hatches behind them as they evacuated, causing the flooding to spread further. There was a loss of electrical power aft, and the ship took on an immediate 11 degree list, enough so that the 5.25-in AA guns on the high side could not depress sufficiently to engage torpedo bombers. Not one of the eight 5.25-inch gun turrets could be trained due to a loss of electrical power. The six mounts of 8-barrel 2-pounder pom-poms had problems with their ammunition, causing the guns to jam. Stoppages were frequent; one of *Prince of Wales'* pom-poms suffered 12 failures, another eight. With power lost all the pom-poms aft were frozen. Sailors tried to train them manually, without success, and in one case they even tried rigging a chain pulley for additional leverage.

With *Prince of Wales'* AA weapons largely out of action, *Repulse* had little to contribute to the defense. She was a WWI vintage ship with only eight hand-operated 4-inch AA and two pom-pom mounts.[23]

And yet, against this anemic AA opposition, the Japanese achieved only 12–16% hits.

A torpedo hit percentage of 15% underway (the historical average during the war in the Pacific) against the fleet off Pearl Harbor would have given six hits out of the 40 torpedo-armed B5N Kate carrier attack bombers. Battleships at sea could be expected to sustain at least four aerial torpedo hits without sinking. So, six hits might have (if concentrated) sunk one battleship; if distributed over several ships, all ought to survive.

Similarly, the hit percentage by 800kg bombs would be reduced from that achieved against the stationary ships on Battleship Row. Hits by level bombers against maneuvering targets were notoriously hard to achieve during all of WWII. A 10% hit rate (5 hits) would have been exceptional, higher than the hit percentage exhibited over the entire war, which was probably less than 1%.[24] Five hits (with a 60% dud or reduced yield rate) would not have done serious damage to the battleline as a whole.

American AA was considerably advanced over the British. The 40 torpedo bombers would have received considerably more attention than that offered by the British battleship and battlecruiser. An apt comparison would be the battle of 12 November 1942, where 21 Japanese twin-engine torpedo bombers attacked six American transports off Guadalcanal protected by three heavy cruisers, two light cruisers and eleven destroyers, about half the AA potential as the seven battleships, three light cruisers, and nineteen destroyers that might have been steaming off Pearl Harbor on 7 December 1941. A view of that action was related by a gunnery officer on the destroyer *Sterrett*:

> Now I gave the gun captains the signal they had been waiting for—"Commence firing! Director control. Rapid, continuous fire." The crews loaded the shells and powder cartridges into the guns, and in four seconds the first salvo was on its way. The concussion was terrific, but by now we were used to it. Our first bursts were low and short, so we changed our trajectories. We were the ship closest to the attackers, and our tracers were headed straight at the lead plane. On our third salvo we made our first kill. With a tremendous explosion and a huge cloud of

smoke our target fell out of the sky, its tail section completely demolished. The plane hit the water with a crash, skidded, tumbled, came to a stop, and burned like all the fires of hell. We shifted our sights to the next plane in line and immediately hit it squarely. It simply disintegrated in the air—big chunks of airplane splashed into the sea across a wide area.

Now every ship opened fire at one target or another. Because we were between the main body of the formation and the attackers, hundreds of shells streaked over our heads and hit the water ahead of the planes. The sky was filled with antiaircraft bursts . . . The Japanese formation broke up and start[ed] dropping torpedoes all over the place. Some fell at such a high speed that they somersaulted, while others ran true but wide. Two passed close astern of us. Two planes that we had hit fell into the water after they had flown directly over us. Our 40- and 20-mm shells made contact with engine nacelles and fuselages. Our automatic weapons gunners were terrific: Kelly, James, Keenum, and Grimm had nursed those guns, firing short bursts every day, and had sometimes slept by them, just waiting for a chance like this. The steady stream of tracers pouring out of those gun barrels was a beautiful sight. . . . twenty of the twenty-one bombers were in the water, most of them on fire and all of them destroyed. Not a single torpedo had reached its target. The wreckage of downed aircraft covered the water in every direction."[25]

This event was 11 months into the Pacific war, after the air threat had been recognized and many warships' anti-aircraft armament had been augmented from pre-war standards. For instance, the armament on the destroyer *Fletcher*, on the ways on 7 December 1941, consisting originally of one four-barrel 1.1-inch mount and six single 20mm mounts. By the end of the war she had five two-barrel 40mm mounts and seven single 20mm guns.[26]

What the battle fleet would have had in 1941 off Hawaii was much greater than what the smaller number of ships had off Guadalcanal on 12 November 1942. They both would have had the same fundamental AA fire control directors that proved so successful throughout the war. There is no reason to believe that the attacking Japanese aircraft would have been any more successful off Oahu than they were off Guadalcanal.

The likely Japanese losses can be calculated as they were in Chapter 9, assuming:

- the heavy AA was engaged for 15 minutes at an average rate of fire of 8 rounds per minute;
- the machine guns engaged for 8 minutes at their practical cyclical rate;
- the fleet consisted of eight battleships, four cruisers, and 20 destroyers with AA-capable main batteries.

Using the 1942 RPB numbers, 158 out of the 186 attackers in the first wave would be shot down, for 85% losses. This does not include losses inflicted by US fighter CAP from Oahu, or that the attackers could have been intercepted on the way to the fleet and on their return by AAC fighters.

In other words, an attack on the fleet underway off Pearl Harbor would have had results more like those seen in the Japanese torpedo plane attack off Guadalcanal than what was seen inside Pearl Harbor on 7 December 1941.

This calculation was based on RPB figures taken from combat experience. The defensive fires would be formidable, the Japanese losses would have been crippling, and the fleet would not have suffered damage anything near the scale that was sustained in the actual attack in the harbor.

The Fleet Is Attacked at Lahaina Roads

Another possibility was that the fleet would be anchored at Lahaina Roads, off Maui, 80 miles southwest of Oahu. The Japanese intelligence officer was sending daily position reports on the location of the fleet. With that in mind, this scenario breaks into two situations.

The first is where the incoming strike was diverted to Lahaina Anchorage after being launched. This case is nearly like that of the "fleet at sea" scenario. An anchor watch would be maintained on each of the ships, with personnel on the bridge and on the foc'sl to watch for the anchor dragging. The steam plant would be hot, with boilers on the line and steam to the nozzle blocks of the main engines. To get underway, it would be a simple procedure to slip the anchor chain, take the main engines off the jacking gear, and open the throttles. Top speed would not be available, but the ship would be able to maneuver.

Some of the ships would not be fast off the mark and might still be at anchor when the attack developed. A higher percentage of hits by the torpedo planes could be expected; however, in the usual fleet anchorage deployment, the torpedo planes would also have to fly close by cruisers and destroyers anchored on the periphery of the anchorage. It could be expected that many more of the torpedo planes would be hit before they could launch their torpedoes. The battle could take on the aspect of the torpedo bombers' attack off Guadalcanal. Six to ten torpedo hits might be a reasonable estimate.

The second case is where the Japanese knew that the force was at Lahaina Anchorage a day before the strike. The plan was for the attack to be executed, with a significant difference. The 50 Kate torpedo bombers that were allocated as high-altitude level bombers would now be armed with torpedoes. These crews had not practiced with torpedoes—many had never even dropped one in training. So, gauging the number of hits this group would achieve is problematic. These crews might be considered at the same training level as the crews assigned to launch torpedoes at the beginning of their training. In the first torpedo-launching exercises, the results were described as "very poor," with hits on the order of 15%.

The targets ships might be underway and maneuvering. The torpedo bombers would be faced with considerable defensive fire. The anchorage waters are shallow (in some places, single digit fathoms), so some torpedoes would strike the bottom. Applying a generous hit percentage of 15% would result in an additional 7 or 8 hits, for a total of 14 torpedo hits. If these hits were distributed over the battleships there would be two hits per battleship (if evenly allocated), or perhaps two or three battleships sunk (if the torpedo hits were concentrated on only a few ships).

This scenario results in about the same number of hits on the battleships as was achieved against the fleet in Pearl Harbor, but not the same losses, since the ships would have Zed set and be active in their damage control. The loss calculations were based on the Japanese estimate that it would take four torpedo hits to sink a battleship, not the US estimate of six to seven when underway in material condition Zed. An additional consideration is that there are good places to beach a sinking battleship within a few hundred yards of the anchorage. So, an attack against the fleet at Lahaina Roads would likely cause less damage then one against the fleet in harbor.

Finally, it must be noted that Lahaina Roads was a "peacetime only" anchorage. The fleet had not used Lahaina Roads for a year due to the submarine threat, so consideration of this scenario is academic.

The oft-stated supposition that the fleet was better off hit in Pearl Harbor than underway does not bear up under analysis. Historians have been caught in the fallacy that the Japanese bombing performance and the American AA performance would have remained as it was in the actual attack. They changed the location, but did not consider what else would change. Damage to the fleet would likely have been much less, while the Japanese air group could have been decimated.

3) "The Japanese should have launched a second strike, targeting the shipyard facilities and the fuel oil tanks." The Re-attack Controversy

Many commentators have asserted that the Japanese missed a great opportunity by not launching follow-up attacks targeting the Navy Yard machine shops and repair facilities, the Submarine Base, and the fuel tank farm. Such criticism is part of the official US Navy account of the battle, where the Japanese are castigated as they "neglected to damage the shoreside facilities at the Pearl Harbor Naval Base, which played an important role in the Allied victory in World War II."[27] This view is echoed by most historical commentators, for example, Goldstein and Dillon (coauthors of *At Dawn We Slept*) and Wenger have asserted that

> One stroke of luck for the Americans on 7 December was the fact that the Pearl Harbor attack plan contained no provision for destroying the Navy Yard. Had the Japanese done so, they would have put the US Pacific Fleet out of action far more effectively than by wrecking individual ships. The fleet would have had no choice but to return to the Pacific Coast. This withdrawal could have significantly altered the course of the war.[28]

This assessment appears to have begun with none other than Admiral Chester Nimitz, Commander in Chief of the Pacific Fleet, who once remarked that destruction of the fuel storage tanks "would have prolonged the war for another two years."[29] The venerable Morison picked up the theme in the semi-official *History of United States Naval Operations in World War II* and made the idea well-known. He asserted:

There is some question, however, whether the aviators were directed to the right targets, even from the Japanese point of view. They knocked out the Battle Force and decimated the striking air power present; but they neglected permanent installations at Pearl Harbor, including the repair shops which were able to do an amazingly quick job on the less severely damaged ships. And they did not even attempt to hit the power plant or the large fuel oil "tank farm," filled to capacity, whose loss (in the opinion of Admiral Hart) would have set back our advance across the Pacific much longer than did the damage to the fleet.[30]

Morison later expressed his opinion on the issue:

Tactically speaking, the Japanese committed the blunder in the Pearl Harbor attack of concentrating their attacks only on warships instead of directing them on land installations and fuel tanks. Not only was it strategically a folly, but politically, too, it was an unredeemable blunder.[31]

Prange, the great historian of the Pearl Harbor attack, added:

By failing to exploit the shock, bewilderment, and confusion on Oahu, by failing to take full advantage of its savage attack against Kimmel's ships, by failing to pulverize the Pearl Harbor base, by failing to destroy Oahu's vast fuel stores, and by failing to seek out and sink America's carriers, Japan committed its first and probably its greatest strategical error of the entire Pacific conflict.[32]

Goldstein, Dillon and Wenger frame the point in these terms:

One stroke of luck for the Americans on 7 December was the fact that the Pearl Harbor attack plan contained no provision for destroying the Navy Yard. Had the Japanese done so, they would have put the US Pacific Fleet out of action far more effectively than by wrecking individual ships. The fleet would have had no choice but to return to the Pacific Coast. This withdrawal could have significantly altered the course of the war.[33]

Van der Vat claimed that the fuel tanks and "vital shoreside facilities" were to be the "prime target of wave number three" and that their destruction "would have rendered the base useless and forced the US Navy back to the West Coast, over two thousand miles to the east,"[34] a claim repeated by Clarke[35] and others. Captain Joseph Taussig, Jr. claimed that "One lucky hit would have sorely curtailed the fuel supplies in the Pacific and created a logistics nightmare. . . . " Admiral Bloch, the Naval District Commander with local defense responsibility, testifying before a post-attack inquiry, said that if Japan had struck the shore installations "we would have been damaged infinitely more than we were."[36] Peattie makes the claim that ". . . there is little doubt that these targets *could* have been destroyed by Nagumo's force."[37] Another claimed that destroying the shipyard would have delayed serious operations in the Pacific by at least a year.[38]

These assessments have been absorbed into the popular consciousness: a television program on "The Myths of Pearl Harbor" asserted that "had the Japanese launched a third wave attack against the fuel tanks and naval shipyard, the United States would have been forced to pull their crippled fleet back to San Francisco . . . leaving Pearl Harbor defenseless."[39]

The tale of the argument on the carrier bridge where stodgy Nagumo turned his back on his aviator's demands for a third strike has been related in many places, based on Fuchida's version of the event:

On his return at midday, Fuchida had told Nagumo that there were still many significant targets worthy of attack. There was a complete infrastructure of dockyard installations, fuel storage tanks, power station and ship repair and maintenance facilities which supported the US Pacific Fleet and without which its rebuilding would have been impossible. There were also plenty of vessels not touched in the first assaults.[40]

According to Toland, the encounter happened this way:

Fuchida returned about an hour later and was greeted by an exultant Genda; then he went to the bridge and reported to Nagumo and Kusaka that at least two battleships had been sunk and four seriously damaged. He begged the admirals to launch another attack at once and this time concentrate on the oil tanks. . . . Kaga's captain, at the urging of Commander Sata, also recommended a strike against installations and fuel tanks. . . . "We should retire as planned," Kusaka advised Nagumo, who nodded. A staff officer suggested that they try and locate and sink the American carriers. Opinion on the bridge was divided. "There will be no more attacks of any kind," said Kusaka. We will withdraw."

Toland added, in a footnote,

Some accounts state that Fuchida and Genda repeatedly pleaded with Nagumo to return. In an interview in 1966, Admiral Kusaka recalled that they merely suggested a second attack and that his words "We will withdraw" ended the discussion; thereafter no one expressed a forceful opinion.[41]

Clearly, Kusaka, the First Air Fleet Chief of Staff, had a different perception of what happened on the *Akagi's* bridge that critical afternoon.

Fuchida published an article in the United States Naval Institute *Proceedings*, which was reprinted in 1969 in an anthology, *The Japanese Navy in World War II*. This article was written as a first-person account.

My plane was just about the last one to get back to *Akagi* where refueled and rearmed planes were being lined up on the busy flight deck in preparation for yet another attack. I was called to the bridge as soon as the plane stopped, and could tell on arriving there that Admiral Nagumo's staff had been engaged in heated discussions about the advisability of launching the next attack. They were waiting for my account of the battle. [After reporting the extent of the damage] I expressed my views saying, "All things considered we have achieved a great amount of destruction, but it would be unwise to assume that we have destroyed everything. There are still many targets remaining which should be hit. Therefore I recommend that another attack be launched." . . . I had done all I could to urge another attack, but the decision rested entirely with Admiral Nagumo, and he chose to retire without launching the next attack.[42]

In this account Fuchida mentions "heated discussions," but only claims that he recommended an additional attack against the "many targets remaining," implying targets from the original target set, ships and aircraft. No mention is made of attacking the shipyard or oil storage tanks. An approximation of this scene was included in the movie *Tora! Tora! Tora!* Fuchida served as one of the principle Japanese advisors to the producers of that film.

There are two other accounts of Fuchida's post-attack report, both by Fuchida as related to Prange, one in *At Dawn We Slept* published in 1981, and another in *God's Samurai,* Prange's biography of Fuchida, published in 1990. Both contain specific, line-by-line conversations, including quotations attributed to Nagumo, Kusaka, Genda, and other staff members.

On departing Pearl Harbor Fuchida claimed that he "mentally earmarked for destruction" the fuel tanks and the "vast repair and maintenance facilities" for the attention of a follow-on strike. Upon his return to *Akagi,* after collecting confirming information from other pilots, he went to the bridge to report to Nagumo. He claimed that "a fierce argument" ensued on the subject of a follow-on strike. In *Dawn* the exchange is related as follows (based on Fuchida's testimony which Prange dramatizes in the third person):

> Then Kusaka took up the questioning. "What do you think the next targets should be?" Fuchida drew a quick breath. The wording seemed to indicate an aggressive intent. He came back swiftly, "The next targets should be the dockyards, the fuel tanks, and an occasional ship." He saw no need to attack the battleships again.[43]

In *God's Samurai,* Fuchida (again through Prange) gives the exchange a different flavor:

> "If we attack again, what should the targets be?" asked Kusaka.
> Fuchida had no difficulty in answering, having thought of little else all the way back to the *Akagi.* "The damaged battleships and the other vessels in the harbor, the dock yards, and the fuel tanks," he informed them. ... Nagumo made no immediate decision, dismissing Fuchida with a word of praise. As soon as

he departed, Genda took up the battle. ... However, Nagumo refused to attack Pearl Harbor again or to hunt for the elusive
[American] flattops. ... *Akagi* hoisted a signal flag indicating retirement to the northwest. Upset, Fuchida scrambled to the
bridge.

"What's happened?" he asked Genda.

His classmate shrugged. "It can't be helped."

That wasn't good enough for Fuchida. He turned to
Nagumo, saluted, and asked bluntly, "Why aren't we attacking
again?"

Kusaka forestalled whatever reply Nagumo might have
made. "The objective of the Pearl Harbor operation is achieved,"
he said. "Now we must prepare for future operations."

Silently, Fuchida saluted and stalked off the bridge. "I was a
bitter and angry man," he recalled, "for I was convinced that
Nagumo should have attacked again."[44]

There are inconsistencies in these accounts that could be picked over
at length. That is unnecessary, since the conversation, in whatever version, the "heated discussion," Genda's "begging," stalking off the bridge
after a second confrontation, re-striking the battleships or not re-striking
the battleships—all, without a doubt, did *not* occur as related.

Kusaka stated in an interview that he had dismissed the subject of a
follow-on attack from the outset. There was a one-question exchange on
the subject initiated by a staff officer, not Fuchida or Genda; he did not
consider the exchange to be sufficiently important to mention it in his
account of the attack.[45]

Nagumo and Kusaka had possibly discussed the question before
Fuchida landed. In Dull's account, intercepted radio traffic inferred to
the Japanese that an estimated fifty land-based bombers were still operational, and they were still concerned over the unlocated American carriers. Nagumo and Kusaka decided that *Kido Butai* should quickly clear
the area. Dull's account did not mention a confrontation with Fuchida.

Genda categorically denied that any confrontation took place or that
a proposal for an additional strike arose. He did not "take up the battle"
for an additional strike, having realized long before that Nagumo had
his mind set against such an attack. Genda believed bringing it up would
be of no use.[46] He stated in his memoirs that he was aware of the scene

in *Tora! Tora! Tora!*, but explicitly denied that any such exchange took place or that a follow-on strike was proposed by Fuchida at all.[47]

Fuchida apparently noted American post-war statements regarding the supposed importance of a third strike against fuel and shipyard facilities and created fictional conversations that raised his perspicacity to heroic stature.[48]

The executive secretary of the US Naval Institute asked Genda why the Japanese did not bomb the fuel tanks. "He replied ingenuously that nobody had thought of this target."[49] When interviewed in 1945 immediately after the war, before all the American comments about striking the shipyard or the oil tanks were available in Japan, Fuchida was asked why there had been no third wave strike against Pearl Harbor. Fuchida made no mention of proposals to further attack the shipyard or the fuel tanks.[50]

Infrastructure targets had been briefly considered by the Japanese planners. Genda rejected them in his initial estimates because there wasn't enough ordnance to spare (recall his dictum that hitting a few critical targets decisively was better than hitting many targets with only minor damage). There wasn't sufficient ordnance to thoroughly attack fleet and OCA targets as it was, and a few odd bombs directed against the shipyard or the oil tank farms during the first or second waves would have been a wasteful half-measure—more like a hundreth-measure.

Thousands of miles away, members of the Combined Fleet staff, including the Chief of Staff Ugaki and Yamamoto, considered follow-on strikes. These officers appear to have been looking towards a more complete annihilation of the Pacific Fleet, and were not considering infrastructure targets.

Genda considered remaining in the Pearl Harbor area for days and dispatching repeated attacks but, as Willmott has noted:

> . . . [Genda] was not necessarily thinking in terms of attacks on port facilities, shore installations and the like. He was thinking primarily in terms of inflicting crippling losses upon the US Pacific Fleet. Indeed, on the morning of the attack Genda limited himself to the proposal that returning Kates should be armed with torpedoes to meet any American forces which tried to mount a counter-attack, but that if none materialized, the Kates should be armed for the normal bombing role. Such deliberation amounted to no more than normal staff procedure, and there

seems to be little evidence to suggest that Genda believed a follow-up attack would be necessary and on his own admission he made no representation to his superiors which suggested he was convinced of the need for such an operation.[51]

Some, particularly the more junior staff officers assigned to the Combined Fleet, were inflamed with fighting spirit, stoked by relief that great things had been accomplished at little cost, and were ready for a repeat performance; some felt that *Kido Butai* was still in dangerous waters, and the additional gains were not worth the additional risk.

One man staunchly against such an attack was Nagumo. He had doubts about the raid from the outset, and had shouldered for weeks the worry that his fragile carriers could be hit while thousands of miles from the nearest friendly port. When the attack met its objectives, he was more than happy to accept an unexpectedly one-sided victory and depart.

The idea that others would suddenly want to champion a return attack to hit shipyard and fuel facilities does not fit with the logistics-blind worldview of Japanese naval officers.

Realizing that the Japanese would likely not have gone after the shipyard and docks and fuel farms does not finalize the debate. Would a third wave attack against those targets been as destructive and as debilitating as so many maintain?

Composition of a Third-Wave Strike

Three hundred fifty aircraft were sent in the two waves of the attack. Of them, 29 (8%) were shot down and another 111 damaged,[52] of which 10 to 15 (perhaps as many as 20) were damaged so severely they were jettisoned. Others were written off as unsalvageable. Of the other damaged aircraft, it is not known how many could not be flown until they were repaired by the ships' maintenance force.[53] Willmott reports that once all the aircraft had returned to the carriers the Japanese had 265 aircraft available for operations.[54]

The Japanese would not have launched another two-wave attack with all available bombers. They were concerned that the US carriers, so far unlocated, would appear and attack. A duplicate two-wave attack would not leave aircraft to search for or strike American carriers. They undoubtedly would have held ready a strike armed with counter-shipping munitions.

If another strike was to be launched, the first order of business would be to launch reconnaissance to ensure the American carriers would not interfere. They could be almost anywhere, to the northeast between Hawaii and San Francisco, east (San Diego), northwest (Midway), west (Johnston Island), or south (Palmyra and the southern training operational areas). Because the Japanese had made a high-speed night transit, they could not even be sure that carriers were not to the north. A 360-degree search out to 250nm would be prudent. If the Japanese used 10-degree search intervals with a single aircraft on each track, 35 aircraft would be required.

The aircraft for this search could come from several sources. First, there were two cruisers accompanying the force, *Tone* and *Chikuma*, specially designed to handle six reconnaissance floatplanes apiece. If they contributed ten aircraft, the balance of 25 would come out of the carriers' complements. These would be B5N Kate carrier attack bombers on the carriers, which had the dual mission of reconnaissance as well as attack. There were the aircraft carried by the two fast battleships that accompanied the carriers, but these aircraft were usually employed in the inner anti-submarine patrol.

The Japanese carriers started with 144 B5N Kate carrier attack planes and 135 D3A Val dive-bombers. 16 Kates were lost or written off after the attack along with 31 Vals, leaving 128 Kates and 104 Vals. The crated spare aircraft would require at least 24 hours to assemble.

If one-third of the remaining aircraft were retained as an anti-shipping reserve, 70 B5N Kate carrier attack bombers (with two or three 250kg bombs each) and 70 D3A Val dive bombers (with one 250kg bomb each) could be employed in a third wave attack. They could deliver 210 to 280 250kg bombs.[55]

This is a high estimate. It is more likely that the Japanese would have retained at least half their aircraft as insurance against enemy carriers, and, as they viewed the B5N Kate as their real ship-killer, they would have retained a greater proportion of them for the anti-shipping strike. 100 of the modified "shallow water" torpedoes were delivered for this operation, and 40 expended in the attack. That might have limited the number of B5N Kates in the anti-shipping strike to 60. However, there may also have been unmodified torpedoes aboard.

Two hundred eighty 250kg bombs can be used as an upper estimate of the ordnance a third wave attack might deliver.

The Japanese Should have Attacked the Shipyard . . .

The first issue is to calculate how much destruction 280 250kg GP bombs could have inflicted on the shipyard.

Shipyard Facilities

Measurements taken from aerial photographs and confirmed by contemporary records give the total area of the naval shipyard and adjoining piers as 498 acres, or 21,692,880 square feet.[56] According to the United States Strategic Bombing Survey, calibrated for the specific bomb scaled from a US 500-pound GP bomb, a Japanese 250kg GP bomb might destroy an area of approximately 4,400 square feet against industrial facilities.[57]

Four assumptions can be made, all favoring the attackers:

- none of the aircraft are shot down before dropping their bomb(s) (an unlikely assumption, considering that defenses would be alert, Army AA batteries would have received their supply of ammunition, the search radars were operational and the remaining fighters would be on alert);
- all of the bombs hit inside the Navy Yard area (possible, if the best Japanese level bombing crews were assigned the attack);
- none of the bomb effects overlap (possible, if the aimpoints were suitably distributed and the bombing precise, but unlikely);
- the lethal area of the Japanese 250kg (551-pound) bomb can be scaled from the US 500-pound GP bomb (the Japanese bomb had a 0.2 second delay, which would mean it would tend to bury itself in the ground before detonating, making a deeper crater but damaging a lesser area than the US bomb. This assumption overestimates the lethality of the Japanese bomb); and
- no duds or low-order detonations (highly unlikely, considering the high dud rates experienced during the actual attack).

Under these assumptions the attack would destroy less than 6% of the area of the Navy Yard. Giving the assumptions a more realistic twist, damage could have been half that or less.[58]

The US Strategic Bombing Survey, when examining bomb damage

on German factories, found that the destruction of a building did not imply destruction of the contents. Often there was only temporary, re-pairable damage to the machines inside, which were rapidly returned to production. In Hawaii's mild climate all that might be required was a solid foundation and canvas to keep out the rain.

The possibility of fires is not included in the above calculation. Fires, unchecked, could greatly spread the extent of the damage. The firefight-ing capacity of the Navy Yard, naval base, and nearby Hickam Field was inadequate, even when augmented by cooperative support from the civil-ian fire fighting organizations at Honolulu. Hickam's sole fire truck was destroyed in the strafing.

When the Japanese bombers struck the Philippines' Naval Yard at Cavite a few days later, the shipyard was largely burned down. However, the Cavite Yard was smaller, crowded, and the buildings largely made out of wood, conditions not duplicated in the Pearl Harbor Yard. Even if fires doubled the area of the shipyard damage, damaging 12% of the navy yard would not place the yard out of commission.

Regenerative Capabilities

The Navy Yard would have considerable regeneration capacity, that is, the ability to repair itself. The submarine base had repair facilities. In ad-dition, there were the civilian facilities at Honolulu—the shipyard there serviced very extensive traffic through the port, on the order of a ship a day. The facilities in place to service that volume of traffic could have helped set damage to the Pearl Harbor Naval Shipyard to rights. There were other civilian companies that could help, and did provide extensive salvage assistance after the attack. Among many others, the Pacific Bridge Company provided divers and underwater concrete for covering torpedo holes in the battleships, and the General Electric Company assisted with restoring salt water-damaged electric motors, particularly the installations in the electric drive battleships.[59]

There was also the very considerable afloat repair capacity:

3 Repair Ships (*Medusa, Vestal,* and *Rigel*),
2 Destroyer Tenders (*Dobbin, Whitney*),
2 Seaplane Tenders (*Curtis, Tangier*).

There were also two small seaplane tenders, two converted destroyer seaplane tenders, and the submarine tender *Pelias*. There were another 12 large capable tenders elsewhere in the Pacific that could have been dispatched to Pearl Harbor.

Of all the tenders at Pearl Harbor on December 7th, the most capable were the three repair ships, two seaplane tenders, two destroyer tenders and the submarine tender. These ships had significant industrial capabilities, were stocked with machine tools and a foundry, and could do anything that a shipyard could do short of drydocking. The repair ships could "do practically anything except build [a battleship] from scratch":[60] rewind motors, cast and machine parts, shape and cut metal, build and repair valves, replace piping and electrical components, and much more. They were very capable of repairing the repair facility.

Skilled manpower was available, with hundreds of machinists' mates and boiler tenders and ship's carpenters released from the damaged battleships. This was a time when most every teenage American boy fixed up his own jalopy or helped repair his family's farm equipment. People were used to making their own repairs, improvising fixes, making do with less. It was an adaptive, adaptable generation.

An example of what resolute American sailors and civilian contractors could accomplish was that of a small group in the Red Sea in 1942.[61] Commander Edward Ellsberg arrived at the port of Massawa, recently abandoned by the Italians, with a small contingent of sailors and six civilian supervisors. He was tasked with restoring the naval shipyard's capability, to make it available to service Allied ships damaged in the intense naval battles in the Mediterranean. The working conditions were horrendous: food was scant and poor, temperatures topped 110 degrees each day at 100% humidity, and the coolest bath and drinking water available steamed when released from the faucet.

To add to the challenge, the Italians had thoroughly destroyed the repair facilities. Every machine tool, power source, or mechanism of any kind had been smashed. Even hand tools did not escape destruction. There remained only a few hand saws, a few screwdrivers, nothing more. This systematic destruction was far worse than what would have resulted if bombs had destroyed a small fraction of the Pearl Harbor facilities.

But, as Commander Ellsberg related:

> I had observed that while there wasn't an unsmashed electric driving motor on any machine, the smashing had not been sym-

metrically done. On some motors, they had smashed one end, on others the opposite end, on still others the main frame. There were hundreds of motors involved of different sizes, but of each size there were dozens at least. That situation was the key to our solution. If only we could disassemble all the broken motors, out of some dozens of broken motors of a given size, I was sure we could find enough undamaged parts of every kind needed to re-assemble a few complete motors at least.

Out of the disparate parts they were able to assemble a lathe and a milling machine. They used them to rebuild other machines. Discarded crucibles were used to cast gears. Quickly a fundamental capability was established, which was used to repair more capability, until ". . . in only one month after my arrival (we) had every sabotaged Italian shop in the naval base working at least the full capacity intended by the Italians themselves; in some cases more."[62]

This feat was accomplished by only a score of Americans with some recruited Italian prisoners of war. This ingenuity would be demonstrated by Americans repeatedly throughout the war under near-impossible conditions.

Compared to the resources Ellsberg had available at Massawa, a Pearl Harbor repair team would have had untouched civilian repair facilities at Honolulu and the Navy's tenders afloat, considerably more manpower, and the support of local civilian contractors, all in a congenial climate. In addition, for special or esoteric needs, the mainland was a week's transit away by steamer, a day by air. Obtaining replacement machines or materials would have been a matter of prioritizing, and with the mood in the Navy in the weeks after the Pearl Harbor attack, prioritization would not have been an obstacle. Obtaining replacement parts and tools for Pearl Harbor would likely have been viewed as a sacred duty.

There is no reason to expect that the Navy Yard could not have restored itself to full capacity faster than was accomplished at Massawa.

Destroying the Power Plant

Morison criticized that the Japanese "did not even attempt to hit the power plant." This was another comment made without considering the means to effect the destruction or the consequences. Morison evidently

made the statement without knowing what constituted the power generation capability at Pearl Harbor. There was not just one power plant, but
several in different locations, along with a new 20,000 kW bombproof
plant that had been under construction since October of 1941. It was not
just a case of allocating one spare Japanese bomb and the lights would
go out and everyone would go home.

If the Japanese wanted to take out the power plants they could have
obtained the necessary intelligence, and could have been able to identify
and target the plants from the air. However, their 250kg bombs were light
for that kind of application. The USSBS found that knocking out gener-
ator halls was extremely difficult, and the damage often could be put to
rights quickly.

The key to determining if the bombs were well employed would be
the duration of the outage. It is likely that power would have been out
for only a few days, perhaps hours. Historians never mention what would
happen after the generators had been destroyed.

Every ship afloat had the capability to generate electric power for itself, often with sufficient overcapacity to allow for battle damage or to
allow systems to be shut down for maintenance. This huge generation
capacity could have been used to power the base.

In 1929 Tacoma, Washington was hit by a drought that cut the water
supply to the city's hydroelectric power plant. The carrier *Lexington* was
directed to proceed to Tacoma to serve as a floating electric power station. *Lexington* arrived on 15 December, and two days later was tied into
the grid and providing power at a cost of one cent per kilowatt-hour for
12 hours a day for the next 30 days. *Lexington* had a new turbo-electric
drive using electricity to power her main propulsion motors, and had the
capacity to generate 140,800 kW, so she was particularly suited to this
task.[63]

Similarly, during the Korean War a destroyer escort provided power
to Korean coastal towns cut off from their regular power sources.[64]

The battleship *Maryland* at Pearl Harbor had a turbo-electric main
propulsion drive system similar to *Lexington*'s. *Maryland*'s plant was
smaller, but the electrical demand from the naval base and shipyard
would have been much smaller than that asked by the city of Tacoma,
and there would be other ships available to augment the supply. *Maryland* had been hit by two AP bombs, but damage was minor, and her engineering plant was unaffected. She was moored inboard of the

Oklahoma and pinned in her berth when that ship capsized, but freed on 10 December. She would have been ideal to provide this service. Alternatively, the tenders could have been used, as these ships were provided with sufficient electrical generation capability to power a nest of destroyers or submarines.

The destruction of the power plants supplying electricity to the Pearl Harbor base would have been a problem, but a temporary problem. It would not have had the strategic effects implied by Morison and Hart.

Conclusions: Attacking Pearl Harbor infrastructure

Admirals in the Pacific learned the great value of the Pearl Harbor Navy Yard throughout the early months of the war. It restored damaged battleships and two torpedoed cruisers and maintained the fast carrier task forces. In one celebrated case, without the Pearl Harbor Navy Yard, *Yorktown* would not have been ready for the Battle of Midway. Certainly admirals would shudder at the thought that the capability might have been taken away in the Japanese attack, as did Admiral Hart and Morison in print.

However, they did not consider what could have done to correct the problem. They did not consider the considerable alternative capacity in the repair ships afloat. Later in the war front line ships were well serviced by these repair ships and tenders far forward of Pearl Harbor. There is no reason why they would not have proven their worth earlier had the Pearl Harbor Navy Yard been incapacitated.

A Japanese third-wave attack simply would not have the firepower to inflict debilitating damage on the Navy Yard. Considering the available restorative capacity on the island, afloat and ashore, military and civilian, any damage could be put to rights in a short time.

Statements that a third wave attack against the shipyard would set the war in the Pacific back by a year are gross exaggerations. These targets were, indeed, as expressed by the Japanese Admiral Hara, "mere secondary objectives."[65]

Attacking the Fuel Oil Storage Tanks

The other target mentioned prominently is the fuel farm. Admiral Kimmel considered that the oil storage would have been an even more lucrative target than the warships: ". . . if they had destroyed the oil . . . it would have forced the withdrawal of the fleet to the coast because there

wasn't any oil anywhere else out there to keep the fleet operating."[66]
Goldstein, Dillon and Wenger claimed that not only would the destruction of the oil tanks have "crippled the entire Pacific Fleet," but they extended the hyperbole by stating, "Their destruction would have rendered
useless every military and naval installation in the islands."[67] Willmott,
Tohmatsu and Johnson have stated that with the destruction of the oil
"an intact Pacific Fleet, even if it suffered not as much as a single loss,
would have been forced to withdraw to San Diego."[68] Admiral Nimitz is
also on record as saying, "We had about 4.5 million barrels of oil out
there and all of it was vulnerable to .50-caliber bullets. Had the Japanese
destroyed the oil, it would have prolonged the war another two years."[69]

Genda wrote after the war that the question of destroying the fuel
tank farms only arose after the attack. "That was an instance of being
given an inch and asking for a mile."[70] The objective was to destroy warships. Oil tanks did not enter into the original concept, and for good reason—when considered as a bomb hauling problem, *Kido Butai's* aircraft
simply could not transport sufficient ordnance to destroy everything it
would have liked. The oil storage was never even on their agenda. Besides
the well-known Japanese dismissal of logistics concerns, all the destruction of the oil storage would do from their viewpoint is to delay the
American counterattack. If it was indeed a two-year delay as suggested
by Admiral Nimitz, that would be about the time when the Pacific Fleet
would have been greatly augmented by new construction and would have
greatly outnumbered the Japanese fleet. A long war is not one the Japanese wanted to fight or thought they could win.

Given that, it remains to test if the Japanese had the capability to destroy the fuel tanks.

The Pearl Harbor fuel farms consisted of 54 major fuel tanks constructed on small hills and slopes in two complexes, one between the
shipyard and Hickam Field, and the other above the submarine base.
There were also aviation fuel storage areas on Ford Island with pipes and
manifolds leading out to the Ford Island fueling pier berth F-4, where
the oiler *Neosho* was moored at the beginning of the attack. The largest
tanks had a capacity of over 10,000 tons of fuel; the total storage capacity
of ships' fuel was 563,000 tons. To place this in context, a full fuel load
for the surface combatants in harbor the day of the attack (eight battleships, eight cruisers, and 30 destroyers) would have been about 61,000
tons.

Prewar, Pearl was serviced by three commercial tankers making a continuous shuttle from the California oil fields. They were delivering about 40–50,000 tons of fuel monthly, enough to meet the fleet's training needs plus build up reserves to near capacity. The Pacific Fleet had a total of 11 tankers, of which four were fitted for underway replenishment.[71]

In addition to the surface tanks, a tremendous underground fuel storage project was begun in late December 1940. Called the Red Hill Underground Fuel Storage Facility, this secret installation eventually had 20 vaults with a total capacity of 5,400,000 barrels of fuel oil and 600,000 barrels of diesel for a total of 818,200 metric tons of fuel, over doubling the fuel storage at Pearl Harbor. The first of the vaults came on line on ten months after the attack, and the project was completed in September of 1943.

Destruction of Oil Storage by Machine Gun Fire

Nimitz believed that the fuel tanks could be set afire by .50-caliber machine gun fire. If this is true, failure to do so represented a significant lost opportunity for the Japanese.

The oil was stored in surface tanks with metal sides and a light conical roof to keep rain out. A flat top floats so there is no vapor space above the fuel, preventing explosive vapors from accumulating and keeping oxygen away from the fuel. The sides of the fuel tank were .75 of an inch to about 1.5 inches in thickness, tapered to increasing thickness near the bottom.

The Japanese aircraft did not carry .50-caliber machine guns. Their standard aircraft machine gun was the 7.7mm machine gun, a close relative of the British .303 machine gun.

Besides two 7.7mm machine guns, the A6M Zero carried two low-velocity 20mm cannon with 60 rounds per gun. The 20mm shell was designed to explode on contact with very light aircraft surfaces, thin aluminum or fabric, and so would not penetrate the tank sides. If hitting the roof, it would explode and hole the roof but likely would do little against the floating top. Fragments might penetrate the floating top, but would not have sufficient energy or any oxygen to ignite the fuel.

For fuel oil or diesel, a bullet would not ignite the fuel. If the bullet penetrates below the liquid level there is no air to support combustion. Even if there was oxygen, the flash point of the fuel is too high, and any bullets hitting a pool of fuel would not carry enough energy to raise any significant volume of fuel to temperatures where ignition could be sustained.[72]

Regarding penetration of the fuel tanks, Edward Rudnicki, a US Army ammunition expert, relates:

> WW2-era rifle-caliber AP typically penetrated its own diameter or a bit more [of metal plate]. The German 7.9x57mm AP was good for 10mm at 100m at 0 incidence, and the US .30 was good for a full half inch. But both of these were more powerful cartridges than the .303 British, which is what the 7.7mm IJN round is. But you'd need API [armor-piercing incendiary ammunition] to ensure fuel ignition, and I don't think [the Japanese] had API. Unfortunately because the IJN 7.7mm is the same as .303 it's hard to find info on the Japanese loadings, but I do note that the IJA's 7.7x58mmSR did not have API, but rather separate AP and I [incendiary] loads.[73]

The idea the Japanese could have achieved a "cheap kill" by machine-gunning the fuel storage tanks is a myth.[74]

Destruction of the Oil Storage Tanks by Bombing

Assumptions that the Japanese attack the oil storage tanks with 280 250kg bombs, all the aircraft release their bombs, and all the bombs hit inside the area of the tank farms, and the wall of the tanks consisted of one inch thick mild rolled steel, a computer simulation was run that distributed the 280 bombs randomly within the target area. Over 1,000 trials, in 90% of the cases between 22 and 35 tanks were hit directly and another three tanks breeched by blast or bomb fragments. This represents 46% to 69% of the fuel tanks, or 259,000–389,000 metric tons of fuel.

Each of the fuel tanks was surrounded by a berm (called a "tank dike") high enough to contain the entire capacity of the tank, plus extra volume to account for sloshing created by oil pouring rapidly out of a wall rupture. The radiant heat from a fire inside one tank dike can eventually ignite oil in neighboring tanks or dikes, but it would take at least an hour. The tank farms had a system of water piping and stray monitors to cool the surrounding areas to prevent the spread of the fire. Every tank would also have a built-in firefighting foam system. Since the Pearl Harbor tanks were relatively new, they likely had a central bunker that controlled the firefighting measures. Fuel from a burning tank or dike area could also simply be pumped from a burning tank into a safe tank. Transfer pumps were installed outside the diked area for this purpose.

There was a 10–15 knot breeze blowing at the time of the attack, so any smoke from upwind tank fires could conceal intact tanks, making the bombing problem more difficult.

The model suggests that about half the oil storage tanks would be destroyed. This is probably a high estimate. Setting fuel tanks on fire is a lot more difficult than it would seem. For example, the Haifa refinery and tank farm was shelled by Italian cruisers during World War II, without starting any fires. During the first Gulf War this refinery was the target of about a dozen Scud missiles. There were no direct hits, but one that exploded in a shopping mall across the street showered the refinery with hot missile parts, some of which hit and penetrated tank roofs. None started a fire.

It is hard to estimate the immediate effect of this loss on Pacific Fleet operations. Fuel certainly limited operations west of Hawaii, but this was because of limited fuel transportation and forward area storage, not a lack of the commodity itself. The main problem with far Pacific operations was a lack of tankers bringing fuel forward from Pearl Harbor, and fast tankers equipped for underway replenishment of the far-ranging carrier task forces.

A real measure of the impact of the destruction of the tanks and fuel would be how long it would have taken to restore the damage.

Oil tanks are simple constructs—a steel shell, a floating top, and a roof. The shell was essentially shaped sheet metal, something easily handled by the shipyard. It would have taken about 5,000 tons of steel to reconstruct the damaged or destroyed tanks. That amount of metal could have been provided by one cargo shipment from the West Coast. The consequences might have been on the order of imposing a two-month delay in the construction of two destroyers.

Replacing the fuel stockpile would require allocating sufficient tankers to provide the cargo lift needed. The table shows the number of tankers that would have to be assigned to the West Coast–Pearl Harbor run to replace the lost stockpile in the stated time.

Months	Tankers Required
1	13–20
2	7–10
3	5–7

At the end of 1941 there were about 120 tankers under US registry, with another 80 in Allied service under Panamanian registry and other flags of convenience. Ships were there—it was a matter of which tasks had the highest priority.

On December 8th, 1941, tankers could have been diverted to the Pacific without disrupting the war effort. Over the following January, February, and March, 43 tankers were sunk along the American eastern seaboard, the Caribbean, and in the Gulf of Mexico by U-boats.[75] Many of these ships were engaged in the US domestic trade delivering oil and gasoline to cities in the northeast. Even with the loss of these ships to the Germans' Operation Drumbeat, and dozens more in the following months, the American European war effort in 1942 was not hampered by fuel shortages. This indicates that some fraction of these 43 lost tankers could have been diverted to the Pacific in December 1941 without affecting the course of the war.

Sending tankers to the Pacific when Admiral King had yet to establish adequate ASW defenses along the Atlantic seaboard would likely have preserved them from the Germans. The Japanese were never effective in interdicting sea lines of communications, even in the opening days of the war when they deployed more than a score of their best submarines to surround and isolate Hawaii, so the ships would have been relatively safe in the Pacific.

The Japanese could have destroyed a significant part of Pearl Harbor's stored oil. However, the consequences of these losses would not have been as bad as represented by Kimmel and Nimitz. The idea that the fleet would have to withdraw from Pearl Harbor is nonsense. Tankers could have served as temporary storage until the surface tanks could be restored, or alternately, the construction of the underground tanks could have been accelerated. As for delaying the war for two years, that idea is hard to accept when the storage tanks could have been rebuilt and the stockpile restored in only a few months.

This analysis indicates that Kimmel's and Nimitz's statements were wrong. There are three reasons why their statements should be taken with the proverbial "grain of salt."

The first is the magnitude of the mental trauma that had been inflicted on them. They had grown up in the service with the feeling of absolute superiority over the Japanese. The sight of sunken American battleships was indeed the shock that Yamamoto expected it to be. It communicated despair thousands of miles away. On 8 December 1941, in Washington, Admiral Nimitz absorbed the news of the attack:

> To his old friend Captain F.E.M. ("Red") Whiting, the Bureau of Navigation's director of recruiting, Nimitz expressed his despair. "Red," he said, "we have suffered a terrible defeat. I don't know whether we can ever recover from it."[76]

In other words, admirals, even brilliant admirals, can be hit by the emotion of the moment.

The other difference appears to be the context that the Admirals were considering. If the entire Pearl Harbor fuel storage was destroyed and not restored, and the United States Navy fully deprived of its mid-Pacific refueling station, then the fleet certainly would have to fall back on its fuel supply at the continental United States, and the war might very well have been extended. If things had remained with the same level of tanker resources assigned to the Pacific, the Admirals' assessments might have been accurate.

But had the admirals considered what could have done to mitigate the problem their answers would have been different. Neither were men to accept setbacks passively. Both would have seen ways to overcome the destruction of the fuel storage tanks. The fact that such informed individuals would have considered it so significant is an indication that corrective measures would have been afforded the highest priority. Tankers would have been diverted from the East Coast and replacement storage tanks shipped to Hawaii and assembled rapidly, with little impact on the course of the war.

Lastly, there was the Red Hill Underground Fuel Storage Facility. This facility was classified "Secret." Nimitz's statement could have been made as "cover" for this facility. If needed, the project could have been accelerated. Indeed, while most documents indicate that the first of 20 tanks was officially placed into service in September of 1942, tour guides at the facility state that on 7 December 1941 there were three completed tanks, one full of fuel.

The idea that the destruction of the fuel tanks would have forced the Pacific Fleet out of Hawaii and extended the war by two years is a myth.

4) *Blocking the Channel*

Fuchida briefed the Japanese aviators to be alert for an opportunity to sink a ship in the channel to "bottle up" the fleet. During the raid *Nevada* got underway and was passing by the naval shipyard when the second-wave dive-bombers arrived. About 14 dive-bombers went after *Nevada*, while seven others went after two underway destroyers, *Dale* and *Helm*. *Nevada* took five hits.

Historians think this was a worthwhile effort. Willmott states, "Had [*Nevada*] been sunk in the channel, especially if she had been sunk in the channel between Ford Island and the gate, the ability of Pearl Harbor to function as a base would have been seriously imperiled."[77] Goldstein, Dillon and Wenger claim that "If a large ship should sink in the narrow channel, it would close the harbor for weeks, perhaps months, not only trapping any ship in the harbor but also denying entrance to those outside."[78] Slackman, showing how these assessments are propagated in the historical community, cites Prange when he claims that the attackers "could turn *Nevada* into a cork which would bottle up Pearl Harbor for weeks, perhaps months, to come." He goes on to make the rather remarkable assertion that "Rendering [the channel] unusable, even temporarily, might well have allowed Japanese forces to drive the U.S. Navy from the Central Pacific and jeopardize American control of Hawaii."[79]

The channel in 1941 was approximately 400 yards (1200 feet) wide. If a battleship with a 100-foot beam sank in the exact middle of the channel, 550 feet of clearance on each side would remain, more than enough for any ship to pass. If the ship was sunk off to the side of the channel, the remaining channel width would have been even greater.

The greatest blockage would come if a ship was at a right angle across the channel. But even if a 600-foot long ship was sunk broadside across the middle of the channel, there still would have remained 300 feet on each side for ships to pass.

The chances that a ship would sink in this way were miniscule. Ships do not sink instantly. A ship's commander would recognize that his ship was sinking and take the ship to the shallows and beach her along one side of the channel, as was done during the attack by *Nevada* and *Vestal*. If she lost power, there were yard tugs available. When *Nevada* was beached off Hospital Point, it was in a controlled manner assisted by a yard tug and a minesweeper.

The solution to any channel blockage would be to dredge a channel around it. Pearl Harbor had a soft bottom of loose silt which required constant dredging. Dredging around a wreck could be done in short order. Aerial photographs taken during the attack show two dredges working the harbor, one that *Nevada* dodged in her sortie.

Getting ships in and out of the harbor might be tricky, but ships routinely transit narrower gaps. At Oran after the North Africa landings 27 French wrecks littered the harbor, with six scuttled in two lines with the intention of blocking the port. There was a gap between two ships that could allow liberty ships to pass with only a few feet of clearance.[80] This took seamanship, but was accomplished. Navy shiphandlers routinely transit the Panama Canal where the channels vary between 500 to 1000 feet wide with two-way traffic. The author navigated the Canal at 40 knots aboard *Pegasus* (PHM-1).

Cutting the channel width to 300 feet would not have eliminated Pearl Harbor's usefulness as a base. The historians are wrong. More significantly, the Japanese attack planners were wrong. Their instructions to try to sink a ship in the channel resulted in wasting over one-fourth of the second-wave dive-bombers.

The only possible excuse for this error was that the planners thought the channel was narrower. In 1941, charts of Pearl Harbor were classified, so this information was not readily available. Even so, an experienced shiphandler could have helped the aviators come to a better decision.

5) *The Tardy Diplomatic Message*
Much has been made of the Japanese failure to deliver on time a diplomatic message that was scheduled to be placed in the hands of the Secretary of State by Ambassador Nomura Kichisaburo at 1300 Washington time, 0800 Pearl Harbor time—the famous "Fourteen Part Message." Delivery was delayed until 1400 Washington time, an hour after the attack had begun.

Historians have explicitly stated that the message was a formal declaration of war.[81] Yamamoto's biographer states that Yamamoto thought a declaration of war was to be delivered, and issued strict orders that the raid should not begin until after war had been declared.

The message delivered by Ambassador Nomura was not a declaration of war. It first reviewed the issues and the status of the negotiations from the Japanese viewpoint, provided an amazing apologia for several

Japanese positions, and accused the Americans of not negotiating in good faith. Then, the last part of the message stated:

> 7. Obviously it is the intention of the American Government to conspire with Great Britain and other countries to obstruct Japan's effort toward the establishment of peace through the creation of a new order in East Asia, and especially to preserve Anglo-American rights and interests by keeping Japan and China at war. This intention has been revealed clearly during the course of the present negotiation.
>
> Thus, the earnest hope of the Japanese Government to adjust Japanese-American relations and to preserve and promote the peace of the Pacific through cooperation with the American Government has finally been lost.
>
> The Japanese Government regrets to have to notify hereby the American Government that in view of the attitude of the American Government it cannot but consider that it is impossible to reach an agreement through further negotiations.
>
> December 7, 1941.[82]

This message was not a declaration of war. It chided the Americans for the developments during the negotiations between the two nations and stated their view that an agreement was impossible "though further negotiations," which returned relations to the *status quo ante* conditions prior to the beginning of negotiations. There was no intimation that the next step was war—there was no mention of resorting to war in the note. The note terminated negotiations, but did not break diplomatic relations or announce the recall their ambassador.

The idea forwarded by historians that the message "signified Japan's intention to resort to war to achieve its aims"[83] cannot be supported anywhere in the text. Certainly the American President did not think so: in his address to Congress on 8 December 1941(the famous "Day of Infamy" speech), Roosevelt referred to the 14-point message, saying that "While this reply stated that it seemed useless to continue the existing diplomatic negotiations, it contained no threat or hint of war or armed attack." Certainly Japan's ambassador to the United States did not interpret the note as signifying war. After delivering the note Nomura was informed of Pearl Harbor. The news of the attack "both surprised and stunned him."[84]

War was officially declared by Japan when the Privy Council met and issued an Imperial Declaration of War against England and the United States, at 1045 Tokyo time (1515 Pearl Harbor time), seven hours after the beginning of the attack.[85] The dramatic race to deliver the Fourteen-Part Message, included in Prange's *At Dawn We Slept*, and afterwards a staple in movies and other historical accounts, is misleading. When Prange quotes the President, after reading the 14th part, as saying, "This means war,"[86] he should have added that there was a world of difference between "This means war" and "This *declares* war *today*."

Did Yamamoto really believe that war was to be declared at 0800 Hawaiian time? Was he intentionally deceived by the government? Or, did he know that the "Fourteen-Part Message" only terminated a particular set of negotiations, and misrepresented it to his staff? If he thought it was a declaration of war and later discovered it was not, why didn't he or the Combined Fleet staff protest to the government?

Or, have Yamamoto's apologists just imaged a 0800 declaration of war so they can disassociate Yamamoto from violating international law? The lack of a 0800 declaration of war can also be claimed to be the cause of the American people's anger and intransigence to a negotiated peace. If a declaration of war had been delayed, it would reduce the apparent significance of Yamamoto's horrendous misjudgment of the American people's reaction to the Pearl Harbor attack.

Even if a declaration of war was to be issued at 0800 Pearl Harbor time, Yamamoto's forces committed numerous acts of war earlier. A Japanese submarine violated American waters when it investigated Lahaina Roads off Maui the day before. Japanese midget submarines violated sovereign waters the night before. American airspace was violated by reconnaissance planes over an hour before. Further afield, Japanese military reconnaissance planes violated Philippine sovereign air space, as well as Singapore's, almost daily for weeks before the commencement of hostilities.

The late delivery of the Fourteen-Part memorandum has been made a thing of high drama in books and movies. In fact, it was irrelevant—the document itself is a vague curiosity, and had it been delivered on time nothing would have changed.

A Japanese midget submarine, captured after her scuttling charge failed to detonate. A truck pulled the submarine onto the beach for salvage. Note the scrapes on the submarine's bow where it grounded on the reefs. The size of the midget submarine can be gauged from the length of the shovels in the right foreground. A wood beam and some sandbags prevent the submarine from rolling. *Source: Naval Archives, Washington DC*

CHAPTER ELEVEN

THE FIFTH MIDGET SUBMARINE:
A CAUTIONARY TALE

Mission and Accomplishments, Known and Presumed

The Japanese transported five two-man midget submarines to the Hawaiian Islands. They were to penetrate into the confines of Pearl Harbor on the night before the beginning of the war, lay on the bottom of the harbor, and in the dark of night after the aerial strike rise up and attack.

This concept did not sit well with the submariners—they wanted to attack at the same time as the aircraft, adding their 10 torpedoes to the 40 carried by the aviators. They petitioned Yamamoto and he granted their request.

If the midget submarines' torpedoes were held until after the air attack they could finish off partially damaged ships or hit remaining undamaged ships. There was no good operational reason to have them attack at the same time as the aviators other than a sense of romanticism.

The submarines first had to penetrate the air and surface anti-submarine patrols off the harbor, get past the torpedo netting stretched across the channel entrance, and navigate the channel in the dark using navigational lines of bearing taken from a small periscope that might only be a foot above the water. This last would be nearly an impossible task—experienced navigators have approached unfamiliar coastlines before, trying to pick out navigation lights from a background of shore lights, and found it difficult even with radar helping to pick out the

328   ATTACK ON PEARL HARBOR

navigation aids. The midgets were "nearly blind."[1] It would require incredible skill coupled with incredible good fortune to penetrate the harbor.

Alternately, one could let the enemy do the navigating, by following behind a ship transiting the channel. At least one midget submarine attempted this, trailing the cargo ship *Antares*. The submarine was visually spotted by the crew of the destroyer *Ward*. This was significant, because it was not always possible to conclusively classify sonar contacts, particularly in the poor sonar conditions around the islands. Whales, schools of fish, temperature inversions, and oil bubbles have often been classified as submarines.

A report of the sighting, identification, attack, and sinking was radioed to the Commandant of the 14th Naval District over an hour before the main attack. This incident illustrates the major flaw in the concept of the midget submarine launch. By attempting to penetrate the harbor before the attack, they ran the risk of putting the defenses on alert. We have earlier shown the possible consequences of early warning.

Just prior to the submariners' departure Yamamoto had second thoughts. He dispatched Captain Takayasu Arima, the torpedo staff officer at Combined Fleet Headquarters, to make it understood that the midgets were to slip into the harbor quietly, without raising any alarm. If they could not do this, they were to abandon the mission.[2]

Considering the restricted sensors on the midget submarines, this restriction was totally unrealistic. The midget submarine commanding officers were specifically selected for dash and determination. Why Yamamoto would think these men would exhibit so little *Yamato damashii* and the spirit of *kesshitai* (self-sacrifice) as to break off their mission is also unknown. Throughout the war, the Japanese had a weakness for expecting unrealistic results from unconventional means of attack, especially any that could be thought of as particularly reliant upon individual bravery, spirit, and force of will.

There was a peculiar psychology surrounding the Japanese planning processes. Failure was dishonorable, something for which one might be expected to apologize to the emperor or even end one's own life; thus, the possibility of failure was a very serious thing. To consider failure as a possibility was almost like an accusation of failure, or an evaluation that the warrior charged with the execution of a mission did not have the requisite fighting spirit or patriotism to succeed, a very serious charge.

To plan for alternative eventualities was almost like an insult to those who were to execute the primary plan. Time and again during the course of the war this resulted in a lack of flexibility in Japanese plans, a lack of alternative courses of action in the planning process, and a hesitation to adapt to alternative circumstance. These factors made the expectation of success from the midget submarine attacks high, and made the staffs overly receptive to optimistic reports of success.

On the evening of the day of the attack, the submarine I-16 received a short radio message transmitting "se, se, se," short for seiko, or success. According to Prange:

> On this slender evidence the Japanese Navy concluded that at least three midget submarines had penetrated Pearl Harbor and, after the raid, had inflicted severe damage, including the destruction of a capital ship. Quickly the word spread that the minisubs had sunk the *Arizona*. During the spring of 1942, the Japanese Navy released this to the press, and the midget submariners were venerated as veritable gods . . . [3]

The Japanese also received a report from a South American embassy source that said a battleship was sunk on the evening of 7 December by midget submarines. Willmott, Tohmatsu and Johnson champion the claim, stating that "two battleships were torpedoed by one midget submarine."[4]

A Matter of Ten Torpedoes

The evidence indicates that the midget submarine attack was a failure. Of the five midget submarines and ten torpedoes:

- One midget submarine penetrated the harbor and was underway west of Ford Island when it was discovered by the destroyer *Monaghan*. It hastily fired its torpedoes. One torpedo exploded near a pier while the other fetched up unexploded on the shore. This submarine was sunk by the destroyer, and eventually raised, inspected, and then buried in a landfill.
- Another was sunk by a 4-inch shell fired by the destroyer *Ward*. This submarine has been located by deep-submergence research submarines with both torpedoes still on board. It

remains in place as a war grave.

- Another suffered from a loss of depth control and a failed gyro, grounded, and was abandoned by her crew after the main battery failed. It washed up onto the shore off Weimanalo, Oahu, with both torpedoes on board.
- Another sank off the harbor entrance in Keehi Lagoon, Oahu, and was recovered in 1960 with both torpedoes still on board.
- The last midget submarine fired one or two torpedos at the light cruiser *St. Louis* as she was heading down the entrance channel for the open sea. As reported in her AR dated 10 December 1941:

When just inside entrance buoy No. 1 two torpedoes were fired at this ship from a distance of approximately 2,000 yards on the starboard beam. The torpedoes, although running shallow, struck the shoal inside buoy No. 1 and exploded, no damage to this vessel resulting. An object near the origin of the torpedo tracks was taken under fire by the 5" battery but no hits were observed.

Another report stated:

At 1004 when just inside the channel entrance buoys (Buoys #1 and 2) two torpedoes were seen approaching the ship from starboard from a range of between 1,000 to 2,000 yards. Just before striking the ship, they hit the reef to westward of the dredged channel and exploded doing no damage to the ship.[5]

Possibly only one torpedo was fired at *St. Louis*. One of the witnesses interviewed post-war said that the two explosions might actually have been one: "Well, it was really one explosion. . . . just, you know, it's practically instantaneous when the one blew up, it blew the other one up.'"[6] Considering that the MRI (minimum release interval) for a midget submarine's torpedoes was 60 seconds, it would have been impossible for two torpedoes to explode at the same point at the same time.

An hour before *St. Louis'* engagement, the destroyer *Helm* appeared to have encountered a midget submarine. From its AR:

0817 Sighted conning tower of submarine to right of channel, northward of buoy #1. [Note: this was in waters too shallow for a conventional submarine to operate.] Gave orders to open fire, pointer fire, but submarine submerged before guns could get on.

0818 Increased speed to 25 knots, cleared entrance buoys, turned right. 0819 Submarine conning tower surfaced.

0820 Opened fire on submarine off Tripod Reef, bearing 290 distance 1200 yards from buoy #1. No hits observed, but there were several close splashes. Submarine appeared to be touching bottom on ledge of reef, and in line of breakers. While still firing at submarine it apparently slipped off ledge and submerged.

0820 Made plain language contact report of Submarine to CinCPAC on 2562 Kc.

0821 Men on after guns and amidships observed torpedo pass close under the stern on a northwesterly course. Report of this did not reach the bridge.[7]

Whether there were two torpedoes fired at *St. Louis*, or one torpedo at her and one at the *Helm*, it appears that a midget submarine was operating just off the entrance to Pearl Harbor in waters right up to (and, perhaps, on) the coral reef, and expended both torpedoes.

Of the ten torpedoes carried by the midget submarines, only four were fired, two at *St. Louis* and possibly *Helm*, and two at *Monaghan*, all of which missed. The only damage inflicted was to a Ford Island pier. All six of the other torpedoes were unfired and have been visually sighted in their submarines' tubes.

Up until recently only four of the midget submarines were located. In 1980 Burl Burlingame was examining one of the Japanese photographs of the attack on Battleship Row and saw in the center of the photograph what looked like a midget submarine with its bow pointed towards Battleship Row, trailed by three plumes of water. Torpedo tracks appear to emanate from the submarine.

Burlingame published his conjectures in a 1991 book, *Advance Force Pearl Harbor*. That was the beginning of an enthusiastic effort by many investigators examining the possibility that the last midget submarine penetrated Pearl Harbor and attacked Battleship Row. In its latest incarnation, researchers hope to prove that the fifth midget submarine penetrated into Pearl Harbor and fired two torpedoes at Battleship Row simultaneously with the torpedo bombers' attack.

The proponents of the "fifth midget submarine in Pearl Harbor" hypothesis have come in two waves.

Wave 1: A Midget Submarine in the Photograph

The first wave of investigations was provoked by the photograph and Burlingame's conjectures. In an investigation published in *Naval History* magazine and broadcast in a television program called *Unsolved History: Myths of Pearl Harbor*,[8] the investigators claimed the image indeed showed a midget submarine. The three plumes in the picture were caused by the midget's props when the submarine oscillated up and down after firing a torpedo. The submarine supposedly lost trim control, broached, and her screws come out of the water kicking up the three plumes, which they called the "rooster tails."

They re-created the geometry of the scene in one-third scale on a lake using a scale model of a midget submarine. The resulting image appeared to closely match the photograph, less the "rooster tails."

The investigators commissioned the University of Michigan Marine Hydrodynamics Laboratories to simulate the event in a hydrodynamic model basin and duplicate the rooster tails. The results looked nothing like those on the photograph, either in size or shape. The University of Michigan investigators concluded that the plumes on the photograph were more likely the signature of Type 91 aerial torpedoes hitting the water.[9] In a rather humorous turn, the proponents then spent nearly an entire magazine article refuting the study that they themselves commissioned (without, in the opinion of many naval experts, much success).

In a letter published later in *Naval History Magazine,* other investigators analyzed the physics of the rooster tails. By using the plume heights as an estimate of the time between splashes and measuring the distance between them, it was calculated that a midget submarine would need to be traveling at well over 30 knots, ten times what a midget could do while launching torpedoes in a harbor. The article pointed out that the theorists had no explanation how a midget sub's small counter-rotating propellers turning at "dead slow" could kick up splashes over 60 feet in the air.[10]

Ignored also was direct empirical evidence. The midget submarine that fired upon *Curtiss* and *Monaghan* lost depth control and broached, but there were no reports of 60-foot rooster tails or, for that matter, any plumes of water at all being kicked up by her screws.

The splashes are more likely to have been generated by splinters from anti-aircraft shells, or by a heavy AA shell that skipped along the surface of the water.[11] A close examination of the plumes does not show any spreading from the brisk wind that was present at the time of the attack, indicating that they were created almost simultaneously, something a midget submarine at three knots could not do.

This first wave of theorists received wide attention. Their theory is repeated on many World War II web sites and in the Wikipedia article on the Pearl Harbor attack. However, it is an example of the worst kind of research, something characterized as "Advocacy Analysis," that is, analysis designed to promote a viewpoint by presenting selected facts and arguments while ignoring all evidence to the contrary. Advocacy Analysis is promoted by postmodernist historians who do not believe in absolute truth, but rather only in viewpoints and opinions.[12] In this case, the "Midget Submarine Myth" promulgators begin their theory based on a dark area on a photograph. Most egregiously, they present arguments in favor of their case but ignore the counterarguments or opposing evidence, such as the torpedoes that were fired at *St. Louis*.

There is also "negative evidence": things that did not occur, but should have, if their story were true. The investigators cannot explain why this midget submarine went unreported after it broached the surface and kicked up three tall plumes of water in an area under the eyes of hundreds of witnesses.

Besides the alleged midget submarine and the three "rooster tails," the photograph also shows an open ship's boat carrying a cluster of standing personnel. This boat is perhaps 20 yards away from the splashes and the supposedly broaching midget submarine, the conning tower of which appears to be five or ten feet above the water and prominent.[13] Two of the boat's occupants have left oral histories, Chaplain William McGuire and Machinist Mate Second Class R.G. Smith. The Chaplain had ordered the boat's coxswain to cross to 1010 Dock, and their path took them directly across the line of attack of the torpedo bombers at-tacking Battleship Row. They were strafed by passing torpedo bombers and their boat was hit four times. The oral histories include no mention of a midget submarine that supposedly broached only yards from their location, kicking 60-foot rooster-tails into the air.[14]

The first wave of investigators pretty much disappeared from public attention as the evidence, and lack of corroborating witnesses, supported the conclusion that the smudge in the photograph is not a midget submarine.

Wave 2: The Fifth Midget Discovered

The theory received another boost when research submarines from the Hawai'i Undersea Research Laboratory (HURL) discovered the last of the midget submarines. It was on the ocean bottom miles outside the harbor, in three pieces, within a debris field containing US amphibious warfare equipment. Both torpedoes were missing, apparently fired at *St. Louis* or *Helm*. This would appear to conclusively prove that the fifth midget submarine played out her career entirely outside the harbor.

This find was featured in a Nova program with the lurid title *Killer Submarines in Pearl Harbor,* first broadcast on 5 January 2010. In it a rather remarkable theory was proposed. Collecting an impressive amount of circumstantial evidence, the program theorized that the midget submarine penetrated into Pearl Harbor and fired her torpedoes, hitting *Arizona* and *Oklahoma*. She then escaped into the West Loch and scuttled. In 1944 there was a terrible accident in that area, an explosion and fire that consumed six LSTs that were preparing for an invasion operation. Navy salvage ships were sent to clean up the wreckage. Destroyed equipment, including amphibious assault vehicles, were taken outside the harbor and dumped. It was in this field of debris that the pieces of the submarine were discovered. The new theorists believe that the salvage operators picked up the midget submarine from inside the harbor and dumped its remains along with the damaged American equipment.

Care must be taken to separate the "Wave 2" investigators and the television producers. These new investigators are mostly a different group from the Wave 1 theorists, although they accept many of their ideas. The Wave 2 investigators uncovered new information to support their hypothesis.

Several of these investigators supported the Nova program. They have written that their own theories, and information that ran counter to the Nova program's arguments, were ignored by the Nova writers and producers, who seemed more intent upon sensationalism rather than serious historical investigation. The Nova writers picked through the arguments and, using innuendo and half-truths, packaged them in such a way as to lead the viewers to a shocking and melodramatic conclusion.

The Nova publicists promoted their program in ways certain to promulgate new myths about Pearl Harbor, and inject new inaccurate information into the folklore.

A hit from a Long Lance torpedo, about twice the size of torpedoes dropped by the Japanese aircraft that bombed Pearl Harbor on December 7th, 1941, would not merely sink a battleship. It would turn it upside down.

That bit of foolishness came from a promotional blurb in *Hollywood Today: Newsmagazine, with Attitude* on 5 January 2010; it was evidently written by the Nova promotional staff and disseminated widely, as the same words appeared verbatim in *rushprnews* and other web sites. It is particularly egregious considering that the Long Lance, a special oxygen-powered 24-inch torpedo carried by surface combatants, was not carried by midget submarines.

The Nova producers ignored their own experts. The fifth submarine was originally found in three pieces in 1992, 2000, and 2001 by HURL. The Nova team worked closely with HURL, filming several of HURL's dives. However, they ignored the HURL team's view, particularly that of Terry Kerby, HURL's Director of Facilities and Submersible Operations,[15] that this submarine was the one that fired on *St. Louis*—indeed, the program does not mention *St. Louis* or *Helm* at all, since any intimation that all ten torpedoes are accounted for explodes their theory that there were two "missing" torpedoes that were fired at Battleship Row. Parks Stephenson, one of the primary technical investigators, related that he attempted to get a more balanced presentation into the script, including consideration of the *St. Louis* and *Helm* attacks, but was rebuffed.

The Nova writers were not averse to implying another bit of sensationalism. In a publicity release, known in the industry as a "teaser," they implied that the midget submarines might have been involved in the sinking (that is, in the "final hours") of the *Arizona*. They wrote:

For decades, it has been thought that the Arizona was brought down by fire from Japanese aircraft. But the discovery of a Japanese "midget sub" displaced from the scene of the battle raises new questions about the Arizona's final hours.[16]

In fact, there is no reason to doubt that *Arizona* was "brought down" by the "fire" from Japanese aircraft, and the idea that a midget submarine was involved in *Arizona*'s "final hours" is acknowledged as speculation even by the Wave 2 investigators. The program itself makes no claim that a midget submarine sank the *Arizona*, but restraint is not evident in the carefully worded innuendo of the press release. Evidently the authors of "teasers" are not held accountable for the violence they do to the historical record.

The Nova program carefully selected the facts they allowed on the program. Besides not mentioning the *St. Louis* and *Helm* attacks, they selectively edited interviews with veterans, sailors on the *Vestal* who claims to have seen a torpedo hit the *Arizona*. Another veteran, Don Stratton, claims to have seen two torpedoes heading for *Arizona*, and in response to critics who doubted his testimony, responded, "They weren't there." The Nova program claims these torpedoes were launched from a midget submarine.

Using witnesses to substantiate information of this kind is very tricky. It is best when substantiated by physical evidence or in some other way corroborated. An example is provided by Herb Garcia, a retired Army colonel who is the curator of the Schofield Barracks base museum. Schofield was not attacked on 7 December—there was an explosion from an improperly fuzed AA shell that fell into a barrel of flour in the kitchen, and a few Japanese rear-seat gunners might have fired their machine guns in Schofield's direction in the course of attacking Wheeler Field, but no aircraft were formally assigned to attack Schofield, and apparently none did.

However, novelist James Jones included an attack on Schofield Barracks in his book *From Here to Eternity*, and the film version compellingly portrayed a heavy attack, with Japanese planes strafing on and off for over an hour and actors dying left and right. This fictitious attack on Schofield Barracks has become embedded in the Pearl Harbor attack folklore. Garcia relates,

> Remember, the soldiers who witnessed this were not trained observers, just excitable Depression-era kids. Then rumors got bigger in the telling and were reinforced by From Here to Eternity. Now, 90 percent of the veterans who return here say, "Yeah, I was bombed, I was strafed." If I argue, they say, "Look, buddy, I was here and you weren't."[17]

Nova sent divers down to inspect *Arizona*. There was no evidence of a torpedo explosion. Therefore, the Nova producers concluded that the torpedo(es) seen by the veterans were duds.

A 2,161-pound Type 97 torpedo striking at almost 50 miles per hour is going to leave an impact crater on the hull. Previous underwater surveys mapped *Arizona*'s hull down to every wrinkle. Nothing like a dud torpedo impact crater was found. A slight possibility exists that such evidence was so low on the hull that it is now buried under the harbor bottom's silt, but the chances of that are slight—the Japanese torpedoes were set to run at a depth of four meters or six meters,[18] which would put any impact point well above the turn of the bilge. If anything, the Japanese torpedoes tended to run a foot or more shallow, as evidenced by the locations of torpedo hits on other battleships.[19]

During the war divers used water jets to expose the hull down to the turn of the bilge while determining if *Arizona* could be salvaged. No evidence was found of a torpedo explosion or the impact of a dud torpedo. No dud torpedoes were found near the hull.

The Nova producers did not show on camera the veterans' *full* testimony. The veterans asserted that the torpedoes that they saw actually hit *and exploded*. They left that part out. That testimony would undermine the program's assertion that the torpedoes were duds. Alternately, the lack of physical evidence of a torpedo explosion would cast doubt on the witnesses' testimony that they saw torpedoes.

Killer Submarines in Pearl Harbor left out anything that cast doubt on their theory. This is about one-tenth of a degree short of mendacity.

Correlating the timing of the veterans' testimony and events, the explosion that the veterans' thought was from a torpedo was made by an AP bomb dropped by *Hiryu*'s level bombers.[20] The torpedo wake was from a torpedo that passed by *Vestal* and hit *Nevada*, the next-to-last torpedo, dropped just before the *Arizona* blew up.

After discarding the Nova program's inaccuracies and innuendo, the actual case put forward by the proponents of the "West Loch Theory" deserves consideration. They have no physical evidence, but a body of circumstantial evidence supports their theory. Most of the circumstantial evidence has alternate explanations, but neither side of the case is conclusive—the controversy boils down to which arguments resonate with a particular reader and which do not.

Calculating the Probability that the Theory Is True

It is possible to perform a subjective, first-order estimate of the probability that the West Loch theory is correct. The following chart shows the flow of the calculation. Each box consists of a specific event that would have to occur to make the theory true. It is possible to examine the arguments surrounding each of these events and, by considering them independently, that is, divorced from whether the preceding events were true or not, to come up with an estimate of the probability that each individual event is correct. Since the events had to happen (mostly) in series, the probabilities of occurrence can then be multiplied to get the net probability that the chain of events occurred in total.

The assigned probabilities are highly subjective. An argument that resonates with one person and assigned a high probability will be unconvincing to another, who might assign it a low probability. Readers are encouraged to substitute their own assessment.

Facts and Initial Assumptions

The assessment begins with what is known about the fifth submarine and its two torpedoes. The submarine:

1) began outside of Pearl Harbor;
2) ended outside Pearl Harbor;
3) was found in three pieces lying in close proximity;
4) one hull separation was caused by explosives, probably the sub's scuttling charge;
5) the other hull separation was caused by unbolting the after section from the amidships section, indicating the sub was subject to some kind of salvage effort;
6) had wire cables attached to all three sections, with their ends cut;
7) had fired its torpedoes.

The theory postulates that the submarine penetrated the harbor, expended its torpedoes against Battleship Row, escaped to the West Loch, scuttled, was discovered, salvaged, disassembled, transported outside Pearl Harbor, and dumped.

The theory must also discredit the alternate explanation that the

(20) The Fifth Midget Submarine: Event Flow Chart

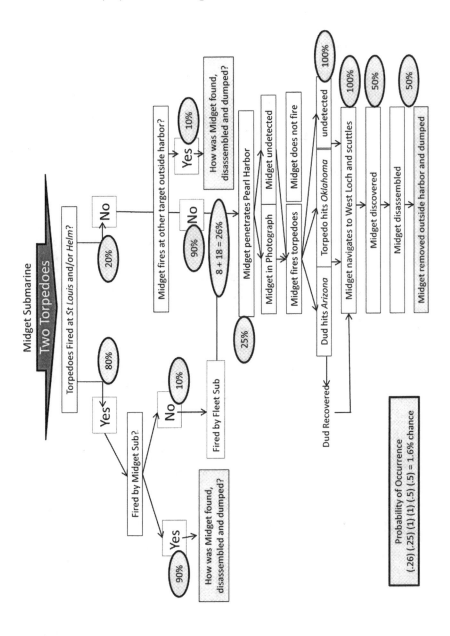

midget submarine remained outside the harbor and fired its torpedoes at *St. Louis* and *Helm*. The midget submarine could not have expended its torpedoes on the morning of the attack and had enough battery power remaining to enter Pearl Harbor.

Event Flow Chart
Was *St. Louis* Attacked by Torpedoes?

The analysis begins at the top of the chart, considering the fate of the two unaccounted torpedoes. The previous belief was that they were expended outside the harbor in an attack on *St. Louis*. In addition to the formal reports, there are surviving crewmembers from the *St. Louis* who witnessed the attack.

The theory must prove that this attack did not happen as recorded.

When *St. Louis* exited the channel she met up with three minesweepers, one of which reported that *St. Louis* took her minesweeping paravane under fire and cut across her sweep line, severing it. The minesweepers' logs do not mention a torpedo explosion.

The proponents suggest that the explosion reported by *St. Louis* was not from a torpedo. They point to the testimony of Douglas Huggins, on board *St. Louis* in Control Aft, who saw what he thought were bombs being dropped all round the ship as she exited the channel. According to one of the leading proponents of the theory, "one would suspect that what was actually seen were anti-aircraft rounds fired from inside the harbour [sic] falling back to earth."[21]

Others suggest that the commanding officer of the *St. Louis* fabricated the story of a torpedo explosion in order to escape responsibility for severing the minesweeper's lines.

A more detailed look at St. Louis' experience is warranted.

At 10:04 a.m., [Captain] Rood saw what appeared to be two torpedoes, one following the other, flashing toward his starboard bow.

"We're going to get smacked good and proper," thought Rood, and he called out to Commander Carl K. Fink, "If you want to see a ship torpedoed, come take a look!" Fink took one look and agreed with the skipper—in the narrow channel there wasn't much they could do. In the foremast structure, with a great view of the oncoming weapons from 1,000 to 2,000 yards,

Lieutenant Charles A. Curtze tensed as he watched the torpedoes arrow toward the ship.

Rood ordered St. Louis, already sprinting at 22 knots, to Emergency Full. At 25 knots, he tried a tentative zigzag, cranking the ship in the narrow, coral-rimmed channel. The first torpedo was aimed directly a the starboard side of turret No. 3, but struck a coral spit near Bouy No. 1, on the west side of the dredged channel, and exploded 200 yards from the ship, sending geysers skyward in an explosive blossom of water and coral.

It drenched the ship with water. "That Jap got over-anxious," observed Rood.

The second torpedo was "running hot" on a diverging track, about 10 degrees off the first, and was apparently caught up in the explosion. The track disappeared.[22]

In this account the torpedo tracks were seen before the explosion, with multiple witnesses. Two torpedoes were seen, one exploded, and the other motored on until it sank after its fuel was exhausted.

Given the existence of the explosion and ignoring the reported torpedo wakes, the argument then turns on whether the *St. Louis'* officers and crewmembers mistook the splash and explosion of a falling AA shell for that of a ~772-pound torpedo warhead when viewed from only two hundred yards. The torpedo plumes shown in photographs of the hits on Battleship Row were over 800 feet high, caused by torpedoes with 452-pound warheads; a 5-inch/25 shell weighed 54 pounds, with about 17 pounds as explosive filler, and would cause a splash 40 to 60 feet high that would not drench the ship if it exploded 200 yards off.

The accusation that the commanding officer fabricated his report to excuse his cutting the minesweepers' lines is rather distasteful, and has no basis other than the theorists' need to discredit the report.

Being generous to the theory, one might estimate that there was an 80% probability that the *St. Louis* was attacked by one or more torpedoes.

Proponents suggest that one of the other 23 Japanese fleet submarines operating in the area might have fired the torpedoes. However, none of the Japanese fleet submarine Tabular Record of Movement (TROM) chronicles any expenditure of torpedoes that day. All of the submarine patrol areas were well away from of the location of the attack. One submarine was later ordered to close on the channel entrance, but became fouled in a net and did not fire any torpedoes.

Some suggest that submarine *I-70*, which was sunk days later, might have delivered the attack on *St. Louis*. Japanese submarines were under strict control by radio by their admiral at Kwajalein Island, both receiving instructions and radioing back contact and attack reports. No orders for *I-70* to change station and approach the channel entrance are recorded in the TROMs, and no report of any attack on that day was radioed by *I-70*. The closest edge of *I-70's* assigned patrol area was 30nm from the harbor entrance.

The chances that a Japanese fleet submarine was responsible for the torpedo attack on *St. Louis* are vanishingly small. It is (generously) assessed at 10%.

If the midget submarine expended its torpedoes against *St. Louis* and never entered the harbor, it is still a mystery how it got to the bottom in three pieces after undergoing some kind of salvage effort.

There remains the possibility that the midget submarine fired its torpedoes outside the harbor in an attack that was not observed or recorded. Lieutenant William Outerbridge, commanding officer of the destroyer *Ward*, stated that

> There was another thing we saw. That was a lot of explosions along the reefs. I thought that they were explosions of torpedoes fired into the reefs. I didn't see any other submarines the whole morning. We didn't actually see any, but we did see a lot of explosions that looked like shallow water explosions of torpedoes.[23]

Numerous other ships in the area claimed to have been missed by torpedoes, although none observed an associated explosion as in the *St. Louis'* case. "Sub Jitters" is a known phenomenon.

The explosions noted by Outerbridge were likely from descending AA shells. The possibility that the midget submarine fired at some other target outside the harbor is small, assessed at 10%.

The two event paths converge with the next step, the submarine penetrating into Pearl Harbor. The net probability up to this point is the combination of the two possible paths, 8% (along the path of a confirmed torpedo attack against *St. Louis*) and 18% along the other, a combined probability of 26%

Did the Midget Penetrate Into Pearl Harbor?

Of the four other midget submarines, one penetrated the harbor, three did not. The locations of all four hulls are confirmed. Based on this operational experience, the probability that the fifth midget submarine penetrated into the harbor is assessed at 25%.

The "Midget in the Photograph" Firing Torpedoes into Battleship Row

As discussed above, the possibility that the photograph captured a view of a midget submarine in the process of delivering a torpedo attack on Battleship Row is vanishingly small.

However, an alternate possibility exists. The midget submarine might have remained in the harbor unobserved. It might have fired its torpedoes from another location in the harbor and the torpedoes missed, all unobserved.

In the absence of any way to discredit this possibility, the event will be given a probability of 10%.

Firing Torpedoes Against Battleship Row

The proponent's have searched for confirmation that the midget submarine fired its torpedoes against Battleship Row targets. Its torpedoes carried almost twice as much explosive as the Type 91 aerial torpedoes, so they have looked for evidence of unusually powerful torpedo explosions. There are several possibilities.

Oklahoma

Sailors in *Oklahoma*'s after steering compartment during the attack described the sounds of the torpedo hits. As related by Seaman First Class Jim Bounds:

> I noticed other torpedo hits, but I noticed [the first] three more than anything else, and then there was an extra loud one . . . it shook the ship, then we got one or two more after that . . . but they wasn't as powerful as that one.

The theory proponents believe that the "extra loud one" was evidence of the detonation of a heavier midget submarine torpedo.

An explosion's sound propagation through a warship's hull is subject to a great deal of variability. Bounds, inside the armored box of after steering, heard the hits distinctly. Gunners Mate Leon Kolb, on *Okla-homa*'s main deck, felt the first hit as more of a thud or vibration rather than an explosion. Boatswain Adolph Bothne, on deck preparing to go over the side on a hull cleaning detail, never felt even one of the hits.[24] Clearly there were differences in sound and shock propagation to different locations.

How loud or heavy a hit might seem is based on:

- what the torpedo hit (against crushable anti-torpedo bulk-heads vs. stiff belt armor anchored to the hull),
- where it hit longitudinally (between 100 to 400 feet away from after steering),
- depth (near the surface, venting most of the explosive force into the air, or deep under the waterline, or even the actual hit that occurred on the second deck above the armored belt as *Oklahoma* capsized),
- the order of the hits and proximity to damaged portions of the hull (a hit forward of a previously damaged section would be less tightly coupled acoustically to transmit sound waves through the structure of the ship from forward to aft).

Torpedoes with the same warhead weight will propagate different sounds, especially when heard from a location at the extreme stern of the ship. One torpedo sounding louder than others would be expected. Differences in perceived volume of noise cannot be reasonably used as conclusive evidence that a larger submarine torpedo warhead hit *Oklahoma*.

Photographs of the *Oklahoma*'s hull taken in drydock after she was raised show much more extensive damage than that inflicted by Type 91 aerial torpedoes on other battleships. One of the Nova program contributors suggests that this was the result of a hit by the heavier Type 97 midget submarine torpedo.

Oklahoma rolled onto her damaged side while capsizing, and was again rolled on that side during the salvage operation. The additional damage resulted from rolling a 27,000-ton hull onto a damaged and weakened structure that was not stressed to handle such loads. If the heavier damage resulted from a single more powerful torpedo hit, the area of heavier damage would have been localized. The heavier damage appears over the entire length of the hull.

There is an area where belt armor plates are missing and one is cracked, but it is unlikely that a torpedo would have been able to create that damage—other aerial torpedoes hitting belt armor deflected belt armor inwards. Increasing the explosive charge would likely just do the more of the same. The missing and cracked plates are more likely the result of the effects of rolling the hull on to them after the plate's support structure was weakened (or removed) by the aerial torpedoes.

Arizona

The Nova program edited testimony from two sailors from the crew of the *Vestal* to make a case that *Arizona* was hit by a dud midget submarine torpedo. There is no corroborating physical evidence.

Witnesses on *Vestal* claim that a torpedo went under their hull to strike *Arizona*. If this had been the case, the same kind of damage would have been inflicted on *Vestal* as that which caused *Oglala* to sink after a torpedo went under her and detonated against *Helena*. *Vestal's* hull showed no evidence of such damage when she was drydocked, only the damage caused by two AP bomb hits.

A photograph taken by a *Kaga* high-altitude level bomber shows oil pouring out of *Nevada*. She was hit by the second-to-last torpedo dropped. There was no oil slick around *Arizona*.[25]

Even assuming that they did see a torpedo, there is nothing to indicate that it was launched from a submarine. Just as in the testimony of the sailors on the *Dale* who testified that they were attacked by AP bombs one hour after the last AP bomb was dropped, and the sailors on the *Shaw* who believed that they were attacked by incendiary bombs when the Japanese had no such weapon, and the soldiers testifying they were strafed at Schofield Barracks, human testimony has to be carefully cross-checked with other testimony and correlated with physical evidence before it is accepted *prima fascia*.

This is not the only case where eyewitness reports were inaccurate. The captain of *Vestal* reported that *Arizona* was hit by a bomb down the battleship's stack in a letter to the Chief of the Bureau of Ships, making it an "official" rumor, repeated to this day.[26] Inspection found the armored grate covering the stack opening was undamaged. There was no evidence of a bomb hit in the vicinity.

This should not in any way be taken as a slur against the veterans. There is a considerable body of literature confirming that eyewitness memories of stressful events are not always accurate—four individuals observing a bank robbery will all give different accounts, to the frustration of law enforcement officers. The brain is a very uncertain recording device when under stress, and memories shift and fade. Veterans' memories can be influenced by things learned after the attack, like reading battle histories, watching war movies or in reunion discussions.

An additional possibility suggested by the proponents is that the torpedo actually went deep and exploded under *Arizona*. Two testimonies are cited to support this theory. First, Admiral Kimmel spoke of what he saw from the front lawn of his quarters. "I saw *Arizona* lift out of the water, then sink back down, way down . . . I knew the ship had been hit hard because even then I could see it begin to list."

He could have witnessed a torpedo hit, although it is difficult to understand how he saw the ship "lift out of the water" when *Vestal* was blocking his line of sight. Or, he could have mistaken *Oklahoma* for *Arizona*, two ships with very similar silhouettes. The movie footage of *Arizona* that recorded the magazine explosion does not show a list on the ship, contradicting Admiral Kimmel's observation.

The water main on Ford Island lost pressure almost immediately after the beginning of the attack. The island's 12-inch fresh water supply pipe passed under *Arizona*. It has always been assumed that *Arizona's* magazine explosion destroyed the water pipes. The proponents speculate that a midget submarine torpedo slipped under *Arizona* and destroyed the pipe.

This is not corroborated by physical evidence. An explosion under the keel is considerably worse than one against a ship's side—the hull would hog from the explosions' gas bubble, then sag down as the bubble collapsed. This would leave cracks in the hull. *Arizona* shows no evidence that a torpedo detonated under her keel.

There was a 6-inch temporary fresh water supply pipe at the south end of the island. This pipe was destroyed by one of the first 250kg GP bombs that hit the island. Water gushing out of that damaged pipe would have depressurized the system. A witness reported that water main pressure was low *before* the *Arizona* exploded (the torpedo hit supposedly within seconds of the magazine explosion). The reported depressurization of the fresh water system was likely the result of the ruptured 6-inch pipe coupled with high demand for water for firefighting.

A Recovered Dud Midget Submarine Torpedo

The best possible evidence to conclusively prove that a midget submarine fired a torpedo at a battleship would be to recover a dud Type 97 torpedo from the mud next to Battleship Row. Researcher Tom Taylor believes he has found references to such a torpedo. He relates:

> The entry "A recovered unexploded torpedo carried a charge of 1,000 pounds of explosive." was made by Admiral Chester W. Nimitz, Commander-in-Chief, United States Pacific Fleet to The Secretary of the Navy via The Commander-in-Chief, United States Fleet and The Chief of Naval Operations.
>
> It is located in the CINCPAC After Action Report (File No. A16-3/Serial 0479 dtd FEB 15 1942) under Part III, Narrative of Events During Japanese Raid, 7 December, 1941, Phase I - 0755-0825 (Combined Torpedo Plane and Dive Bomber Attacks), (A) Torpedo planes, paragraph 1.
>
> 1. Of the four separate torpedo plane attacks made in this Phase, as distinguished by sectors of origin, the major effort was that conducted by 12 torpedo planes which swung in generally from the Southeast, over the tank form, Merry Point, and environs; launching their torpedoes from very low altitudes, and at very short distances, toward the battleships on the South side of Ford Island. All of the outboard battleships were effectively hit by one or more torpedoes. Strafing was simultaneously conducted from the rear cockpits. A recovered unexploded torpedo carried a charge of 1,000 pounds of explosive.[27]

Taylor asserts that the torpedo with "a charge of 1,000 pounds of explosive" refers to a dud midget submarine torpedo.

Reference to a recovered torpedo with a "1,000 pound warhead" does not necessarily indicate a midget submarine torpedo. The Type 97 torpedo used on the midgets had a warhead explosive weight under 800 pounds. The warhead weights do not match. The figure quoted in the report could have been an underestimate of the total weight of a recovered aerial torpedo, or a typographical error, or a reference to the total weight of an aerial torpedo rather than just the warhead, or some other problem in the documentation.[28] Taylor believes otherwise, asserting that the entry must be correct since Nimitz signed the report.[29] To accept that he must also believe that Nimitz wrongly associated that torpedo with the aerial attack, so, according to Taylor, Nimitz was both right and wrong. Taylor chooses which facts to accept and which to reject based on which best forward his theory.

Several aerial torpedoes were recovered, one from the Naval Shipyard's woodpile after it was jettisoned, most likely that of Petty Officer First Class Kitahara Syuzo. There are eyewitness accounts of another torpedo that slid up a muddy beach and spun its prop to exhaustion, "buzzing its life out in a parking lot."[30] So, the Americans had samples of Japanese aerial torpedoes. They also had samples of the Type 97 torpedo as two were recovered on the midget submarine that beached off Bellows Field.

Since a warhead weighing 1,000 pounds does not match the two torpedo types employed at Pearl Harbor or, for that matter, *none of the torpedoes that ever existed in the Japanese inventory*, the entry is simply an error. Erroneous information cannot be used to either prove or disprove a hypothesis. It is like finding a document where a man says he found a 20 cent coin. Taylor would have us accept that since 20 cents is closer to a quarter than a dime, the man therefore found a quarter. But it could have been a typographical error, either substituting a "2" for a "1," meaning the man found a dime, or a "0" for a "5," meaning the man found a quarter. Erroneous information cannot be used to support an argument either way.

Others feel that further documentation would be helpful, hopefully in the form of an ordnance intelligence exploitation report documenting a Type 97 torpedo recovered from Battleship Row. Such a document has yet to be found. If such a report is found, it hopefully will specify the locations from which the torpedo was recovered.

It is impossible to either prove or disprove the possibility that the missing Japanese midget submarine fired its torpedoes inside Pearl Harbor. There is always the possibility that the weapons were expended without anyone noticing—unlikely, considering the thousands of witnesses surrounding the harbor that day—but impossible to disprove without indisputable evidence of how the torpedoes were used. So as to not bias the calculation, a probability of 100% will be assigned to this event.

The Midget Navigates to West Loch

After expending its torpedoes the midget submarine must navigate to the

West Loch and scuttle. Proponents point to several sightings of periscopes in the areas between Battleship Row and the entrance to the West Loch between 0837 and 0900, heading outbound.

Alternate explanations are again possible. The "periscope sightings" occurred 40 minutes to an hour after *Arizona* exploded and *Oklahoma* capsized. Both of these catastrophes threw massive amounts of debris into the water, all of which would be floating with the current out of the harbor, down the channel and past the entrance to West Loch. Photographs show evidence of this debris.

The periscope sightings were about a mile downstream from Battleship Row. There was a brisk current. The locations and times of the sightings are such that they could be from debris floating in the current.

Debris has often been misidentified as submarine periscopes. In the Atlantic, German submarines used to throw swabs into the water ahead of convoys. The mop head would become saturated and sink, leaving the wooden handle floating straight up and down and looking remarkably like a periscope. Many swabs suffered crippling damage from depth charge attacks by Allied escorts.

Ships store their swabs in racks on the weather decks to allow them to dry in the sun without introducing a bad odor into the ship. Many were dumped in the water when *Oklahoma* capsized.

There is the very human propensity to see things that are not quite so. "Submarine Jitters" has already been mentioned. For example, during the Falklands War in 1982 the British were concerned about the Argentine submarine threat. They maintained close attention to their ASW searches. A number of contacts were prosecuted but all eventually proved to be false alarms. However, when British intelligence reported that an Argentine submarine had left her berth in a port hundreds of miles away, the number of submarine contacts went up by a factor of ten. The British began to run short of ASW torpedoes as they attacked whales, schools of fish, and thermoclines. The contact rate returned to normal when the Argentine submarine was found to have moved to a different berth.

A similar thing happened to the Japanese battleline, which was at sea the day of the Pearl Harbor raid. On 10 December reconnaissance flights and patrol boats reported five enemy submarines in the vicinity of the Japanese Main Body. They decided to return to port. Combined Fleet Chief of Staff Ugaki recorded in his diary, "How dangerous our invisible enemy is!" [31] There were no American submarines within 1,500nm.

After *Ward's* engagement with a midget submarine outside the harbor, and *Monaghan's* engagement inside the harbor, it would be natural for people to mistake swabs for periscopes.

This explanation aside, there is no concrete evidence to prove that a midget submarine did not make it into the West Loch. Looking at it as an independent event, and assuming that all the previous events had occurred, there is nothing to say that a midget submarine could not have escaped and navigated to the West Loch, and scuttled. So, while an informed analyst might find this difficult to accept, this probability will be set at 100%.

Midget Discovered, Midget Disassembled, Midget Dumped

The last of the series of events in the theory is that the midget submarine was salvaged, taken outside the harbor, and dumped. The theory's proponents believe that this happened in the course of the salvage operations associated with the West Loch Disaster.

There is again a lack of any evidence, records, or witness accounts to support this hypothesis.

The theory requires people to press the "I believe" button several times. First, they must believe that the submarine was found in 1944 and that this discovery was kept a secret, as no publicity or notice was circulated announcing the find. It would have been natural for the discovery to have been reported to higher authorities and to the intelligence community, as the midget submarine might have been evidence of attempts to penetrate the harbor after 7 December, and the intelligence community (as well as those in charge of harbor defense) would want to know about it. No such reports have been discovered. No reports to higher authority, no reports of salvage activity, and no requests for instructions on how to proceed have been found.

The salvage activity was well documented by photographers, as evidenced by the many photographs of the cleanup activity in the archives. No photographs of a midget submarine have been found. Any photographer assigned to document the salvage operation would have jumped at the chance to photograph a salvaged Japanese midget submarine.

It is hard to believe that, if they existed, all these reports and photographs and documents have been lost, and that no one who worked on the West Loch Disaster has subsequently come forward with the revelation of a previously unreported Japanese midget submarine.

The possibility that the midget submarine was discovered in the West Loch (and kept secret) is remote. A probability for this event is assigned at a generous 50%.

Assuming that it was found in the West Loch, the midget submarine then had to be salvaged and disassembled. Again, there are no records of instruction passed to the salvage teams, no log entries, or any other documentation. A probability for this event is also generous at 50%.

There is physical evidence that the midget submarine was salvaged, disassembled, and rigged with wires that might have been for lifting or towing tackle. Those wires were apparently cut and remain connected to the submarine's remains outside Pearl Harbor. No Navy records of this activity have been found.

There are several possibilities. First, that the midget submarine was found in the West Loch and salvaged. The records exist but have not been located, or they have been discarded or destroyed.

Second, the salvage was accomplished by people other than Navy salvage teams, perhaps civilians who did not have any bureaucratic need for records.

A third possibility is that the midget submarine did not penetrate into Pearl Harbor, but was discovered outside the harbor, salvaged, and dumped. If this happened after the war, there would be no need to exploit the midget for intelligence. The midget had had no torpedoes or remaining scuttling charge, so there would be no issues regarding unexploded ordnance and no need to call in explosives experts. If salvaged by a civilian firm, the operation might not leave Navy records. If this happened during the Korean War, the Navy might not want to raise memories of the attack on Pearl Harbor while it was undertaking wartime operations out of Japanese ports.

This event chain would have a much higher probability of occurrence than the one proposed in the Nova television program.

Final Assessment

The probability that the *Killer Sub in Pearl Harbor* theory is correct in all its components is determined by multiplying the probabilities of all the independent components. The result of this calculation is that there is a less than 2% chance that it is correct—and this with probability numbers that are very generous.

A problem with this type of analysis is that it is almost impossible to prove that something did not occur. Known events can be substantiated by witness reports, documents, logs, and photographs—but how does one disprove that an unobserved submarine fired unobserved torpedoes that did not explode? If the two "100%" assessments were changed to 10%, a number with which reasonable observers might feel comfortable, the chances drop to under one in 6,000.

Only by proving what the midget submarine did do could all other courses of action be eliminated. In the case of the fifth midget submarine, there are witnesses that saw evidence of her attack on the *St. Louis*, but if the torpedo misses, there are always those who can claim that the witnesses were mistaken.

Without concrete proof, there will be no curbs on speculation. Theories, no matter how unlikely, will continue to be explored by ratings-inclined television producers or researchers.

A lingering possibility exists that the American copy of the photograph that started the controversy simply had a smudge or imperfection that only looks like a submarine. The area of the photograph under question is tiny.

The Japanese originally used this photograph during their BDA assessment. They annotated the photograph in detail, down to mentioning the torpedo tracks in the loch. They examined the original of this photograph very closely. There was no mention of midget submarines on their copies.

The last word on this controversy ought to be left to the Japanese. A program on NHK Broadcasting, *The Mystery of Pearl Harbor: The Tragedy of the Special Submarines* was broadcast on 6 December 2009. It was a joint production with the US Public Broadcasting station WGBH, which funded and broadcast the *Killer Sub in Pearl Harbor* program, and used much of the same footage.

To the Japanese audience the program renounced their government's previous report that one of their midget submarines sank *Arizona*. They concluded that the fifth midget submarine expended its torpedoes against *St. Louis*. The midget submarine crews were appropriately honored for their bravery and sacrifice.

Conclusion

The West Loch theory has several components that could represent single point failures; for example, if the torpedoes could be somehow confirmed as being fired outside the harbor. But there are also single pieces of evidence that, if discovered, could signal the theory is correct; for example, discovery of an intelligence report of a dud Type 97 torpedo recovered from the vicinity of Battleship Row, or reports dealing with a previously unknown midget submarine salvaged from the West Loch.

Until such evidence is discovered, the search will continue. If the theory is eventually confirmed, its proponents will have achieved one of the more remarkable cases of historical detective work in modern history.

Evaluation of the Midget Submarine Operation

The midget submarine operation was only scheduled after a personal appeal to Yamamoto. He authorized it over the opposition of most of the air staff officers, who feared that the midget submarines might be detected. Yamamoto's emotional decision ought to have been overridden by cold calculation.

Crews were killed in training when depth control was lost and the submarines nosed into the bottom muck and could not surface. American anti-submarine technology and tactics were known to be good.[32] With all these factors in play, all that could be expected even by the most optimistic planners was that one or two submarines might penetrate into the harbor and achieve a hit, maybe two.

The downside was huge. If detected, the element of surprise could be lost for the attack as a whole. The Americans would be given hours to go on alert, shift their mental outlook into wartime thinking, and ready themselves for war. The attacking aircraft would lose the element of surprise and possibly be greeted by the defenses outlined in Chapter 9. The cream of the Imperial Naval Carrier Aviation Corps was at risk.

Any Western naval officer who accepted such odds would be labeled a fool. But the Imperial Japanese Navy did not operate on Western standards of rationality, but rather depended upon the "favor of providential help" and the "supremacy of mental power."[33] To any other way of thinking, risking thousands of men and the future of your country in order to accommodate the knight-errant ambitions of a few junior officers in an unproven weapon makes no sense whatsoever.

But, to deny young warriors such a chance for glory? That was not Yamamoto's way of war.

CHAPTER TWELVE

REASSESSING THE PARTICIPANTS

Most of the historical treatment of the Pearl Harbor attack has centered upon the human tragedy of the events and the story of the decisions that shaped those events. This analysis has developed a dramatically new assessment of the Pearl Harbor attack. This, in turn, requires a reassessment of some of the key participants.

The Americans
General Short, Commander of Pearl Harbor's Defenses

Pearl Harbor was supposed to be a sanctuary, a place where the Pacific Fleet could rest, break down equipment for maintenance (including AA guns and directors), and allow crews rest and liberty, all of which were needed considering the Fleet's intense training schedule. General Short, the commander in charge of the air and ground defenses of the islands, was tasked to provide that sanctuary.

He had maintained a high level of alert up until the eve of the attack. Then, inexplicably, after receiving a "war warning" message, he returned the ammunition to the magazines, parked the mobile AA batteries in storage, allowed the fighter pilots off base, allowed fighters to be placed out of service for maintenance, and locked up their ammunition in hangars. The Air Information Center remained inoperative. In effect, he disarmed his air defenses.

Fearful of the Islands' Japanese immigrants and nationalized citizens, he made the decision to park his aircraft wingtip-to-wingtip as an anti-sabotage measure, rather than dispersing them into their revetments.

This was all done after he received intelligence that war was imminent and that the Japanese fleet was on the move. It was as if he knew that the war was coming but rejected any possibility of an attack on the islands, so he was giving his men a last weekend of rest before the balloon went up.

General Short had sufficient forces and equipment to do his job. If the AIC had been active and his air defenses alert, the Army defenders would likely have given the Japanese a very bloody nose and the fleet would have been well defended. The anti-sabotage parking measure alone tripled the US aircraft losses on the ground.

General Short was held responsible for his decisions, and rightly so.

Admiral Kimmel, Commander in Chief, Pacific Fleet

Many feel that Kimmel was ill-treated and made a scapegoat. Kimmel argued that Washington withheld information that would have prompted different decisions. Placing that aside, he remains worthy of censure on other grounds.

Kimmel was responsible for deep reconnaissance around the islands. His argument for not fulfilling this responsibility was that he had insufficient aircraft for a continuous, full 360-degree search over the months of the developing war crisis, the only kind he contended would be useful. Such patrolling would indeed have worn his force to the nub quickly.

However, short-term patrols during high-risk periods were possible. Before 7 December Kimmel had in hand a "war warning" message from Washington, something truly special, and well beyond previous advisories of rising tensions or the status of negotiations. He also had reports of major Japanese fleet units moving towards an invasion of Southeast Asia—in fact, 90% of the Japanese Navy was underway on 6 December 1941. This should have triggered a decision to initiate patrolling.

His intelligence chief reported he had lost track of the Japanese carriers. Kimmel asked the right question: "Do you mean to say that they could be rounding Diamond Head this minute and we wouldn't know?" He did not act on the answer.

Kimmel's own instructions to the fleet highlighted the possibility of a Japanese aerial attack. Instead, he, too, gave his men the weekend off. A reasonable alternative, never mentioned, was the possibility of employing an "Outer Air Patrol" designed to detect incoming air raids. Such a patrol could have detected the approach of the Japanese air strike and provided 40 minutes warning. An Outer Air Patrol was doctrine in the fleet while underway,[1] and required far fewer aircraft than those needed for a 700nm, 360-degree search. Forty minutes would have been sufficient to disperse the aircraft on the ground,[2] get any "ready" fighters aloft, and make the ships and their AA defenses ready to repel attackers.

The most significant deficiency was that the Air Information Center was inactive. Had the AIC been up and operational, 40 minutes warning would have been given the fleet and the Army AA units. Kimmel bears a portion of the responsibility for not insisting that the AIC be activated after its successful operational test. Lack of manpower was the excuse for not activating the Center. Kimmel could have provided the needed Navy officers and ought to have insisted that the Army follow suit.

Kimmel knew his battleships were vulnerable to torpedoes. He knew about Taranto, and he had been informed by the CNO that he could not assume that harbor depth would preclude a torpedo attack.[3] He rejected torpedo nets for operational considerations, but there were other countermeasures possible. He could have shielded the battleships with less-valuable deep draft auxiliaries moored outboard, or just obtained some hulks from the local boneyard and ballasted them down as a torpedo shield. A barge anchored in the shipyard turning basin mounting a few dozen .50-cal machine guns would, if the performance of *Bagley*'s AA gunners was duplicated, have gone a long way towards thwarting the attack. But, as one naval officer has observed, "He just wasn't interested, in plain truth."

Those championing Kimmel's cause contend that he should be exonerated since he was not in charge of the harbor's defenses. The Navy has a long tradition of responsibility epitomized by the saying, "You get what you *in*spect, not what you *ex*pect." Aboard ship, responsibility has to be delegated; a captain cannot run every piece of machinery and make every decision. However, the captain still bears the responsibility, and is expected to perform sufficient inspections and oversight to ensure his ship is run effectively and safely. The saying is akin to Ronald Reagan's famous "Trust, but verify."

While Kimmel was not responsible for the air defenses of the island, he was responsible for the safety of the fleet. He did not "inspect" to get what he "expected." As Prange noted,

> he never looked over the Army's antiaircraft batteries, did not know that Short had three types of alert, and did not visit the Information Center to see for himself how the radar setup operated, although these were essential factors in the defense of his precious anchorage and of the Fleet at its moorings.[4]

When General Short relaxed readiness, Kimmel should have recognized what the new condition of readiness constituted, and taken action to reverse that egregious decision. He expected his fleet to be defended, but did not ensure that the defense was in place. He did not inspect. He did not verify.

Kimmel's standing orders to the fleet of 14 October 1941, a short seven weeks before the attack, stated that "a declaration of war may be preceded by 1) a surprise attack on ships in Pearl Harbor; 2) a surprise submarine attack on ships in operating area; or 3) a combination of these two."[5] He lost sight of his own standing orders. He was more concerned with preparing a plan to lure the Japanese fleet into an early contest between the battlelines in the Central Pacific. His actions were conditioned by his assumptions: "I never thought those little yellow sons of bitches could pull off such an attack so far from Japan."[6]

Prange contends that there was no action open to Kimmel on 7 December with more than a negligible bearing on the outcome.[7] That obfuscates what Kimmel could have done, the simplest thing of all: keeping his people informed. If he had informed his command that war was imminent, something he could have done without revealing any code-breaking secrets, there were things that could have been accomplished even in minutes before the attack. For example, no ship CO in the fleet would have allowed voids to remain open over a weekend had they known what Kimmel knew on 6 December.

Kimmel informed Rear Admiral William Halsey of the imminence of war. When Halsey took Task Force Eight to sea he placed it on a war footing, under radio silence, magazines unlocked and aircraft fully armed. What Halsey did, Kimmel should have done; had others been kept informed, their actions could not have been as overt as Halsey's, but still could have saved hundreds of lives.

Kimmel bears an appropriate degree of responsibility for what happened. His failure remains an example of the consequences of insufficient oversight. To exonerate him decades removed from the events would only obscure that lesson.

The Japanese
Genda, the Brilliant Planner

Genda has been praised for putting together a brilliant attack plan. He has been lauded as a genius.[8] Analysis leads to a different impression.

Genda was operating under significant constraints, particularly in the experience level of his aviators. Many of his aircrews were nuggets; the air groups of two of his six carriers had only recently been formed and were green. His available A6M Zero fighter pilots were especially so. Consequently, he decided early the roles to be played by each of his squadrons in order to allow his aviators to concentrate on their specific roles. He left no flexibility to change those roles based on the hit percentages achieved during training or if the problem of delivering torpedoes in shallow water was or was not solved. He decided early in the planning process the numbers of torpedo bombers, high-altitude level bombers, and OCA aircraft. His solution achieved the strike's objectives and should be praised as such, even though his plan received the unexpected assistance of some really bad command decisions by the Americans.

Otherwise, Genda's attack plan was simple and uncomplicated. He divided the bombers up into groups, gave them their targets, and expected them to hit. He allocated sufficient firepower to cripple the battleships, which was his boss's objective; but he allocated just a bit more to follow his own lodestar, the destruction of the carriers, including a follow-on attack by dive bombers assigned to hit carriers even if they were capsized hulks. True to his boss, yes; but even more true to his own vision.

The plan was simple, constrained by the training level of the personnel with which he had to work. But it also was so simple that it could have been disastrous. There was no attempt to have the aircraft arrive over their targets simultaneously in a time-on-target strike. There was no control over the fighters to have them maintain a CAP with their bombers and over the airfields. There was no provision for SEAD, even though SEAD tactics were practiced for attacks against fleet units at sea. Probably worst of all, the torpedo aircrews were given a complicated prioritization scheme for the selection of their targets that was unworkable under combat conditions, one of the reasons for the poor distribution of weapons over the available targets. The second-wave dive-bombers were to hit targets of opportunity also in accordance with a prioritization scheme, which became a muddled affair when their objectives were changed literally at the last moment before take-off, and upon arrival over the target, smoke and cloud cover restricted visibility at the dive-bombers' normal pitch-over altitude. The plan for the employment of fighters ignored any responsibility to protect the strike's heavy hitters, the torpedo bombers, in favor of slap-dash strafing attacks against scattered airfields. Even then, the distribution of fighters against airfields made little sense: more first-wave fighters were sent against a base serving reconnaissance seaplanes rather than against bases serving fighters and bombers.

Genda did not include a full rehearsal of the specific attack in his timetable, allowing only two days for all the aircraft types and formations to practice in a group setting against fleet units anchored in an open bay—a setting dissimilar to what the attackers would find at Pearl Harbor. This allowed several planning problems to slip through. Practicing the attack against a mock-up of the carrier moorings might have discovered the problem of making torpedo runs into the rising sun, and perhaps could have prevented wasting valuable torpedoes on the *Utah*. The co-ordination and deconfliction of crossing torpedo bomber attack routes did not happen. The problem of overconcentration on some targets was noted, but apparently no action was taken to resolve the issue. The problem of deploying the torpedo bombers into long strings was not practiced, and was to be a serious problem in the actual attack.

Prior to sailing, all of Genda's plans assumed that surprise would be achieved. This is astonishing, particularly considering that he had almost a year to work on alternatives, and that the operations order specified that the attack would be launched even if *Kido Butai* was detected as much as a day prior to the attack. Several other plans based on other sets of assumptions were put together during the transit to the target, but they were only minor riffs on the original theme. They were not well thought out, as exemplified by the flare signaling method that was supposed to shift the attackers from one plan to another. The confusion that resulted directly led to most of the B5N Kate losses, and the premature bombing alerted the American AA fire that may have contributed to the low percentage of hits by the torpedo bombers.

Overall, the attack plan created by Genda (with assistance from Fuchida and other Japanese experts) was simplistic and much less than state of the art for the period. It was not the product of genius. It succeeded because there were 40 aircrews in B5N Kate torpedo bombers who struck with fortitude, overcoming the plan's problems to deliver their attacks with skill and determination, and 15 of them managed to hit the targets they needed to hit. Aside from that, to paraphrase the intrepid World War I pilot Manfred von Richtofen, "Anything else is rubbish."

Fuchida, the Intrepid Warrior

Fuchida's reputation has waned over the last several decades.

He began by having a tremendous influence on the postwar history of the early engagements of the Pacific War. His reputation and influence hit its zenith with the adulatory depictions of his actions by Prange in *At Dawn We Slept* and Prange's biography of Fuchida, *God's Samurai*, along with the publication of Fuchida's own book, *Midway, the Battle that Doomed Japan*. It began to diminish with the discovery of serious discrepancies in his accounts. His Midway tale, where he claimed that the Japanese carriers were minutes from launching their own strike when the American dive-bombers struck, has been shown to be a fabrication.[9] His claim that he was on the deck of the *Missouri* during the surrender ceremony is a wistful fabrication.

With these cracks in the façade, it was appropriate to go back over all of Fuchida's statements regarding Pearl Harbor and look on them with analytic scrutiny. Many of the statements have been found to be suspect. Many apparently are the product of a man trying to inflate his own reputation and blame Japan's failures on others—"If they would only have listened to me . . ." Others are the product of complex professional, personal, and cultural pressures.

This analysis has found additional problems with Fuchida's judgment regarding the planning and execution of the attack. In addition, there were statements that he made postwar that did not stand up to scrutiny:

- He claimed he pointed out to Genda the need for level bombers employing AP bombs. The timeline of weapons development does not support this claim.

- He claimed he informed Genda of the double berthing of battleships and the possibility of torpedo nets. He claimed he was the one to put these factors together to realize that level bombers were needed, and convinced Genda to include level bombers with AP bombs in the plan. Considering the reputed brilliance of Genda, and the fact that AP bombs were on order well before Fuchida joined the program, these claims are suspect.

- He claimed he ordered his level bombers to concentrate on one battleship in order to ensure that at least one of the US heavies was destroyed. The level bombers' attacks were nearly evenly distributed over the inboard ships along Battleship Row, making it questionable if such instructions were actually issued. He might have been trying to indirectly claim credit for the *Arizona's* magazine explosion. If it was given, that instruction might have been spread to the torpedo bomber aircrews and could assume some of the blame for the over-concentration of torpedoes against *Oklahoma* and *West Virginia*.

- The planned torpedo attack technique, four long strings of bombers with many crossing routes from which to choose, coupled with Fuchida's blunder with the flares, resulted in an uncontrolled attack with mutual interference, aborted runs, and at least one jettisoned torpedo. The aborted runs forced re-attacks, which dragged out the duration of the torpedo attack, allowing AA resistance to intensify, which may have contributed to the torpedo misses and to torpedo bomber losses. While it is likely that Fuchida did not put together these routes, he was a supervisory planner and a B5N Kate crewmember, and ought to have noted that the planned routes required deconfliction.

- He shares blame with Genda and the other planners for the unworkable prioritization plan for matching aircraft with targets, which was impossible to execute under combat conditions.

- He shares blame with Genda for refusing to adjust the attack plan to account for the latest intelligence reporting the absence of carriers in the harbor. This directly contributed to wasting six torpedoes against ships moored at the carrier anchorages.

- The planning did not provide fighter cover for the torpedo bombers all the way to the target. He did not ask for appropriate SEAD support for the torpedo bombers, even though he was a torpedo bomber pilot, and such support was considered necessary for attacks against fleet targets.
- He chose an approach route to the target different from what was planned. While that may have been forced on him by the clouds over northern Oahu, he could have regained his planned track, but made no effort to do so. This eliminated the possibility that the torpedo attacks on the east and west sides of Ford Island could be delivered simultaneously.
- His decisions led to the loss of five B5N Kate torpedo bombers, and to the inaccurate delivery of many torpedoes.
- He acquiesced to the decision to send dive-bombers against the *Nevada* to sink her in the channel, when the chances of that happening using GP bombs were close to nil. His belief that sinking a ship in the channel would bottle up the fleet was ill-informed.
- He approved a report crediting more torpedo hits than were reported by his subordinate commanders. He estimated almost double the number of torpedo hits than actually occurred.
- He approved a report that grossly inflated the number of GP bomb hits attributed to the dive-bombers of the second wave on fleet targets, and the effects of those hits.
- He approved a report that assessed *Neosho* as sunk when photographic evidence would have shown the berth to be empty. He inexplicably failed to note *Neosho*'s movement away from Battleship Row.
- He similarly approved a report that *Vestal* was sunk, with inadequate evidence.

There were a lot of cultural and institutional pressures on Fuchida as he put together the BDA Report. He was part of a community of aviators looking to prove themselves; he had friends who participated in the attack who he did not want to put "on report" for poor performance; he would not want to over exaggerate the results of the attack, as this might lead his nation into disastrous strategic decisions in the future; he wanted his component of the aviation community, and the aviation community as a whole, plus himself, to look good in front of the Imperial Navy, the Japanese government, as well as before his god-emperor. And he craved attention, a sense of self-significance. Mark Twain described such men as "The bride at every wedding, the corpse at every funeral." Or, in this case, at every surrender ceremony.

In the early postwar years, Fuchida said that he felt he "was like a star that had fallen. At one moment I was Captain Mitsuo Fuchida, and the next I was nobody!" When he converted to Christianity, he grabbed a microphone from the missionaries and shouted, "I am Mitsuo Fuchida who led the air raid on Pearl Harbor. I have now surrendered my heart and my life to Jesus Christ."[10] It was typical of Fuchida that he would mention his name and fame as if God would be impressed.

Fuchida's report of the net damage to the Pacific Fleet, in spite of individual distortions and exaggerations and falsifications, was in the aggregate remarkably accurate. It is in the details that his accounts suffer.

There is one last clue that would suggest that any machinations in the BDA report to make the dive bombers look good became known during the war. Looking at Fuchida's wartime record, he served as the strike leader of the attack on Pearl Harbor, and then served afloat as a key leader on board Kido Butai's flagship for the first six months of the war. At Midway he broke both of his ankles jumping down from the bridge to the flight deck to escape the fire that engulfed the island superstructure. After Midway, he never again served in a front-line billet. He ended the war as an obscure aviation staff officer at an obscure airfield. With the horrendous losses the Japanese experienced in aviation personnel and their need for experienced aviation leaders, why was the hero of Pearl Harbor, a proven combat leader, sidelined in a backwater assignment?

The key might be the "Japanese Study of the Pearl Harbor Operation," a review of the Pearl Harbor attack conducted in August of 1942. This study significantly pared back the number of hits credited to the second wave dive bombers. This study could have discovered that Fuchida had inflated the returns, and concluded that he no longer could be trusted with a front-line leadership role. Perhaps. Again, there is no definitive answer.

In Japan, Fuchida is recognized as an unreliable source. They are amazed that this is unknown in the Western world. As more is learned about Fuchida and more scrutiny given to his decisions and statements, the more his reputation suffers, a sad legacy for a pioneer aviation warrior.

Nagumo, the Timid Commander

Nagumo has been castigated by historians, depicted as a timid commander who did not really understand air power. His decision to forgo a third wave strike has been criticized as a monumental lost opportunity, under the presumption that destruction of the naval shipyard or the fuel storage facilities would have changed the course of the war.

Analysis indicates that a third wave strike would not have had the devastating consequences most writers have assumed. It could not have destroyed the shipyard, and any damage that could have been done would likely have been quickly repaired. Significant damage could have been inflicted on the fuel storage tanks had the Japanese concentrated all their third effort against them, but the damage could have been put to rights in a few months, would have only required a relatively minor redirection of American oil transportation assets and materials, and likely would not have had any great impact on operations.

Under this light, Nagumo's decisions look much better than before. In two sets of wargames he had been conditioned to expect losses. He was burdened with custody of Japan's consolidated fleet carrier striking force in a navy that revered the offensive; damage to or loss of *Kido Butai* would severely curtail Japanese offensive potential, or could lose the war at the outset. His recommendations regarding the planning of the attack were mostly ignored, which had to prey on his mind. He was burdened with the worry that a careless IJN submarine would be spotted, causing loss of the element of surprise.[11]

In the face of these responsibilities and pressures, he fully accomplished his mission with miniscule losses, something that the Japanese had no right to expect. Additional strikes would have risked everything for diminishing returns. Unlocated American carriers remained a threat.

Nagumo's reputation stemming from his decisions during the Pearl Harbor expedition ought to be at least partially rehabilitated by what has been learned in this analysis.

Yamamoto the Daring Gambler

"As Commander-in-Chief I have resolved to carry out the Pearl Harbor attack no matter what the cost."[12]

In the light of what has been learned in this study, this statement takes on an entirely new significance.

Yamamoto's attack on Pearl Harbor was not just a tactical operation designed to damage the US Pacific Fleet. It perforce represented an entirely new strategy to win the war. The objective "sold" to the Naval General Staff was for the attack to immobilize the Pacific Fleet for six months, allowing the Japanese to make their conquests to the south unhampered by a risk to their flank. It actually eliminated the Naval General Staff's "short war" strategy, the basis upon which the fleet had originally been designed.

Yamamoto's intent was to shock the Americans to the negotiating table, not immediately, but after the completion of the two-phase invasion of the south. If the Americans were not sufficiently intimidated, if instead they found the resolve to fight an extended war, if the Pearl Harbor attack required them to wait for six months to recover their strength, there was nothing to stop the Americans from waiting another six months or a year and thereafter confronting the Japanese with an overwhelming material superiority.

The Americans had no imperatives to meet the Japanese in a decisive battle under any conditions that might lead to a Japanese victory. The Japanese could not force that battle without American cooperation. The Japanese did not have access to any American center of gravity, the destruction of which would bring the war to an end on their terms. When Yamamoto stated that he would "dictate his terms in Washington" perhaps, subconsciously, he had this very limitation in mind, because he certainly could not dictate them from anywhere else. The Japanese Army and Navy could not get him to Washington; Washington would have to extend an invitation.

Yamamoto gambled with the core of the air striking power of his navy without a guarantee that there would be a pot of gold as a reward. The gamble was, from its outset, flawed; the odds that it would succeed, low; the chances that it would accomplish its purpose, unimaginable to the American people.

Authors have excused Yamamoto's failed strategic judgment. Historians like Prange have implied that it was not Yamamoto's fault that the Pearl Harbor attack stoked an incredible desire for retribution in the American people, it was really the fault of incompetent diplomats who did not deliver Japan's declaration of war in a timely manner. But the

Fourteen-Part Message delivered to the American Secretary of state hours after the attack was not a declaration of war. Even if delivered promptly, it would not have assuaged American rage at Japan's "sneak attack." Indeed, Yamamoto was warned by his own subordinates that he should not attack Hawaii because Japan should avoid anything that would get "America's back up too badly." The warning was ignored, as was all other opposition to his plan.

Some authors claim that Yamamoto thought that the Fourteen-Part Message was actually a declaration of war. Was Yamamoto deceived by his government, or have historians gotten this wrong? Historians have not addressed this issue, which has deep implications for pre-war government-Navy relationships. It is more likely that Yamamoto was accurately informed as to its contents and that postwar apologists have used this as a smokescreen to obscure Yamamoto's remarkably bad judgment regarding his prediction of the American people's response to his surprise attack.

Eventually, as the planning process brought the attack into focus, it is evident that the attack became an end in itself. If weather prevented underway refueling, the force would proceed with only *Kaga*, *Shokaku* and *Zuikaku*, and would attack the Pacific Fleet battleships with twelve torpedoes and fifteen AP bombs.[13] If *Kido Butai* was discovered within a day's steaming of Pearl Harbor they were still to attack, even though the element of surprise was gone and the losses to Japan's nearly irreplaceable ships and aircrews were calculated to be horrendous. Clearly, the attack on Pearl Harbor had departed from the category of a "calculated risk" into something more akin to a schoolyard dare.

Some Japanese historians contend that Yamamoto inherited a clan memory of mistreatment by the Americans.

> Yamamoto executed the attack on Pearl Harbor in order to establish a "balance of vengeance" between the two countries, to make good the humiliation of the Japanese nation by Perry's gunboat diplomacy in 1853. It was likely that in 1941 the majority of the Japanese, even if they were unaware of the detail of events in 1853, more or less shared Yamamoto's sentiments.[14]

Such sentiments are not unusual in the world. The events in Kosovo in the late 1990s and many of the genocides in sub-Sahara Africa can be traced to tribal, clan, or religious animosities dating back centuries.

Whether he was driven by motives of revenge or by calculation, a significant finding in this study is that Yamamoto should have had his head handed to him on a platter. Had the Americans' been in their usual state of readiness, conditions that existed just one weekend before and had been maintained for weeks before that, the Japanese would likely have lost half of their attacking aircraft, perhaps as many as three quarters, and the damage to the Pacific Fleet would have been considerably lighter than was experienced. There might also have been opportunities for counterattacks by American land-based and carrier aircraft. Yamamoto could very well have ended up trading a few torpedo hits on salvageable battleships for the loss of three carriers and half his aircraft and aviators. This reassessment of the most likely outcome (in OR terms, the "expected value") of Yamamoto's gamble puts a different light on the level of risk he assumed.

This has to be viewed from the perspective of Yamamoto's personality and goals. As one respected historian has noted, "Yamamoto took a huge risk, but is this any surprise given his gambling tendencies, and the relative value he assigned to his carriers compared to a psychological victory over the US?"[15]

Yamamoto was "resigned at the outset to losing at least half the carriers taking part in the Hawaiian operation."[16] His objective was to cripple four battleships. If things went as he expected he would have initiated a battle where the expected outcome was to exchange three fleet carriers, forever lost, for four Treaty battleships, crippled for six months. When 1942 arrived, not an admiral in the Pacific would have permanently given up three carriers to put four battleships temporarily out of action.

Historians must now reassess Yamamoto's views on the relative importance of carriers vs. battleships. This decision reveals Yamamoto as more of a traditionalist than "The Father of Japanese Naval Aviation" has been previously portrayed. It puts into perspective his decision later in the war to set up his headquarters on the battleship *Yamato*, 400 miles behind his carriers, for the Battle of Midway. Perhaps Yamamoto really considered his carriers as a raiding force, albeit a powerful one, and that the force of decision was in *Yamato* and the Japanese battleline. For one with that viewpoint, trading carriers for battleships appears attractive. This makes Yamamoto appear much less prescient than his cheerleaders have claimed.[17]

As another example of questionable judgment, Yamamoto allowed the midget submarine samurai fantasy to proceed. If the midget submarines attacked after the aerial attack was finished, their effort is defensible. But to surrender to the entreaties of a midget submarine lieutenant who wanted the honor of firing a torpedo at the same time as the air strike for nothing other than a sense of participation is absolutely irresponsible. If the midgets were detected and the Americans put on alert, the aircrews of hundreds of aircraft and the whole of *Kido Butai* would be at risk—all for the remote chance of a few torpedoes hits.

According to Ugaki, Yamamoto's Chief of Staff, "how much damage they will be able to inflict is not the point," but rather the demonstration of "the spirit of *kesshitan*" (self-sacrifice). After the battle, however, Yamamoto's thoughts were not on *kesshitan* but on torpedo hits. When he learned that none of the midget submarine crews returned, he looked grave and said, "I would have never sent them if I'd known we'd achieve so much with air units alone."[18] In other words, before the attack Yamamoto wanted every means possible working to inflict damage on the Pacific Fleet. He had doubts about how much damage the air units would mete out, so he included attacks by midget and fleet submarines. At the same time he was absolutely oblivious to the risks he was imposing on *Kido Butai*. This shows remarkably poor judgment; either that, or a direct line to the gods assuring him that all his favorable assumptions would come true. It makes little sense under Western logic; few of his subordinates under Eastern logic were convinced.

Studies of people making high-risk decisions have found that someone engaged in a reckless course of action is prone to add more risk thoughtlessly. There is a loss of perspective. Yamamoto demonstrated this in his decision regarding the midget submarines.

Willmott, Tohmatsu, and Johnson have concluded, "Yamamoto's inclusion of the submarines in the attack would almost seem to indicate a lack of confidence in his carrier aircraft, and must cast doubt upon his strategic judgment."[19] Agreed.

The Japanese Naval General Staff felt that Yamamoto's Pearl Harbor attack was foolhardy. Many experienced officers did not support it. The commander of *Kido Butai* did not want to conduct the operation. Historians have portrayed these objections as a product of obsolete thinking, and cheer what they see as Yamamoto's incredible perspicacity and determination.

This evaluation is wrong. Yamamoto was not a strategic genius—his strategic vision was seriously flawed. Better was the foresight of Rear Admiral Kusaka Ryunosuje, Nagumo's chief of staff. In September of 1941 he stated, "Tactically the attack might succeed, but strategically the chances are limited." Kusaka believed that the attack might afford Japan a temporary advantage, but without any measurable long-range return.[20]

Historians have depicted Yamamoto's plan as "bold and original."[21] A more accurate assessment would be "foolhardy and wrongheaded."

Yamamoto's decision to attack Pearl Harbor was tantamount to the CEO of a bank withdrawing all the company's core cash reserves to buy a lottery ticket. Just because the bet came through does not make the gambler a wise man.

CHAPTER THIRTEEN

SUMMARY AND CONCLUSIONS

This study of the attack on Pearl Harbor is at odds with many of the myths and much of the conventional wisdom regarding the attack. A summary reveals the breadth and depth of these new revelations.

During the pre-war years, thve Japanese Navy had painstakingly prepared its fleet for one particular strategy: a "decisive battle" to be held in its home waters, after the US fleet had been whittled down by aircraft and submarines during its long transit from Pearl Harbor into Japanese waters. The fleet was designed for this task, where fuel endurance and habitability and (in some cases) ships' stability was sacrificed for speed and firepower. Logistics ships, tenders, repair ships, and developed forward support bases were unneeded in this strategy. Bases were to receive only minimal development, enough to support long-range reconnaissance and bombing aircraft and a sacrificial garrison. They were only speed bumps in the path of the American fleet and likely to be lost to the Americans' advance. Fleet auxiliaries were not needed, because the most intense combat was expected to occur near the Japanese homeland in one cataclysmic decisive battle.

When the Japanese government decided on a war of conquest, this strategy was set on its ear. Now, the Navy would be required to take and hold outlying islands as a way to prevent the Allies from retaking the vital natural resources areas the Japanese would conquer in order to

371

sustain their warfighting machine. The decisive battle was moved further and further from Empire waters until it eventually was in the vicinity of the Marshall Islands, 2,300nm from Japan. Now bases would be needed and auxiliaries commissioned to service the fleet far from its homeports, but the very lack of resources that would force Japan into the war would also prevent her from establishing the needed bases and auxiliaries.

But first, the Japanese had to achieve the desired conquests, a process which, even in the force vacuum in the Pacific caused by the war in Europe, was likely to take months. The Japanese would need most of their fleet for the offensive, scattered over thousands of miles supporting multiple simultaneous thrusts. The wild card was the United States Pacific Fleet. While it consisted of less than half the Americans' commissioned battleships, it could be reinforced, and a move by the fleet to the Philippines would cut off the Japanese lines of communication to the southern advance, cut off resources returning to Japan, and threaten the Japanese with defeat.

Yamamoto proposed a strike against the Pacific Fleet's main base at Pearl Harbor, using all his available fleet carrier strength. What is clear is that Yamamoto was after battleships, mainly to strike a psychological blow against the United States, hoping that it would result in a negotiated peace after the Japanese had secured their conquests. In the shadow of the historical results of the Pearl Harbor attack, what is little understood is that Yamamoto (and the rest of the Japanese command structure) was expecting to sacrifice at least two fleet carriers to this goal and perhaps more, making it a "carriers for battleships" swap. This realization belies the previous general assumption that Yamamoto was an aviation visionary who believed battleships to be obsolete. This is confirmed by Yamamoto's instructions to *Kido Butai*, ordering them to press their attack even if they were detected 24 hours before the strike, and to attack even if there were no carriers in Pearl Harbor. Clearly, Yamamoto was willing to put his fragile carriers in harm's way in order to cripple battleships.

Japanese testimony indicates that they needed to cripple four American battleships. This number was likely based on the calculations used to determine the needed force ratios to defeat the American fleet after a trans-Pacific advance. This number is confirmed by back-calculating from the targeted ratios that the Japanese attempted to obtain in negotiations during the various naval arms limitations conferences between 1922 and 1936. Even then, there would be little margin for a Japanese victory—

they admitted that, if the confrontation occurred as planned, they had only a 50-50 chance of victory, a rather low chance of success considering that the fate of the country was at risk.

Yamamoto's avowed objective was to cripple the Pacific Fleet sufficiently to prevent it from moving against the flank of the Japanese advance for at least six months. What is not commonly recognized is that this objective put the torch to the conventional Japanese plans for a decisive battle between the fleets at odds that would allow a Japanese victory. In fact, if the Americans were delayed by six months, they would have no incentive to engage the Japanese in a fleet action until their strength was sufficiently reinforced by the oncoming flood of new construction. A successful attack against Pearl Harbor would force the Americans into a "long war" strategy from the outset, exactly the kind of war that the Japanese knew they could not win. Yamamoto recognized this. After the conquest of resource areas, he had to force the Americans' hand. He needed a decisive battle by whatever means possible. He tried to force one in the middle of the Pacific, which then led to defeat at the Battle of Midway.

The most telling indictment against the Japanese strategists and intelligence service is that they did not need an attack on Pearl Harbor to get their needed six months. It would have taken six months for the Americans to assemble sufficient oilers and auxiliaries to permit significant offensive operations, assuming that the course of the war in Europe allowed such a concentration. Raids would have been possible, but nothing serious enough to influence the course and outcome of Japan's phase-one expansion to the south. Generally blind to logistics constraints, the Japanese did not care to visualize or understand the constraints under which the Americans would operate.

Contrary to the accolades of most chroniclers, the planning and execution of the Pearl Harbor attack was imperfect; in many ways it was not state-of-the-art.

- The planning was inflexible. The battleship-killers, the B5N Kates, the only Japanese carrier attack bombers that could carry either heavy armor-piercing bombs or torpedoes, were allocated their weapons very early in the planning process. This allocation was not adjusted to account for the results of training and tests, or intelligence regarding the presence or absence of torpedo nets in Pearl Harbor. The problems associated with delivering torpedoes in shallow water were solved literally only two weeks before the expedition departed home waters.

- The planners were to execute the attack even if the torpedo delivery problem had not been solved, or if the battleships were protected by torpedo nets. This contributed to the decision to over-allocate B5N Kates to the high-altitude bombing role.
- Although the level bombers exceeded accuracy expectations, a disgraceful number of their AP bombs failed to properly explode.
- In another example of inflexibility, the Japanese received a detailed intelligence report 24 hours ahead of the attack, yet did not adjust their plan to the observed conditions. The staff planners were so intent upon sinking carriers that they decided to allow an attack against the carrier anchorage to remain in place after learning there were no carriers in port.
- Had more B5N Kates been assigned to carry torpedoes the attack would have been considerably more lethal. As it was, three of the eight viable torpedo targets were untouched, and one was hit only by mistake.
- The plan was based entirely upon achieving a surprise attack, and provided for no SEAD support for the torpedo bombers. Even when a "no surprise" plan option was included, the torpedo bombers were not provided with any support—indeed, they were not even escorted the entire way to the target by fighters.
- The plan for the torpedo bombers was faulty. Planned attack routes were not deconflicted and caused mutual interference.
- The Japanese scheme of prioritizing targets was unexecutable. The burden of responsibility was put onto the individual aircrews, who could not have the information needed to appropriately execute the plan, and did not have the needed communications to mutually coordinate their efforts. The result was an overconcentration on the easiest targets, wasted torpedoes, and the escape of half the major targets on the torpedo prioritization list. Eleven torpedoes accomplished the

mission—the rest were misses, overkills, or hits on inappropriate targets.

- Fuchida's mistake with the flares, rather than an inconsequential error, threw the torpedo bombers' attack into some confusion and rushed their approach. This gaffe was a contributing factor to the problems the torpedo bombers faced, including mutual interference, aborted runs, and likely a reduction in delivery accuracy and reliability. Fuchida's error directly contributed to the B5N Kate aircraft losses.
- The loss of *Arizona* was the result of a bomb that penetrated the ship's forward magazine, not the convoluted explanation in the Navy's official report. Simulation modeling shows that the hit was not a "one in a million" outlier, but the most probable result for the attack.
- Japanese aerial communications were ineffective.
  - The Japanese leaders could not exert effective control over the strike, especially after Fuchida's error with the flares turned the first wave into an aerial Preakness.
  - The attack formation adopted for the torpedo bombers, long strings of up to 12 bombers separated by 500 yards or more (which often became 1,500 to 1,800 yards under combat conditions), eliminated any possibility of anything but the most basic "follow the leader" control of targeting.
- The attacks by the dive-bombers on *Nevada* were an inappropriate employment of the planes' ordnance. These bombs did nothing towards accomplishing the mission of the attack.
- The idea of sinking a warship in the channel in order to bottle up the Pacific Fleet was a quixotic half-measure, an exceedingly poor decision.
- The dive-bombers assigned to fleet targets contributed little. Of 81 bombers tasked with this mission only two hits were accomplished against what should have been their primary target, cruisers. Six of the eight cruisers in harbor escaped significant damage, with the other two were damaged by torpedo hits. Much of the damage caused by the dive-bombers came from bombs that missed their intended targets.
- A disgraceful percentage of the dive-bombers' 250kg bombs were defective.

- The dive-bombers' target identification was exceedingly poor. Tenders were identified as battleships and cruisers, destroyers identified as cruisers, drydocks identified as battleships.
- The plan for the employment of the fighters was poor. Fighter cover for the first wave's bombers was not in accordance with the importance of the attack groups. Unbelievably, the torpedo bombers were not escorted all the way to the target, and had no top cover for the duration of their attack.
- Much of the "conventional wisdom" about the attack is false:
  - The Japanese did not employ a corps of "super aviators" for the attack.
  - Any third wave attack directed against the shipyard could have damaged only a small part of Pearl Harbor's total repair capacity. Any damage could have been put to rights rapidly, and would not have caused the war in the Pacific to be extended by any appreciable period.
  - While the fuel tanks were vulnerable and the majority of them could have been destroyed in a third wave attack, the effects of their destruction could have been mitigated. Damage to the fuel tanks would not have put back the course of the war by any significant duration and would not have forced the Pacific Fleet to abandon Pearl Harbor as some have asserted.
  - The Japanese fourteen-part diplomatic message, delivered late and after the attack, was not a declaration of war. An on-time delivery would not have changed the American people's righteous anger catalyzed by the Japanese "sneak attack."
  - The probability that the fifth midget submarine penetrated into the waters adjacent to Battleship Row and torpedoed *Oklahoma* or *Arizona* is vanishingly small.

One significant discovery is the extent to which many historians have been wrong in their opinions of the battle. This has in turn led to much distortion in the historical assessments of the roles, skills, and judgment of the participants. Care must be taken before previous historians' value judgments are accepted. Even the most prestigious of the contemporary warfighters might be wrong.

The Questions

In the introduction a number of questions were posed which now can be addressed.

Were there flaws in the attack planning?
Was anything forgotten or neglected in the planning?

In contrast to popular perceptions, the plan was not the "brilliant" effort that has been portrayed. It was not even state of the art for the period. It neglected to take advance of the full capabilities of the attackers, use appropriate existing doctrines, or use the aircraft types in a cooperative manner.

The plan was too inflexible to take into account last-minute intelligence. Unnecessary reconnaissance flights by floatplanes in advance of the attack were flown, with the potential to forewarn the Americans of the attack, as did the remarkably poor decision to allow the midget submarines to attempt to penetrate the harbor prior to the strike.

Command and control was not well considered. The plan provided no means for commanders to control their forces during the attack.

The means to communicate changes in the plan when airborne was ill-considered. The torpedo attack prioritization scheme was faulty.

Fighter support to guarantee the arrival of the torpedo bombers to their attack points was nonexistent, and first-wave fighter support was not allocated in accordance with the importance of the bomber groups. The fighters were not employed in any organized manner; rather, they were just turned loose to shoot up whatever they discovered, without providing the bombers with escort or SEAD support. There was no provision to post guards over the American airfields, which could have been done employing the excellent endurance of the A6M Zero.

The plan to deal with torpedo nets was bizarre (but very Japanese). The concept of operations for the torpedo bombers' attack was not robust, both in the method of target selection and the potential for mutual interference.

The differences between the "surprise" and "no surprise" plans were miniscule and ineffectual, and the changes insufficient to deal with the threat if indeed the Americans were waiting with their defenses active.

The plan for delivering the torpedo attack was too hard to execute. Not only were the attack routes in conflict, but the prioritization scheme for selecting targets asked too much of the combat aircrews. The result was that there were only 13 hits (out of 40 torpedo bombers) that effectively advanced the objectives of the attack; it was something of a miracle that these were enough.

There were many other flaws of omission and commission. The planning was anything but brilliant, even by the standards of 1941.

If there is a flaw in this analysis, it is that too many of the defects in the attack have been charged against the planners' account. The planners were working in most cases within the constraints of doctrine, and many of the poor choices (such as target selection methodology, command and control, and communications methodology) might better be attributed to doctrine. The problem is that doctrine was fluid in this period, and in a tantalizing number of cases the planners threw off the constraints of doctrine to embrace innovative solutions (such as reducing the formation size of the level bombers). This analysis blames the planners for not recognizing the need to overturn doctrine in more cases, perhaps unfairly. The point is that there were significant flaws in the attack plan; attributing them to the planners or to the state of the art in doctrine will make for interesting future debates.

Was the plan state-of-the-art, or were existing useful attack techniques not used? Why not?

The plan neglected many tools existing at the time that could have contributed to a greater success. There was no SEAD to support the torpedo bombers' attack, either by strafing fighters or dive-bombers. Fighters were not assigned as a standing CAP to deal with any American fighters that might get airborne. The Japanese simply did not have a combined-arms mindset—it was not in their worldview to have one type of aircraft provide support to the others.

What was the balance between risk and reward? Were Japanese expectations reasonable, or the products of over-optimism, or even self-delusion?

Yamamoto was risking his fleet carrier force in totality—the platforms, the aircraft, the aircrews, the core of the navy's aircraft maintenance men, and the sailors that manned the fleet. This was the cream of the Japanese navy's warfighting power, at the peak of its effectiveness—thereafter, effectiveness could only be expected to deteriorate, and replacements would be limited.

In wargames it was shown that he possibly would trade two or three of his six fleet carriers and half his aviators to disable four of the US Navy's 17 commissioned battleships. The odds that he would be able to achieve surprise ought to have been low. Yamamoto was taking on much risk for little relative reward.

The risk-reward equation was even more unfavorable considering the combat conditions that Yamamoto was willing to accept. He willed the attack to continue even if the fleet was discovered 24 hours in advance. He willed the attack to continue even if the problem of launching torpedoes in shallow water was not solved, or if the American capital ships were protected by torpedo nets. Under these conditions he was willing to trade half his fleet carriers, aircraft and aircrews for only one battleship (the likely result of the level bombers' attack) and whatever carriers were in port (destroyed by the dive-bombers). And, he willed the attack to continue even if the carriers were not in port.

In other words, there were a wide range of combat conditions that Yamamoto was willing to accept that would have yielded massive risk for little potential gain.

In the end, any operation that relies for its success on "divine guidance" and "the favor of the gods" accepts the possibility that the gods might choose to favor the other side.

Was the operation executed properly?

No.

Fuchida's fumble with the flares turned the air over Pearl Harbor into a scrambled affair. The torpedo bombers' planned 90-second attack turned into a 11-minute furball. The second-wave dive-bombers went after inappropriate targets, and even then did not hit them. Only the OCA effort was executed as planned, and was rewarded by unforeseen success.

Most historians have accepted Prange's assessment:

> The deeper one probes into the technical methods of the attack, the more one realizes how much depended upon surprise, exquisite timing, teamwork, fortitude, and a whole combination of refined skills. Genda and Fuchida's strategical [sic] and technical brainwork reveals a close attention to detail as well as flexibility.[1]

Prange was a historian, not a professional naval officer. He did not know what to look for when evaluating timing, tactics, and teamwork. He mainly took the word of Fuchida and others that he interviewed, Japanese officers who, in the wake of postwar defeat, were not likely to denigrate their great victory. As a result, that great work, *At Dawn We Slept*, a work which has conditioned the thinking of three generations of historians, is not accurate in its assessment of the objectives, the wargames, the planning, or the execution of the attack.

Surprise was achieved. Surprise, and the mistakes made by the defenders' commanders, forgave a multitude of errors in the planning and execution of the attack. Prange's "exquisite timing" was not achieved; "teamwork" was little evident; "flexibility" on a command level did not exist. The "refined skills" were not evident in the accuracy of the dive-bombing attack on the fleet or in the target selection or precision delivery of the torpedo attack.

Japanese torpedoes worked well. It will never be determined how many of the approximately ten torpedoes that ended up in the mud were placed there by pilot error or torpedo malfunction, but enough were properly launched to do the job. The 250kg GP bombs were plagued with duds and fuze timing inconsistencies, as well as low order and incomplete detonations. The AP bomb performance was miserable. Aviators risking their lives deserve better.

Did the attack meet expectations?
Yes. And no.

The great paradox of the battle, in spite of all the errors and confusion and poor execution that occurred, is that the Japanese tactical expectations were exceeded. At the same time, they came up short in their strategic expectations.

They needed to disable four battleships to, in their estimation, keep the US Pacific Fleet out of the Western Pacific in any strength. In their wargames, they calculated that they would disable a sufficient number of battleships to change the odds of a battleline confrontation to that which they felt they could win, albeit with only a small margin of victory. They believed that if that level of damage was inflicted, they could delay the counterattack of the Pacific Fleet until after their Phase One conquests were completed.

The Americans did not steam to the relief of the Philippines until

1944. However, it is questionable whether this was because of the losses inflicted at Pearl Harbor or because of other constraints. Taking the long view, the United States only lost two Treaty battleships and one demilitarized target ship to the attack, along with the services of 15 other ships for periods ranging from a few weeks to 34 months. The 34-month period is deceptive, as those were battleships that underwent extensive modernization, essentially rebuilt from the main deck up, as well as receiving augmented torpedo defenses, work that dragged because their priority for material and shipyard labor was low.

The OCA effort totally disrupted American airpower, so that, while the Japanese expected to lose up to half of their carriers, their fleet was not attacked at all, again exceeding their expectations.

The Japanese failed in their greatest of all expectations—that the shock of having their Pacific Fleet eviscerated would bring the Americans to the negotiating table. This did not happen; this miscalculation was The Great Strategic Error of the Pacific War.

Did the attack meet its potential?

No, yes, no, and yes.

Looking first at the torpedo bombers, at the end of their training the B5N Kate aircrews scored 82.5% delivery accuracy, which, if duplicated in the attack, would have meant 33 hits. As a rule of thumb, combat conditions reduce the expected results of an attack by a third, giving an expected 22 effective hits. The Japanese expected 27 hits, and actually hit with 19 torpedoes, less than their expectation. Poor target identification, poor target selection, and overkill reduced the number of effective hits—those hits that advanced the objective of the attack—to 11, while half of the targets high on the priority list, heavy and light cruisers, were untouched. The torpedo attack did not meet its potential.

The level bombers put in a good performance under difficult conditions. They were both lucky and unlucky: lucky that one bomb hit at just the right spot to detonate *Arizona's* magazine; unlucky in that most of their bombs malfunctioned. The Japanese were ecstatic over the results of an attack by a weapons system that was really only an insurance backup to the primary assault weapon, the torpedo.

The second-wave dive-bombers allocated to fleet targets performed poorly, probably due to the poor visibility, smoke and cloud cover that prevented them from attacking in the way in which they had trained.

These aircraft scored only a few hits.

The attacks against the airfields went spectacularly well. They destroyed two to three times the number of aircraft as could be expected, and totally thwarted any ability of the Americans to perform reconnaissance and assemble a counterattack.

What would a perfect attack have looked like?

With the wisdom of hindsight, based on the state-of-the-art of naval aviation attack in 1941 (and its limitations), it is possible to put together the characteristics of a perfect attack.

It would have begun with flexible planning and training.

First, the torpedo bombers would be recognized as the core of the attack. They would be expected to inflict most of the damage on the fleet. High-altitude level bombers would be the secondary weapon of choice against inboard battleships, or in the event the Americans decided to employ torpedo nets. Because of the importance of these missions, the more experienced B5N Kate aircrew from *Kaga, Akagi, Hiryu*, and *Soryu* would be assigned to strike the enemy fleet. Using the most experienced aircrews would have simplified their training, as some of the aircrew would be asked to train in both roles.

The Japanese method of level bombing, where all the aircraft in a formation would release when the lead bombardier dropped, could have facilitated planning flexibility. A core of B5N aircrew, the best level bombers, perhaps 20, could have trained exclusively in the role of lead bombers. Another group would train exclusively as torpedo bombers. But the majority of the pilots would train not only to drop torpedoes but also to fly formation in the level bombing roles. These aircrews could fly to the training areas in formation, then practice torpedo delivery, then fly back again in formation. Based on the last-minute intelligence, these aircrews could be assigned to carry either bombs or torpedoes as the last-minute intelligence dictated.

Better use would have been made of the second-wave dive-bombers against the fleet targets.

(Appendix D includes a fictionalized account of how a perfect attack against the Pacific Fleet might have been executed.)

Might the flaws in planning and execution portend things to come?

The Japanese planning problems would persist throughout the war. There continued to be a lack of cooperation between the combat arms, adding to the catastrophic lack of cooperation between the Army and the Navy. The greatest failures were in a lack of flexibility, and a lack of consideration for contingencies. Japanese plans were made assuming that events would unfold in accordance with their schedule and concept of operations, with little consideration in advance of what to do if other results intruded. There was generally little consideration of alternative scenarios, and little consideration for logistics. But, as has been shown repeatedly, no plan survives contact with the enemy. Yet the Japanese rarely abandoned a plan when the underlying premises upon which it was founded were discovered to be wrong. If the plan exploded, control was mostly lost, as was seen in the Pearl Harbor attack.

All this suggests a systemic problem with Japanese staffs. Japanese culture may have had a large hand in the problem, including the uncomfortable union of the individualistic samurai tradition, and the extreme consequences of errors or failures in a culture that values consensus and accord. However, these thoughts are nescient, and this question would be a valuable field for future research.

What could have happened if the Japanese attack had not benefited from the fortuitous blunders of the American high command?

The calculations indicate that the American command decision blunders before the attack had a huge impact on the results of the action. In the best-case scenario where the Navy and Army were at the level of alert of the previous weeks, and the Air Information Center activated, the Japanese strike would have encountered massive resistance. Perhaps half the Japanese aircraft would have been shot down, a result calculated in the Japanese wargames, the US Naval War College Maneuver Rules, and through historical data analysis, and is not far off the loss rates experienced in the first four carrier vs. carrier actions. An American counterattack with the available land-based bombers might have succeeded in sinking or damaging one or more of the Japanese carriers. Losses to the Pacific Fleet battleships would have been much more limited.

Coming out of this action would have been a much different concept of naval warfare, one more balanced between employment of battleships and carriers than what was experienced in the war. A battleline action could very well have been seen earlier than the historic battleship confrontations at Guadalcanal and Surigao Strait.

In spite of these differences, there would likely have been little difference in the course of the Japanese Phase One program of conquest. The American countermoves were dictated more by logistics than availability of forces—historically, the Americans had plenty of battleships in the Atlantic that could have been transferred to the Pacific, but were not, as what governed Allied action was the availability of fuel and food, and the transportation needed to get these commodities to the western Pacific. The Japanese would have had to rebuild their carrier air wings earlier than what were historically required, meaning that the skill and lethality of the Japanese carriers would have been reduced from the skill levels encountered in the Coral Sea and at Midway. American domination of carrier exchanges would have come earlier than the Battle of the Philippine Sea. Whenever the Americans created the required logistics base, the course of the war, until Japan's defeat, would have been accelerated.

Probably the most significant impact of the attack was on the professional worldview of key American naval officers. In the aftermath of the attack, the perception must have been communicated that the battleship force was a weak reed. Yes, *Oklahoma* and *West Virginia* were sunk, but no battleship of the period was expected to withstand so many torpedo hits in so short an interval. It was *Nevada*, sunk after only one torpedo hit and a few bombs, and *California*, sunk by two torpedoes, and *Arizona*, blasted into flinders by AP bombs, that stunned the naval establishment. Battleships were expected to take this kind of punishment and survive.

The American battleships' design philosophy purposely sacrificed high speed in favor of survivability. Were the designs wrong? Was the concept wrong? If *Arizona* succumbed to a few AP bombs made out of battleship shells, would not other battleships succumb to a few plunging armor-piercing 16-inch gun rounds? Would American battleships replicate the performance of the British battlecruisers at Jutland, where ship after ship disappeared in awesome magazine detonations, causing Admiral Beatty to lament that "something is wrong with our bloody ships"? Is this, perhaps, the reason why the investigation into the *Arizona*'s detonation concluded that her loss was attributable to open hatches, rather than admitting that their battleships were vulnerable to armor piercing bombs and exploding magazines?

Granted, there were qualifiers. The American battleships were not ready for battle, but the intellectual understanding that the battleships were in an unusually vulnerable condition would not overcome the emotional blow of the photographs on newspaper front pages worldwide showing smoking hulls lying in the mud on the bottom of Pearl Harbor.

Probably the most significant reaction must have been in the mind of Admiral Chester Nimitz, who became the Commander in Chief of the Pacific Fleet after the debacle. In the first months after the attack Nimitz sent the battleships to the West Coast, where they could be overhauled, repaired, modernized, fueled, fed, and trained without straining his logistical resources. For a few months, battle damage kept the battleships out of the front lines. Then, logistics kept the battleships where they were.

Later, when the logistics strains eased and the battleships were cocked and ready, Nimitz hesitated. As a submariner he was not an official member of the "Gun Club," in spite of a tour as commanding officer of a battleship, so he did not have the professional and emotional commitment to the battlewagons and nowhere near as much faith in their capabilities as the True Believers. Although pressed by the Chief of Naval Operations, Admiral King, to get the battleship forces into combat, Nimitz was hesitant—there were always reasons to keep them out of the theater, and when he finally sent them forward, reasons to keep them out of the fight. They were too slow. They were ill-suited for combat in the constrained waters of the Solomons. They sucked up too much fuel.

The battleships that did get to the Southwest Pacific mostly swung at anchor, their combat edge deteriorating as their crews idled.

Overall, one suspects that the Pearl Harbor attack influenced Nimitz's perceptions of the utility and survivability of the Treaty battleships in the early months of the war. It was not until the end of 1943 that these ships came to take a more prominent place in the war. They were afforded a place in the 5th Fleet's surface action plans during the Gilbert and Marshall Islands campaigns, perhaps an essential place. They eventually displayed their ship-to-ship combat capabilities in the constrained waters of Surigao Strait. Perhaps they could have done as well in the constrained waters of the Solomons in 1942.

So, perhaps the greatest impact of the Pearl Harbor attack was in its influence on how the war would be fought. Overall, a change in the results of the Pearl Harbor attack would have resulted more in a change in the characteristics of combat in the Pacific war, with little change in the pace, and no change in the outcome.

At the same time, the Pearl Harbor attack distorted the Japanese view of war. Commanders take the results of every battle and subconsciously build internal mental models of how modern war is fought, including the expected results when different forces are pitted against each other. Pearl Harbor contributed to these mental models. Out of it, the Japanese would have found a renewed faith in the concept of a decisive battle. They saw how a relatively small force operating far from home could attack the hub of the enemy's power and inflict debilitating losses at little cost. If this could happen, perhaps the Japanese could be victorious in a later decisive battle as well. The Japanese victories at Pearl Harbor, Darwin, the Java Sea, and the Indian Ocean not only contributed to "Victory Disease," that fatal underestimation of American capabilities, but also to a mental model of warfare that held out the hope that all the losses of 1943 and 1944 could be reversed in one powerful blow supported, as was the Pearl Harbor attack, by chance and the favor of the gods. The Pearl Harbor attack not only forced a long war strategy onto the Americans, it added hope to the Japanese that they could win such a war.

At Pearl Harbor, the efforts of tens of thousands of Japanese culminated in the skills and dedication of the aviators on 15 torpedo bombers, men who successfully "dedicated their life to that one torpedo." Had they faltered, the history of the Pacific War would have been dramatically different.

APPENDIX A

TABULATION OF SECOND-WAVE DIVE-BOMBER ATTACKS

Ship (Hull number)— # of Bombs; reasons and sources

Aylwin (DD-355)—1

One bomb dropped off *Aylwin*'s bow. *Henley* (DD-391) also observed a bomb strike in this area, with a different time recorded. Time records in the logs can be very imprecise, with some ships recording the beginning of an event, some the end of the event, and some the time of the log entry (which might be minutes after the event). It was assumed that these two entries were a record of the same bomb. Sources: *Aylwin* (DD-355) AR, *Henley* (DD-391) AR.

Solace (AH-5)—1

One bomb 400 yards off *Solace*. Sources: Chronology, *Allen* (DD-355) AR. Note that *Solace*, a hospital ship, did not report that she was attacked. The bomb was likely a very badly aimed bomb directed at *Dobbin* or *Whitney*'s destroyer nest, or was jettisoned from a damaged bomber.

Dobbin (AD-3)—3

Three dive-bombers in a single attack against *Dobbin*. One was shot down prior to bomb release, two others dropped their bombs (the ComDesFlotOne AR reported that all three dropped bombs). Sources: *Dobbin* (AD-3), *Breeze* (DM-18), *Dewey* (DD-

349), *Hull* (DD-350) ARs; *Chronology*.

Raleigh (CL-7)—3

A single *shotai* of three bombers attacked *Raleigh*. *Raleigh* AR says "many," *Chronology* states five, but this may be confusion in numbers with the five (see below) that attacked *Tangier*. Number of bomb splashes not recorded. One hit scored on *Raleigh*. A conservative estimate of one three-aircraft *shotai* was used, which is apparently confirmed by the postwar testimony of Lt. Zenji Abe, who reported that he led three bombers against *Raleigh*. His rear-seater reported:

Formation leader short. Second plane short. Third plane hit! Adjustment correct. Second echelon successful!' I was later able to identify our target as an Omaha-class light cruiser–Raleigh.

Sources: http://www.historynet.com/lieutenant-zenji-abe-a-japanese-pilot-remembers.htm, *Raleigh* (CL-7) AR, *Chronology*.

Tangier (AV-8)—5

A single attack on Tangier likely with elements of two *shotai*. *Tangier* AR indicates four near-miss splashes and one bomb that hit Ford Island, and is considered authoritative. The possibility was considered that the *Raleigh* and *Tangier* attacks were the same, but both ship's AR report how close the bomb misses were, so it is unlikely the bomb misses would be double counted, since the ships were located 800 yards apart. Source: *Tangier* (AV-8) AR.

Curtiss (AV-4)—6

Two attacks on *Curtiss*, each by three aircraft. One aircraft crashed into *Curtiss'* crane. One bomb hit from the second attack. The time of attacks were reported as 0910 and 1913. *Medusa* (AR-1) (about 200 yards away) claimed an attack where one bomb was aimed at *Curtiss* and four aimed at *Medusa*, claiming four bomb misses close aboard *Medusa*. These two claims have been consolidated. Sources: *Curtiss* (AV-4) AR, *Medusa* (AR-1) AR, *Zane* (DMS-4) AR.

Helm (DD-388)—2

Helm was attacked outside the entrance buoy. *Helm* reported only one aircraft sighted, but two bombs in distinctly different locations close aboard, causing some shock damage. Since the attack was evidently a surprise, and the aircraft evidently sighted by only a few crewmembers, it is evident that one of the attacking D3A Vals was unobserved. Source: *Helm* (DD-388) AR.

Dale (DD-353)—5

> *Dale* was attacked on two occasions, first by at least two dive-bombers while in the channel, and three more just outside the entrance buoy. Sources: *Dale* (DD-353) AR, Olson *Tales of a Tin Can*, crew interviews with Miller at http://www.historynet.com/first-hand-accounts-from-the-crew-of-uss-dales-escape-from-pearl-harbor.htm, accessed 1/27/10.

Shaw (DD-373)—8

> *Shaw* was in the floating drydock. Eight bombers attacked. Three bombs hit *Shaw*, and five hit in or around the floating drydock, which received 155 holes from splinters that had to be welded or plugged before she was raised on 9 January 1942. Sources: NAV-SHIPS A (374), *Shaw* (DD-373) AR and War Damage Report, *Chronology*, Wallin 205.

Nevada (BB-36)—14

> The testimony on the attack on *Nevada* is contradictory and subject to inflation by the drama of the event. Smith, in his biography of Egusa, says Egusa's section of 18 aircraft attacked *Nevada*; in his book on the D3A Val, he intimates one attack of eight and a second wave of six, without being specific. *Chronology* states that 15 dive bombers attacked the *Nevada* and a destroyer, which would likely be the first attack against *Dale*; other ships' ARs list as many as 21 attackers, but also state that some of them (one-third in one account) broke off to attack the floating drydock. The Japanese dive-bombing techniques used a dive angle of 60 degrees initiated at 15,000 feet, so it was difficult for observers to differentiate the attacks delivered against targets in close proximity, as were *Nevada*, the floating drydock containing *Shaw*, the permanent drydock containing *Pennsylvania*, and the Navy Yard. Some of the bombs that hit in the water near *Shaw* could have been interpreted as attacks against *Nevada*. All that appears firm is that *Nevada* took five hits in two waves of attackers. After balancing accounts and considering the aircraft accounted in attacks against other nearby targets, 14 attackers appears a reasonable estimate.

Pennsylvania (BB-38)—9

> This number was arrived at by bomb count. This includes the misses on *Pennsylvania* that hit *Cassin* (2) and *Downes* (1), the hit on *Pennsylvania* (1), the DNM near *Pennsylvania*'s bow (1), hits on the edge

of the drydock (2), and at least two bombs that splashed just outside the caisson. Sources: *Pennsylvania* (BB-38), *Cassin* (DD-373), *Downes* (DD-375), *Tracy* (DM-19) ARs, Lord 132, Wallin.

California (BB-44)—3

According to Prange, Ofuchi attacked *California*. It may have been a solo attack, but likely his *shotai* of 3 bombers. The attack resulted in one 250kg DNM by the bow.

Helena (CL-50)—4

By bomb count. Sources: Lord, 119, *Helena* AR. Fuchida gave the dive-bombers credit for 6 hits.

Neosho (AO-23)—2

By bomb count. *Neosho's* AR states that "several bombs fell close to the stern jarring the ship appreciably." At the time of the attack *Neosho* was well into the channel and possibly passing the Naval Shipyard piers, so these bombs must have been directed at her and not at Battleship Row. There is a possibility that these bombs were simply wide misses by bombs directed at the Yard.

Pyro (AE-1)—1

By bomb count. *Pyro* was at the ammunition piers in the West Loch when she was attacked by a single dive-bomber, which put its bomb on the pier. *Pyro* AR.

Navy Yard—10

An accurate number is difficult to determine because the various accounts tended to mix attacks on the Navy Yard with attacks on the Drydocks and attacks on 1010 Dock. This number is intended to include attacks only on the repair basin area and piers. *Chronology* claims 30 dive-bombers attacked the Yard; *Sumner's* AR states 10 went against the Navy Yard and docks; *Tautog* claimed 18 attacked at 0900; and *Chronology* states that 10-12 attacked the repair basin at 0910. The final number came through a count of bomb detonations reported and some interpretation in the ARs of *Honolulu* (CL-48), *Rigel* (ARB-1), *Tautog* (SS-199), *Sumner* (AG-32), *Ramapo* (AO-12), *Pyro* (AE-1), and *Preble* (DM-20) ARs.

APPENDIX B

ABBREVIATIONS, ACRONYMS, AND JAPANESE TERMS

AA	Anti-Aircraft
AAC	Army Air Corps
AR	Action Report
AP	Armor piercing
AS	Anti-Submarine
BB	Battleship
BC	Battlecruiser
CA	Heavy cruiser
CAG	Commander Air Group
CAP	Combat Air Patrol
CEP	Circular Error Probable
chutai	a flight of nine aircraft, usually made up of three *shotai*
CinCPACFLT	Commander in Chief, Pacific Fleet
CL	Light cruiser
CNA	Center for Naval Analyses
CNO	Chief of Naval Operations
CONOPS	Concept of Operations
CV	Fleet carrier
CVL	Light carrier

CW	Continuous Wave (keyed HF radio transmission)
daitai	27 aircraft, usually made up of three *chutai*
DC	Damage control
DD	Destroyer
DEAD	Destruction of Enemy Air Defenses
DP	Duel Purpose
DNM	Damaging Near Miss
FMC	Fully Mission Capable
GP	General Purpose
GQ	General Quarters (i.e. battle stations are manned)
HF	High frequency
HURL	Hawa'ii Undersea Research Laboratory
IJN	Imperial Japanese Navy
IP	Initial Point
kg	kilogram
Kaigun Daigakko	Naval Staff College
Kido Butai	literally "Mobile Force," the Japanese carrier-centric striking force
Mod	Modification, as in the Type 91 Mod 1 torpedo
MPI	Mean Point of Impact
MRI	Minimum release interval
nm	nautical miles
NSFO	Navy Standard Fuel Oil
NWC	Naval War College
OBE	overtaken by events
OCA	Offensive Counter-Air
OR	Operations Research
RPB	Rounds Per Bird
rpm	rounds per minute
SAP	Semi Armor Piercing
SEAD	Suppression of Enemy Air Defense
shotai	a flight of 3 aircraft, the fundamental tactical unit in Japanese naval aviation
SNAFU	"Situation Normal, All Fouled Up"
TOT	Time on Target

US	United States
USN	United States Navy
USNWC	United States Naval War College
USSBS	United States Strategic Bombing Survey
VB	Bomber
VF	Fighter
VT	Torpedo bomber
WDR	War Damage Report

APPENDIX C

SHIPS IN PEARL HARBOR AND VICINITY, 7 DECEMBER 1941

(• = Sunk or destroyed)

Battleships (BB)
  Pennsylvania (BB-38) (in Dry Dock No.1)
  •*Arizona* (BB-39)
  •*Nevada* (BB-36)
  •*Oklahoma* (BB-37)
  Tennessee (BB-43)
  •*California* (BB-44)
  Maryland (BB-46)
  • *West Virginia* (BB-48)
Heavy Cruisers (CA)
  New Orleans (CA-32)
  San Francisco (CA-38)
Light Cruisers (CL)
  Raleigh (CL-7)
  Detroit (CL-8)
  Phoenix (CL-46)
  Honolulu (CL-48)
  St. Louis (CL-49)
  Helena (CL-50)

Destroyers (DD)
  Allen (DD-66)
  Schley (DD-103)
  Chew (DD-106)
  Ward (DD-139) (patrolling entrance to Pearl Harbor)
  Dewey (DD-349)
  Farragut (DD-348)
  Hull (DD-350)
  MacDonough (DD-351)
  Worden (DD-352)
  Dale (DD-353)
  Monaghan (DD-354)
  Alywin (DD-355)
  Selfridge (DD-357)
  Phelps (DD-360)
  Cummings (DD-365)
  Reid (DD-369)
  Case (DD-370)
  Conyngham (DD-371)
  Cassin (DD-372) (in Dry Dock No.1)
  Shaw (DD-373) (in floating drydock YFD 2)
  Tucker (DD-374)
  Downes (DD-375) (in Dry Dock No.1)
  Bagley (DD-386)
  Blue (DD-387)
  Helm (DD-388) (underway, nearing West Loch)
  Mugford (DD-389)
  Ralph Talbot (DD-390)
  Henley (DD-391)
  Patterson (DD-392)
  Jarvis (DD-393)
Submarines (SS)
  Narwhal (SS-167)
  Dolphin (SS-169)
  Cachalot (SS-170)
  Tautog (SS-199)
Minelayer (CM)
  • *Oglala* (CM-4)

Minesweepers (AM)
Turkey (AM-13)
Bobolink (AM-20)
Rail (AM-26)
Tern (AM-31)
Grebe (AM-43)
Vireo (AM-52)
Coastal Minesweepers (AMc)
Cockatoo (AMc-8)
Crossbill (AMc-9)
Condor (AMc-14)
Reedbird (AMc-30)
Light Minelayers (DM)
Gamble (DM-15)
Ramsay (DM-16)
Montgomery (DM-17)
Breese (DM-18)
Tracy (DM-19)
Preble (DM-20)
Sicard (DM-21)
Pruitt (DM-22)
High Speed Minesweepers (DMS)
Zane (DMS-14)
Wasmuth (DMS-15)
Trever (DMS-16)
Perry (DMS-17)
Gunboat (PG)
Sacramento (PG-19)
Destroyer Tenders (AD)
Dobbin (AD-3)
Whitney (AD-4)
Seaplane Tenders (AV)
Curtiss (AV-4)
Tangier (AV-8)
Seaplane Tenders (Small) (AVP)
Avocet (AVP-4)
Swan (AVP-7) (on Marine Railway)

Seaplane Tenders (Destroyer) (AVD)
  Hulbert (AVD-6)
  Thornton (AVD-11)
Ammunition Ship (AE)
  Pyro (AE-1) (at Naval Ammunition Depot, West Loch)
Oilers (AO)
  Ramapo (AO-12)
  Neosho (AO-23)
Repair Ships (AR)
  Medusa (AR-1)
  Vestal (AR-4)
Base Repair Ship (ARb)
  Rigel (ARb-1)
Submarine Tender (AS)
  Pelias (AS-14)
Submarine Rescue Ship (ASR)
  Widgeon (ASR-1)
Hospital Ship (AH)
  Solace (AH-5)
Cargo Ship (AK)
  Vega (AK-17) (at Honolulu)
General-Stores-Issue Ships (AKS)
  Castor (AKS-1)
  Antares (AKS-3) (at Pearl Harbor entrance)
Ocean-going Tugs (AT)
  Ontario (AT-13)
  Sunnadin (AT-28)
  Keosanqua (AT-38) (at Pearl Harbor entrance)
  Navajo (AT-64) (12 miles outside Pearl Harbor entrance)
Miscellaneous Auxiliaries (AG)
  •*Utah* (AG-16)
  Argonne (AG-31)
  Sumner (AG-32)
Motor Torpedo Boats (PT)
  PT-20
  PT-21
  PT-22

PT-23
PT-24
PT-25
PT-26 (on pier, Navy Yard)
PT-27 (on board Ramapo)
PT-28 (on pier, Navy Yard)
PT-29 (on board Ramapo)
PT-30 (on board Ramapo)
PT-42 (on board Ramapo)

District Craft

Harbor Tugs (YT)
YT 5
Sotoyomo (YT 9) (in YFD 2 with Shaw)
YT 119
Osceola (YT 129)
YT 130
YT 142
Hoga (YT 146)
YT 152
YT 153 (underway in channel)

Motor Tug (YMT)
YMT 5

Torpedo Testing Barge (YTT)
YTT 3

Net Tenders (YN)
Ash (YN 2)
Cinchona (YN 7)
Cockenoe (YN 47) (Honolulu Harbor)
Marin (YN 53)
Wapello (YN 56)

District Patrol Vessel (YP)
YP 109

Floating Drydock (YFD)
YFD 2 (with Shaw and Sotoyomo docked)

Salvage Pontoons (YSP)
YSP 11
YSP 12
YSP 13

YSP 14
YSP 15
YSP 16
YSP 17
YSP 18
YSP 19
YSP 20

Floating Workshops (YR)
YR 20
YR 22 (alongside Cachalot)

Miscellaneous (Unclassified) (IX)
Cheng Ho (IX 52)

Gate Vessel (YNg)
YNg 17

Garbage Lighters (YG)
YG 15
YG 17
YG 21

Ferryboat (YFB)
Nihoa (YFB 19)

Fuel Oil Barges (YO)
YO 30
YO 43
YO 44

Seaplane Wrecking Derrick (YSD)
YSD 9

Hulk
Ex-Baltimore (CM 1)

Covered Lighters (YF)
YF 240
YF 241

Open Lighters (YC)
YC 429
YC 470
YC 473
YC 477
YC 651
YC 699

Pontoon Storage Barges (YPK)
    YPK-2
    YPK-3
Submarine Rescue Chamber (YRC)
    YRC 5
Ash Lighter (YA)
    YA 66
Water Barge (YW)
    YW 10

APPENDIX D

THE PERFECT ATTACK

*The following vignette offers a scenario of what a "perfect attack"
might well have looked like, written from the viewpoint of an idealized
Commander Fuchida, the Strike Commander.*

Commander Fuchida sat in the wardroom of the *Akagi*, tapping his feet impatiently, drinking his tea with the air of a man who really would rather be away doing something else. He had told the communications watch officer where he would be; what was taking those sluggards in Tokyo so long? It was not as if they had anything to do other than retransmit the report.

A sailor opened the door to the wardroom, bowed respectfully, and cast his eyes over the officers scattered about the large compartment. Fuchida assumed a look of calm disregard. It was important to set an example.

The sailor's eyes lit on to Fuchida, and he skipped forward with an excited glint in his eye. He came to attention, bowed quickly, and proffered a flimsy piece of paper to Fuchida.

Fuchida looked it over quickly, and could not repress a smile. He rose and hurried out of the wardroom en route to Genda's stateroom, ordering the messenger to follow.

A quick rap of the knuckles on the door, and Fuchida entered. Genda looked up from behind the tiny desk that folded out from the bulkhead.

Fuchida grinned. "No barrage balloons. No torpedo nets!"

"Ah," replied Genda. "Very good. So, no level bombers."

"Three battleships double-berthed," Fuchida responded. "Two behind battleships, one behind a repair ship. One in drydock"

"So. *Some* level bombers." He offered a slight smile to Fuchida. "Carriers?"

"No carriers."

"So. They have been out of port for quite a while. Perhaps they'll come in today. We'll leave a reserve for them, should it happen."

The two planners pulled out the chart of Pearl Harbor and revisited the calculations first made so many months ago. They marked the latest information from the message. There were four battleships inaccessible to torpedoes. Previously they had decided to try for two AP bomb hits on each inaccessible battleship along Battleship Row, hoping for an engine room or magazine hit to put the ship out of action for the months needed to complete the Southern Advance. Eight formations of five bombers each would do the trick, leaving fifty with torpedoes. The battleship in drydock they decided to leave alone, since if the bombs were successful there would be no water to flood into the ship and magnify the damage. Better to save the bombs for where they could do the most damage.

They decided on the aircrews for each payload, checking them off on a previously prepared message form.

Genda thrust a finger at the chart where the battleship was double berthed behind the repair ship. "Do you think we could slip a torpedo or two past this auxiliary?"

Fuchida pulled out a copy of the venerable *Jane's Fighting Ships*, and flipped through the pages. "Their repair ships are just under 500 feet long. That pretty much covers the length of the battleship. But its draft is under 20 feet. Maybe we go under. Set five torpedoes for eight meters, and assign those crews to hit those ships in particular."

The initial assignments and targeting was worked out. The initial torpedo attack would go down the Southeast Loch. The attack would be delivered in waves of five aircraft in an echelon-left formation with about 50 yards between aircraft. The leader would attack the leftmost battleships, the next torpedo bomber the next to the right of the leader's target, and so on until the entire wave was lined up with a target. The most difficult attack paths went to the trailing aircraft in each group. They would have to pass the supply depot and immediately rack around into a nearly 60-degree turn in order to line up their torpedo.

Five groups of five torpedo bombers would make the initial attack. The second through fifth groups would bore in to their targets regardless of the results of previous attacks; hit or miss, they were to concentrate their lives on their one torpedo and their one target. With steady crews, that would mean five torpedoes per battleship, likely four hits per battleship, enough to sink them all.

Fuchida and Genda allocated another four *shotai* of torpedo bombers, twelve B5N Kates in all, to seek out and destroy the cruisers reported to be to the north and northwest of Ford Island. That totaled 37 torpedo bombers for the initial charge. Thirteen would remain with Fuchida as an attack reserve, to be assigned after the results of the first charge were ascertained. Their task would be most dangerous, going into the teeth of the awakened American defenses.

Genda handed the message to the communications messenger. "Take this to the Chief of Staff. He is expecting it. It is to go out immediately by flashing light." The messenger saluted and left, clearly excited.

Fuchida himself would command the strike from a B5N Kate loaded only with two 250kg GP bombs. His first responsibility was to ensure that the torpedo attack went in successfully, and then assign targets for the second wave dive-bombers based on the damage inflicted by the torpedo bombers. His command responsibilities were more important than any damage he might inflict.

But the B5N Kate carrier attack bomber had a range far in excess of what was needed, and his pilot was skilled in fuel conservation. He had enough endurance to carry a few bombs. Between the attack waves, he would allow his pilot, Ohno, and their bombardier to join in with the true samurai spirit of the attack—Fuchida did not have the heart to ask them to go up unarmed as just a command platform, and he did not want to go up unarmed himself, either. His crew had smiled happily when he told them of the bombs.

During the evening meal, in the company of all of the carrier's aviators, Ohno announced to all his ambition to sink Pearl Harbor's garbage scow. Without that boat to remove their garbage the rich American ships would soon all sink from the weight of their own trash, he proclaimed, thus winning the war for Japan in a single, sublime blow.

His companions in the aviators' mess hooted in derision. What if the rich Americans had *two* garbage scows?

But this only caused him to sit proudly, with a coy glint in his eye.

"From Sun Tzu we know, 'To see victory only when it is within the ken of the common herd is not the acme of excellence,'" Ohno recited with an academic air. He ended with a snort, his eyes scanning the common herd around him.

"He quotes a Chinaman!" someone cried. The laughter was general.

A short day later, Fuchida was in the observer's seat of his B5N Kate as the first wave of *Kido Butai's* strike turned toward Oahu. The sun was just beginning to peek above the horizon, a glorious visage illuminating the heavens with rays of red and gold. As the aircraft droned south, they sorted themselves out into the attack groupings, one formation for each of the target areas, each a mix of aircraft types. Around Fuchida formed up the fifty torpedo bombers destined for the harbor, along with three *chutai* of fighters, 27 in all, that were to be their cover and SEAD support. One *chutai* of D3A Val divebombers would attack the AA positions on the ships. Thirty-nine B5N Kates carrying 800kg AP bombs followed.

Ahead, Fuchida saw Oahu forming up out of the misty sky. He adjusted their course to pass over Kahuku Point, the northernmost tip of Oahu. There was no evidence of the enemy, so he allowed the default plan, which assumed that they had achieved surprise, to remain operative.

As his B5N Kate passed over the Point, he shouted "Mark time!" and his bombardier-radioman began to broadcast, "To, To, To," marking the first time tick to synchronize the attack. He looked around, and saw that all the bomber formation leaders were waggling their wings, indicating they had received the message. The fighter leaders did not all respond, but that did not make any difference, as their initial job was to follow the bombers and cover their movements.

The formation turned south to pass along the Koolau Range, mountains more spectacular for their beauty than their elevation, which did not top 600 meters. This course would lead them inland to pass to the east of Pearl Harbor. As the hands on Fuchida's stopwatch clicked the time, groups pulled away from the main formation on schedule and orbited in racetrack patterns. First to depart were the attackers destined for Wheeler Field, then the Ewa Field attack group departed, then the Kaneohe attack group, the Bellows attack group, and at last the Hickam group. They all would watch their clocks and at the pre-calculated times turn toward their objectives. It was a simple "time and distance" method to ensure that all the attacks were delivered simultaneously.

On schedule, Ohno banked to the right, and the formation headed west toward Pearl Harbor. With the sun at his back Fuchida could easily recognize the ships in the harbor. The scene looked just like that picture post card of the harbor that naval intelligence had given to all the bomber pilots. They had numbered all the mooring locations on it. It was faintly ridiculous that the blow-ups provided to his pilots should have "Souvenir of Hawa'ii" printed across the bottom. But then again, what self-respecting samurai went into Intelligence?

He scanned the harbor. No carriers. Too, too bad.

He looked at Battleship Row. The intelligence was correct—there was a line five battleships long, with three sets double berthed. An oiler could be ignored. They would proceed as planned.

As they passed Hickam Field, the formation broke apart. The first 25 torpedo bombers, five groups of five, formed up in their echeloned lines with 500 meters between groups. They pushed their noses down to drop to low altitude to begin their runs. The dive-bombers accelerated, pushing ahead with one *chutai* of fighters in support. Fuchida's B5N Kate, accompanied by the remaining reserve of torpedo bombers and a *chutai* of fighters, angled to the south to where the action could best be observed.

First in were five A6M Zero fighters. Fuchida could see the tracers from their 7.7mm machine guns, one tracer for every four rounds of armor piercing, as they searched out the machine gun positions on the high fighting tops of the battleships. They gracefully turned away. No fire came from the battleships.

Fuchida saw the D3A Vals pitch over to the attack in three chains of three, not enough for all five of the battleships, but doctrine had the *shotais* attack as a team, and three *shotais* were all that could be spared. The leaders released their bombs—Fuchida groaned as all three missed, long and to the left. The leaders had not recognized the strength of the wind. He squeezed his fist around his pencil.

The second and third bombers in each team, as they were trained, adjusted their aim points based on the results of their leader's bomb. Then, in rapid succession, three, no, four hits erupted on three battleships in the middle of Battleship Row. Two hits were squarely on the AA gun decks on different battleships. Fires blossomed.

The first group of five torpedo bombers crossed south of the submarine base, low and slow, heading along the Southeast Loch, the full formation extending almost entirely across the loch so that, when the turns were required, each plane would have the most room to line up on their target and the least amount to turn. There was no indication of enemy AA fire. The leader eased left, crossed the formation heading for the southernmost mooring, a *Tennessee* class battleship. Like a ballet perfectly synchronized, each following aircraft made its course adjustment to line up on its target as they had practiced so often together.

"Too low," mumbled Fuchida, as he watched the last bomber bank right to begin its difficult turn towards the northernmost target. The pilot evidently had been flustered by the aircraft crossing ahead of him closer than they had practiced, and momentarily pulled back on his throttle. Fuchida saw a ripple of wake on the water below the torpedo bomber's right wing and then, to his horror, saw the wing catch a wave top. Instantly the four tons of aircraft, aircrew and torpedo were spinning a cartwheel like a crazed circus acrobat, flipping over and over above the water, finally settling in a vast spray of water.

Fuchida had a flash of anxiety. Would the other pilots flinch from their attack on the northernmost part of Battleship Row? Before he could be visited by more apprehensive thoughts, the second group of attackers flashed down the loch, fifteen seconds behind the lead formation. The same ballet ensued, aircraft lining up their drops, this time with the clearances as they had practiced. Fuchida locked his eyes on the last aircraft, willing it to stay aloft. The torpedo bomber banked, turned right, seemed to shudder a little in the air, then the wings leveled. Fuchida saw the splash as this aircraft released its weapon. A good attack!

"A hit! Number 1 position!" shouted his pilot and bombardier together. "A hit! Number 2 position! A hit! Number 3 position!"

"Three hits in the first wave," thought Fuchida, as he pulled out his clipboard with the chart of the harbor. He made pencil tic marks next to each ship that was hit.

Another wave appeared at the end of the loch. Arcs of machine gun fire streamed out from a destroyer moored against the quay at the Navy Yard. Two streams converged on one of the torpedo bombers, releasing a flow of red flame from its wing root. Its torpedo tumbled away, jettisoned. The bomber pulled up, stalled, and like a fluttering cherry blossom hit the ground inside the Navy Yard. A red balloon of fire brightened the sky.

"Damnation," muttered Fuchida.

Three of the covering A6M Zero fighters rolled over and streaked down, aiming for the offending destroyer. Streams of machine gun bullets lashed up and down the destroyer's deck. Fuchida could hear the distant deeper, rapid "chug chug chug" sound as the fighter pilots added their 20mm cannon to the fire of their 7.7mm machine guns. The third fighter pulled up. Nothing more came from the destroyer. The next formation of torpedo bombers slipped by, unimpeded.

"A hit! Number 2 position! A hit! Number three position! A hit! Number 5 position!"

In less than ninety seconds 25 torpedo bombers had completed their attack. Fuchida and his crew had counted sixteen hits. Position 2 and 3, the simplest runs, had taken the brunt of the attack, five hits. Both ships looked on the verge of capsizing. Position 1 had taken three hits, and position 5 one. Position 4 had taken two hits, but it was difficult to say if the hits were on the repair ship or the battleship. Certainly the repair ship took at least one, as it appeared to be broken in half. Fuchida scribbled notes on his kneeboard, his mind calculating ferociously.

"A hit! Number seventeen position! A hit! Number twenty-one position!"

Fuchida jerked his eyes out of the cockpit and looked out over the harbor. To the north, plumes of cascading water were settling alongside two cruisers. As he watched, another plume climbed skyward.

"A hit! Number seventeen position!" The bombardier's voice was getting hoarse with excitement. Fuchida could feel his own pulse pounding. Somehow, two miles south of the events, he thought he caught a whiff of raw fuel oil.

As his eyes gazed over the harbor, he saw five poppy seeds arc down from high in the sky and fall around the number-two position battleship. They exploded and kicked up huge columns of water seventy feet high. The level bombers were attacking. Five water columns—five misses. He sent his prayers to will the hand of providence to guide the bombs of his compatriots—Genda-san would never let him live it down if his level bombers failed.

Another set of water columns rose up. Four columns and one dull flash. A hit.

Fuchida looked down to his clipboard to record the information, marking the AP bomb hit, searching the chart for Number Seventeen position to record the torpedo hits. Suddenly the cockpit lit up—his skin almost seemed to peel from the radiance of the white flash of light, impossibly bright for a second, then two—and he looked up to see the most incredible explosion envelope the northern part of Battleship Row.

"The Heavens have struck number four position," Fuchida heard Ohno intone as he watched smoke and flying, burning pieces of debris cast up 500 meters into the sky. While a part of his mind was dumbfounded at the power of the explosion, another part said that he would not need to worry about striking the battleship berthed next to the repair ship. Were any of his bombers caught in the blast?

He shook his head to bring himself back to reality. Speed was needed, quickness. Looking down at his chart, he circled the positions of ships needing more attention. He snapped an order to Ohno, who put more power to the engine and edged over to where the reserve torpedo bombers were flying their racetrack, waiting expectantly. He pulled alongside one, and Fuchida pulled out his prepared cardboard sheets with large numbers printed on them, one for each mooring position in the harbor. He showed the number to the aircrew of the first B5N Kate. The pilot nodded, saluted, and dropped back in formation. One by one he gave the reserves their assignments. It was now perhaps five minutes since the first torpedo had hit, and ugly black puffs of AA fire were beginning to soil the sky.

He gave out the last of the assignments, ticking off the last circled numbers as he did. When all the circles were checked, he still had three torpedo bombers left. He had assigned attackers to the outlying cruisers, the cruiser moored next to 1010 Dock, the cruisers at the carrier moorings, the battleships that could use another hole or two. What to do with this last three? He sent two against the cruisers at the Navy Yard piers—even if the targets were foreshortened into slivers by the angle of approach, they would be bound to hit something valuable if the torpedo survived the launch. The last torpedo? His friend Lt. Suzuki grinned at him across the gulf between the two aircraft. He had told him back on the *Akagi* that he wanted a challenge. Let him have a go at the drydock caisson.

He fired a Black Dragon flare. The reserve torpedo bombers broke formation to attack their targets as nearly simultaneously as possible.

He watched them swoop into position. Black puffs of AA fire seemed dark and ugly compared to the white water splashed up as the torpedoes fell into the harbor.

"A hit! Number 14 position!" New hits were announced. Fuchida continued to record damage. Eventually, the last of the torpedoes were launched, the last hits recorded. Fuchida glanced at his watch. It seemed impossible, but it was a bare fifteen minutes from when the attack had started.

Fuchida fired a Red Dragon flare. In doing so he released his escort fighters and SEAD support. They banked away, heading for their assigned airfields. They would strafe the air bases, and then the fighters would fly top cover to ensure that no American aircraft got aloft. They would remain as guards until the second wave arrived to relieve them.

He watched as Suzuki's plane descended to attack altitude.

He heard Ohno say, "Our turn, sir?" It interrupted his concentration, but Fuchida assented, and directed the pilot towards the Navy Yard piers. They climbed to 2,000 meters—good level bombing altitude against a fixed target, low enough for accuracy, high enough to be out of machine gun range.

Fuchida was inspecting the cruisers with his binoculars when he felt the bomber suddenly lift. "Bombs released!" shouted the bombardier, who kept his eyes pressed to his bombsight. Fuchida could not resist—he went down on his knees and looked out the observer's sight in the floor of the bomber. At this altitude the details on the ground were in sharp focus, he could even see small figures of men rushing along the piers heading for the ships. He spotted their two 250kg bombs gracefully descending, becoming smaller and smaller, and saw the shipyard piers far, far ahead of them, he could not see how the bombs could possibly get there—then, in a rush, bombs and targets merged. There was a red flash along the line where the pier and a class "A" cruiser met, and further along a huge splash in the turning basin.

"One hit!" Fuchida called out.

"What did we get?" Ohno asked.

Fuchida paused to heighten the pilot's anxiety.

"A garbage scow, I think," he said tonelessly. Ohno seemed to slump in his seat. Fuchida reached forward and patted him on the side of the head. "Ohno-san, the Yankees have 10,000-ton garbage scows with gun turrets, it appears." The pilot laughed.

Fuchida had now about 30 minutes to consider the next necessary decisions. Egusa would be arriving with the second-wave dive-bombers. He ordered his pilot to climb to 3,000 meters to meet them while he inspected the harbor. His crew had counted 30 hits of the 50 torpedoes, not as many as expected but the distribution was good. Five of the battleships along Ford Island were finished, two capsized, two with water over their main decks, and one blasted apart and sending up a tremendous cloud of smoke that obscured most of Battleship Row. All the torpedo-accessible cruisers had taken one or two torpedo hits, one class "B" cruiser was capsized, another obviously sinking. It was impossible to tell what the torpedoes had done to the ships at the Navy Yard piers, but something had happened from the amount of smoke.

"Did you see Suzuki-san?" he called to the bombardier. The man pointed to a column of smoke and burning debris. The Yankees were awake and shooting. He would meet Suzuki-san at the Yasukuni Shrine when he, too, gave his life for the Emperor.

Fuchida saw a large tanker backing out of its berth at Ford Island. Centered in the channel, the froth at its stern meant the captain was trying to twist the ship to line up to go hide in the loch beyond the Navy Yard.

"Good, we'll sink you right there," he thought.

The dive-bombers appeared on the horizon—they were 15 minutes early, excellent timing. Fuchida made his last decisions, and his pilot turned the plane to join up with the dive-bombers' command elements. There was no time to give individual assignments, so Fuchida pulled up to each of the nine *chutai* leaders and flashed the number of their target assignment to them. Two *chutai* would put the tanker on the bottom. Four *chutai* would hit the four cruisers at the Navy Yard Piers. The remaining three would hit the surviving cruisers anchored north of Ford Island or put some bombs in the nests of destroyers.

The dive-bombing conditions were horrible, with smoke obscuring the targets and a layer of 70% cloud cover at 1,500 meters altitude over parts of the harbor that threw off all chances of bombing as the crews had been trained. The American AA fire was suddenly tremendous—far better than what would come from a Japanese fleet under similar circumstances; but then again, AA fire was defensive, and the Japanese did not honor the defensive.

But through it all the dive-bombers attacked bravely.

The two *chutai* attacking the oiler put six hits into the huge hull, and it lit up like a Chinese fireworks fountain, gushing red flames and oily black smoke. But sinking that oiler, with all her separate storage tanks only partially filled with a cargo that was lighter than water, proved to be more difficult than expected. The bombs missed the relatively small engineering spaces, so the oiler remained under way. Her captain put her aground off Hospital Point, well out of the channel. Later, the current twisted her off the shore, but Navy tugs got lines across her at the extreme bow and stern and, with the help of her engines, put her firmly aground on the other side of the channel. Burning fuel streamed down the channel, halting all movement out of the harbor.

Otherwise, the performance of the dive-bombers was less than what was expected, but good under the circumstances. Egusa had expected half the bombs to hit, but the actual score appeared to be well short of that. The smoke, the clouds, the brisk wind and the even brisker AA fire seemed to take away the favor of providence from the dive-bombers. But attacking targets further away from the smoke clouds around Ford Island was a good decision, and so while the hit percentage was down, many useful hits were scored.

Finally, the dive-bombers completed their attacks, and after a last flurry of strafing, they abandoned the harbor to their new enemies.

Fuchida directed his pilot to take a last tour of the harbor. His bombardier took photographs to help with the battle damage assessment.

Four battleships sunk by torpedoes, five or six hits apiece. There would be very little left of them to salvage, particularly the two that capsized. One battleship was blown apart by the mighty 800kg bombs, a point that Fuchida would report with particular pride. It, too, would never float again. There were several AP bomb hits on the other inboard battleships which hopefully detonated in their engineering spaces, crippling them for six months to a year. It appeared that only one battleship escaped heavy damage, the ship in the drydock, but the gods do not favor the greedy, it would have been unreasonable to expect more and that ship was not vulnerable enough to warrant expending limited ammunition on it.

They had exceeded Yamamoto's goal of one battleship sunk and a total of four battleships crippled—they had achieved five battleships sunk, and crippled two more. Yamamoto would be pleased.

Damage to lower priority targets was also excellent. Of the eight cruisers in port, the four anchored scattered around the harbor were all put down by a combination of torpedoes and bombs. The smoke over the Navy Yard piers made damage assessment difficult, but where there is smoke there is fire, and it looked to Fuchida's eye that two of the four cruisers there were burning fiercely, and another one leaning against the pier, half-sunk. Smoke also came out of five of the nests of destroyers, indicating that the dive-bombers had some successes there. The photographs later would show another four destroyers sunk, one destroyer-minelayer sunk, and six destroyers damaged.

Five battleships sunk, seven cruisers sunk or destroyed, eleven destroyer-class vessels sunk or heavily damaged, a huge oiler grounded and melting. As Fuchida tallied the results, he could not see how they could have been better. Perhaps better dive-bombing could have added to the margins with a few more of the smaller warships, but it was nearly a clean sweep of the most important targets.

As he departed the Pearl Harbor area for a quick tour of Ewa and Wheeler fields before heading back to the carrier, Fuchida's eyes were drawn to the huge oil storage tanks lined up like soldiers marching up the hills on the periphery of the harbor.

"How foolish are the Americans," he thought. "They make all this effort to bring out millions of liters of fuel for their fleet, and then do not protect the fleet. Of what use is oil without warships? The Americans make war like accountants. They have no *Yamato damashii,* no *kesshitai.* Clearly providence favors we Japanese. We will take the southern resource areas, the Philippines and Singapore, and the Americans and British accountants will see that war is too costly to defend places that they can hardly spell. They will be pleased to have done with it all and bow to us across a negotiating table. Then they will give all this oil to us as war reparations."

With this thought his plane turned away from the white fuel tanks, and Fuchida's heart was glad that he did not have to bother with such dishonorable targets.

APPENDIX E

ACKNOWLEDGMENTS

I am told in the publishing business that a book has two positions of especial importance: what is said first, and what is said last. The subject of the book should surely have first priority. However, next must come acknowledgement of the many people who made substantive contributions to this work.

All good books are necessarily the result of the efforts of many people who take the time to help the author get the facts right and keep him from straying into ideas that cannot be substantiated. I have been blessed by many experts who have given freely their time, shared their research, and provided valued criticism. Their contributions have done nothing but improve this work. I cannot mention them all, but must mention a few, as they contributed immensely.

William O'Neil, Captain USNR (ret) and a senior analyst at the Center for Naval Analyses, was generous with his time and talents. He provided references, important documents and excellent comments throughout the manuscript. Chapter 9 was extensively modified from his input.

Christopher Powers, Captain USN (ret) provided extensive and valuable comments, along with the perspective of a strike fighter pilot and Air Boss.

Trent Hone provided valued research material and extensive comments. Under his cogent criticism arguments were strengthened and alternative explanations suggested.

Tim Lazendorfer provided almost a page-by-page critique of the work which proved exceptionally valuable.

David Aiken of the Pearl Harbor History Associates provided references and comments. He generously shared his research and comprehensive knowledge of the Japanese torpedo attack and other areas.

Jon Parshall, David Dickson, and (soon to be) Dr. David Flannigan provided comments and criticism. Mark Campbell made the suggestion that resulted in the "pop history" portion of the introduction. Terry Sofian shared his compilation of information on the Japanese aircraft groups' attack missions.

Nathan Okun, a respected expert in World War II ordnance and armor penetration technology, contributed comments throughout, along with specific help on the construction and performance of Japanese bombs and ship damage.

Terry Kirby of HURL provided information on the creation of the NOVA television program. Parks Stephenson (one of the good guys who fell into evil company) and I engaged in a spirited exchange on the fate of the fifth midget submarine. I look forward to his book.

Ralph Norton, a petroleum expert, generously provided extensive information on fuel oil storage tank construction and firefighting measures dating back to the 1930s. He provided much of the information on fuel tank specifications, operations, and fire prevention measures, along with information on the experiences of the Haifa refinery. Edward Rudnicki, an Army ordnance expert, assisted with several technical points.

My thanks to the "Fire Control Group," of naval history experts with many publication credits, who have been generous with their time and assistance over the years. They provided many valued documents, insights, inspiration and, when needed, correction. Thank you, all.

My valued critics would have me point out that some of what is discussed in this book still has room for additional research and debate, which I encourage—it can only improve our understanding of World War II naval history and of the Pearl Harbor Raid. Many of the best points made in this study were at their suggestion. They held everything to a high standard, for which I am grateful.

My sincere thanks to my dear wife Deborah and daughter Natalie. Thank you for putting up with my disappearances into the basement book cave for so many months.

BIBLIOGRAPHY

Books

Agawa, Hiroyuki. *The Reluctant Admiral: Yamamoto and the Imperial Navy*. New York: Kodansha International, LTD, 1982.

Aldrich, Richard James. *Intelligence and the War Against Japan: Britain, America and the Politics of Secret Service*. Cambridge, UK: Cambridge University Press, 2000.

Arakaki, Leatrice R. and Kuborn, John R. *7 December 1941, The Air Force Story*. Honolulu: University Press of the Pacific, 2005.

Asada, Sadao. *From Mahan to Pearl Harbor: The Imperial Japanese Navy and the United States*. Annapolis: Naval Institute Press, 2006.

Barnhart, Michael A. *Japan Prepares for Total War: The Search for Economic Security, 1919–1941*. Ithaca: Cornell University Press, 1987.

Belote, James H. and Belote, William M. *Titans of the Seas: The Development and Operations of the Japanese and American Carrier Task Forces During World War II*. New York: Harper and Row, 1975.

Bisson, T.A. *Japan's War Economy*. New York: The Macmillan Company, 1945.

Brown, David K. *Nelson to Vanguard: Warship Development 1923–1945*. Annapolis: Naval Institute Press, 2000.

Burlingame, Burl. *Advance Force Pearl Harbor*. Annapolis: Naval Institute Press, 1992.

Bywater, Hector. *The Great Pacific War*. Boston: Houghton Mifflin Company, 1942.

Calhoun, C. Raymond. *Tin Can Sailor: Life Aboard the USS Sterett, 1939–1945*. Annapolis: Naval Institute Press, 1993.

Campbell, John.1985. *Naval Weapons of World War II*. London: Conway Maritime Press Ltd., 1985.

Clarke, Thurston. *Pearl Harbor Ghosts: The Legacy of December 7, 1941*. New York: Ballantine Books, 1991.

Cohen, Jerome B.1949. *Japanese Economic History 1930–1960, Volume II, Japan's Economy in War and Reconstruction*. New York: Routledge, 1949.

Cohen, Stan. *East Wind Rain: A Pictorial History of the Pearl Harbor Attack*. Missoula: Pictorial Histories Publishing Company, 1981.

DeBlanc, Colonel Jefferson. *The Guadalcanal Air War*. Gretna: Pelican Publishing Company, 2008.

Drea, Edward. *Japan's Imperial Army: Its Rise and Fall, 1853–1945*. Lawrence: University of Kansas Press, 2009.

Dull, Paul S. *A Battle History of the Imperial Japanese Navy (1941–1945)*. Annapolis: Naval Institute Press, 1978.

Edwards, Bernard. *Japan's Blitzkrieg: The Allied Collapse in the East 1941–42*. Barnsley: Pen and Sword Books Ltd, 2006.

Ellsberg, Edward. *No Banners, No Bugles*. New York: Dodd, Mead & Company, 1949.

Evans, David C. and Peattie, Mark R. *Kaigun: Strategy, Tactics, and Technology in the Imperial Japanese Navy, 1887–1941*. Annapolis: Naval Institute Press, 1997.

Fiske, Rear Admiral Bradley A. *The Navy as a Fighting Machine*. New York: Charles Scribner's Sons, 1918.

Francillon, Rene J. *Japanese Aircraft of the Pacific War*. Annapolis: Naval Institute Press, 1970.

Fuchida, Mitsuo and Okumiya, Masatake. *Midway: The Battle that Doomed Japan*. New York: Ballantine Books, 1958.

Friedman, Norman. *US Aircraft Carriers: An Illustrated Design History*. Annapolis: Naval Institute Press, 1983.

Friedman, Norman. *US Battleships: An Illustrated Design History*. Annapolis: Naval Institute Press, 1985.

Gannon, Michael. *Pearl Harbor Betrayed*. Annapolis: Naval Institute Press, 2001.

Goldstein, Donald M. and Dillon, Katherine V. (ed.). *Fading Victory: The Diary of Admiral Matome Ugaki, 1941–1945*. Pittsburgh: University of Pittsburgh Press, 1991.

Goldstein, Donald M. and Dillon, Katherine V. (ed). *The Pearl Harbor Papers: Inside the Japanese Plans*. McLean: Brassey's, 1993.

Goldstein, Donald M. and Dillon, Katherine V. and Wenger, J. Michael. *The Way It Was: Pearl Harbor, the Original Photographs*. Washington, DC: Brassey's, 1991.

Hearings Before the Joint Committee on the Investigation of the Pearl Harbor Attack, Seventy-Ninth Congress. Washington: Government Printing Office, 1946.

Kinoaki, Matsuo. *How Japan Plans to Win*. Boston: Little, Brown and Company, 1942.

Lambert, John W. and Polmar, Norman. *Defenseless: Command Failure at Pearl Harbor*. St. Paul: Motorbooks International, 2003.

Lea, Homer. *The Valor of Ignorance*. New York: Harper & Brothers Publishers, 1942.

Lenton, H.T. *American Fleet and Escort Destroyers, Volume I*. New York: Doubleday & Company, 1971.

Lord, Walter. *Day of Infamy*. New York: Henry Holt and Company, 1957.

Lundstom, John. *The First Team and the Guadalcanal Campaign*. Annapolis: Naval Institute Press, 1993.

Madsen, Daniel. *Resurrection: Salvaging the Battle Fleet at Pearl Harbor*. Annapolis: Naval Institute Press, 2003.

McFarland, Stephen L. *America's Pursuit of Precision Bombing, 1910–1945*. Washington, DC: Smithsonian Institution Press, 1995.

Middlebrook, Martin and Mahoney, Patrick. *The Sinking of the Prince of Wales and Repulse: The End of the Battleship Era*. Barnsley, South Yorkshire: Pen & Sword Books Limited, 2004.

Miller, Edward S. *War Plan Orange: The US Strategy to Defeat Japan, 1897–1945*. Annapolis: Naval Institute Press, 1991.

Monday, David. *American Aircraft of World War II*. London: Chancellor Press, 1996.

Morison, Samuel Eliot. *The Rising Sun in the Pacific, 1931–April 1942*. Edison: Castle Books, 2001.

Mrazek, Robert J. *A Dawn Like Thunder: The True Story of Torpedo Squadron Eight*. New York: Back Bay Books, 2008.

O'Connell, Robert L. *Sacred Vessels: The Cult of the Battleship and the Rise of the US Navy*. New York: Oxford University Press, 1991.

Olson, Michael Keith. *Tales from a Tin Can: The USS Dale from Pearl Harbor to Tokyo Bay*. St. Paul: Zenith Press, 2007.

Parshall, Jon and Tully, Anthony. *Shattered Sword: The Untold Story of the Battle of Midway*. Washington, DC: Potomac Books, 2005.

Peattie, Mark R. *Sunburst: The Rise of Japanese Naval Air Power, 1909–1941*. Annapolis: Naval Institute Press, 2001.

Pelz, Stephen E. *The Race to Pearl Harbor: The Failure of the Second London Naval Conference and the Onset of World War II*. Cambride: Harvard University Press, 1975.

Poolman, Kenneth. *The Winning Edge: Naval Technology in Action, 1939–1945*. Annapolis: Naval Institute Press, 1997.

Potter, E.B. *Nimitz*. Annapolis: Naval Institute Press, 1976.

Prange, Gordon W. *At Dawn We Slept: The Untold Story of Pearl Harbor*. New York: Penguin Books, 1981.

Prange, Gordon W. *Pearl Harbor: The Verdict of History*. New York: McGraw-Hill Book Company, 1986.

Naval Analysis Division, United States Strategic Bombing Survey (Pacific). *Campaigns of the Pacific* War. Washington, DC: Government Printing Office, 1946.

Prange, Gordon W. with Goldstein Donald M. and Dillon, Katherine V. *God's Samurai: Lead Pilot at Pearl Harbor*. Washington, DC: Brassey's (US), 1990.

Rusbridger, James and Nave, Eric. *Betrayal at Pearl Harbor: How Churchill Lured Roosevelt into WW II*. New York: Summit Books, 1991.

Slackman, Michael. *Target: Pearl Harbor*. Honolulu: University of Hawaii Press, 1990.

Smith, Carl. *Pearl Harbor 1941: The day of infamy*. New York: Osprey Publishing Ltd., 2001.

Smith, Peter C. The *History of Dive Bombing*. Annapolis: The Nautical & Aviation Publishing Company, 1981.

Smith, Peter C. *Aichi D3A1/2 Val*. Ramsbury: The Crowood Press, 1999.

Smith, Peter C. *Fist From the Sky: Japan's Dive-Bomber Ace of WWII*. Mechanicsburg: Stackpole Books, 2005.

Smith, Douglas. *Carrier Battles: Command Decision in Harm's Way*. Annapolis: Naval Institute Press, 2006.

Stephan, John J. *Hawaii Under the Rising Sun: Japan's Plans for Conquest After Pearl Harbor*. Honolulu: University of Hawaii Press, 1984.

Stern, Robert C. *The Lexington Class Carriers*. Annapolis: Naval Institute Press, 1993.

Stillwell, Paul (ed). *Air Raid: Pearl Harbor! Recollections of a Day of Infamy*. Annapolis: United States Naval Institute, 1981.

Stillwell, Paul. *Battleship Arizona: An Illustrated History*. Annapolis: Naval Institute Press, 1991.

Stinnett, Robert B. *Day of Deceit: The Truth about FDR and Pearl Harbor*. New York: The Free Press, 2001.

Theobald, Rear Admiral Robert A. USN (ret). *The Final Secret of Pearl Harbor: The Washington Contribution to the Japanese Attack*. New York: Devin-Adair Company, 1954.

Thorpe, George C. *Pure Logistics: The Science of War Preparation*. Washington: National Defense University Press, 1986 (reprint).

Toland, John. *The Rising Sun: The Decline and Fall of the Japanese Empire, 1936–1945*. New York: Random House, 1970.

United States Naval Institute. *The Japanese Navy in World War II*. Annapolis: Naval Institute Press, 1969.

Vat, Dan van der. *The Pacific Campaign: World War II, the US—Japanese Naval War, 1941–1945*. New York: Simon & Schuster, 1991.

Wallin, Vice Admiral Homer N. USN (Retired). *Pearl Harbor: Why, How, Fleet Salvage and Final Appraisal*. Washington DC: Naval History Division, 1968.

Watts, Anthony J. and Gordon, Brian G. *The Imperial Japanese Navy*. Garden City: Doubleday & Company Inc, 1971.

Weinberg, Gerhard L. *Germany, Hitler, and World War II*. New York: Cambridge University Press, 1995.

Werneth, Ron. *Beyond Pearl Harbor: The Untold Stories of Japan's Naval Airmen*. Atglen: Schiffer Military History, 2008.

Willmott, H.P. *Empires in the Balance: Japanese and Allied Pacific Strategies to April 1942*. Annapolis: Naval Institute Press, 1982.

Willmott, H.P. *Pearl Harbor*. New York: Galahad Books, 1982.

Willmott, H.P. with Tohmatsu, Haruo and Johnson, W. Spencer. *Pearl Harbor*. London: Cassell and Company, 2001.

Yoshimura, Akira. *Build the Musashi! The Birth and Death of the*

World's Greatest Battleship. New York: Kodansha International, 1991.

Yoshimura, Akira. *Zero Fighter*. Westport: Praeger, 1996.

Journal Articles and Reports

Aiken, David. "Torpedoing Pearl Harbor." *Military History Magazine*, December 2001.

Burke, Frederick W. Jr. "Unidentified Ships at Pearl Harbor on 7 December 1941." *Warship International*, vol. 46 No. 2, 2009.

De Virgilio, John F. "Japanese Thunderfish." *Naval History* Vol. 5 No. 4, Winter 1991.

De Virgilio, John F. "Seven Seconds to Infamy." *United States Naval Institute Proceedings*, December 1997.

Gaines, William. "Antiaircraft Defense of Oahu 1916–1945." *The Coast Defense Journal*, Vol. 15, Issue 2, May 2001.

Hone, Trent "The Evolution of Fleet Tactical Doctrine in the US Navy, 1922–1941." *Journal of Military History*, October 2003.

Hone, Thomas C. "The Destruction of the Battle Line at Pearl Harbor." *United States Naval Institute Proceedings*, December 1977.

Leonard, Rich. "Early Intel on the Japanese Zero." www.midway42.org/temp/leonard-zero.html

Miller, Edward S. "Kimmel's Hidden Agenda." *Military History Quarterly*, Volume 4 No. 1, Autumn 1991.

Oberg, Dan. "*Gyokusai* and *Yamato-damashii*—Discourses on Organized Suicide attacks during the Pacific War." Institution of Warstudies, Swedish Defense College.

O'Neil, William D. "Transformation Billy Mitchell Style." United States Naval Institute *Proceedings*, March 2002.

O'Neil, William D. "Interwar US and Japanese National Product and Defense Expenditure." Center for Naval Analyses, CIM D0007249,A1 / Final, June 2003.

Parshall, Jonathan. "Reflecting on Fuchida, or "A Tale of Three Whoppers"". Naval War College Review, Spring 2010, Vol. 63 No 2.

Peattie, Mark and Evans, David C. "Planning Pearl Harbor." Hoover Digest, No. 2 1998. www.hoover.org/publications/digest/3531646.html

Wright, Christopher C. (ed), "The US Navy's Study of the Loss of Battleship *Arizona*." Warship International, Vol. No. 39, No. 3, 2002.

Zimm, Alan D. et al. "A Midget Sub in the Picture?" Naval History, April 2005

Zimm, Alan D. "Modern Theories and the Practice of Analysis." *Phalanx*, vol. 34 No. 2, June 2001.

Documents

Admiralty, Naval Staff, Tactical Section. , *Instruction for Tactical and Strategic Exercises Carried out on Tables or Boards.* O.U. 5243. January 1921.

Air Intelligence Group, Division of Naval Intelligence. *Striking Power of Air-Borne Weapons.* OPNAV-16-V A 43, July, 1944.

Chief of Naval Operations to Commander in Chief, United States Fleet, Letter classified SECRET, 10 December 1934.

Commander Aircraft Battle Force. *Current Tactical Orders and Doctrine US Fleet Aircraft Volume One Carrier Aircraft USF-74 (Revised),* March 1941.

Commander in Chief, Pacific Fleet. *The Battle of Midway.* Report A16 0 1849.

Commander, Navy Yard, Pearl Harbor, to The Chief of the Bureau of Ships. Subject: USS Arizona (BB 39)—War Damage Report. C-L11-1/BB/NY10 Serial Y-02149, 7 October 1943.

Commanding Officer, Administrative Office, USS Arizona, to The Chief of the Bureau of Ships. Subject: Material Damage Sustained in Attack on December 7, 1941. BB39/A9/L11-1, January 28, 1942.

Commanding Officer, USS California (BB-44). Report of Raid (Revised), December 7, 1941. BB44/A16-3, 22 December 1941

Commanding Officer, USS Nevada, Report of December 7, 1941 Raid. BB36/A9/A1615, December 1941.

Commanding Officer, U. S. S. North Carolina. Action of August 24, 1942, report of. BB55/A16-3 Serial 0109, 26 August 1942.

Data Sheet 2-C5a. Perforation of Armor: Bombs. August, 1944.

Department of Intelligence, Naval War College. "Blue and Orange Fleets." TEC-1B-36, June, 1936.

General Headquarters, US Army Forces Pacific. Anti-Aircraft Artillery Activities in the Pacific. October, 1946.

Headquarters of the Commander in Chief, United States Navy. Antiaircraft Action Summary—World War II. Information Bulletin No. 29, 8 October 1945.

Memorandum for File, ANALYSIS OF THE LOSS OF ARIZONA, 31 October 1944.

Military Analysis Division, United States Strategic Bombing Survey (Pacific): "Japanese Air Power." July 1946.

Military History Section, Headquarters, Army Forces Far East. Japanese Monograph No. 97: "Pearl Harbor Operations: General Outline of Orders and Plans."

Military History Section, Headquarters, Army Forces Far East. Japanese Monograph No.118 "Operational History of Naval Communications, December 1941–August 1945."

Operations Evaluation Group Study No. 428, "Number of Torpedo Hits Required to Sink a Ship." 27 September 1950.

Operations Evaluation Group, Study No. 431, "Maneuver Rules for Dive Bombing. Torpedo Bombing, and Level-Pattern Bombing of Surface Ships, 27 February 1951.

Preliminary Design Section, Bureau of Ships, Navy Department. "Summary of War Damage to U.S. Battleships, Carriers, Cruisers and Destroyers, 17 October 1941 to 7 December 1942." NavShips A (374), 15 September 1943.

Preliminary Report, USS Shaw (373) War Damage Report, and USS Shaw (373) Bomb Damage Report, 29 January 1942.

US Naval Technical Mission to Japan. Japanese Bombs. December, 1945.

US Naval Technical Mission to Japan. Japanese Torpedoes and Tubes, Article 2—Aircraft Torpedoes. 7 March 1946.

US Naval Technical Mission to Europe, Technical Report No. 372–45. German Fire Effect Tables. 21 Sept 1945.

US Naval War College. Maneuver Rules. Issues of June, 1925; June 1927; June 1936; May 1939; June, 1940; June, 1941; June, 1943; 20 January 1948.

United States Strategic Bombing Survey. Ships' Bombardment of Japan— 1945.

Television

"Unsolved History: the Myths of Pearl Harbor." Military History Channel, broadcast on11/14/09

"Killer Submarines in Pearl Harbor," Nova, broadcast on 5 January 2010.

Web Sites

Carrier Striking Task Force Operations Order No. 3. http://www.ibiblio. org/pha/myths/jm-097.htms, 12. Accessed 1/8/2007

Commanding Officer, USS Dale (353). Detailed report of offensive measures taken during Air Raid, December 7, 1941.

Commanding Officer, USS *St. Louis* (CL-49), report to Commander-in-Chief, US Pacific Fleet, dated 25 December 1941, from http://i-16tou.com/stlou/, accessed 2/24/10.

http://www.history.navy.mil/docs/wwii/pearl/ph36.htm, accessed 1/2/09

Czarnecki, Joseph and Worth, Richard and Noch, Matthias C. and Horan, Mark E. and DiGiulian, Tony. Order of Battle Pearl Harbor 7 December 1941

"The Fourteen Part Message." http://www.ibiblio.org/pha/myths/14_part.html

Gannon, Michael. "Admiral Kimmel and the Question of Shallow Water Torpedoes." pearlharbor911attacks.com/ . . . /GANNON_PAPER_SHALLOW_WATER_TORPEDOES.pdf, accessed 11/25/09.

Hough, Ludwig, Shaw. History of US Marine Corps Operations in World War II. Chapter 4: Midway Versus the Japanese, 4–5 June 1942. http://www.ibiblio.org/hyperwar/USMC/I/USMC-I-V-4.html, accessed January 31, 2007

Parshall, Jon. http://www.combinedfleet.com/battles/Attack_on_Pearl_Harbor, accessed July 22, 2009.

Robinson, Bruce. *Pearl Harbor: a Rude Awakening.* BBC History. http://www.bbc.co.uk/history/worldwars/wwtwo/pearl_harbour_01.s html, accessed 3/30/10.

Roundtable Forum, the Official Newsletter of the Battle of Midway Roundtable. Issue 2010–07, http://www.midway42.org/forum-current.html. 21 February 2010.

Sanborne, Bill. J-aircraft.com 2001 PH group project data sheet. http://www.j-aircraft.com/research/bill_sanborn/phmod21.pdf, accessed 2/12/09.

http://www.kickasstorrents.com/pbs-nova-killer-subs-in-pearl-harbor-s37e09-ws-pdtv-xvid-ekolb-t3354799.html, accessed 1/7/10.

Stephenson, Parks. http://www.j-aircraft.org/smf/index.php?topic=8601. 1080, accessed 3/1/10.

http://www.heritage.nf.ca/law/royal_air.html, accessed 12/26/08

http://www.historynet.com/lieutenant-zenji-abe-a-japanese-pilot-remem-
bers.htm, accessed 1/17/10.
http://www.navweaps.com/index_oob/OOB_WWII_Pacific/OOB_WWII
_Pearl_Harbor.htm, accessed 12/21/08.
http://www.navweaps.com/index_oob/OOB_WWII_Pacific/OOB_Pearl_
Harbor.htm, accessed 12/22/06
http://www.combinedfleet.com/sensuikan.htm
http://i-16tou.com/stlou/stlou2.html, accessed 2/25/10
http://www.engin.umich.edu/dept/name/facilities/mhl/projects/televised_
programs.html, accessed 3/9/10.
The Myths of Pearl Harbor. http://www.ibiblio.org/pha/myths/taranto.
html
USS Helm Action Report, 10 December 1941. http://www.history.navy.
mil/docs/wwii/pearl/CinCPac.htm
Usmm.org/sunk42a.html#anchor331462, accessed 11/28/09.

ENDNOTES

Introduction: Folklore, Viewed With a Critical Eye

1. Letter from Ensign William Robinson in Mrazek, xv.
2. Lambert and Polmar, 8. Rusbridger and Nave. Stinnett. Gannon. Theobald.
3. Slackman, 76. Prange, 1981. 203. Slackman, 9. "Unsolved History: the Myths of Pearl Harbor." Military History Channel, 14 November 2009.
4. Most histories accept the "brilliant" label. See Robinson, bbc.co.uk/history/worldswars/wwtwo/pearl_harbor_05.shtml. The only major history that questions a perfect performance by the attackers is Willmott, 1982, 134. He criticizes over-concentration on battleships. Clarke, 114. O'Connell, 314. Edwards, 14. Hone, Trent, 2003, 1107.
5. Toland, 236.
6. Agawa, 229.
7. Prange, 1981, 437, 419, 338.
8. Werneth, 109.
9. Willmott, et al, 2001, 61.
10. A Japanese retrospective study was conducted circa August 1942. It is included as Chapter 18, "Japanese Study of the Pearl Harbor Operation," in Goldstein and Dillon, 1993. 278–311. This document has been little cited in general histories. The report, referred to as *Lessons*, will be discussed later.
11. Slackman, 119.
12. Parshall. http://www.combinedfleet.com/battles/Attack_on_Pearl_Harbor, accessed 22 July 2009.
13. Poolman, 130.

14. "Unsolved History: Myths of Pearl Harbor." The Military Channel, 14 November 2009.

15. Stephan, 27.

16. Repeated in many places, such as Rear Admiral Grossgean (USN, ret), in "Unsolved History: Myths of Pearl Harbor."

17. Willmott, et al, 2001, 70–71.

18. See McFarland, O'Neil, March 2002.

19. Smith, Douglas, 23.

Chapter 1: Strategic and Operational Setting

1. Drea, 102.

2. Willmott, et al, 2001, 50, 52. Agawa, 193.

3. Stephan, 74.

4. Stephan, 75. Asada, 18.

5. Pelz, 42.

6. Prange, 1981, 33.

7. Evans and Peattie.

8. Burlingame, 19.

9. *The Great Pacific War* was published while Yamamoto was serving as naval attaché in Washington. Toland, 150.

10. Stephan, 2.

11. Lambert and Polmar, 23. The use of Pearl Harbor as a target for raiding forces during US Navy Fleet Exercises has been misinterpreted in most histories. The Fleet did most of its exercises in the Pacific or the Caribbean to take advantage of good weather at a location remote from civilian activities (anyone who has attempted to clear a firing range of civilian shipping, fishing boats and curiosity-seekers can testify to the desire for remoteness). The fleet trained to seize and hold advanced operating bases. The war plans expected the initial objective to be the Marshall Islands, with the force based out of Pearl Harbor. This movement could be practiced over similar distances by a transit from the US west coast terminating at Pearl Harbor. At the same time, the Pearl Harbor defenses needed to be exercised, and could serve as opposition. The repeated use of Pearl Harbor as a Fleet Exercise target was more a consequence of geography than a prophecy of a surprise attack on the fleet's base. Similarly, in 1941 the Army held large-scale maneuvers in Louisiana, but that did not mean that an invasion of Louisiana was expected.

12. Pelz, 26.

13. Agawa, 31.

14. Agawa, 195.

15. Pelz, 35.

16. Willmott, et al, 2001, 37.

17. Willmott, et al, 2001, 38
18. Stephan, 73.
19. Agawa, 175.
20. Evans and Peattie, 2.
21. Prange, 1981, 16. Toland, 152.
22. Agawa, 399. Toland, 152.
23. Agawa, 91–3.
24. Asada, 184.
25. Prange, 1981, 99.
26. Prange, 1981, 34.
27. Francillon, 350.
28. Agawa, 71, 105–6.
29. An obvious question is, "What else could Yamamoto have done?" The Japanese fleet had precious few reserves and was stretched thin over thousands of miles of attacks. But there were reserves—in particular, there were six battleships and two light carriers in the Inland Sea that were uncommitted, and could have been deployed to augment the two fast battleships and seven heavy cruisers in the South China Sea. The six days from the British warship's well-publicized arrival at Singapore to the beginning of the war would not have provided sufficient time for the battleships to arrive in the South China Sea for the beginning of hostilities, but they could have arrive a few days thereafter.
30. Willmott, et al, 2001, 83.
31. Some historians have erroneously stated that the objective of the attack was the American aircraft carriers, such as the television program "Unsolved History: Myths of Pearl Harbor." Carriers were indeed included in the Operations Order priority list, but as a second priority target: "The order of targets will be battleships and then aircraft carriers." Carrier Striking Task Force Operations Order No. 3, 23 November 1941, in Goldstein and Dillon, 1993, 101.
32. Werneth, 247.
33. The reserve force of battleships, based out of the Inland Sea, was cruising south of the Bonins to "support" *Kido Butai* as it retired from the Pearl Harbor strike. These forces were over 2,000 miles apart, making support problematic. The battleships undoubtedly got underway as a morale measure, to avoid the shame of remaining in port while the rest of the fleet fought. After several submarine scares, the battleships cranked on knots for home, realizing that pride was not worth exposing the precious battleships to damage.
34. Japanese battleships and battlecruisers were located as follows: off Indo China, 2: (BC *Haruna*, BC *Kongo*); Empire, 6: (BB *Nagato*, BB *Mutsu*, BB *Fuso*, BB *Yamashiro*, BB *Hyuga*, BB *Ise*); with the carrier striking force, 2: (BC *Kirishima*, BC *Hiei*). Under construction, Empire: 4: (BB *Yamato*, fitting

out, in service 5/19/42; BB *Musashi*, to be commissioned 8/5/42; BB *Shinano*; BB Hull No. 111). American operational battleships totaled 14: Pearl Harbor, 7: (BB-36 *Nevada*, BB-37 *Oklahoma*, BB-39 *Arizona*, BB-43 *Tennessee*; BB-44 *California*; BB-46 *Maryland*, BB-48 *West Virginia*); East Coast US, 7: Casco Bay, 4 (BB-35 *Texas*, BB-33 *Arkansas*, BB-40 *New Mexico*, BB-41 *Mississippi*); Norfolk, 1 (BB-56 *Washington*); Iceland, 1 (BB-42 *Idaho*); Caribbean, 1 (BB-55 *North Carolina*,). There were 11 battleships in the pipeline: Bremerton, 1: overhaul, (BB-45 *Colorado*, completed 31 Mar 42); Norfolk, 1: overhaul (BB-34 *New York*, completed Dec 41); Pearl Harbor, 1: refit, 1 (BB-38 *Pennsylvania*, completed Dec 41). US East Coast, 8: under construction, 8 (BB-57 *South Dakota*, commissioned 3/20/42; BB-58 *Indiana*, commissioned 4/30/42; BB-59 *Massachusetts*, commissioned 5/15/42; BB-60 *Alabama*, commissioned 8/16/42; BB-61 *Iowa*, commissioned 2/22/43; BB-62 *New Jersey*, commissioned 5/23/43; BB-63 *Missouri*, commissioned 6/11/44; BB-64 *Wisconsin*, commissioned 4/16/44).

35. Willmott, et al, 2001, 157.
36. Prange, 1981, 374.
37. Not included are the ships assigned to the Asiatic Fleet, one heavy cruiser, two light cruiser and 13 destroyers, which were in the immediate path of the Japanese advance and would likely not participate in any sorties of the Pacific Fleet from Pearl Harbor.
38. Weinberg, 195–204.
39. Agawa, 292.
40. Willmott, 1982, 8.
41. Asada, 108–9.
42. Agawa, 196.
43. Kinoaki, 208.
44. SECRET letter, Chief of Naval Operations to Commander in Chief, United States Fleet, 10 December 1934.
45. Asada, 181. Stephan, 80.
46. Agawa, 196, 200, 202.
47. Asada, 263.
48. Agawa, 197.
49. Miller, 286–7.
50. Miller, 308.
51. This practice also is a hint that the fuel tanks mentioned above were constructed during the war and not before.
52. Agawa, 197.
53. Stephan, 99. Agawa, 217.
54. Stephan, 115.
55. Aldrich, 64.

56. OPNAV 16 V # A43, 2.
57. This includes the *Yamato* class, whose bulk concealed a number of damage control flaws. According to Nathan Okun, "The anti-torpedo protection of *Yamato* was improperly designed. It used deep empty voids between the side and the innermost NVNC "holding" bulkhead (also the very thick—8" at the top and 3" at the bottom—anti-diving-shell lower belt). There was nothing to stop the concussion of the [torpedo] detonation shockwave, blast, and considerable number of high-speed fragments but a few thin bulkheads prior to hitting the innermost holding bulkhead. If even a few feet of water had been used to soak up part of the blast and almost all of the fragments, the protection would have worked better. A single torpedo hit snapped *Yamato*'s holding bulkhead off at the top where it joined the heavy waterline VH belt since it was not keyed to the belt. This led to very large amounts of flooding. This was never remedied, though somewhat reinforced later."
58. Agawa, 196.
59. In the first six months of the war these ships served at the following locations: *Akashi* at Palau, Davao, Staring Bay, Ambon, and joined the Midway invasion force; *Asahi* at Camrahn Bay, Singapore, and then sunk by submarine on 25 May 1942; *Yamabiko Maru* at Takao, Balikpapan, Makassar, and Singapore; *Matsue Maru* at Truk, sunk by submarine on12 May 1942; *Urakami Maru* was evidently as much a coal transport ship as repair ship. She served a route between Truk, Kwajalein, and Ponape, delivering coal and making repairs as necessary.
60. Agawa, 195–6.
61. The Japanese would go to such extremes as to convert a musical instrument factory into aircraft propeller production. On the Japanese economy, see O'Neil, 2003, Cohen, Bisson, Barnhart.
62. Prange, 1981, 298.
63. There was another possible objective, an internal political goal within the context of war. Zenshiro Hoshima was the Secretary General of the Imperial Navy and Emperor Hirohito's naval advisor. He argued strenuously against war with America. He "came to believe that Yamamoto, who also opposed war with America, staged the brilliant strike at Pearl Harbor not only to cripple the US Fleet, but to give the Imperial Navy parity with the Japanese Army." Burlingame, 47.
64. Willmott, et al, 2001, 39.
65. Prange, 1981, 21.
66. Agawa, 243–4.

Chapter 2: Targets, Weapons, and Weapon-Target Pairings
1. Prange, 1981, 19.

2. Agawa, 221.

3. At the time of Genda's study carriers *Shokaku* and *Zuikaku* were still fitting out. The original dates of the attack would have been before they were operational.

4. Prange, 1981, 27.

5. Ships put into shipyard for underwater damage repair usually also undergo overhaul and modernization, which might add months to the total duration. For example, *California* and *West Virginia* were extensively rebuilt and modernized after their damage at Pearl Harbor, and would not emerge from the shipyards until January and September, 1944, 26 and 34 months after Pearl Harbor. They were delayed by low priorities and the crush of other work in West Coast shipyards. In contrast, when Saratoga was torpedoed in January 1942, BuShips estimated she could be placed back in action in four to six weeks if necessary. The decision was made to modernize her. She had her 8-inch and 5"/25 guns replaced with sixteen 5"/38s taken from new construction ships, a hull blister installed, her flight deck widened and lengthened forward, her light AA battery augmented, new radar and gun directors installed, and was still out of the shipyard in four months. The priority of work and state of modernization of the ship had a huge influence on repair times. Friedman, 1983, 51.

6. *German Fire Effect Tables*, 15–16.

7. Prange, 1981, 21–22, 99.

8. Werneth, 199.

9. Captain Baron Tomioka from the Operations Section of the First Bureau. Prange, 1981, 104–5.

10. Sakai, 48. The only Allied fighter at that time with "strategic" range was the P-38 Lightning, just coming into service at the end of 1941. Similar range-extending fuel conservation techniques were developed for the P-38 Lightning but were not in place in the Pacific until 1943. Lindbergh, the famed pilot who first crossed the Atlantic in solo flight, made a tour of front-line squadrons to help train the pilots and "popularize" the techniques, which almost doubled the combat radius of the aircraft.

11. Sakai states that the development of the strategic range capability in the A6M Zero freed up three light carriers. This probably is not exactly correct. In addition to the six fleet carriers, on 8 December 1941 the Japanese had six light and escort carriers available or in the latter stages of workups. The two escort carriers, *Kasuga Maru* and *Chuyo*, were engaged in aircraft ferry missions. Light carriers *Hosho* and *Zuiho* were attached as aviation support to the battleships of the First Fleet operating out of Hashirajima Anchorage. Light carrier *Shoho* was in the final stages of workups and not ready for active operations. Light carrier *Ryujo* was attached to the Southern Philippines

Seizure Force operating off the east coast of the Philippines. From examining the dispositions of the fleet on 8 December, it would appear that CarDiv 5 (fleet carriers *Shokaku* and *Zuikaku*) was originally intended to provide air support for strikes against Clark Field, Cavite, and Manila, followed by the invasion of Davao, and possibly followed thereafter by a quick transit around north of Luzon to the west coast to support the Lingayen Gulf invasion. This support became unnecessary with the increase in range of the A6M Zero, allowing the Japanese to immediately strike the Philippine air bases from Formosa. In addition, fighter bases were established after the landing at Bataan Island (north of Luzon) on 8 December 1941, and on Philippine soil after the landings at Vigan and Aparri on Northern Luzon, 11–12 December 1941. MacArthur incorrectly evaluated those landings as a feint designed to draw his forces away from the main landing site at Lingayen Gulf, which was not invaded until the 21st of December. He allowed the 5th Air Army to become established on Luzon and elements of the 21st and 23rd Air Flotillas at Davao without opposition. MacArthur did not understanding the significance of allowing Japanese air power to become established on the Philippines.

12. Prange, 1981, 158.
13. Peattie, 2001, 102.
14. Peattie, 2001, 108.
15. Yoshimura, 27.
16. Peattie, 2001, 113.
17. Oberg.
18. Francillon, 112–120.
19. Watts and Gordon. Aircraft capacity numbers should not be considered fixed or standard. A carrier's rated capacity would change as larger or smaller aircraft models were introduced, doctrine was changed, or the ships modified. In addition, most fleet carriers stowed additional disassembled spare aircraft that might be assembled before a battle in anticipation of losses.
20. Operational were fleet carriers *Kaga, Akagi, Hiryu* and *Soryu*, light carriers *Hosho* and *Ryujo*, and escort carrier *Kasuga Maru*. Fleet carriers *Shokaku, Zuikaku, Junyo, Hiyo,* and *Taiho* were in the pipeline, along with light carriers *Shoho* and *Ryuho* and escort carriers *Unyo* and *Kaiyo*. The term "escort carrier" was not used until later in the war. The Japanese escort carriers listed here were considered as auxiliaries by the Japanese, and more often used as aircraft transports.
21. The B5N Kate had the lifting capacity for three 250-kg bombs, and this capacity is listed in many references. However, only two were carried on the Pearl Harbor mission. The possibility exists that at this time the bomber had only the hard point attachments for two.

22. This would include the carriers, considering that two of the potential target carriers, *Lexington* (CV-2) and *Saratoga* (CV-3), were built on battle cruiser hulls.

23. *Japanese Torpedoes and Tubes, Article 2—Aircraft Torpedoes.*

24. NavShips A (374), 7–9.

25. Peattie, 2001, 36.

26. *Japanese Bombs.*

27. This shell has been variously identified as 15-inch, 40 cm, or 16-inch, even in official Navy documents. Initial estimates were taken from measuring the curvature of shell fragments recovered from the battleships, a process subject to some uncertainty. Most of the information cited on this weapon, correcting several errors in official documents, was provided by Nathan Okun, correspondence. Data Page on Type 99 No. 80 Mark 5 armor piercing bomb, from US Naval Technical Mission to Japan, *Japanese Bombs*. December 1945, 35. Note that it incorrectly identifies the original shell as "40 cm AP."

28. *Striking Power of Air-borne Weapons,* v.

29. *Japanese Bombs,* 35. Also Richard Worth, correspondence with the author.

30. Prange, 1981, 268.

31. Brown, 208.

32. Data Sheet 2-C5a. Perforation of Armor: Bombs. August, 1944.

33. The US Naval War College Maneuver Rules (USNWCMR) and Fire Effect Tables represented the most advanced mathematical modeling of naval combat developed in the interwar years. It was a tremendous collaboration between the War College, BuOrd, and BuC&R to develop the most advanced training and analytical tool ever created. The rules and data tables were several inches thick of legal-sized paper. The rules and data were constantly updated with new releases nearly every year between 1922 and 1946. The calculations and values incorporated into the Maneuver Rules represent the official US Navy view of such things as gunnery effectiveness, armor penetration, and resistance of ships to damage, the effectiveness of bombers and fighters and submarines and torpedoes, and many other technical topics.

34. Prange, 1981, 160.

35. *Striking Power of Air-borne Weapons,* v.

36. Prange, 1981, 259.

37. *Japanese Bombs,* 19.

38. *Striking Power of Air-borne Weapons.*

39. Campbell, 1985, 172.

40. Peattie, 2001, 143.

41. USNWCMR, 12 March 1940, j-24, j-25.

42. USNWRMR, 19 June 1944, j-24.

43. Peattie, 2001, 146.

44. Olson, 43.
45. This was before the invention of NAPALM or other jellied gasoline weapons. NAPALM was first employed operationally in 1944 against ground targets. NAPALM was never used against warships underway during WW II.
46. *Downes* AAR, Commander, Battleships, Battle Force AAR.
47. Preliminary Report, *USS Shaw* (373) War Damage Report, and *USS Shaw* (373) Bomb Damage Report, 29 January 1942.
48. Also reported at 500 rounds per gun

Chapter 3: Wargames
1. Prange, 1981, 113.
2. Admiralty, Naval Staff, Tactical Section. *Instruction for Tactical and Strategic Exercises Carried out on Tables or Boards.* O.U. 5243, January 1921.
3. Willmott, et al, 2001, 60.
4. Prange, 1981, 30–39.
5. Prange, 1981, 31.
6. Prange, 1981, 381.
7. Prange, 1981, 35–36.
8. Fuchida and Okumiya, 92.
9. Prange, 1981, 34.
10. Prange, 1981, 404. In footnote 22 for Chapter 4 Prange cites Fuchida's Midway book as his source, going on to say, "Similar cheating occurred during the war games for Pearl Harbor."
11. Prange, 1981. Toland, 161, states that one-third were shot down.
12. The number of "130 aircraft" is from Prange. Agawa, 228, states that 180 aircraft were "shot down."
13. Prange, 1981, 229–230.
14. Willmott, et al, 2001, 57.
15. Prange, 1981, 161–3.
16. Prange, 1981, 389.
17. Prange, 1981, 234.
18. Willmott, et al, 2001, 57.
19. Willmott, et al, 2001, 57.
20. Prange, 1981, 282.
21. Prange, 1981, 229–230.
22. Prange, 1981, 234.
23. Burlingame, 50.
24. Prange, 1981, 338.
25. Agawa, 230.
26. Prange, 1981, 263, 285.

Chapter 4: Planning the Attack

1. The Japanese solved the range problem by converting some voids in some of their carriers to carry fuel, by carrying fuel in drums on the hangar deck, and by underway replenishment from oilers. Another option that could have precluded the problem would have been for the carriers to refuel at the Marshall Islands from oilers at anchor after the strike. The destroyers would still require underway replenishment to make the trip. No satisfactory explanation has ever been offered why this option was not considered, although it is possible the Japanese were concerned that Pacific Fleet carriers might follow them to the islands and strike the carriers while at anchor, a remote possibility.

2. Thomas Hone to the author.

3. The A6M Zero was about 30 feet long, the D3A Val 33 feet, and the B5N Kate 45 feet, although they could be parked in overlapping configurations.

4. Japanese aircraft carriers had closed hangars, so engines could not be warmed below decks. Applying full power for takeoff on a cold engine could crack the cylinder block or blow out engine gaskets. A proper warm-up would require about 15 minutes. The Japanese lost one A6M Zero in the water from engine failure after launch.

5. Willmott, et al, 2001, 81. Werneth, 100.

6. The American doctrine was different. When two carriers were operating together, one would be assigned as "duty carrier," responsible for launching and recovering all the search aircraft, ASW patrols and CAP needed. The other carrier would spot all possible aircraft on the flight deck ready to launch a "full deck" strike. As aircraft got larger, not all the aircraft could fit on deck, so the full deckload would be launched and then orbit the carrier while the remaining aircraft were brought up from the hangar deck (where they had already been warmed, allowable in the Americans' open hangar deck design). The process was awkward and cut down the range of the strike. Eventually the Americans adopted what they called a half-deck strike, which was similar to the Japanese doctrine but employed mixed groups of bombers.

7. Chapter 12 contains a more detailed discussion of the experience level of the Japanese aircrew.

8. Prange, 1981, 163, relates that Japanese naval fighters before 1941 never operated more than 100 miles from its base or carrier, which was also the maximum range of their radiotelephone. Since the Pearl Harbor raid would be at a range "250 to 300 miles from the carriers," fighter pilots were trained in morse code. These statements appear to be erroneous, since fighters were not equipped with CW radios, and Japanese radiotelephones are reputed to have a much shorter range.

9. Werneth, 35.

10. *Operational History of Naval Communications, December 1941—August 1945.*
11. Werneth, 214.
12. The Roundtable Forum, the Official Newsletter of the Battle of Midway Roundtable. Issue 2010-07, 21 February 2010.
13. Lieutenant Commander William Widhelm, quoted in Belote and Belote, 168.
14. In all the interviews and reminiscences of the Pearl Harbor attackers, the author has not found one reference to the use of voice radio, and many places where voice radio ought to have been used if it was available, but was not.
15. Sakai.
16. Prange, 1990, 28.
17. Prange, 1981, 161.
18. Prange, 1990, 27–8.
19. Prange, 1981, 160–162.
20. Prange, 1981, 268.
21. Aiken.
22. Not all the planned aircraft launched due to deck aborts. One fighter crashed on takeoff. Aircraft totals that hit Pearl Harbor were 183 in the first wave and 167 in the second. Arakaki and Kuborn, 61, 67.
23. Czarnecki, et al. Order of Battle Pearl Harbor 7 December 1941.
24. Lambert and Polmar, 40.
25. The accuracy standard for Japanese dive bombers is not known, but is likely as good or better. This estimate is taken from results achieved by Western dive bombers of the period. Smith, 1981, 37, 41, 53, 68, 69. CEP, Circular Error Probable, is a circle of a radius where 50% of the bombs would fall inside the circle.
26. Prange, 1981, 415.
27. McFarland, 99.
28. Mondey, 36, 73–77.
29. Lambert and Polmar.
30. Prange, 1981, 403.
31. Carrier Striking Task Force Operations Order No. 3, para. 3a: "The targets of Fighter Combat Units will be enemy aircraft in the air and on the ground."
32. Genda, in Goldstein and Dillon, 1993, 25.
33. Haleiwa, Wheeler, Kaneohe, Bellows, Hickam, Ford, and Ewa.
34. Prange, 1981, 366.
35. Smith, 2001, 40. Note that the total of fighters shown is the 45 planned. There were 2 deck aborts, one from the *chutai* assigned to the torpedo bombers and one from the groups assigned to Kaneohe Field.
36. Carrier Striking Task Force Operations Order No. 3.
37. Sakai, 48.

38. Clarke, 15.
39. Arakaki and Kuborn, 47.
40. Willmott, et al, 2001, 63.
41. Willmott, et al, 2001, 63
42. Goldstein and Dillon, 1993, 101.
43. Prange, 1981, 332, quotes two candidate sets of launch parameters: A) 20 meters altitude, 120 knots, attitude level, and B) 10 meters altitude, 100 knots, and a 1 ½ degree nose down attitude. He states that the first was selected as being the easiest to execute. Goldstein and Dillon, 1993, 284, provides a translation of a Japanese staff study which cites the two conditions were A) 20 meters altitude, 140 knots, 0 degrees elevation, and B) 10 meters altitude, 100 knots, 4.5 degrees nose up. The staff study does not indicate that one method was preferred or selected over the other. Genda, in "Analysis No. 1 of the Pearl Harbor Attack, Operation AI," in Goldstein and Dillon, 1993. 29, gives the conditions as A) 150 knots, 65 foot altitude, and B) 100 knots (with lowered landing gear), 35 foot altitude. Gannon, in *Admiral Kimmel and the Question of Shallow Water Torpedoes* states that the approach settled on was "20 meters (66 feet) off the deck at 100 knots and with trim set to place the torpedo in the water at 17–20 degree incidence." Following the author's experience piloting propeller aircraft, and after discussions with Captain Chris Powers USN (ret.), a former carrier Air Boss and F-18 pilot, it is probable that launching at 20 meters altitude, 140–150 knots, level attitude, gear and flaps up was probably the selected approach. 10 meters at 100 knots would likely be perilously close to stall speed with the heavy torpedo load attached; the 140 knot approach would also allow sufficient speed to pull up and turn after weapons release, to avoid overflying the battleships and getting too close to their defensive AA automatic weapons. Even then, flying this profile in a heavily-laden torpedo bomber within the constraints of Pearl Harbor after clearing the turbulence and updrafts off the buildings of the Naval Supply Base (and while being shot at) would be tricky, requiring airmanship of the first order. Flaps and gear down would prevent immediate acceleration to clear the area and avoid defensive fires, making it a less-preferred method.
44. Aiken, 2001, 47.
45. Gannon.
46. Prange, 1981, 328.
47. Prange, 1981, 367.
48. Lord, 22.
49. http://www.historynet.com/lieutenant-zenji-abe-a-japanese-pilot-remembers.htm. Italics are the author's.
50. Prange, 1981, 269–70.
51. The office of the Chief of Naval Operations knew in July 1941 that the Royal

Navy Fleet Air Arm had made fin modifications to its Mark XII aerial torpedo so it could be employed in water as shallow as 24 feet. According to Gannon in *Admiral Kimmel and the Question of Shallow Water Torpedoes,* this information was not provided to the Pacific Fleet Commander, a charge Gannon repeated at the National Press Club on 6 November 2003. However, in Gannon's 2001 defense of Kimmel, *Pearl Harbor Betrayed,* he admits that Kimmel was warned by the CNO that ships in harbor should not be assumed to be safe from torpedoes. See 175–177. Thanks to Captain William O'Neil USNR (ret) for noting the discrepancies.

52. Toland, 185
53. The primary testimony on this discussion is Prange, 1981. Prange never mentioned that the Japanese considered this option. Willmott, et al, 2001, 81. It is unlikely that they considered using 250-kg GP bombs against torpedo nets, as the first wave D3A Val dive bombers were assigned to OCA, and the Japanese had shown resistance throughout the process to changing aircraft assignments. The Japanese 250-kg bombs with their 0.2 second delay fuzes could have been effective if adequate delivery accuracy was achieved. However, this solution would delay the torpedo bombers' attack, which the Japanese did not relish.
54. Toland, 196. Willmott, et al, 2001, 81.
55. Werneth, 160–161.
56. Fuchida was in Japan at that time recuperating from broken ankles suffered during the Battle of Midway.
57. Goldstein and Dillon, 1993, 283–4.
58. Goldstein and Dillon, 1993, 202.
59. Willmott, et al, 2001, 63.
60. Smith, 1999, 61.
61. Smith, 2005, 155. Presumably this is per aircraft, and not per shotai.
62. OEG 431, 3.
63. There are many examples in Edwards.

Chapter 5: Pre-Attack: Training, Rehearsals, Briefings and Contingency Planning
1. David Aiken, Pearl Harbor History Associates, letter to the author.
2. Prange, 1981, 328–330.
3. Prange, 1981, 382.
4. Prange, 1981, 384.
5. There were five other plans to cover the possibility that the fleet was outside of Pearl Harbor, but no details are available.
6. Prange, 1981, 344.
7. Prange, 1981, 351.
8. Prange, 1981, 351.

Chapter 6: Execution of the Attack

1. Stillwell, 1981, 6.
2. Burlingame, 153.
3. Prange, 1981, 384.
4. Prange, Goldstein, Dillon, 1990, 34.
5. Agawa, 257.
6. Exact times are impossible to determine. Wheeler and Kaneohe were struck within minutes of each other. Kaneohe is a ten minute flight from Wheeler. It apparent that the standard track chart of the Japanese approach taken out of the official Navy account, *Campaigns of the Pacific War*, is incorrect, as it shows the Kaneohe attackers overflying Wheeler en route to their target. The Kaneohe attackers more likely split off upon landfall and headed directly to their target, perhaps along the northeast coast or slightly inland. Willmott, et al, 2001, 123.
7. Smith, 2001, 40. Aiken, 48. Goldstein and Dillon, 1993, 293.
8. Aiken, 48–52.
9. Aiken, 48. The cruisers were *Raleigh* (CL-7) commissioned in 1924, and *Detroit* (CL-8) commissioned in 1923. These ships participated in the Aleutians campaigns.
10. Lord, 65.
11. Aiken, 51.
12. This time is in accordance with *New Orleans* (CA-32) and *Bagley* (DD-386) ARs, those ships being pierside in the Navy Yard along one of the direct attack lanes for the torpedo bombers. Aiken indicates that the first Japanese torpedo against Battleship Row hit the water at 0757.
13. Likely the dredge that was working the channel south of Battleship Row.
14. Toland, 214.
15. Aiken, 50–51.
16. Aiken, 50–51.
17. Aiken, 51.
18. Commanding Officer, USS *Nevada*, Report of December 7, 1941 Raid, BB36/A9/A1615, December 1941.
19. Aiken, 51.
20. Madsen.
21. Slackman, 130.
22. Stillwell, 1981, 11.
23. Stillwell, 1981, 13.
24. David Aiken, from a forthcoming article on the attack.
25. Werneth, 43.
26. Prange, 1981, 535. Smith, 1999, 63, claims that the second wave dive bombers were given new orders *while airborne* to attack targets of opportu-

nity, principally any heavy ships that had survived the earlier attacks. It is more likely, given the state of Japanese radio communications and airborne command and control, that these instructions were given prior to launch.
27. Goldstein, Dillon and Wenger, 101.

Chapter 7: Assessment of the Attack

1. Ensign Taisuke Maruyama, quoted in Werneth, 177.
2. The CinCPAC Action Report gives these times as that required to bring the *full* anti-aircraft battery into action, which they said was based on the ships' after-action reports. However, reading the ships' reports, they almost always reported the time when they first opened fire (often with only one gun or a machine gun), not when the full battery was manned and ready. CincPAC had a vested interest in reporting a quick time, since it reflected on his efforts training the fleet and the readiness level he required in port.
3. Aiken, 50–52.
4. The US Naval War College Maneuver Rules (May, 1940) assigned a "Life" to each ship in terms of equivalent penetrating 14-inch shell hits. The battleships at Pearl Harbor had Life values of between 16.1 and 18.5 (Department of Intelligence, Naval War College. "Blue and Orange Fleets." TEC-1B-36, June, 1936). The Japanese 18-inch aerial torpedo was valued at 3.0 equivalent penetrative 14-inch shell hits. Additional torpedo hits within 15 minutes of another had their effect increased by one-third, by two-thirds for any succeeding hits after that. Four hits achieved within 15 minutes would be scored as $3 + 4 + 5 + 5 = 17$. *Nevada* and *Oklahoma* had a Life of 16.1, *Pennsylvania* and *Arizona* 17.2 and 17.1 respectively, *New Mexico* 17.3, *Tennessee* and *California* 17.7, and *Maryland* and *West Virginia* 18.5. The bonus value for hits within a small spaced of time reflects the fact that flooding would not have a chance to disperse over the full width of the compartment, and the free surface effect would accentuate the list. Longer intervals between hits also allowed ship's damage control teams to control flooding and to counterflood.
5. OEG 428.
6. *Washington* (BB-47) was partially completed but had to be expended due to limits imposed by the Washington Naval Treaty.
7. Firemain water was used in some spaces for dewatering using eductors.
8. The "World at War" television series featured comments from Fuchida, who claimed that the attack on Taranto was of great interest to the Japanese.
9. The "Torpedo Attack Plan Against Ships Moored Around Ford Island" from Prange, 1981, 385.
10. Toland, 213. *Utah* had its main battery turrets removed and the barbettes enclosed within wooden deck houses. Otherwise, her superstructure was intact and her lattice foremast in place, making it impossible to believe that

anyone would mistake her for *Enterprise* or *Lexington*. Toland's description of her "stripped decks covered with planks," implying that she looked enough like a carrier to justify the attack, is misleading. She looked enough like an operational battleship to neophyte torpedo bomber crews skimming over Pearl City 60 feet above the water to have them decide to attack. For pilots with twelve days in transit to brush up their ship identification skills, pilots who were warned about the presence of *Utah*, the error remains inexcusable. De Virgilio, 64, states that "Despite popular belief the Japanese did not mistake the *Utah* for an American aircraft carrier." Aiken also attests from veterans' interviews that the Japanese misidentified *Utah* as an operational battleship.

11. Aiken, 48.
12. During the war, the US WW I-vintage light cruisers operated out of South American ports patrolling for German merchant raiders and blockade runners. This was useful duty, but certainly not one that would have an impact on the course or outcome of the war in the Pacific. Sinking them would have had limited value to the Japanese.
13. Slackman, 77.
14. Aiken, correspondence with the author.
15. Prange, Goldstein, Dillon, 1993, 287. This could also describe Mori's effort, where he broke off from attacking *Helena* to attack *California*.
16. Goldstein and Dillon, 1991, 173.
17. Commander, Navy Yard, Pearl Harbor, to The Chief of the Bureau of Ships. Subject: USS *Arizona* (BB 39)—War Damage Report. C-L11-1/BB/NY10 Serial Y-02149, 7 October 1943.
18. Memorandum for File, ANALYSIS OF THE LOSS OF *ARIZONA*, 31 October 1944. In Christopher C. Wright (ed), "The US Navy's Study of the Loss of Battleship *Arizona*." Warship International, Vol. No. 39, No. 3, 2002. 285.
19. Stillwell, 1991. De Virgilio, 1997.
20. The official American report gives the attack duration at 15 minutes. One Japanese veteran estimated the duration at 20 minutes from when the first bomb hit Ford Island to when he delivered his torpedo.
21. The official *Dictionary of American Naval Fighting Ships* recorded that *Arizona* sounded the air raid alarm at 0755.
22. Stillwell, 1991, 233.
23. The numbers of torpedo hits has been a subject of considerable debate. Some historians argue for more hits than were finally decided upon by Navy salvage and repair crews. They argue that some of the torpedoes may have hit near the blast hole caused by an earlier torpedo, and thus did not leave an individual hole in the ship. The ships were moored so close together that the shock

of a hit on one ship was often misinterpreted as a hit aboard other ships, inflating the reports by witnesses.

24. The British attack at Taranto was executed at night, against a very heavy and alert AA defense employing blinding searchlights, and with the lines of approach defended by barrage balloons and torpedo nets. There were considerably fewer attackers to split the enemy fire, and they arrived in two waves, allowing more fire to be concentrated on each aircraft.

25. Prange, 1981, 382.

26. Peattie,146.

27. During modifications all of the battleships received a heavily-augmented AA armament, including 5"/38 guns in either single or twin enclosed armored mounts. The heavy automatic weapons (40mm and 1.1"/75 guns) were mounted in gun tubs surrounded by splinter shields.

28. OEG 431, 10.

29. Nathan Okun, correspondence with the author.

30. 81 D3A Vals were planned, with three deck aborts.

31. Prange, 1981, 536.

32. Damaging near misses (DNM) are scored if the near miss required shipyard assistance to repair the damage, thus disregarding incidental fragmentation damage. The *Pennsylvania* (BB-38) DNM was on the dock off the bow which caused fragmentation damage in an area where the ship was also damaged by fire and fragments from explosions on the *Cassin* (DD-372) and *Downes* (DD-375). Not included are one near miss on *Cummins* (DD-365), which dented some bulkheads, put two holes in the superstructure, and wounded three, or those that inflicted incidental damage on *Rigel* (AR-11), multiple near misses which caused about 150 small holes in the port quarter (repaired by ship's force) and destroyed a motor whale boat in the water, with a total of seven wounded. These bombs might have been aimed at New Orleans (CA-32) or San Francisco (CA-38) in the shipyard.

33. Smith, 2005, 174, puts the hit percentage at "between 26 percent and 27 percent." However, he counts as hits fragmentation damage against *Cummings* (DD-365), *Rigel* (AR-11), and *New Orleans* (CA-38). *New Orleans'* damage was similarly inconsequential, consisting of a few dozen holes in thin plating, none of which impaired the ship's combat capability, and an easily-repaired severed aviation fuel line, with no personnel casualties. These have not been assessed as hits or DNMs as they contributed nothing to the Japanese mission objectives.

34. Smith, 2005, 152.

35. *Striking Power of Air-Borne Weapons,* 15.

36. Air Operations Staff Officer, 1st Air Fleet, in Goldstein and Dillon, 1993, 87.

37. Fuchida attested that he considered ordering an attack on *Nevada*, so presumably he felt he had the command and control to order such an attack to occur or not to occur.
38. Stillwell, 1981, 148.
39. Madsen, 15–16.
40. Madsen, 17.
41. Cohen, 112.
42. Lord, 150.
43. "Gedunk" was sailor's slang for snacks such as ice cream and candy bars. This vehicle is also known as the "Roach Coach." The traditional announcement on the 1MC, "the Roach Coach is making its approach," is often banned by modern skippers.
44. Slackman, 126–7.
45. Okun, correspondence with the author.
46. Arakaki and Kuborn, 76.
47. Peattie, 113.
48. Peattie, 133.
49. Peattie, 44–45.
50. Goldstein, Dillon and Wenger, 1991, 142–3.
51. Prange, 1981, 533.
52. Goldstein and Dillon, 1993, 280.
53. Military Analysis Division, 2.
54. Goldstein and Dillon, 1993, 290.
55. Peattie, 146.
56. Lord, 139.
57. Lord, 110.
58. Lambert and Polmar, 109–150.
59. Some of this strafing may have been conducted by bombers, but Japanese veterans did not indicate that bombers engaged in much strafing. Some of the damage might actually have been caused by AA rounds descending from the harbor. It is impossible to separate out these actions from those of the fighters. The extent of strafing of civilian targets was much less than initially reported.
60. Prange, 1981, 529.
61. Slackman, 148.
62. Wallin, 195.
63. Washington Naval Treaty, Chapter II Part 3 Section 1.
64. Stephen, 99.
65. Stephenson, http://www.j-aircraft.org/smf/index.php?topic=8601.1080

Chapter 8: Battle Damage Assessment

1. Goldstein and Dillon, 1993, 135.

2. Goldstein and Dillon, 1993, 162.

3. Prange, 1981, 573.

4. Goldstein and Dillon, 1993, 202.

5. Likely *Utah* (AG-16).

6. Goldstein and Dillon, 1993, 200–201.

7. Prange, 1981, 579.

8. Fuchida's chart survived the war. It was discovered and reproduced in color inside the covers of Goldstein and Dillon, *The Pearl Harbor Papers*. Brassey's (US), now Potomac Books, was the publisher, and retains the right to publish the chart themselves, although they do not have the right to allow others to publish it. The original map was put up for auction, purchased by an anonymous buyer, and has disappeared.

9. Compiled by Yokosuka Naval Air Corps. Possibly August 1942. *Lessons [air operation] of the Sea Battle off Hawaii, Vol. I.* in Goldstein and Dillon, 1993, 287.

10. Preliminary Design Section, Bureau of Ships, 9.

11. Lord, 91.

12. Willmott, et al, 2001, 106.

13. De Virgilio.

14. One aircraft in Fuchda's group prematurely dropped its bomb due to a material failure caused by AA damage. One B5N Kate level bomber was a deck abort. Goldstein, and Dillon, 1993, 287.

15. Slackman, 107.

16. Commander in Chief, Pacific Fleet. Report of Japanese Raid on Pearl Harbor, 15 February 1942. Enclosure C.

17. Hone, T.C., December, 1977, 56–57.

18. De Virgilio. Okun and Aiken correspondence with the author.

19. Willmott, et al, 2001, 116.

20. *Soryu* and *Hiryu* constituted Carrier Division (CarDiv) Two. The carrier division issued a consolidated report.

21. Willmott, et al, 2001, 191.

22. There were 30 destroyers in Pearl Harbor or on patrol in the immediate vicinity. There were another 15 on exercises in the general area, and 9 at various CONUS locations, for a total of 54 destroyers, not counting the Asiatic Fleet. Hitting three destroyers was inconsequential towards achieving the Japanese mission as compared to other available targets.

23. Prange, 1981, 535.

24. Werneth, 17, 274.

25. Werneth, 43.

26. Only one AR mentions a dive bomber attack on Battleship Row during this time frame, that of *Allen*, anchored northeast of Ford Island about a thousand

yards from Battleship Row. Her AR states, "Bridge personnel observed dive bombing attacks on battleship row approaching from both east and west." The smoke from the burning *Arizona* was between her and most of Battleship Row. *Allen* more likely observed the attacks on *Tangier* and *Raleigh* and *Nevada* and recorded them as attacks on Battleship Row. Aircraft attacking *Pennsylvania* and *Helena*, seen from *Allen*'s position, would also have lined up with Battleship Row.

27. Slackman, 168–9.
28. Werneth, 205.
29. Gordon, et al, 1990, 26
30. Olson, 43. This work erroneously says that the *Dale* was attacked by 16-inch AP bombs. By the time *Dale* (DD-353) was attacked, all the AP bombs had been expended against Battleship Row. *Dale* was attacked by D3A Val dive bombers employing 250-kg GP bombs.
31. Commanding Officer, USS *Dale* (353). Detailed report of offensive measures taken during Air Raid, December 7, 1941.
32. Goldstein, Dillon, and Wenger, 1991, 99.
33. Prange, 1981, 544–47; Prange, et al, 1990, 40.
34. Toland, 223.
35. Prange, et al, 1990, 77.
36. Fuchida and Okumiya, 155–6.
37. Prange, et al, 1982, 264.
38. Parshall, letter to the author.
39. Parshall and Tully, 230–231.
40. Prange, et al, 1990, 174. My thanks to Jonathan Parshall for bringing this to my attention.
41. Correspondence with Michael Weidenbach, Curator of the USS Missouri Memorial, and Jonathan Parshall.
42. Parshall and Tully, 135.
43. Parshall, correspondence with the author. Parshall is a co-author of *Shattered Sword,* the definitive account of the Japanese' side of the Battle of Midway.
44. Prange, 1981, 542.
45. Goldstein and Dillon, 1993.

Chapter 9: What Might Have Been: Alerted Pearl Harbor Defenses

1. Burlingame, 32.
2. One of the scandalous command failures was that, while junior officers of both services and the War Department wanted to make the full AWS operational immediately, Navy and Army senior officers refused to release the needed watch officers. The ownership of the system muddied the waters: the Signal Corp built the system and was supposed to turn it over to the Air

Corps, but dragged their feet. The War Department issued a directive on 15 September 1941 ordering the system be activated, to which General Martin, the air commander, responded that he hoped to have the AIC in operation "within 30 days" (or, prior to 25 October 1941). The successful 27 September exercise should have been the final demonstration before full-time operation. On 24 November the joint-services AWS steering committee (with the senior Army officer a lieutenant colonel, and the senior Navy representative a lieutenant commander) tried to prod their superiors onward by recommended that the AIC should be made operational "as early as possible." However, the senior officers decided that the system would become operational only after the war started. See Lambert and Polmar, 65–67.

3. In a letter dated 7 February 1941, the Secretary of War informed the Secretary of the Navy that there were currently 82 3-inch, 20 37mm, and 109 .50-cal AA gun in the Army establishment at Oahu. The "total program" was to be 98 3-inch, 120 37mm, and 308 .50-cal machine guns. A date for the delivery of the additional weapons was not provided. http://www.ibiblio.org/pha/timeline/410207awar.html. The numbers on 7 December are from Hearings, 320.

4. General Headquarters, US Army Forces Pacific, 17.

5. Lambert and Polmar, 99.

6. General Headquarters, US Army Forces Pacific, 19.

7. Lambert and Polmar, 40.

8. www.navweaps.com/index_oob/OOB_WWII_Pacific/OOB_Pearl_Harbor.htm, accessed 12/22/06. Lambert and Polmar, 97. Arakaki and Kuborn, 78–9 assess 10 aircraft shot down by the defending fighters, plus one that might have been shot down by Lieutenant Dains. Radar operators observed a P-40 shoot down a Zero, which might have been an engagement by Dains. Returning from a third sortie, Dains was shot down by US AA guns over Schofield Barracks and killed, so he never made a report.

9. Not counted are three P-40 aircraft that were destroyed while taking off.

10. www.navweaps.com/index_oob/OOB_WWII_Pacific/OOB_WWII_Pearl_Harbor.htm, accessed 12/18/08

11. Czarnecki, et al.

12. Campbell, 106.

13. Commander in Chief, United States Fleet, October 1945.

14. Wallin, 106.

15. The AA fire could be considered more effective still, if six USN Dauntless dive bombers and four Wildcat fighters Blue-on-Blue losses are included in the total of kills for the ammunition expended. These aircraft were flown in from the carrier *Enterprise* (CV-6) after the attack, and were shot down by jumpy defenders. An additional tribute to the accuracy of the defender's fire is that approximately 20 Japanese aircraft were pitched overboard after

landing as damaged beyond repair, and another 35 were immediately unflyable. 111 aircraft that landed on the carriers had some degree of damage, or 36% of the aircraft that returned.

16. Goldstein, Dillon, and Wenger, 112.

17. Joint Congressional Committee on the Investigation of the Pearl Harbor Attack, 69.

18. Commanding Officer, USS *California* (BB-44). Report of Raid (Revised), December 7, 1941. BB44/A16-3, 22 December 1941.

19. This 1946 report would not have been able to correlate data with Japanese records. A review of John Lundstom's *The First Team and the Guadalcanal Campaign* found that USMC 90mm AA batteries tended to claim 50–100% more aircraft than were actually shot down. One cause was joint engagements, where the AA guns fired on aircraft that were later shot down by fighters. The AA batteries might see the larger bomber but not the smaller fighter, see the bomber go down, and thus claim the bomber as their kill. Many aircraft claimed as AA kills actually managed to limp home, though perhaps in the end they were good only for the scrap heap.

20. Prange, 1981, 569.

21. The eight rounds per minute figure was taken from the overall rate of fire of heavy AA guns on *North Carolina* (BB-55) on 24 August 1942 at the Battle of the Eastern Solomons during an intense, coordinated air attack, assuming that one half of the battery could bear on targets at a time. This appears to be a good estimate, as the commanding officer estimated that the 5"/38 guns were firing at a rate of 17 rounds per minute when they engaged, using a fuze setting dead time of 3 seconds. He specifically mentions that this high rate of fire was a product of long training hours during the transit to the battle area. While the Army gunners might not have had as much sustained practice, they also would be handling ammunition that weighed less than half that of the 5"/38 round—the 5"/38 projectile was about 55 pounds and the powder and case 35 pounds, while the 3"/50 fired a fixed round (projectile + powder and case) of 26 pounds. Commanding Officer, U. S. S. *North Carolina*. Action of August 24, 1942, report of. BB55/A16-3 Serial 0109, 26 August 1942.

22. Lambert and Polmar, 68.

23. Clarke, 61.

24. Arakaki and Kuborn, 16.

25. Official AAF claims were 9 kills, 4 probable, 2 damaged.

26. Hough, et al.

27. Commander in Chief, Pacific Fleet. "The Battle of Midway." Report A16 0 1849.

28. First Air Fleet's Detailed Battle Report #6, "Midway operation from 27 May

1942 to 9 June 1942." Reprinted in The ONI Review, May 1947. There are conflicting numbers of kills given in various sections of the report. The number used, eight kills, comes from the tally of losses from each of carriers, which has five aircraft lost to enemy aircraft, three aircraft lost to ground fire, and one lost to an unspecified cause. In addition, the report of the *Hiryu* fighters states that "nine suffered hits (of which two became inoperational)." In many other reports the Japanese tended to count aircraft as "shot down" only if they were immediately destroyed in the air-to-air combat. Aircraft that were damaged but ditched or crashed on the return flight were not reported as air-to-air kills, but using some euphemism (such as "became inoperational"). However, this could also mean that the aircraft were deemed unflyable after they had returned and landed on the carrier. Thus, this analysis will use five kills as a lower bound and eight kills as the upper bound of kills achieved by the Midway fighters.

29. This kill ratio would be less inflated than usually seen in air-to-air kill claims, because the Flying Tiger pilots were paid a bonus for each kill, which required strict documentation of the kill, usually by recovering parts of the crashed aircraft as evidence.

30. US pilots left training with about 300 hours. Perhaps 100 of that would be in fighter-type aircraft, mostly in older biplanes. Pilots in the groups reinforcing the Philippines were mostly taken directly out of flight school, assigned, waited for transportation, and then shipped via sea, a process which took months, during which they did not fly. Upon arrival some of them got hours in the Philippine Air Force P-36 aircraft, but most had to wait until their P-40 aircraft were unboxed and assembled. Aircraft were still being assembled and tested when the war began.

31. Lambert and Polmar, 68.

32. *Japanese Air Power,* 5.

33. Lambert and Polmar, 68–9.

34. Leonard.

35. Prange, 1981, 228.

36. Arakaki and Kuborn, 58.

37. Clarke, 60.

38. Lambert and Polmar, 40, gives 76 mobile Army guns, and an additional 8 USMC guns were at Ewa Field. There were also 16 of the new SCR-268 radar gun directors available. The calculation does not include the Ewa guns, as the duration of the attack on that field is not available. At the time of the battle, ammunition transport vehicles had to be dispatched to the central magazine at Aliamanu Crater, where each battery was issued 1200 rounds, or 300 rounds per gun. Allowing 40 minutes of driving time plus loading time would mean that resupply during the course of the action would not have been

possible, particularly considering the huge traffic jam that existed at the magazine.

Chapter 10: Assessing the Folklore

1. Slackman, 63.
2. Slackman, 152.
3. Burton, xiv.
4. Belote and Belote, 3.
5. Peattie, 31.
6. Genda, in Goldstein and Dillon, 1993, 12.
7. Prange, 1981, 271.
8. Lieutenant Commander Hirata Matsumura, quoted in Werneth, 172.
9. Goldstein and Dillon, 1993, 284–5.
10. There are different figures given for the numbers of aircraft carried by Japanese ships. In addition to their normal operational complement, they would also carry spare aircraft fully or partially disassembled, and might also carry additional experimental aircraft or aircraft to be ferried to another location on an overload basis. The numbers might also change as the war progressed, reflecting modifications to the ship or its operational doctrine. The above numbers reflect the usual published figures for their pre-war operational capacities.
11. Werneth, 199–200.
12. Goldstein and Dillon, 1993, 23.
13. The Japanese light carriers *Ryujo*, *Zuiho*, and *Hosho* went to war carrying the previous-generation A5M Claude fighter. Francillon, 346.
14. Prange, 1981, 272. It is noteworthy that, in spite of the need for carriers to support the movement south, *Shoho* began the war in port Nagaski. She worked up a new air group for all of December and January, first becoming operational on 4 February 1942 when she transited from Empire waters to Truk. This provides an indication of how short the Japanese were of carrier-qualified aviators.
15. Willmott, et al, 2001, 58.
16. Goldstein and Dillon, 1993, 284–5.
17. Smith, 2005, 155.
18. DeBlanc, 17.
19. http://www.heritage.nf.ca/law/royal_air.html, accessed 12/26/08.
20. Prange, 1991, 28.
21. Willmott, et al, 2001, 77. Prange, 1981, 237.
22. "Unsolved History: Myths of Pearl Harbor." The Military Channel. The two luminaries were Larry Bond of Harpoon fame, and Captain Chris Carlson (USN, ret).

23. Middlebrook and Mahoney, 40, 44, 184.

24. In one training run Japanese level bombers scored 40% hits on the underway target ship *Settsu*, a remarkable achievement considering that the B5N Kate did not have a mechanical bomb sight. However, training against maneuvering ships had been abandoned in favor of training against stationary targets, as the US battleships were expected to be at anchor.

25. Calhoun, 71–3.

26. Lenton, 107.

27. http://www.history.navy.mil/faqs/faq66-1.htm.

28. Goldstein, Dillon and Wenger, 1991, 24.

29. Yergin, 327.

30. Morison, 125.

31. Morison, quoted in Willmott, et al, 2001, 142.

32. Prange, 1981, 550.

33. Goldstein, Dillon and Wenger, 1991, 24.

34. van der Vat, 21–2.

35. Clarke, 119.

36. Prange, 1986, 509.

37. Peattie, 168. Emphasis as in the original.

38. Gailey.

39. "Myths of Pearl Harbor." The Military Channel.

40. Imperial War Museum web site, www.iwm.org.uk/upload/package/25/pearl_harbor/index.htm.

41. Toland, 223.

42. United States Naval Institute, 27.

43. Prange, 1983, 542

44. Prange, 1990, 40–1.

45. Goldstein and Dillon, 1993. Willmott, et al, 2001, 156.

46. Willmott, et al, 2001, 156–7.

47. Parshall, 130.

48. Willmott, et al, 2001. 155–157.

49. Stillwell,1981, 139.

50. Parshall, 130.

51. Willmott, et al, 2001, 155–6.

52. Prange, 1981, 545, reports 74 damaged: 23 fighters, 41 bombers and 10 torpedo planes.

53. The carriers had 54 aircraft spares. A few of the spares were assembled before December 8th. If 59–64 aircraft were lost or immediately unflyable, replaced by the 54 spare aircraft, then the net loss in combat power was only 5–10 aircraft (less any deficit in aircrews).

54. Willmott, et al, 2001, 186.

55. Most sources show the B5N Kate payload as "800 kg of bombs," which would seem to allow the plane to carry three 250-kg bombs. However, some B5N Kates from *Shokaku* and *Zuikaku* carried two 250-kg bombs on their OCA mission against the airfields. Possibly the B5N Kate at this time did not have the mountings to carry three 250-kg bombs.

56. *Pearl Harbor and the Outlying Islands: US Navy Base Construction in World War II.*
http://www.history.navy.mil/library/online/constructpearlww2.htm.

57. United States Strategic Bombing Survey, *Ships' Bombardment of Japan— 1945*, 4.

58. The area of 498 acres for the shipyard given according to the official sources may include areas that were open ground for storage or undeveloped at the time of the attack. Estimates made by measurements of the area containing large buildings and warehouses from photographs taken in late 1941 give an area of less than 7,500,000 square feet. Using the same assumptions, this might result in a possibility of 17% damage to the shipyard, likely 12–15%. The conclusions remain unchanged.

59. Wallin, 222–242.

60. Prange, 1981, 469.

61. Ellsberg, 1946, 134.

62. Ellsberg, 1946, 139.

63. Stern, 57–9.

64. Burke, 128.

65. Prange, 1981, 392.

66. Prange, 1981, 549.

67. Goldstein, Dillon and Wenger, 1991, 26.

68. Willmott, et al, 2001, 161.

69. Prange, 1986, 510.

70. Prange, 1986, 509.

71. Prange, 1981, 66.

72. "The flash point of NSFO is above 140F and unless the bulk fuel is already at that or very close it is easy to calculate that there is simply not enough energy in a 7.7mm ball round raise any significant volume of fuel to flash point and ignite it. If the bulk fuel was already at flash point then a 7.7mm might possibly serve as an ignition source under some circumstances, but there is zero chance that those tanks were even close to that hot on 7 Dec 1941. Even if you get an ignition it is by no means certain that the fire won't sputter out, since you need to have enough energy to raise the temperature another 40F to 50F in the vicinity of the fire to sustain it, and a small initial flash may not be sufficient to do this. It would definitely take a pretty energetic source to set these tanks alight. A bomb would do it, at least if not too deep, but no

other air-launched weapon available to the Japanese [would do]. Even too small a bomb might very well not work. Having watched Boiler Techs struggle to get NSFO to light off from cold iron impressed me greatly with how hard it is to get this stuff burning well." Captain William O'Neil, USN (ret.), letter to the author.

"As to the 7.7mm solid shot projectile igniting diesel or NSFO, that is impossible. If you have been following [the Mythbusters television series], they have done much of the tests of this kind of thing and it turns out that in most cases, the chance of such a thing is so small that they give it a complete "BUST". Even with explosives, setting off such non-flammable material as these is not easy, even when they added sparks on purpose to try to enhance the chance. Some materials that would seem to be flammable are not since it is almost impossible for any small flame that is started to spread beyond the initial ignition point (only fumes can burn, not the liquid or solid material itself, unless, like black powder, it has its own oxidizer inside it)." Nathan Okun, letter to the author.

73. Edward Rudnicki, letter to the author.
74. Jim O'Neil, William O'Neil, Nathan Okun, Ralph Norton and Lonnie Gill provided information addressing this question.
75. Information courtesy of Ralph Norton. Usmm.org/sunk42a.html#anchor331462.
76. Potter, 7.
77. Willmott, et al, 2001, 120.
78. Goldstein, Dillon and Wenger, 1991, 24.
79. Slackman, 165, 167.
80. Ellsberg, 1949, 65–87.
81. Dull, 15.
82. "The Fourteen Part Message." http://www.ibiblio.org/pha/myths/14_part. html
83. Slackman, 60.
84. Prange, 1981, 554.
85. Goldstein and Dillon, 1991, 44.
86. Prange, 1981, 475.

Chapter 11: The Fifth Midget Submarine: A Cautionary Tale

1. Burlingame, 60.
2. Burlingame, 129–130.
3. Prange, quoted in Warship International, v 46 nr 4, 2009. 316.
4. Willmott, et al, 2001, 57.
5. Commanding Officer, USS St. Louis (CL-49), report to Commander-in-Chief, US Pacific Fleet, dated 25 December 1941, from http://i-16tou.com/stlou/.

6. http://i-16tou.com/stlou/stlou2.html.
7. USS Helm Action Report, 10 December 1941. http://www.history.navy.mil/docs/wwii/pearl/CinCPac.htm.
8. The Military Channel, 14 November 2009.
9. http://www.engin.umich.edu/dept/name/facilities/mhl/projects/televised_programs.html.
10. Zimm, et al, 2005.
11. A photograph of a pre-war bombardment near Diamond Head shows shell splinters hitting the water that look remarkably like the splashes in the subject photograph. Burlingame, 148.
12. Zimm, 2001, 24.
13. Aiken, Director, Pearl Harbor History Associates, correspondence with the author.
14. Credits to David Aiken for discovering the oral history evidence.
15. http://www.combinedfleet.com/Pearl.htm includes an article on the midget submarines which cites Kirby's theory.
16. http://www.kickasstorrents.com/pbs-nova-killer-subs-in-pearl-harbor-s37e09-ws-pdtv-xvid-ekolb-t3354799.html.
17. Clarke, 147–8.
18. This is the depth that the Japanese set their Type 91 aerial torpedoes for the attack. No information is available on the depth setting of the Type 97 midget submarine torpedoes, but it is likely to be similar to that used by the aviators. Aiken, 47.
19. Friedman, 1985, 415–8.
20. Aiken, 53.
21. http://i-16tou.com/stlou/stlou3.html.
22. Burlingame, 225–6.
23. http://i-16tou.com/stlou/stlou4.html.
24. Slackman, 99–100.
25. Aiken.
26. Commanding Officer, Administrative Office, USS *Arizona*, to The Chief of the Bureau of Ships. Subject: Material Damage Sustained in Attack on December 7, 1941. BB39/A9/L11-1, January 28, 1942.
27. http://www.j-aircraft.org/smf/index.php?topic=8601.1050.
28. Taylor claims that in naval jargon torpedo warheads were rounded off to "1000 pounds" and "500 pounds," and so the entry just represented naval slang. He provides no evidence of this rather remarkable assertion. In 40 years of naval service and researching naval documents in the archives, the author has never encountered a case where torpedo warheads were referred to in increments of 500 pounds.

29. Tom Taylor, posting on the http://www.j-aircraft.org/smf/index.php?board=5.0 message board.
30. Anthony Lovell, letter to the author.
31. Goldstein and Dillon, 1991, 50.
32. Burlingame, 131.
33. Prange, Goldstein, Dillon, 1993, 280, 282.

Chapter 12: Reassessing the Participants
1. USF-74, March 1941, Section V, "Patrol."
2. Prange, 1981, 411.
3. "It may be stated that it cannot be assumed that any capital ship or other valuable vessel is safe when at anchor from this type of attack if surrounded by water at a sufficient run to arm the torpedo." http://www.ibiblio.org/pha/myths/taranto.html
4. Prange, 1981, 701.
5. Lambert and Polmar, 134.
6. Prange, 1981, 460.
7. Prange, 1981, 654.
8. Prange, 1981, 260.
9. See Parshall and Tully, *Shattered Sword,* for an in-depth analysis.
10. Clarke, 119–120.
11. Prange, 1981, 281.
12. Prange, 1981, 263, 285.
13. Willmott, et al, 2001, 63–4.
14. Willmott, et al, 2001, 180.
15. Hone, T.C., correspondence.
16. Agawa, 264.
17. William O'Neil, correspondence.
18. Agawa, 266.
19. Willmott, et al, 2001, 88, 70–1.
20. Prange, 1981, 235.
21. Slackman, 9.

Chapter 13: Summary and Conclusions
1. Prange, 1981, 386.

INDEX